1971

THE
NEW BOOK
OF
KNOWLEDGE
ANNUAL

THE YOUNG PEOPLES
BOOK OF THE YEAR

A REVIEW OF THE EVENTS OF 1970

Grolier
INCORPORATED
NEW YORK

ISBN 0-7172-0602-5
The Library of Congress Catalog Card Number: 40-3092

STAFF

CONTENTS

10 MAN AND HIS ENVIRONMENT *Matthew J. Brennan*
17   NOISE POLLUTION *Mark O. Hatfield*
20   AUTOMOBILES AND AIR POLLUTION *Henry Ford II*
32   SAVING OUR ENVIRONMENT *Gaylord Nelson*

37 TOP OF THE NEWS *Walter Cronkite*

64 AFRICA *Alphonso and Margaret Castagno*
76 AGRICULTURE AND FOOD *Jerry A. Carlson*
86 THE ARTS
88   PHOTOGRAPHY *Ralph Hattersley*
96   PAINTING *Robert Taylor*
100   SCULPTURE *Robert Taylor*
102   ARCHITECTURE *Walter F. Wagner, Jr.*
108 ASIA *Arnold C. Brackman*
126 AUSTRALIA, NEW ZEALAND, AND THE PACIFIC ISLANDS
      E. J. Tapp
134 CANADA *Guy Birch*
144 ECONOMY *Wilbur Martin*
154 EDUCATION *Leonard Buder*
162 ENTERTAINMENT
164   MOTION PICTURES *Haig P. Manoogian*
168   DANCE *Lydia Joel*
170   MUSIC *Herbert Kupferberg*
171   POPULAR MUSIC *Arnold Shaw*
174   TELEVISION *Richard K. Doan*
180   THEATER *Marilyn Stasio*
182 ENVIRONMENT *Gladwin Hill*
192 EUROPE
196   WESTERN EUROPE *J. J. Meehan*
202   SOVIET UNION AND EAST EUROPE *Harry Schwartz*
206 HOBBIES
208   ARTS AND HANDICRAFTS *Sybil C. Harp*
210   STAMPS *Herman Herst, Jr.*
213   COINS *Clifford Mishler*
214 LATIN AMERICA *James N. Goodsell*
224 LITERATURE *Roger Jellinek*
230   LITERATURE FOR YOUNG PEOPLE *Charles P. May*
236 MEDICINE AND HEALTH *Leonard I. Gordon*

246 MIDDLE EAST *Harry J. Psomiades*
262 MODERN LIVING
264 FASHION *Jo Ahern Segal*
268 GAMES FOR OUR TIMES
270 DECORATING ROOMS FOR YOUNG PEOPLE *William Pahlmann*
274 PERSONALITIES
280 DEATHS
288 RELIGION
290 PROTESTANTISM *Kenneth L. Wilson*
291 ROMAN CATHOLICISM *Robert G. Hoyt*
293 JEWS AND JUDAISM *Meir Ben-Horin*
294 SCIENCE
298 BIOLOGICAL SCIENCES *Susan Zolla*
299 PHYSICAL SCIENCES *Lewis Friedman*
300 OCEANOGRAPHY *Jenny E. Tesar*
301 ANCIENT SOUTH POLE IN THE SAHARA *Rhodes W. Fairbridge*
302 DIGGING UP OUR PAST
304 PHOTOGRAPHING THE HEAVENS
306 ON THE TRAIL OF THE DINOSAUR
308 SPACE *John Newbauer*
318 SPORTS *Steve Singer*
342 TRANSPORTATION *Roderick Craib*
352 UNITED NATIONS *Pauline Frederick*
362 UNITED STATES *John B. Duff*
382 WEST INDIES *Sir Philip Sherlock*
388 YOUTH ORGANIZATIONS
390 GIRL SCOUTS *Richard Knox*
392 BOY SCOUTS *Alden G. Barber*
393 4-H CLUBS *E. Dean Vaughan*
393 CAMP FIRE GIRLS *Audrey M. Hudson*
394 BOYS' CLUBS *E. J. Stapleton*
395 FUTURE FARMERS OF AMERICA *A. D. Reuwee*
396 YOUNG PEOPLE IN THE NEWS

398 STATISTICAL SUPPLEMENT

410 DICTIONARY INDEX

423 ILLUSTRATION CREDITS

CONTRIBUTORS

Barber, Alden G., L.H.D.
Chief Scout Executive, Boy Scouts of America
  Boy Scouts   page 392

Ben-Horin, Meir, Ph.D.
Professor of Education and Chairman, Division of Education, The Dropsie University
  Jews and Judaism   page 293

Birch, Guy
News Editor, *Toronto Star*
  Canada   page 134

Bohle, Bruce, A.B.
Usage Editor, American Heritage Dictionaries
  New Words in Dictionary Index
  page 410

Brackman, Arnold C.
Consultant, Asian affairs; Author, *The Communist Collapse in Indonesia*
  Asia   page 108

Brennan, Matthew J., Ed. D.
Director, Pinchot Institute for Conservation Studies
  Man and His Environment
  page 10

Buder, Leonard
Education Writer, *The New York Times*
  Education   page 154

Carlson, Jerry A., M.S.
Managing Editor, *Farm Journal*
  Agriculture and Food   page 76

Castagno, Alphonso A., Ph.D.
Director, African Studies Center, Boston University
Castagno, Margaret F., B.A.
Free-lance editor
  Africa   page 64

Craib, Roderick, A.M.
Contributing Editor, *Business Week;* Author, *A Picture History of U.S. Transportation*
  Transportation   page 342

Cronkite, Walter
CBS News Correspondent
  Top of the News   page 36

Doan, Richard K.
Columnist, *TV Guide*
  Television   page 174

Duff, John B., Ph.D.
Professor of History, Seton Hall University
  United States   page 362

Fairbridge, Rhodes W., D.Sc.
Professor of Geology, Columbia University
  South Pole in the Sahara
  page 301

Ford, Henry II
Chairman of the Board, Ford Motor Company
  Automobiles and Air Pollution
  page 20

Frederick, Pauline, A.M.
NBC News United Nations Correspondent
  United Nations   page 352

Friedman, Lewis, Ph.D.
Senior Chemist, Brookhaven National Laboratory; Co-author, *Ion Molecule Reactions*
  Physical Sciences   page 299

Goodsell, James Nelson, Ph.D.
Latin America Editor, *The Christian Science Monitor;* Author, *The Quest for Change in Latin America*
  Latin America   page 214

Gordon, Leonard I., B.S., M.D.
Consultant, *Medical Tribune*
  Medicine and Health   page 236

Harp, Sybil C., B.A.
Editor, *Creative Crafts Magazine*
  Arts and Handicrafts   page 208

Hatfield, Mark O.
United States Senator from Oregon
  Noise Pollution   page 17

Hattersley, Ralph
Contributing Editor, *Popular Photography*
  Photography   page 88

Herst, Herman, Jr., B.A.
Author, *Nassau Street; Fun and Profit in Stamp Collecting*
  Stamps   page 210

Hill, Gladwin, B.S.
National Environmental Correspondent, *The New York Times*
  Environment   page 182

Hoyt, Robert G., A.B.
Editor, *National Catholic Reporter*
  Roman Catholicism   page 291

Hudson, Audrey M.
Assistant National Public Relations Director, Camp Fire Girls
  Camp Fire Girls   page 393

Jellinek, Roger, M.A.
Editor, *The New York Times Book Review*
  Literature   page 224

Joel, Lydia, B.A.
Director, Lydia Joel Associates, Dance Consultants
  Dance   page 168

Knox, Richard
Director, Public Relations Department, Girl Scouts of the United States of America
Girl Scouts   page 390

Kupferberg, Herbert, M.A., M.S.
Music Critic, *The National Observer;* Author, *Those Fabulous Philadelphians*
Music   page 170

Manoogian, Haig P., B.S., M.F.A.
Professor, Institute of Film and Television, New York University
Motion Pictures   page 164

Martin, Wilbur
Managing Editor, *Nation's Business*
Economy   page 144

May, Charles Paul, M.A.
Free-lance author, photographer, and book reviewer; Author, *The Early Indians; Natural and Imaginary Worlds*
Literature for Young People page 230

Meehan, J. J., B.A.
Editor, United Press International
Europe, Western   page 196

Mishler, Clifford
Numismatic Editor, *Coins Magazine* and *Numismatic News*
Coins and Coin Collecting page 213

Nelson, Gaylord
United States Senator from Wisconsin; received a 1970 National Congressional Award for his work to improve the quality of the environment
Saving Our Environment page 32

Newbauer, John, A.B.
Editor in Chief, *Astronautics & Aeronautics*
Space   page 308

Pahlmann, William, F.A.I.D.
President, William Pahlmann Associates, Inc.; Author, *The Pahlmann Book of Interior Design*
Decorating Rooms for Young People   page 270

Psomiades, Harry J., Ph.D.
Chairman, Department of Political Science, Queens College, The City University of New York
Middle East   page 246

Reuwee, A.D., M.A.
Director of Information, Future Farmers of America
Future Farmers of America page 395

Schwartz, Harry, Ph.D.
Specialist in Soviet affairs, *The New York Times*
Soviet Union and Eastern Europe page 202

Segal, Jo Ahern, B.S.
Fashion Editor, *Look* magazine
Fashion   page 264

Shaw, Arnold, M.A.
Author, *The Rock Revolution: What's Happening in Today's Music*
Music, Popular   page 171

Sherlock, Sir Philip, K.B.E.
Secretary-General, Association of Caribbean Universities and Research Institutes
West Indies   page 382

Singer, Steve
Free-lance sports writer
Sports   page 318

Stapleton, E. J.
Director, Public Information, Boys' Clubs of America
Boys' Clubs of America   page 394

Stasio, Marilyn, M.A.
Theater Critic, *Cue* magazine
Theater   page 180

Tapp, E. J., M.A.
Associate Professor of History, The University of New England, New South Wales, Australia
Australia, New Zealand, and the Pacific Islands   page 126

Taylor, Robert, A.B.
Arts Critic, *Boston Globe;* Lecturer in English, Wheaton College
Painting   page 96
Sculpture   page 100

Tesar, Jenny E., M.S.
Senior Editor, *The Book of Popular Science* and *Encyclopedia Science Supplement*
Oceanography   page 300

Vaughan, E. Dean, Ph.D.
Director, 4-H and Youth Development Division, Federal Extension Service, U.S. Department of Agriculture
4-H clubs   page 393

Wagner, Walter F., Jr., A.I.A.
Editor, *Architectural Record*
Architecture   page 102

Wilson, Kenneth L., Lit.D.
Editor, *Christian Herald Magazine*
Protestantism   page 290

Zolla, Susan, Ph.D.
Assistant Professor of Pathology, New York University Medical School
Biological Sciences   page 298

MAN AND HIS

IN 1965, the famous American statesman, Adlai E. Stevenson, said, "We all travel together, passengers on a little space ship, dependent on its vulnerable supplies of air and soil." We manage to survive only by ". . . the care, work, and love we give our fragile craft."

ENVIRONMENT

By MATTHEW J. BRENNAN

Director, Pinchot Institute for Conservation Studies

The earth is our environment. This environment comprises everything in our surroundings, and all the conditions that affect our lives. In the short time man has been on earth, he has learned to change the environment to provide for his needs and luxuries. He has raised plants and domesticated animals; he has cleared away forests to open up land for farming. He has mined and refined the earth's minerals; he has learned to use minerals for fuel and as materials to make tools, houses, and machines. In doing all these things, man has brought about great changes in his home, the earth.

In recent years we have begun to ask questions about the quality of our environment. Can the earth support an unlimited number of people? We have started to think deeply about things once taken for granted: the supply of clean air to breathe, pure water to drink, and room in which to live.

As a result of what man has done to his environment, there is today a great interest in the science of ecology. The word comes from the Greek *oikos,* which means house or home, and *logos,* which means a science. Ecology is the science that ex-

Plants need solar energy (1), together with carbon dioxide, water, and minerals from the soil, to make food. The plants, in turn, provide food for animals (2). When plants and animals die (3) they decompose (4) and the minerals are returned to the soil. A similar cycle takes place in the sea (5). In the water cycle, water evaporates into the air (6) and later falls back to earth as rain (7). Man-made changes in our environment have upset both cycles.

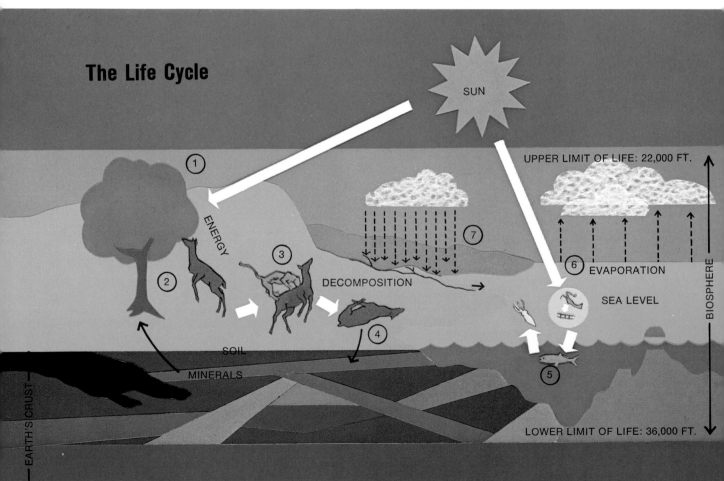

The Life Cycle

SUN

ENERGY

UPPER LIMIT OF LIFE: 22,000 FT.

1

2

3

DECOMPOSITION

7

6 EVAPORATION

SEA LEVEL

SOIL

4

MINERALS

5

BIOSPHERE

EARTH'S CRUST

LOWER LIMIT OF LIFE: 36,000 FT.

Man-made wastes are now being produced faster than they can be reused.

amines our home, the earth, and the ways in which all living organisms are related to each other and to their surroundings.

No living thing, including man, lives entirely on its own. It affects other living things, and it is affected by them. It also affects its nonliving surroundings and is affected by them.

All life on earth depends on the sun. Living things must have energy to stay alive, and energy comes from the sun. Green plants, in a process called photosynthesis, use the energy in the sun's light to combine water and carbon dioxide gas to form sugar. A by-product of photosynthesis is oxygen gas, which animals need for breathing.

Animals cannot make food. They eat plants or they eat other animals that have eaten plants. In either case, the animals thus depend on plants for the food they need for energy. So both plants and animals owe their energy to the energy of the sun.

The materials that make up living things are used and reused continually. As a plant grows, it takes minerals from the soil. When the plant dies it decays, and the minerals return to the soil. They are a resource, not a waste, for they can be absorbed by another growing plant. In time that plant may be eaten by an animal. Then the minerals are absorbed by the animal. When the animal dies the "waste" minerals will again return to the soil as a resource.

The changes that man makes in the environment have upset the balance of wastes and resources. Wastes are now produced faster than they can be reused. They are no longer resources. They are pollutants: substances that can damage the environment.

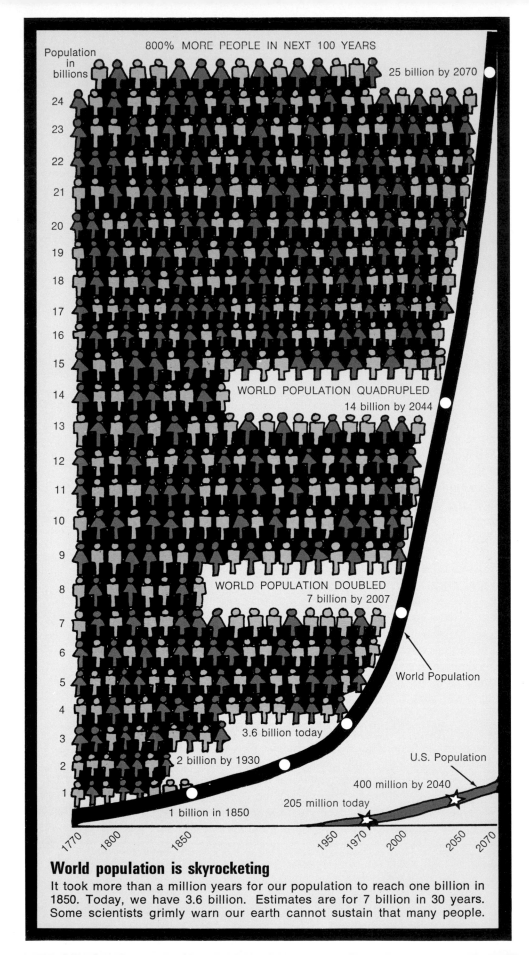

World population is skyrocketing

It took more than a million years for our population to reach one billion in 1850. Today, we have 3.6 billion. Estimates are for 7 billion in 30 years. Some scientists grimly warn our earth cannot sustain that many people.

The population explosion is probably the greatest danger facing man. By the year 2000 there will be 7,000,000,000 people living on earth. This will place an unacceptable drain on the world's limited resources.

▶POPULATION

The earth's population has nearly doubled since World War II. More babies than ever have been born, but this is only part of the reason for the increase. More and better food and medical care have kept alive many people who would otherwise have died.

This enormous increase in the number of people is called the "population explosion." Many experts believe that it is the greatest danger facing man. They estimate that the population will almost double again by the end of this century. This would mean that shortly after the year 2000, there would be 7,000,000,000 people.

Would there be enough food for so many people? Even today, more than one half of the people in the world do not have enough to eat. Agricultural experts have developed new types of rice and wheat plants that yield bigger crops per acre. These cereal grains can keep more people from being hungry, but they do not contain the proteins necessary for good health and proper growth. Cattle and poultry provide these proteins, but they must be nourished on scarce grain. Fish also provide protein, but some experts believe that overfishing and pollution have already dangerously reduced the number of fish.

Can anything be done to feed a doubled world population? Ways will have to be found to obtain more protein from the sea, both by using plants now found in the oceans and by growing others. Synthetic (man-made) chemical foods must be manufactured. Yields of present crops will have to be increased

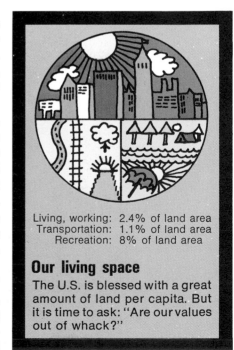

Living, working: 2.4% of land area
Transportation: 1.1% of land area
Recreation: 8% of land area

Our living space
The U.S. is blessed with a great amount of land per capita. But it is time to ask: "Are our values out of whack?"

The sign, in Hindi, reads "Happiness is a two-child family." Further destruction of the environment will take place if the number of births is not limited.

tremendously. The way that food is now distributed will have to be changed. If mass hunger is to be avoided, the nations with sufficient food will have to make sacrifices to help the underfed countries.

A doubled population means a greater drain on the world's limited resources. Lumber is needed to provide decent housing. So are iron, copper, aluminum, and other metals. Vehicles to carry people and goods require tremendous amounts of metals. Some of these metals are already scarce.

A doubled population will need more electricity. Waterpower, which now generates about one third of the world's electricity, is limited because there are only a limited number of rivers that can be dammed. Coal, oil, and gas are used to make steam to provide about two thirds of the electricity generated today. The supply of these fuels seems to be adequate. But no one can be sure how long they would last in the face of a vastly increased population. A small amount of electricity is now produced by using atomic energy, but the use of atomic reactors in great numbers might present problems of pollution by radioactivity.

A doubled population means that more land will be needed to raise food. More land will be used for building roads for the increased number of vehicles.

Biologists are concerned about the many tensions that arise from overcrowding. They feel that the population should not grow beyond the capacity of the earth to house people in some comfort. Some scientists believe that even today the number of people is close to the limit that the earth can support. Many countries have begun family-planning programs. In these programs people are urged to limit the number of their children. Some experts fear that these voluntary programs will not be effective and that laws limiting the size of families will be needed.

(*text continued on page 18*)

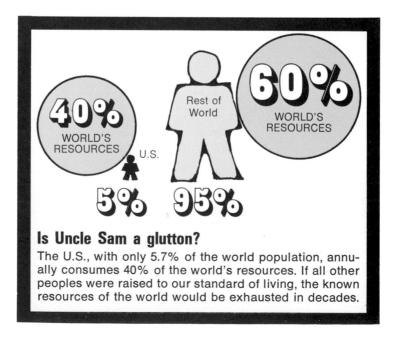

Is Uncle Sam a glutton?

The U.S., with only 5.7% of the world population, annually consumes 40% of the world's resources. If all other peoples were raised to our standard of living, the known resources of the world would be exhausted in decades.

NOISE POLLUTION

By MARK HATFIELD

*. . . the senior senator from Oregon sets forth a
plan to remedy a serious environmental problem*

Pollution usually refers to the presence of unwanted substances in the environment. This could be the smoke that pours out of a factory chimney. It could be the chemicals and sewage that contaminate our rivers and lakes. Or it could be the junked cars that clutter the landscape. Noise, or unwanted sound, is different from these forms of pollution because it is not a physical substance. Rather, it is a form of energy made up of sound waves. Still, noise is a major environmental problem.

We are all aware of the terrible noise in our environment. Near an airport, we hear the piercing scream of jetliners. In the city streets, we hear the roar of traffic and the staccato sound of jackhammers. Even in the discotheques we are assaulted by noise: the blasting of rock music. These noises certainly irritate. But they can do much worse: they can make us deaf. Most people realize that very loud noise can cause permanent or temporary deafness. However, most people do not realize that repeated moderate noises can build up to produce the same effect. It has also been charged that noise contributes to such conditions as fatigue, hypertension, and high blood pressure. It also decreases our mental efficiency.

Because of this, the problem of how to control noise has been receiving increased attention. In 1968, for example, Congress gave the Federal Aviation Agency the authority to set limits on the noise produced by aircraft. The Government also promised that if the supersonic transport is built, supersonic flights over land will be banned unless the sonic-boom problem is solved.

The Walsh-Healey Act sets limits on the amount of noise in factories and plants that do a great deal of business with the Government. The Federal Government is also sponsoring a number of research programs on how to control noise.

State and local governments are also trying to solve the noise-pollution problem. New York City, for example, set up a Mayor's Task Force on Noise Control. It made several recommendations on how to reduce noise in the United States' largest and perhaps noisiest city. Los Angeles is making an effort to reduce noise levels at the Los Angeles International Airport. And legislation on noise abatement, particularly in the area of traffic noise, is under consideration in New York, New Jersey, Minnesota, California, and other states.

In the private sector, the aircraft industry is trying to produce quieter jet engines. And construction companies have shown that buildings can be constructed more quietly. Many now weld materials together instead of riveting or bolting.

Though there has been some effort to control noise in our environment, much more needs to be done. Federal legislation may be needed to set national standards for environmental noise levels. State and local governments should direct their attention to problems best handled at the local level, such as traffic noise and community and construction noise. And the public should be educated so that there will be a demand for quieter jobs, products, and homes.

In addition, scientific research should continue into the question of noise-induced health problems. Research will also give us better methods of suppressing noise. Industry should step up its efforts to quiet factories and machinery.

Noise can and must be controlled. It is a danger to the public health and the economy. It makes living in our urban centers a less-than-civilized experience.

▶MACHINES

People in many parts of the earth live in a world of machines. They have machines that do much of their work, and machines carry them about quickly and comfortably. Still other machines can solve many very complex problems almost instantly. In the poorer countries of the world, people hope that someday they too may have machines to make life easier, more comfortable, and more enjoyable.

Some machines have caused serious changes in our environment. The greatest single offender is the automobile. As more automobiles are bought, more highways are needed. Each year, in the United States alone, over one million acres of forest and grassland are cleared and paved over for roads. Trees and other plants that produced oxygen for breathing are gone forever. In Paris, Tokyo, Los Angeles, and almost any other large city, automobiles fill the streets with exhaust gases as they creep along in bumper-to-bumper traffic.

Some city planners and government officials say there will have to be a big change in our thinking about transportation on the ground. They think that more money should be spent to

Automobiles have made the American people mobile, and trucks have moved their goods. But motor vehicles have also damaged the environment. Besides contributing to air pollution, autos have made it necessary to pave over more than one million acres of forests so that highways could be built.

build and improve subways and railroads and provide more buses. They reason that fast, comfortable mass transportation would persuade people to make less use of their automobiles.

The jet airplane has revolutionized travel. It has brought people and cultures closer together. It has made world travel easy. But it has also created environmental problems. Harmful chemicals sift down from the smoky trails of low-flying jets. The scream of jet engines is constantly heard by people who live near big-city airports. A new, more widespread noise problem is connected with the supersonic transport (SST). A supersonic plane flies faster than sound. At these speeds, the plane produces a "sonic boom," a thunderlike cracking noise that is heard on the ground. A sonic boom frightens and upsets many people. It can shatter windows thousands of feet below.

With more people traveling by plane, more airports are needed to serve large cities. Building more airports means extending the noise and air pollution to new areas. Many people are asking whether the environmental problems created by big jets may not be too great a price to pay for faster travel.

(*text continued on page 21*)

Jet planes get us where we want to go—and they get us there fast. But they also spray the air with gasoline, and damage buildings with their sonic booms. These loud noises also cause physical discomfort.

19

AUTOMOBILES AND AIR POLLUTION

By HENRY FORD II

. . . the chairman of the board of the Ford Motor Company details efforts by the auto industry to curb air pollution by producing low-emission vehicles

The more than 100,000,000 motor vehicles in the United States play a key part in American life. According to the Council on Environmental Quality, they also account for 40 per cent of air pollution by weight. However, when the harmfulness of different pollutants is considered, the automobile's share of responsibility drops to about 12 per cent.

In most cities, the most serious air-pollution problems are caused by sulfur oxides and particulates, or small particles, in the air. Industry and electric power plants cause most of this type of pollution. Automobiles contribute only about 1 per cent of the sulfur oxides and 3 per cent of the particulates. In heavy traffic areas, however, the automobile is an important factor in air pollution. This makes the development of low-emission vehicles a top-priority item.

During the 1960's, rapid progress was made toward reducing automotive emissions. Indeed, a 1971 car produces less than one fifth as much as hydrocarbon (unburned gasoline) and about one third as much carbon monoxide as a 1960 car.

As newer cars have replaced older cars, the amount of automotive pollutants in the air has decreased. In Los Angeles, for example, the peak output of hydrocarbons and carbon monoxide was reached in 1966. It has been dropping ever since. By 1980 nearly all cars in use will be 1970 models or later. It is estimated that by that date—even if no further improvements in emission controls are made—Los Angeles will have less hydrocarbons in its air than it had in 1940. And its carbon-monoxide levels will be back to where they were in the late 1940's.

Actually, progress toward cleaner air will come faster than that. This is because emission controls are being greatly improved. Control of nitrogen oxides began with 1971 cars in California. These controls will be extended nationwide in 1973. Nearly all new cars are now being built to run on gasoline that contains little or no lead. This will permit the use of certain devices in autos that will further reduce exhaust emissions. These devices are already being tested in experimental vehicles. When they come into use, hydrocarbon emissions will be reduced to about 5 per cent of the amount from a vehicle lacking emission controls. Carbon monoxide and nitrogen oxide emissions will be reduced to about 15 per cent of the precontrol levels.

Despite research, no alternative power source to the combustion engine has been perfected. None can match the combustion engine's degree of cleanliness and its economy, usefulness, and efficiency.

Sufficiently powerful lightweight batteries are not available for electric cars. And even if they were, they would still need to be recharged. This would require more electric power plants—another source of pollution. Steam engines, low-emission gas turbine engines, and engines using compressed natural gas are not suitable for passenger cars.

A better gasoline-burning internal-combustion engine, therefore, still appears to be the best answer. With such an engine we will have a low-emission vehicle that can serve our transportation needs reliably, safely, and economically with little damage to our environment. Much remains to be done. But we in the automobile industry feel that motor-vehicle emissions already are under better control and closer to final solution than any other major aspect of the air-pollution problem.

▶POLLUTION BY INSECTICIDES

Some insects damage crops and carry disease. Certain kinds of mosquitoes, for example, carry malaria. Other insects destroy food crops.

Chemists have developed substances, called insecticides, that are useful for killing insects. During World War II a new insecticide, DDT (dichloro-diphenyl-trichloro-ethane), was introduced. It seemed to be the perfect insecticide. It was cheap, easy to use, amazingly effective against insects, and long lasting. After the war, DDT and other chemicals related to it were used all over the world. But the long-lasting quality that made them so useful turned out to be an environmental problem. Their effects are seen

Spraying crops with DDT and other insecticides will kill harmful and destructive insects. It can also kill birds, fish, and other animal life.

Habitat, DDT problems

DDT causes many birds to lay infertile and fragile eggs. Wildlife loses 1.5 million acres of habitat each year.

in many ways. If a bird eats insects that were sprayed with DDT, the insecticide remains in the body of the bird. If enough DDT accumulates, the bird dies. So the bird, a natural insect killer, is lost to an insecticide.

When DDT is sprayed on crops and trees, some of it may be blown onto grass that is later eaten by cows. Before long the DDT can be detected in the cows' milk. DDT is often sprayed in swamps to kill mosquitoes. Some of the DDT may be carried into a stream or lake, where tiny organisms that live on the bottom absorb the chemical. Fish eat these organisms, and gradually build up a store of DDT in their bodies.

DDT and other long-lasting insecticides may prove to be the most serious and damaging pollutants of the ocean. Insecticides washed off plants by rainwater are carried down rivers. In time they reach oceans. There is evidence that insecticides interfere with the process of photosynthesis in one-celled water plants called plankton. Like other green plants, plankton make their food by photosynthesis and give off oxygen. It is estimated that 70 per cent of the world's oxygen is produced by plant plankton. Plankton are eaten by tiny shrimplike animals called copepods. Small fish eat copepods and in turn are eaten by bigger fish. Less photosynthesis by plankton could result in a lowered number of fish available for humans to eat. At a time when the world's population is booming, this possibility is an example of the balances in the environment so easily upset by man. An insecticide used to ensure increased food production on farms could cause a decrease in food available from the sea.

Biologists have studied the effects of DDT on dogs. The dogs had the same concentration of DDT in their bodies as that in the bodies of people who work with DDT. The offspring (young) of these dogs had a very high death rate: on the average, 5 of every 6 died. In a control group (a group used for comparison) of dogs not exposed to DDT, 5 out of 6 of the offspring survived. Other studies by biologists have shown some evidence that DDT and related insecticides may be harmful to humans. The United States Government is phasing out the use of these insecticides for most agricultural purposes.

Scientists are searching for new insecticides that will not have the dangerous environmental effects of DDT and its relatives. In the meantime, there are other but less effective ways to kill undesirable insects. Changing the type of crop grown in a field (rotation of crops) is effective against some insects. Another method is the use of the natural insect enemies. When an insect comes into a new area, it often multiplies very fast. This happens because the insect's particular natural enemies, usually other insects, are not present. Introducing the natural enemy into the area helps to control the insect pest. Birds eat huge amounts of insects. Conserving birdlife is a big step toward insect control.

Fertilizers. Fertilizers are materials added to the soil to help plant growth. They may be organic or inorganic. An organic fertilizer is one that was once alive or that comes from a living thing. Fish meal and animal manures (wastes) are examples of organic fertilizers. Inorganic, or chemical, fertilizers are mined or made in a chemical factory.

When cheap chemical fertilizers became available, farmers added them freely to the soil. This resulted in great harvests, but something else happened, too. The excess fertilizer drained away from the soil and was carried down into ponds and lakes. There it stimulated the growth of algae. (The green scummy growths floating on ponds are one form of algae.) The fast-growing algae filled the lakes, crowding other plant and animal life.

The huge masses of algae died. As they decayed, they used up the oxygen in the water. This killed off the fish and other water animals. In time, slimy, foul-smelling mats of dead algae and fish floated on lakes that once had served for drinking water, swimming, and fishing.

This is an example of the delicate balance that exists between a resource and a waste. Fertilizer properly used is a resource that produces better crops. Used too freely, it becomes a waste that pollutes the environment.

Detergents. Chemists invented detergents and gave housewives of some countries the whitest washes in the world. But these detergents became a source of pollution. They flow into sewers leading to streams or lakes. Wastes in sewage are attacked by bacteria, which change the wastes into simpler substances. But

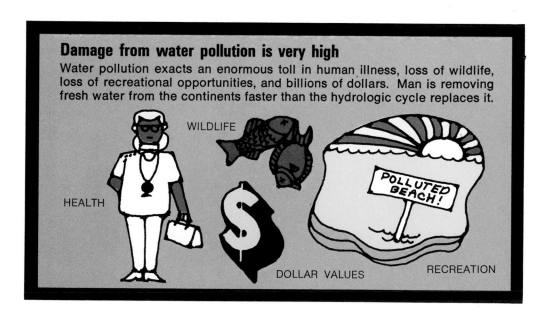

Damage from water pollution is very high

Water pollution exacts an enormous toll in human illness, loss of wildlife, loss of recreational opportunities, and billions of dollars. Man is removing fresh water from the continents faster than the hydrologic cycle replaces it.

HEALTH

WILDLIFE

$

DOLLAR VALUES

POLLUTED BEACH!

RECREATION

For those concerned about pollution, Jewel Food Stores list detergents' phosphate content.

Detergents with phosphates may make washes whiter, but the effect on fish is all too evident.

the detergents proved to be non-biodegradable—that is, the bacteria could not change them into simpler substances. As a result, masses of foaming detergent piled up. People became concerned when suds began to appear in their drinking water, and a search for a new kind of detergent began.

The new detergent was degradable, but it became a pollutant of a different kind. It contained phosphorus, which stimulated the growth of algae when it reached streams. The search for a suitable detergent continues, with the hope of finding one that will not damage man's environment.

Sewage. The most serious water pollutant, as far as public health is concerned, is sewage. This is water collected by sewer

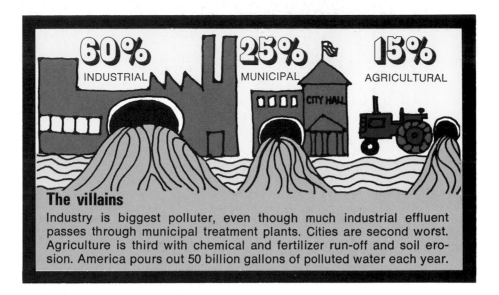

The villains

Industry is biggest polluter, even though much industrial effluent passes through municipal treatment plants. Cities are second worst. Agriculture is third with chemical and fertilizer run-off and soil erosion. America pours out 50 billion gallons of polluted water each year.

pipes leading from homes and factories, and it carries many types of waste, including the wastes from the human body.

The solid wastes from the body contain large numbers of bacteria and viruses. Most of these are harmless, but disease-carrying organisms can also be found. If these get into drinking water they may cause epidemics.

At first all communities merely dumped their sewage into nearby water. (Many still do.) The flowing water diluted the sewage. Bacteria of decay in the water broke down the wastes into simpler substances. But as the population increased in cities and towns, flowing water alone was not enough to dispose of the increased amounts of sewage. Sewage-treatment plants were built. Most of these plants remove the solid materials and harmful organisms from the sewage. The remaining water is dumped into a stream or lake. Unfortunately, only a few treatment systems also remove the elements that act as fertilizers. These elements are responsible for ruin of hundreds of bodies of water.

The pollution of water can be ended by building advanced sewer systems, sewage-treatment plants, and installations to block fertilizers and insecticides. The cost will be enormous. The United States alone will have to spend more than $25,000,000,000. In the meantime, polluted lakes and streams will continue to "die."

Even the oceans, which cover 70 per cent of the earth's surface, have not escaped pollution. Sewage sludge—the solid material remaining after sewage is treated—is dumped at sea. In studies made in one of these dumping areas, no living things could be found. Wastes from mines, factories, and refineries are dumped directly into the ocean, or they reach it through rivers. The ocean has even been used as a dumping place for radioactive wastes and unused wartime poison gases.

Oil. Oil is now a common ocean pollutant. It may get into the water when an oil tanker springs a leak or sinks. Drilling for oil offshore has also caused pollution. The thick, sticky oil floating on the water coats and kills fish, birds, and seals, and other living things. It spoils beaches and coastal waters, making them useless for swimming.

Agencies of the United Nations are conducting studies of ocean pollution and planning ways to deal with the problem. If the oceans of the world are to be saved, the nations of the world must act together to save them.

Oil kills seabirds. Shell Oil Company is trying to dispose of oil spills by spraying them with chemically treated sand; the oil-sand mixture sinks.

▶AIR POLLUTION

A great deal of power is needed to run the factories of modern industrial nations. Automobiles, trains, planes, and buses need power too. Nearly all this power is produced in the same way— by burning fuels. The burning produces wastes. Some of the wastes get into the air, causing air pollution. In 1970, United States Government officials estimated that 200,000,000 tons of these wastes enter the air each year—one ton for each man, woman, and child in the country!

A curtain of smog often hangs over big cities. It irritates the eyes, throat, and chest. The word "smog" is a combination of the words smoke and fog, but smog itself is a mixture of many more ingredients. It begins with some of the pollutants from burning: soot, carbon monoxide, hydrocarbons, and nitrogen oxides are among them. Some of the pollutants react with one another, like chemicals in a test tube, to form new irritating substances. Energy is needed for the reactions, and it is supplied by the light of the sun. The resulting mixture is photochemical smog (photo means light). It can be deadly.

In London, Tokyo, New York, and other cities a weather condition called a temperature inversion has allowed smog to hang over the city for several days at a time. When this happens thousands of people become ill. The death rate among elderly people and people with lung disorders climbs rapidly.

About half of the pollutants in the air come from the engines of motor vehicles. As they burn fuel, they give off carbon monoxide

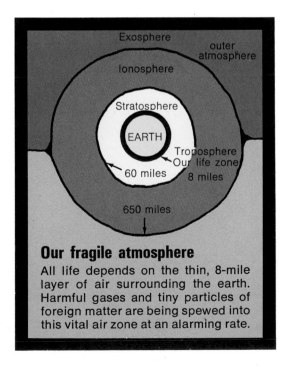

Our fragile atmosphere

All life depends on the thin, 8-mile layer of air surrounding the earth. Harmful gases and tiny particles of foreign matter are being spewed into this vital air zone at an alarming rate.

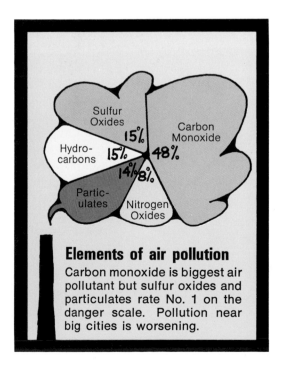

Elements of air pollution

Carbon monoxide is biggest air pollutant but sulfur oxides and particulates rate No. 1 on the danger scale. Pollution near big cities is worsening.

as a waste. Carbon monoxide is a colorless, odorless gas, and a deadly poison. The amount of carbon monoxide that an engine gives off can be reduced with special devices designed to make the engine burn the fuel more efficiently.

Governments of some countries are sponsoring programs to develop low-pollution automobiles. Some automobile manufacturers are working on experimental cars run by electricity or other means that will reduce pollution. City governments in various parts of the world have begun to close certain streets to automobile traffic, hoping to lower pollution levels. Many city planners believe that cities, or at least their central areas, should be kept free of automobiles.

Motor vehicles are not the only air polluters. Coal and oil, used to heat homes and factories and to generate electricity, contain small amounts of sulfur. When the fuels are burned, sulfur dioxide, a poisonous gas, is produced. It is irritating to the lungs. Some cities have passed laws that permit coal and oil to be burned only if their sulfur content is low.

Sources of air pollution In millions of tons annually (1968 figures)	Carbon Monoxide	Sulfur Oxides	Nitrogen Oxides	Hydro-carbons	Partic-ulates	Totals
Transportation	63.8	.8	8.1	16.6	1.2	90.5
Fuel combustion	1.9	24.4	10.0	.7	8.9	45.9
Industrial processes	9.7	7.3	.2	4.6	7.5	29.3
Solid waste disposal	7.8	.1	.6	1.6	1.1	11.2
Miscellaneous	16.9	.6	1.7	8.5	9.6	37.3
Totals	100.1	33.2	20.6	32.0	28.3	214.2

Major sources of air pollution

Since 1966, the U.S. has increased its air pollution rate by 5 million tons of pollutants annually. Motor vehicles are by far the biggest contributor to air pollution.

In 1970, some 200,000,000 tons of waste entered the air in the United States alone. Motor vehicles were the major contributors to air pollution. But the most harmful pollutants came from industrial plants.

Most electricity is generated by steam turbines. About half of the sulfur dioxide in the air comes from burning fuel to make steam. Nuclear power plants do not burn fuel, so there is no air pollution of the ordinary kind. But the radioactive materials in these plants could present a danger in an accident. Also, there is a problem in disposing of the radioactive wastes in a way that will not endanger the environment.

Another type of pollution, called thermal (heat) pollution, is caused by both the fuel-burning and nuclear plants. Both require huge amounts of cold water, which cool the steam. The water is warmed as it cools the steam. When it is returned to the river, the warm water may stimulate the growth of weeds. It may also kill fish and their eggs, or interfere with their growth.

Physicists are studying new ways of generating electricity that may be less damaging to the environment. In the meantime, many power plants are being modernized to give off less polluting material. Also, engineers try to design and locate new power plants to do minimal damage to the environment.

▶ SOLID-WASTE POLLUTION

As cities grow, the problem of what to do with solid waste material grows too. Solid waste includes litter, garbage, papers, refrigerators, furniture, and rubble from buildings. Millions of old automobiles each year become part of the solid-waste problem.

What should be done with all this refuse? Formerly the answer was to take it to the city dump or incinerator. But now many cities have run out of dumping space. Refuse can be burned in incinerators, but this causes air pollution. Dumping into marshes, bays, or even the ocean causes water pollution.

Researchers have suggested many solutions of the problem. Nearly all of them will cost more than our present ways of disposing of refuse. Some materials, such as paper, glass, and various metals, can be separated from the refuse, then processed for reuse. This method would also help to save some valuable resources. Experiments have been made in reducing certain solid wastes to compact bricks for building materials. Packages and containers made of materials that will decay after use can be used in place of disposable glass and aluminum containers.

Each year, millions of automobiles end up in auto graveyards.
These eyesores have contributed to the uglification of America.

▶ OUR FUTURE ENVIRONMENT

Man has learned innumerable ways of changing his environment to make work easier and life more comfortable and secure. But now we have begun to see that much of our recent progress was made at the cost of enormous damage to our environment. Our continued existence depends on the way we use the environment in the future.

Putting the environment in better order will not be cheap or easy. The environmental damage is worldwide. Working out the solutions will require planning on an international level. People will have to think over some hard questions. Are we willing to limit population? Are we ready to pay the staggering costs of ending air and water pollution? Are we ready to make less use of automobiles and electric power if that is part of the price?

The answers to questions like these must be "Yes!"

Rachel Carson, an American biologist and writer, once wrote: "No organism in biological history has survived for long if its environment became in some way unfit for it. But no organism before man has deliberately polluted its environment."

SAVING OUR ENVIRONMENT

By SENATOR GAYLORD NELSON

In recent years man has achieved great things. He has harnessed the power of the atom. He has prolonged life by transferring a living heart from one human being to another. He has escaped the bonds of the earth to walk on the surface of the moon. But during the same time, man has poisoned, scarred, and polluted the land. Indeed, the faster man has built and created, the faster he has destroyed.

Today there is no unpolluted air left in the United States. There is no river or lake that has not been affected by the wastes of our society. And now the oceans are threatened. The United States alone dumps tens of millions of tons of raw sewage and industrial wastes into the fragile sea environment every year. Scientists have predicted that in twenty to fifty years, all life in the sea may be destroyed. It has also been predicted that air pollution will become so serious that man will have to live in domed cities to survive.

On all levels of society, there is a growing disgust with this kind of "progress." There is a rising demand for action. The participation of thousands of colleges, high schools, and grade schools in the Earth Day teach-ins on April 22, 1970, was proof that people want action now.

The fight to save the environment will be long, tough, and expensive. First we must realize that we are only a part of the world's life system, and that whatever we do affects the entire system. Then we must establish new policies to protect this life system.

A National Land Use Policy will be necessary. It will have to be tough enough to halt the kind of development for industry, highways, and housing that is needlessly ravaging the countryside. Strip mining has already laid open lands equal to a trench 100 feet wide and 1,500,000 miles long. Changing these methods will require a Federal law providing that the land be filled and reforested once mining is finished.

We must halt the dredging and filling that in the past 20 years have wiped out 900 square miles of coastal wetlands. The coastal wetlands are an important habitat for bird and animal life, and a key link in the life systems of the sea.

We must begin a massive program to protect the remaining undeveloped ocean and Great Lakes shorelines for the public.

Another policy to be established is a National Policy on Air and Water Quality. Such a policy would require every industry, municipality, and government facility to install immediately the best pollution-control equipment available. And 1975 must be set as a deadline for producing an automobile engine that is nearly pollution-free. The technology is available to make an automobile engine that is nearly pollution-free. Industry must be required to apply it.

A third policy that must be established is a National Policy on Resource Management. Such a policy will stop the plunder of the country's mineral, timber, and public-land resources. The drilling of new oil wells in the ocean must be delayed until we can learn to control oil spills from the wells. And the forests and wilderness must be protected for future generations.

A fourth vital policy is a National Policy on Population. This would include a program of research into family-planning methods. Then a broad educational effort must be undertaken to make family-planning information available to all who desire it. No plans to rebuild and preserve the environment will endure in the face of an exploding population.

To do all this, vast quantities of human and material resources must be marshaled. Everyone from grade-school pupils to the heads of giant corporations must take part in the environmental crusade. We must realize that we are not just citizens of one country. We are citizens of the total environment in which we live. A New Environmental Citizenship must be recognized, in which preservation and protection are as important as progress. The environment can be saved. But it will take large amounts of time, hard work, and caring.

Earth Day, April 22, 1970

HOW YOU CAN HELP

Everyone will have to take an active part if we are to stop the destruction of our environment. The task cannot be left to government and industry alone. Earth Day was a start in the right direction. Many people were made aware of the great task ahead. Some of them have already joined the fight against pollution.

Signing a petition to stop smog (left) is one way to join the fight. Other people, especially young people, prefer to get outdoors and work with their hands. The young boy and his mother (below) are collecting aluminum cans. These will be returned to the manufacturer so that they can be recycled. This not only improves our environment, it saves metals that someday will be in short supply. Girl Scouts (right) in 1970 helped clean up riverbanks, clearing away tons of debris. Many urban youths tried to make their city (New York) a nicer place in which to live, by planting flowers on an island in the middle of Broadway, the busiest street in the world.

George Rottung

TOP OF THE NEWS

By WALTER CRONKITE

THE community of nations could find a measure of comfort from world events as 1970 came to an end. To be sure, there were many problems to be solved, many areas of conflict that could explode into war. Still, at the end of 1970 there was more peace—or less war—than there had been at the beginning of the year. The civil war in Nigeria, Africa's most populous nation, ended in January. Despite the extension of the Indochina war to Cambodia, the war in Vietnam seemed to be winding down, with more and more American troops being withdrawn. And an American-sponsored cease-fire plan brought a halt to much of the fighting in the Middle East. In December, Israel decided to rejoin indirect peace talks with the United Arab Republic and Jordan, giving some hope, however slight, that a durable peace could be worked out.

In other areas, the United States and the Soviet Union continued their talks on limiting the production and deployment of strategic nuclear weapons; and the United Nations approved a treaty banning the placement of nuclear weapons on the seabed.

Perhaps the most dramatic developments toward an East-West *détente* took place in Europe. West German Chancellor Willy Brandt signed a historic treaty with the Soviet Union. The treaty pledged both nations to abstain from using force to settle disputes between them. It also recognized all existing European boundaries, including the one between Poland and East Germany. After World War II, Poland had annexed thousands of square miles of German territory. This treaty, and one between West Germany and Poland, recognize these boundaries, thus removing a major source of tension in Europe.

The Vietnam war has caused grave domestic problems for the United States. It is primarily responsible for the polarization of American society. And it is responsible for such economic woes as soaring prices and growing joblessness. As a result, 1970 saw a retrenchment on the part of the United States, as the nation sought to reorder its priorities. The results of the November elections indicated that the American people were more anxious than ever to turn inward and to solve such domestic problems as pollution, crime, inflation, and unemployment. The people's growing awareness of these problems (witness Earth Day) and their willingness to take an active part in solving them was an encouraging sign.

			1	2	3
4	5	6	7	8	9	10
11	12	13	14	15	16	17
18	19	20	21	22	23	24
25	26	27	28	29	30	31

5. United Mine Workers official Joseph A. Yablonski, his wife and daughter were found murdered in their home in Pennsylvania. In December 1969, Yablonski had lost a UMW presidential election after waging a bitter campaign.

11. The Kansas City Chiefs, American Football League champions, won the Super Bowl by downing the Minnesota Vikings 23–7 in New Orleans.

16. The leader of Libya's Revolutionary Command Council, Muammar al-Qaddafi, formed a new Cabinet and assumed the posts of premier and defense minister.

19. A Florida judge, G. Harrold Carswell, was nominated to the Supreme Court by President Richard Nixon.

20. After a two-year suspension of talks, the United States and Communist China met in Warsaw, Poland.

28. South Africa refused to allow black American tennis player Arthur Ashe to play in the South African Open Championships. . . . During a two-day visit to the United States, British Prime Minister Harold Wilson joined President Richard Nixon at a National Security Council session in Washington, D.C.

NIGERIAN CIVIL WAR ENDS. On January 12, after 31 months of fighting, the Republic of Biafra gave up its fight to remain independent. On May 30, 1967, the Ibo people of Biafra had declared their independence from Nigeria. The civil war followed, as Nigerian troops invaded Biafra in an effort to keep their country united. Nigerian leader Yakubu Gowon accepted the Biafran surrender and immediately announced programs to send food to Biafra, where the civil war had caused mass starvation, and to better relations between the defeated Ibos and Nigeria's other major tribes, the Yoruba and the Hausa.

Nigerians in Lagos, their capital city, cheer the news that the civil war is over. At right: Young, hungry children in Biafra wait for someone to give them food.

FEBRUARY

1	2	3	4	5	6	7
8	9	10	11	12	13	14
15	16	17	18	19	20	21
22	23	24	25	26	27	28

1. Jose Figueres Ferrer was elected president of Costa Rica. He had held the same office from 1953 to 1958. . . . In Buenos Aires, Argentina, a passenger train smashed into a parked commuter train, killing 136 people.

6. Yugoslavia and the European Economic Community signed a three-year trade agreement, the first such pact between the EEC and a communist country.

10. The worst avalanche in French history killed 42 people in the Alpine resort of Val d'Isère.

23. Switzerland imposed strong restrictions on the admission of Arab travelers into the country. Two days earlier a Swiss airliner on a flight to Israel exploded and crashed killing all 47 persons aboard. An Arab guerrilla group had claimed responsibility for the crash, but later denied it. . . . The South American country of Guyana became a republic, formally ending 139 years of association with Great Britain. Guyana will remain within the British Commonwealth.

24. Mrs. Margaret Kienast, 27, of Far Hills, New Jersey, gave birth to quintuplets, three girls and two boys, at Columbia Presbyterian Medical Center in New York.

CHICAGO 7 TRIAL ENDS. On February 18, David Dellinger, Rennie Davis, Thomas Hayden, Abbie Hoffman, and Jerry Rubin were found guilty of crossing state lines with intent to riot. All five were sentenced to five years in prison and fined $5,000. Two other defendants, John Froines and Lee Weiner, were acquitted. They were, however, sentenced to jail for contempt of court. The lawyers for the Chicago 7, William Kunstler and Leonard Weinglass, were also given jail terms by Judge Julius Hoffman for being in contempt of court.

Originally, the Chicago 7 were the Chicago 8. The eighth defendant, Black Panther leader Bobby Seale, was separated from the trial in November 1969 and sentenced to four years in prison

Julius J. Hoffman, presiding judge at the Chicago 7 trial. Hoffman accused the defense lawyers of "disrupting the administration of justice." In reply, defense lawyer William Kunstler stated that "this is not a fair trial."

for contempt of court. The Chicago 8 initially were charged with *conspiracy* to incite a riot at the 1968 Democratic national convention in Chicago. (This was the convention at which Chicago police and thousands of antiwar demonstrators battled in full view of television audiences.) After forty hours of deliberation, however, the jury found the defendants guilty not of conspiracy to incite a riot but of crossing state lines with intent to incite a riot and giving inflammatory speeches to further their goal.

Immediately after the defendants were sentenced, on February 18, students and Leftists held demonstrations in many parts of the country. All the defendants were released on bail on February 28 pending appeal of the sentences.

The Chicago 7 and their lawyers (clockwise from right foreground): Leonard Weinglass (lawyer), Rennie Davis, David Dellinger, John Froines, Thomas Hayden, Lee Weiner, Jerry Rubin, Abbie Hoffman, William Kunstler (lawyer).
© 1970 Verna Sadock—NBC News

1	2	3	4	5	6	7
8	9	10	11	12	13	14
15	16	17	18	19	20	21
22	23	24	25	26	27	28
29	30	31				

2. Rhodesia officially declared itself a republic, ending its last ties with Great Britain.

7. Millions of people on the North American continent witnessed a total eclipse, as the sun, moon, and earth fell into complete alignment.

12. President Richard Nixon nominated Curtis W. Tarr to be director of the Selective Service System, to replace General Lewis B. Hershey.

15. EXPO'70, Japan's world's fair, opened in Osaka.

17. For the first time, the United States used a veto in the UN Security Council. The United States rejected a resolution to condemn Britain .for not using force to overthrow the Government of Rhodesia.

19. In Erfurt, East Germany, Chancellor Willy Brandt of West Germany and East German Premier Willi Stoph held talks. It was the first time that leaders of both governments had met since the division of Germany 25 years before.

29. More than 1,000 people died, and 90,000 were left homeless, in an earthquake in western Turkey.

National Guardsmen deliver the mail in New York City.

POSTAL STRIKE. The first strike in American history by post-office workers began on March 18. It quickly spread across the country, with more than 200,000 postal workers walking off their jobs and demanding higher wages. On March 23, President Nixon ordered National Guard troops into New York City to sort and deliver the mail. Two days later the post-office workers were back on the job, and the Guardsmen were sent home. The postal unions began bargaining with the Government for an increase in wages.

Prince Sihanouk, ousted Cambodian leader.

SIHANOUK OF CAMBODIA OUSTED. On March 18, while Cambodian Chief of State Norodom Sihanouk was visiting the Soviet Union, right-wing military leaders seized control of the Government. Headed by General Lon Nol, the new Government announced that it would force Vietcong and North Vietnamese troops out of Cambodia. These troops had set up camps and supply dumps along the Cambodian border with South Vietnam. According to Cambodia's new leaders, they had ousted Sihanouk because he had not taken action against the communist troops. By the end of March, Cambodian soldiers, aided by American spotter planes from South Vietnam as well as South Vietnamese soldiers, began attacking the Communists. One result was that the Communists began moving deeper into Cambodia. Another result was that the Indochina war, previously confined to two countries—South Vietnam and Laos—had now spread to a third country.

General Lon Nol (center) with his new foreign minister (left) and deputy premier.

APRIL

			1	2	3	4
5	6	7	8	9	10	11
12	13	14	15	16	17	18
19	20	21	22	23	24	25
26	27	28	29	30		

5. West German Ambassador to Guatemala, Count Karl von Spreti, was found dead after the Guatemalan Government would not meet the ransom demands of guerrilla terrorists who had kidnaped Von Spreti on March 31.

8. In Osaka, Japan, 73 people were killed when a series of gas explosions tore through an underground subway-construction site.

14. Judge Harry A. Blackmun of Minnesota was nominated to the Supreme Court by President Richard Nixon. The Senate had rejected the nomination of G. Harrold Carswell six days before.

20. In a nationally televised address, President Nixon pledged to withdraw 150,000 more troops from Vietnam by April 1971; this would leave about 284,000 troops still there.

22. Millions of Americans across the nation participated in Earth Day, the largest demonstration ever organized to protest the pollution of the environment.

24. Gambia, the smallest country in Africa, became a republic within the British Commonwealth. . . . Communist China launched its first space satellite; it weighed 380 pounds.

APOLLO 13. On April 11, astronauts James A. Lovell, Jr., Fred W. Haise, Jr., and John L. Swigert, Jr., were launched into space aboard Apollo 13. Their goal was to make the United States' third manned lunar landing. But on April 13, as the spacecraft neared the moon, the astronauts heard and felt an explosion. An oxygen tank had blown up, damaging the command module. The lunar landing was canceled, and Apollo 13 swung around the moon for the long and dangerous trip back to earth. The astronauts returned in the lunar module, which still had its power and oxygen supply. They transferred back to the damaged command module for re-entry, and splashed down on target about 3½ miles from the recovery carrier USS *Iwo Jima* on April 17.

U.S. TROOPS ENTER CAMBODIA. On April 30, President Nixon announced that United States and South Vietnamese troops were being sent into Cambodia "not for the purpose of expanding the war into Cambodia, but for the purpose of ending the war in Vietnam." The immediate goal, the President said, was to destroy communist supplies and bases. The President's action was expected to trigger dissent by antiwar students, congressmen, and others.

An American GI in the Fishhook section of southeastern Cambodia. This area is just seventy miles from Saigon, the capital of South Vietnam.

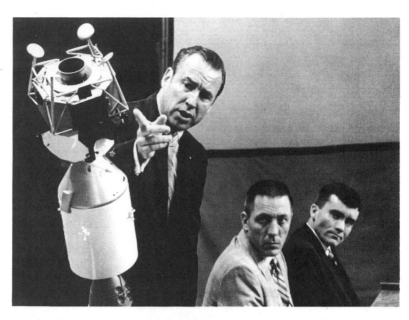

Apollo 13 commander James Lovell explains how he and fellow astronauts John Swigert (center) and Fred Haise (right) were saved by the lunar module.

In a TV address to the nation on April 30, President Nixon announces that American troops have entered Cambodia to destroy communist bases and supplies.

MAY

8. In New York City, hundreds of construction workers and anti-war student demonstrators clashed in the Wall Street area, leaving seventy people injured.

12. In racial rioting involving looting, fires, and sniper shooting, six Negroes were killed in Augusta, Georgia. . . . After defeating two of President Nixon's nominations to the Supreme Court, the Senate unanimously confirmed Judge Harry A. Blackmun.

15. South Africa was expelled from all Olympic Games competition because of its racially discriminating sports policies.

22. Palestinian guerrillas ambushed an Israeli school bus near the Lebanese border, killing 12 persons, most of them children. In retaliation, Israel attacked 4 Lebanese villages, killing about 20 persons.

27. Mrs. Sirimavo Bandaranaike, heading a three-party Leftist coalition, was elected prime minister of Ceylon. She had won the same office in 1960, when she became the world's first woman prime minister.

31. An earthquake devastated northern Peru, leaving 50,000 people dead, 100,000 injured, and 800,000 homeless.

THE KENT STATE TRAGEDY. After President Nixon's announcement on April 30 that he had ordered U.S. troops into Cambodia, antiwar demonstrations were held on many college campuses. Most of these demonstrations were peaceful. Some, however, resulted in violence. On May 4, at Kent State University in Ohio, National Guardsmen fired their rifles into a crowd of demonstrators. Four students were killed and several others wounded. The deaths of Allison Krause, 19, Sandra Lee Scheuer, 20, William Schroeder, 19, and Jeffrey Glenn Miller, 20, shocked the nation. Kent State was closed down for the remainder of the semester, and students in many colleges held memorial services for the dead students. The shootings also added to the fervor of antiwar demonstrators. On May 9, 60,000 to 100,000 students and others protested the war in Washington, D.C. And for the remainder of the month, campus demonstrations continued. The National Guard was again called out, or alerted, in several states, including Kentucky, South Carolina, Illinois, Colorado, Iowa, Maryland, and Ohio.

Two other students—Phillip Gibbs and Earl Green, both Negroes—were killed on May 14 at Jackson State College in Jackson Mississippi, this time by State Police, who had been called in to quell disturbances on the campus. The Federal Bureau of Investigation announced that it would send agents to investigate the shooting.

National Guardsmen at Kent State. Moments later four students lay dead.

A bullet-scarred building at Jackson State, where two youths were killed by police.

JUNE

4. Tonga, a Polynesian island group that had been a British protectorate for seventy years, became an independent nation within the British Commonwealth.

6. Robert H. Finch, secretary of health, education, and welfare, was shifted from his cabinet post to become an adviser to President Nixon. Elliot L. Richardson was named to succeed Finch.

10. George P. Shultz, secretary of labor, was named director of a new agency, the Office of Management and Budget. James D. Hodgson was nominated to succeed Shultz in the cabinet post.

16. Kenneth A. Gibson became the first Negro to be elected mayor of a major Eastern city when he defeated incumbent Hugh J. Addonizio in Newark, New Jersey.

19. Ending an earth-orbit mission, Soyuz 9, with cosmonauts Vitaly I. Sevastyanov and Colonel Andrian G. Nikolayev aboard, landed in the Soviet Union; they set a manned space-flight endurance record of 17 days 16 hours 59 minutes.

29. After two months of military operations, the last American troops were withdrawn from Cambodia, one day before President Nixon's deadline.

Edward Heath, Conservative prime minister of Great Britain.

CONSERVATIVES WIN BRITISH ELECTIONS. In May, certain that his ruling Labor Party would win, British Prime Minister Harold Wilson called for national elections. His optimism was backed up by the public-opinion polls. Right up to election day, four out of five polls predicted a Labor victory. Nevertheless, in June 18 national elections, the Conservative Party scored an impressive victory. The Conservatives won 330 seats in the House of Commons, for a gain of 68 seats and a clear majority of 31 seats over all other parties combined. The Labor Party lost 59 seats, and Harold Wilson lost his post as prime minister. He was replaced by Conservative Party leader, 53-year-old Edward Richard George Heath.

The most important election issue was the state of the British economy. However, a divisive note was injected when Conservative Enoch Powell stressed the issue of race. Powell, who easily won re-election to the House of Commons, is against allowing nonwhites into Great Britain. Many thousands of Pakistanis, Indians, and West Indians now live there and hold British citizenship. Powell was denounced by Heath, who called for better relations between races.

Robert Finch, President Nixon, and Elliot Richardson at a news conference.

George Shultz

James Hodgson

Kenneth Gibson

JULY

1. President Nixon named David K. E. Bruce to be the new chief negotiator at the Paris peace talks on Vietnam. Bruce, who had been ambassador to Britain, France, and Germany, would take up his post on August 1, 1970.

4. Thousands of people with many different political beliefs gathered in Washington, D.C., to celebrate Honor America Day on the 194th birthday of the nation.

6. Italy's 31st Government since the end of World War II fell after Premier Mariano Rumor and his four-party coalition Cabinet resigned.

10. Iceland's Prime Minister, Bjarni Benediktsson, his wife, and 4-year-old grandson were killed when their summer cottage was destroyed by fire. Johann Hafstein was named acting prime minister. . . . After spending 12 years imprisoned in Communist China, 79-year-old Reverend James E. Walsh was released. The Roman Catholic Bishop from Maryland had been sentenced to 20 years on charges of spying and subversion.

26. It was announced that the Sultan of Muscat and Oman, Said ibn Taimur, had been overthrown by his 28-year-old son, Qabus ibn Said.

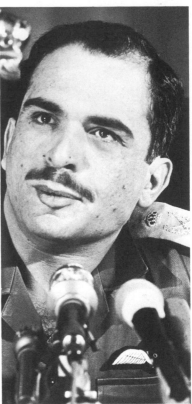

U.A.R. President Nasser (above left), Jordanian King Hussein (above right), and Israeli Prime Minister Meir (right) agreed to a cease-fire in July.

MIDDLE EAST CEASE-FIRE ACCEPTED. During the last week of July, the United Arab Republic (U.A.R.), then Jordan, and finally Israel agreed to a ninety-day cease-fire in the Middle East. The plan had been proposed on June 25 by United States Secretary of State William P. Rogers. In addition to the cease-fire, the Rogers plan called for United Nations mediator Gunnar Jarring to hold talks with representatives from Israel and the two Arab nations. The aim of the talks would be to bring about a permanent peace based on the UN Security Council resolution of November 22, 1967. This resolution calls for the withdrawal of Israel's forces from Arab territories it had occupied during the six-day war in June 1967. It also calls for Arab acceptance of Israel's right to exist within secure boundaries. Syria, Iraq, and the Palestinians denounced the cease-fire plan. But U.A.R. President Nasser called it the "final opportunity" to gain peace in the Middle East. Israel's acceptance of the plan came on the last day of the month, after a week-long, very bitter cabinet debate. Israel's right-wing Gahal Party threatened to resign from the Government if Israel accepted the plan.

						1
2	3	4	5	6	7	8
9	10	11	12	13	14	15
16	17	18	19	20	21	22
23	24	25	26	27	28	29
30	31					

6. The United States and Spain signed a five-year treaty permitting Americans the continued use of their military bases in Spain. In return, the United States will provide military equipment, grants, and loans. . . . . Ending a month-long government crisis, Emilio Colombo was sworn in as premier of Italy.

12. A bill creating an independent government agency to replace the 181-year-old Post Office Department was signed by President Nixon, ending Congressional authority over the mail system.

18. A 66-ton cargo of deadly nerve gas encased in concrete-and-steel containers was sunk by the U.S. Army off the Florida coast after legal battles failed to prevent the dumping.

20. Mexico and the United States agreed on a plan to settle all border disputes, ending nearly a century of minor border problems that had caused friction between the two countries.

24. A bomb blast tore through the Army Mathematics Research Center at the University of Wisconsin, killing a graduate student and causing damage estimated at $6,000,000. The Center had often been a target of antiwar demonstrations.

Soviet Premier Aleksei Kosygin (left) and West German Chancellor Willy Brandt (right), before the signing of the Soviet-West German treaty.

An Israeli officer relaxes in front of a bunker on the east bank of the Suez Canal while UN mediator Gunnar Jarring (above right) discusses the cease-fire with Egyptian representative Mohammad al-Zayyat.

MIDEAST CEASE-FIRE IN EFFECT. The Middle East cease-fire went into effect on August 7. Fighting stopped immediately along the Suez Canal, but Israeli forces and Palestinian commandos clashed inside Israel and in Jordan and Lebanon. On August 25, UN mediator Gunnar Jarring met with representatives from Israel, Jordan, and the United Arab Republic. Israel charged that the U.A.R. had violated the cease-fire by moving missiles closer to the Suez Canal.

SOVIET-WEST GERMAN TREATY. On August 12, West German Chancellor Willy Brandt and Soviet Premier Aleksei Kosygin signed a treaty by which their nations agreed to renounce the use of force in settling disputes. The two nations also agreed to recognize existing national boundaries in Europe. West Germany thus accepted Poland's annexation of the areas east of the Oder and Neisse rivers. Before 1945 this territory had been German.

SEPTEMBER

		1	2	3	4	5
6	7	8	9	10	11	12
13	14	15	16	17	18	19
20	21	22	23	24	25	26
27	28	29	30			

1. Nigeria resumed its ties with Tanzania, Gabon, Ivory Coast, and Zambia, the four African countries that had recognized secessionist Biafra. The reconciliation was announced at a summit meeting of the 41-nation Organization of African Unity, held in Addis Ababa, Ethiopia.

4. Salvador Allende Gossens received the most votes in Chile's presidential elections. However, because he did not win a majority (over 50%) of the votes, Chile's Congress was to make the final decision. If chosen, Allende would become the first Marxist to be democratically elected president of a noncommunist country. . . . Natalya Makarova, a leading ballerina of the Soviet Union's Kirov Ballet, was granted political asylum in Great Britain.

8. A three-day world summit conference of nonaligned nations opened in Lusaka, Zambia, with representatives from 54 neutral countries.

24. Luna 16 landed safely in the Soviet Union, becoming the first unmanned spacecraft to land on the moon, successfully lift itself off and return to earth. Mechanically-obtained lunar material was brought back from the Sea of Fertility, an area of the moon never before explored.

MIDDLE EAST: A MONTH OF TURMOIL. During September, violence and problems in the Middle East multiplied day by day. Israel walked out of the peace talks. Palestinian commandos hijacked and destroyed four airplanes. Civil war erupted in Jordan. And Egyptian President Nasser died of a heart attack.

During the first week of September, Israel accused the United Arab Republic of violating the cease-fire by moving missiles closer to the Suez Canal. Israel withdrew from the peace talks, saying it would not return until the missiles were removed.

On September 6, the same day Israel withdrew from the talks, Palestinian commandos hijacked 3 Western-owned civilian planes. One jet was forced to fly to Cairo, where it was blown up after the passengers were removed. The other 2 were flown to a desert airstrip in Jordan. Three days later the commandos hijacked a British plane. The Popular Front for the Liberation of Palestine claimed credit for the hijackings. A PFLP spokesman said the planes and passengers would be released when Arab commandos held in Western jails were released. This demand was not immediately met, and the commandos blew up the 3 planes. About 50 passengers were held as hostages for further bargaining; all others were released.

Meanwhile, hostility between the commandos and forces loyal to King Hussein of Jordan exploded into civil war. Thousands of people were killed before the fighting ended on September 25. Within the next few days the rest of the passengers were released. Arab commandos held in jail in Great Britain, West Germany, and Switzerland were set free.

The month ended on yet another tragic note: On September 28, Egyptian President Nasser died of a heart attack. Vice-President Anwar al-Sadat was named acting president.

Below: A hijacked TWA plane on a desert airstrip in Jordan. Right: An emotional scene at the funeral of Egyptian President Gamal Abdel Nasser.

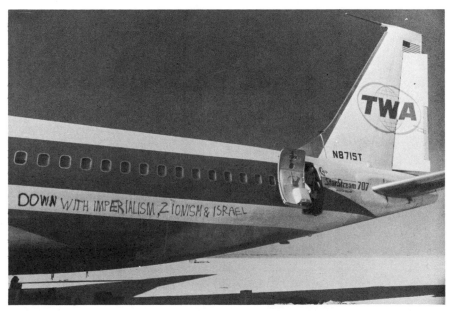

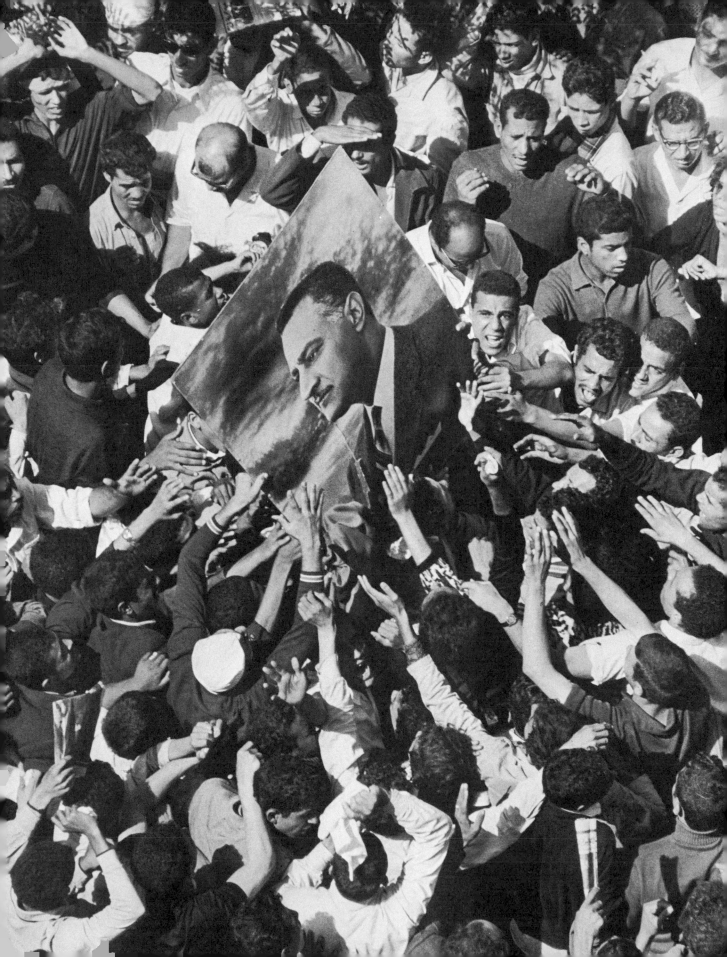

			1	2	3
4	5	6	7	8	9	10
11	12	13	14	15	16	17
18	19	20	21	22	23	24
25	26	27	28	29	30	31

7. After a political power struggle in Bolivia, Leftist general Juan Jose Torres assumed the powers of president. One day earlier, President Alfredo Ovando Candia had been forced to resign by right-wing-conservative elements in the Army.

9. Cambodia, a 1,168-year-old monarchy, became a republic.

10. Fiji, a group of South Pacific islands, became independent, ending 96 years of British rule.

13. Canada and Communist China established diplomatic relations.

15. The first successful hijacking of a Soviet airliner occurred when two hijackers forced the plane to land in Turkey. A stewardess was killed, and the pilot and copilot were injured. . . . In a plebiscite in the United Arab Republic, Acting President Anwar al-Sadat was elected to succeed the late President, Gamal Abdel Nasser.

24. Chile's Congress elected Salvador Allende Gossens, a Marxist, president of the country for a six-year term.

28. The United States and Russia agreed to develop "mutually compatible" rendezvous and docking systems for spacecraft.

James R. Cross, a British diplomat, was kidnaped from his home on October 5 by Quebec separatists.

Pierre Laporte, the Quebec labor minister, was kidnaped and then murdered by the separatists.

QUEBEC SEPARATISTS KILL DIPLOMAT. On October 5, the Front de Liberation du Quebec (FLQ), a group of Quebec separatists, kidnaped British diplomat James Cross. The FLQ demanded $500,000 in gold and the release of FLQ members being held in jail. On October 10, Quebec Labor Minister Pierre Laporte was kidnaped. The FLQ repeated its demands, but the Canadian Government refused to give in. On October 18 Laporte was found murdered. Two days earlier, Canadian Prime Minister Trudeau had invoked the War Measures Act and called in Army troops. At month's end, neither Cross nor the kidnapers had been found.

After the kidnapings, Prime Minister Trudeau called out Army troops.

NOVEMBER

1	2	3	4	5	6	7
8	9	10	11	12	13	14
15	16	17	18	19	20	21
22	23	24	25	26	27	28
29	30					

1. In Saint-Laurent-du-Pont, France, a fire in a dance hall killed 146 people, all 17 to 25 years of age.

6. Italy and Communist China established diplomatic relations.

10. The Soviet Union released two U.S. generals and a Turkish colonel, held since October 21 when their plane accidentally landed in Soviet Armenia.

17. The Soviet Union landed a "robot" moon rover on the lunar surface. The vehicle, Lunokhod 1, was transported to the moon by the spacecraft Luna 17.

18. Poland and West Germany concluded a treaty to normalize relations between the two countries.

20. A small unit of Army and Air Force men landed near Hanoi in an unsuccessful attempt to free American prisoners thought to be held there.

25. President Nixon dismissed Secretary of the Interior Walter J. Hickel.

27. A 35-year-old Bolivian artist attempted to assassinate Pope Paul VI in Manila, the Philippines, one stop in the Pontiff's tour of Asia and the Pacific.

On November 25, Secretary of the Interior Walter Hickel was dismissed by President Nixon. Relations between the two had been strained since May, when Hickel accused the President of failing America's youth.

CYCLONE HITS EAST PAKISTAN. On November 13 the southern coast of East Pakistan was struck by a cyclone. Winds reaching 150 miles an hour caused tidal waves 25 feet high to roar across the low-lying islands in the Bay of Bengal. The storm struck in the middle of the night, and when daybreak came the area was a scene of near-total devastation. How many people were actually killed may never be known. But entire villages were washed away, and early estimates put the number of dead in the hundreds of thousands. This was clearly one of the greatest tragedies of all times.

East Pakistani children, orphaned by the cyclone and tidal wave, wait for food. Relief supplies were flown in by the United States, West Germany, and other nations.

DECEMBER

	1	2	3	4	5
6	7	8	9	10	11	12
13	14	15	16	17	18	19
20	21	22	23	24	25	26
27	28	29	30	31

3. James R. Cross, the British official kidnaped by Quebec separatist militants on October 5, was released unharmed.

8. The United Nations Security Council condemned Portugal for "its invasion of the Republic of Guinea" in November.

11. Republican Congressman George Bush was nominated to succeed Charles W. Yost as U.S. delegate to the United Nations.

14. It was announced that former Democratic governor of Texas John B. Connally, Jr., was to replace David M. Kennedy as secretary of the treasury.

25. Eugen Biehl, West German honorary consul to Spain, was released by the Basques who had kidnaped him on December 1.

28. After a four-month boycott, Israel decided to resume Middle East peace talks at the UN.

30. Spanish leader Francisco Franco commuted the 6 death sentences imposed after a military trial of 15 Basque separatists.

31. The Russian Supreme Court commuted the death sentences of 2 Jews. They and 9 other defendants had been convicted on December 24 of planning to hijack a Russian airliner.

RIOTS IN POLAND. On December 14, after the Polish Government announced that fuel, food, and clothing prices would be increased, workers in the port city of Gdansk began rioting. When the rioting spread to Gdynia, Szczecin, and other urban areas, the Government declared a state of emergency. Militiamen and Army troops were called in to quell the riots. In the fighting that followed, dozens of people were killed and hundreds injured. On December 20, Polish Communist Party leader Wladyslaw Gomulka resigned along with four other top-ranking Communists. Gomulka was replaced by Edward Gierek. The state of emergency was lifted on December 22.

Wladyslaw Gomulka: former Communist Party chief of Poland.

Edward Gierek: successor to Gomulka as Poland's most powerful figure.

John B. Connally, Jr., former governor of Texas, was picked by President Nixon to replace David Kennedy as secretary of the treasury.

President Nixon announces the appointment of Texas Republican George Bush (left) to be U.S. ambassador to the United Nations. He will replace Charles Yost (right).

THE
YEAR
IN
REVIEW

1970

AFRICA

IN 1970, Sub-Saharan Africa had fewer wars, coups, and revolutions than in any year since 1960. During the 1960's, many coups had toppled governments. Two major civil wars had taken place: in the Congo (Kinshasa) from 1960 to 1963 and in Nigeria from 1967 to January 1970. The Nigerian civil war was fought to prevent the Eastern Region (Biafra) from withdrawing.

One new and possibly major problem arose late in 1970. Guinea President Sékou Touré said that Portuguese-led forces had invaded his country. Portugal denied the charges. But United Nations investigators said that the invaders had been trained in Portuguese Guinea and led by Portuguese officers.

The problems of poverty and tribal rivalry plagued every part of Africa. There are 16 African countries where less than 20 per cent of the adults can read, and the income per person per year is less than $100. Tribal rivalries are a common cause of political unrest. One-man rule or military government is the means most used to counter this, since African countries lack experience in real democracy. Ten African countries were run by the military in 1970.

In January 1970, Nigeria's 2½-year civil war came to an end. Biafran leader Odumegwu Ojukwu fled the country, and Major General Philip Effiong (below) took command. He made arrangements to surrender to the Federal Government.

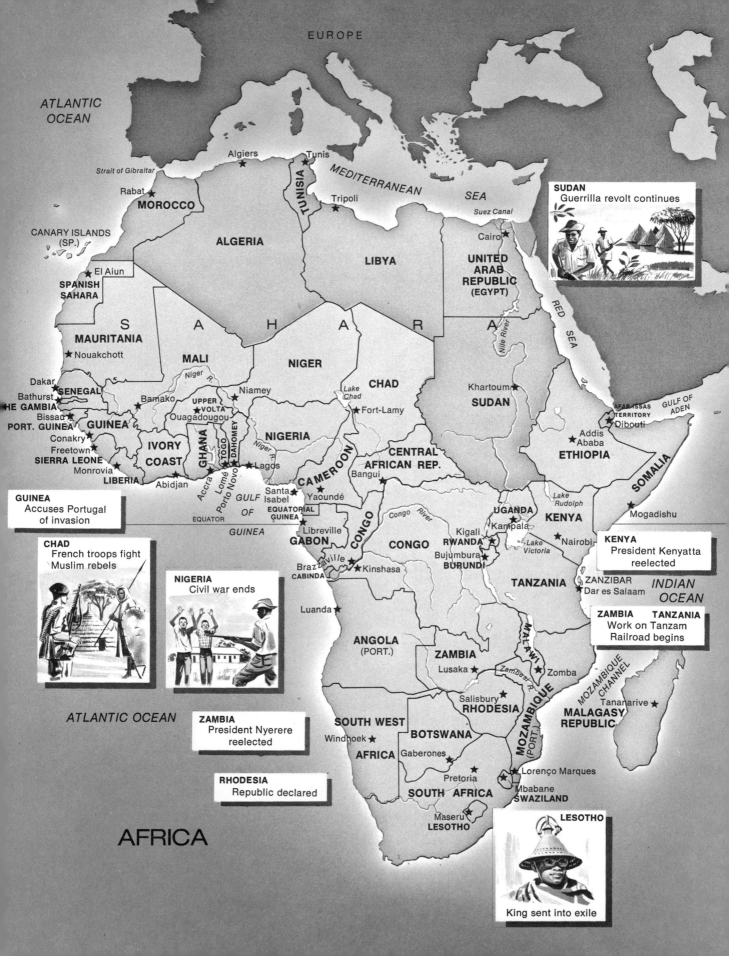

EUROPE

ATLANTIC
OCEAN

SUDAN
Guerrilla revolt continues

Strait of Gibraltar

MEDITERRANEAN   SEA

Algiers ★   Tunis ★

Rabat ★

MOROCCO

Tripoli ★

Suez Canal

Cairo ★

CANARY ISLANDS
(SP.)

ALGERIA

LIBYA

**UNITED
ARAB
REPUBLIC
(EGYPT)**

El Aiun ★

**SPANISH
SAHARA**

S   A   H   A   R   A

RED
SEA

Nile River

MAURITANIA

MALI

NIGER

Khartoum ★

Nouakchott ★

Niger R.

CHAD

SUDAN

AFAR-ISSAS   GULF OF
TERRITORY   ADEN
Dibouti

Dakar ★
Bathurst ★ **SENEGAL**
HE GAMBIA
Bissau ★
PORT. GUINEA **GUINEA**
Conakry ★
Freetown ★
SIERRA LEONE
Monrovia ★
LIBERIA

Bamako ★

Niamey ★

Fort-Lamy ★

**UPPER
VOLTA**
Ouagadougou ★

Lake
Chad

Addis
Ababa ★

NIGERIA

ETHIOPIA

Niger R.

CHAD
French troops fight
Muslim rebels

**IVORY
COAST**

GHANA
TOGO
DAHOMEY

Lagos ★

CAMEROON

**CENTRAL
AFRICAN REP.**

Abidjan ★
Accra ★
Lomé ★
Porto Novo ★

EQUATOR

Santa
Isabel ★ Yaoundé ★

Bangui ★

Lake
Rudolph

SOMALIA

GUINEA
Accuses Portugal
of invasion

GULF
OF
GUINEA

**EQUATORIAL
GUINEA**

Libreville ★

Congo River

UGANDA
Kampala ★

KENYA

Mogadishu ★

NIGERIA
Civil war ends

GABON

CONGO

CONGO

Kigali ★
RWANDA
Bujumbura ★
BURUNDI

Lake
Victoria

Nairobi ★

KENYA
President Kenyatta
reelected

Brazzaville ★
CABINDA

★ Kinshasa

TANZANIA

ZANZIBAR
Dar es Salaam ★

INDIAN
OCEAN

Luanda ★

**ANGOLA
(PORT.)**

ZAMBIA   TANZANIA
Work on Tanzam
Railroad begins

ATLANTIC OCEAN

ZAMBIA

Lusaka ★

Zambesi R.

MALAWI
Zomba ★

MOZAMBIQUE
CHANNEL

ZAMBIA
President Nyerere
reelected

Salisbury ★
RHODESIA

Tananarive ★

**MALAGASY
REPUBLIC**

SOUTH WEST

Windhoek ★

BOTSWANA
Gaberones ★

**MOZAMBIQUE
(PORT.)**

RHODESIA
Republic declared

AFRICA

Pretoria ★

Lorenço Marques ★
Mbabane ★
SWAZILAND

SOUTH   AFRICA

LESOTHO

Maseru ★
LESOTHO

King sent into exile

AFRICA

1970 was generally a year of friendly relations among African states. In early September, Ethiopian Emperor Haile Selassie (right) opened a summit meeting of the Organization of African Unity with the announcement that there had been a reconciliation between Nigeria and the four African states that had recognized Biafra as an independent state. At the second session of the OAU meeting (below) the 41 member states decided to press Western nations to stop supplying arms to the Republic of South Africa.

Lesotho, which is completely surrounded by the Republic of South Africa, had its share of political problems in 1970. Prime Minister Leabua Jonathan (left) canceled the results of January elections and declared himself head of state. He later sent King Moshoeshoe II into exile. Fighting between the supporters of the King and supporters of the Prime Minister resulted in many deaths. While southern Africa experienced turmoil, eastern Africa was quite tranquil. In Nairobi, Kenya, President Milton Obote of Uganda, President Jomo Kenyatta of Kenya, and President Julius Nyerere of Tanzania (below, left to right) met to discuss Zambia's application for membership in the East African Community.

NIGERIA: AFTERMATH OF THE CIVIL WAR

In January 1970, after 2½ years of bitter fighting, the Nigerian civil war ended. With his Army defeated, General Odumegwu Ojukwu, leader of the Biafrans, fled to neighboring Ivory Coast. The Nigerian Government began the difficult task of healing the wounds of war and rebuilding the country.

Although it had been feared that the Nigerian soldiers would loot the Ibo (Biafran) villages and harm the people, few such incidents took place. The most pressing problem for the Army was to bring in food and medical supplies for the civilian population. This was hindered at first by the bad condition of the roads, which had gone unrepaired during the thirty-month war. Many nations offered the Nigerian Government supplies and the planes, trucks, and jeeps to transport them.

At the end of 1970 the ravages of war were still felt in most parts of former Biafra.

The many children who had suffered illness and near-starvation needed special care. Many towns and cities still needed rebuilding. Yet the East-Central State was beginning to return to normal. Schools were open and places of business were operating. The government of Rivers State took revenge against the Ibos, though. Ibos were prevented from returning to their jobs, businesses, and lands in Port Harcourt, second-largest port in Nigeria and center of the oil industry. Before the civil war, Port Harcourt, which is on an arm of the Niger River, had been an Ibo city.

In October, Major General Yakubu Gowon, the Nigerian head of state, announced that Nigeria would return to civilian rule by 1976. Time was needed, he said, to wipe out the traces of the war and rebuild the economy. Time was also needed to write a new constitution and to take a national census before elections could be held.

Ibo refugees begin the long trip home after the end of the Nigerian civil war. For them the major task is to rebuild their homes.

WEST AFRICA

Dahomey, Nigeria's small neighbor to the west, has had a *coup d'état* every two years since it gained independence in 1960. The latest coup was in December 1969. During 1970, elections were held, and a unique form of government was set up. There are three presidents—one from each of the major ethnic groups. Each of the presidents is supposed to have a 2-year term in office before new elections are held. During the years they are not actually in the presidential seat, the second and third presidents are considered "assistant presidents." This is Dahomey's way of trying to solve the problem of political rivalry among its various groups.

Ghana, too, experienced a unique political event. The country returned to civilian government headed by Prime Minister Kofi A. Busia. But in 1969 its former military rulers kept a veto power over the new government and served as members of a three-man Presidential Commission. In 1970, the National Assembly asked the Commission to resign and allow the election of a civilian president. The Commission members agreed not only to dissolve the Commission but also to resign their military and police posts. Brigadier A. A. Afrifa, who had headed the military-police Government and was a member of the Commission, said that the Commission agreed to the request, "to put across a lesson—that people in power should not try to stay in office and keep control of the government" forever, as if it were their "property." Edward Akufo-Addo was elected president, and Ghana completed its return to civilian rule.

President Sékou Touré of Guinea announced on November 22 that Portuguese forces from neighboring Portuguese Guinea had invaded his country. Portugal denied responsibility, but a UN fact-finding mission supported Touré's charges. Portuguese officers, according to the mission, had led the 350-man invading force. The UN Security Council condemned Portugal by a vote of 11–0 on December 8.

Earlier in the year, Guinea had an outbreak of cholera. At least sixty people died of the disease.

CENTRAL AND EAST AFRICA

A military coup took place in Somalia in late 1969. The Government is now controlled by Major General Mohammad Siad Barre. The ousted leaders, who were more pro-West than the present Government, were arrested. In May, the Government nationalized foreign-owned banks. It also nationalized an electric-power company, a sugar company, and oil-distributing companies. The owners of the companies were promised full compensation.

In Sudan too the military Government, which took power in 1969, nationalized foreign banks and other businesses. The Government promised compensation in Sudanese bonds, repayable between 1980 and 1985. The owners of the nationalized companies think this compensation unsatisfactory.

A long-term guerrilla rebellion against Sudan's Muslim-dominated Government by black non-Muslim separatists in the south continued in 1970. The new Sudanese ruler, Gaafar al-Nimeiry, had promised the rebels more self-rule when he took power in 1969, but mutual mistrust caused continued fighting. The rebels accused the Government of bombing villages and destroying crops.

In November 1970, important talks were held between al-Nimeiry of Sudan and the leaders of the United Arab Republic and Libya. The leaders decided to make plans for a federation of their three Muslim nations.

In sparsely-populated Chad, to the west of Sudan, a nagging, five-year-old rebellion continued in 1970. Even the presence of three thousand French soldiers, first sent in in 1968, failed to halt it. The situation was the reverse of that in Sudan. In Chad the rebellion was carried on by Muslim tribesmen of the north, center, and east against a Government dominated by the black Sara people of the south.

In Ethiopia, Muslim separatists of Eritrea Province remained a thorn in the side of the Christian Government. Though the rebels (thought to be about one thousand strong) have little influence in the towns, they are a threat to peace in the Eritrean countryside. In March they kidnaped a

In Chad, a French soldier guards a prisoner. A rebellion by Muslim tribesmen who live in the north of Chad has been going on for five years.

team of researchers from the *National Geographic* magazine and held them 16 days. The Government believes the rebels are a Pan-Arab extremist group directed from abroad and not a real separatist movement.

Kenya re-elected President Jomo Kenyatta in late 1969. In May 1970, the Government declared that Swahili would become Kenya's national language. Swahili is a Bantu language of the East African coastal areas. It contains many Arabic, Portuguese, English, and Indian words. When the British ruled Kenya, they required that all government employees know Swahili. But after independence the Kenyans came to use English more and more. The new government order—written in English—stated that people must now speak Swahili both at work

and at home. People who speak tribal languages can now only use them when meeting with members of their tribe.

In 1970, Kenya stepped up its policy of expelling Asians (mostly East Indians). Many Asians had lived in Kenya for generations and in some cases were Kenyan citizens. The Asians did not often mix socially with the blacks, but they owned many of the country's businesses. The Government decided the Asians are depriving blacks of the chance to go into business and began to shut Asian businesses down.

When the Asians are ordered to leave Kenya (or neighboring Uganda), they often have nowhere to go. The majority hold British passports—but Britain does not permit nearly so many Asians to enter as Kenya plans to expel.

A street scene in Nairobi, Kenya. The sign is partly in Swahili, which is to become Kenya's national language.

President Julius K. Nyerere of Tanzania was returned to office in an October election. He continued his policy of turning Tanzania into a socialist state. In February he had announced that the Government would take over all wholesaling activities. The Government also took over *The Standard,* Tanzania's largest English-language newspaper.

A highlight of 1970 for Tanzania and for Zambia, its neighbor to the southwest, was the start of work on the Tanzam railroad. The railroad, which will cross both countries, will connect Zambia with Tanzania's Indian Ocean port of Dar es Salaam. It will provide an outlet through black Africa for Zambia's copper. Zambia will no longer have to depend on rail routes through white-dominated Rhodesia, Angola, and Mozambique.

The People's Republic of China is financing the railroad with an interest-free loan and is providing about half the manpower to build it. The 1,116-mile railroad, China's largest foreign-aid project, should be finished by 1975.

In September, Zambia hosted a meeting of nonaligned nations. Representatives from 54 countries met in Lusaka for a 3-day conference. They passed resolutions favoring "liberation movements" in the Middle East, Southeast Asia, and southern Africa.

▶SOUTHERN AFRICA

The one *coup d'état* in Africa in 1970 occurred in the tiny kingdom of Lesotho. The Prime Minister, Leabua Jonathan, canceled the January 27 election results and declared himself head of state. He accused the King, Moshoeshoe II, of interfering in politics and exiled him. The Prime Minister arrested his political opponents. In the following months the police carried out raids in which over two hundred people were killed. Great Britain, which supplies 90 per cent of Lesotho's economic aid, did not recognize Jonathan's take-over and cut off the aid. Later Jonathan met with his imprisoned opponents to seek a compromise. Jonathan is said to be a friend of South Africa, which surrounds Lesotho on all sides. The opposition leaders favor a Pan-African policy and seek to reduce Lesotho's ties with South Africa.

In South Africa, the Government has been trying to move the country toward complete apartheid (separate development of the races). Though the policy was still championed by the ruling Nationalist Party in 1970, certain flaws in the policy were showing up. Apartheid's goal is to get all the country's 15,000,000 blacks to move to special homelands called Bantustans. But the 1970 census shows that there are now 8,000,000 blacks living in white areas, whereas there were 5,000,000 blacks in white areas in 1951. Thus the policy is not working.

More and more white South Africans are beginning to realize that if the blacks all

Communist China increased its economic and political penetration of Africa in 1970. Chinese technicians and laborers began work on the Tanzam railroad (above) while Chinese entertainers (below) performed in Dar es Salaam, Tanzania.

Clifford Dupont, the first president of the Republic of Rhodesia.

move to Bantustans there will be a serious labor shortage in the white areas, where all the country's industries are. And the blacks point out that if the Bantustans are to function the South African Government must give them much more money.

The whites' awareness of the drawbacks of total apartheid caused the opposition United Party to gain a total of 17 seats in the Federal Parliament and provincial councils in 1970. The United Party supports a less strict form of apartheid. The Progressive Party, which opposes apartheid, retained its one seat in Parliament.

The Government of Rhodesia, South Africa's northern neighbor, declared the country a republic on March 2, 1970. On the same date, a new republican constitution came into effect. Under the constitution, income requirements for voting prevent all but token participation in the government by Rhodesia's 4,500,000 black majority.

Britain continued to regard Rhodesia as a self-governing colony in a state of rebellion. But the new Conservative Government in Britain said in November that it would have one more try at reaching a compromise with Rhodesia on the racial issue. It was because of Rhodesia's white-supremacist racial policies that Britain withdrew its approval for Rhodesian independence in 1965. Economic sanctions against Rhodesia by most nations continued in 1970 but had a limited effect.

▶ **REFUGEES**

More than a million refugees from 12 African countries are aided by the United Nations High Commission for Refugees. Most of the refugees are members of tribal groups who have left their countries to avoid political persecution. Some national policies are creating refugees more directly. Kenya and Uganda, for example, are simply expelling British Asians. The Government of Ghana expelled about 200,000 people in 1970. Ghana explained that most were traders who lived off the country but did not pay income tax. Actually the people expelled included many longtime residents and migrant workers on the cacao farms. Ghana allowed those foreigners to remain who held valid work permits.

MARGARET F. CASTAGNO
ALPHONSO A. CASTAGNO, Director
African Studies Center, Boston University

AFRICAN GAME PARKS

A sixth-grader in Boston asked a visiting diplomat from Ghana, "Do you often see lions and tigers in Africa?" The Ghanaian replied that he had not seen tigers because they come from Asia. As for lions, though they come from Africa, he had seen them only in zoos.

It seems that the diplomat, like his young host, was a city dweller. To see wild animals, many Africans must do what visitors to Africa do—go to one of Africa's many large game parks. Most countries have at least two or three. Kenya has 12!

The most famous game park is probably Kruger National Park in South Africa.

Kruger is eight thousand square miles in area, the size of the state of Massachusetts. Kafue National Park in Zambia and Tsavo in Kenya are just as big.

Most of Africa's large wild animals—lions, elephants, giraffes, rhinoceroses, hippopotamuses, zebras, antelopes, leopards, buffaloes, and okapi—roam at will throughout the parks. They live just as they did in the distant past, before man began to build cities and use deadly weapons.

Hunting is not allowed in the parks. The tourists come to watch the animals and "shoot" them with cameras. Each park is cared for by a staff of rangers or wardens. They keep out poachers (illegal hunters) and also watch for signs of animal diseases, brush fires, and floods.

A tourist "shoots" an elephant with a camera in the Kruger National Park in South Africa. Hunting is not allowed in any of Africa's game parks.

A young visitor plays with a baby monkey in Kruger National Park. Constant contact with tourists has made many animals very tame.

A pride of lions seems to be holding up traffic in this national park. Lions have the right-of-way, and wise motorists will stay in their cars.

Zebras, a giraffe, and some Cape buffalo share a drink at a water hole while another giraffe, who is probably 18 or 19 feet tall, feeds on tree leaves.

AGRICULTURE AND FOOD

IN the less-advanced nations of the world, most of the people must spend most of their time just finding enough to eat. Even in the Soviet Union, a third of the work force is on farms. In the United States, only 5 per cent of the people live on farms and produce the food needed by the nation. Indeed, because American farms are so productive, the average farm worker produces enough food to feed 45 people. One week's grocery list for those people would include 225 pounds of meat and fish, 180 quarts of milk, 400 pounds of fruits and vegetables, and 172 pounds of bakery goods as well as breakfast cereal and flour.

In 1970 an imaginary "average" United States farmer farmed almost 400 acres. He sold $25,000 worth of farm products. His

profit from farming was only about $5,700. However, some of his family worked in town part of the time. This income, plus money from other nonfarm investments, added about $5,300 to his income, giving him a total of nearly $11,000 for family living and investment.

The figure sounds comfortable. But it is the average of the income of very different kinds of farmers. Of America's 2,900,000 farms, the 1,000,000 largest produce most of the nation's food. 1970 brought continued growth in this group. Most of the other 1,900,000 farms are worked by part-time farmers who depend on jobs in town. Or they are farms of a few acres on which poor people scratch out a living. More of these farm families move to cities and suburbs every year.

In 1970 much of the Midwest fought wet weather during the corn-planting season. Blight struck the corn in the summer. Yet farmers produced one of the most abundant total crops ever. The crop was so abundant that food prices dropped late in the year, helping to cool inflation. Farmers rode out the business slump in better shape than most other businessmen. Even when business is bad, people must still buy food.

During 1970, American farms continued to be the most productive in the world. The average farm worker produced enough food to feed 45 people.

At the start of 1970, the average American farmer was managing $100,000 worth of land, buildings, machinery, livestock, and supplies. He still owed about $30,000 on his mortgage, and in the course of the year would have to borrow almost $30,000 to meet his bills.

Early in the year, farm experts made a number of predictions to help farmers in their planning. The experts guessed that 1970 would bring slightly improved prices for corn and soybeans and fairly good prices for livestock. The experts also predicted that farmers would take in about 3 per cent more from farm-product sales than in 1969. But expenses would run 4 per cent higher.

Major farm-machinery builders offered awesome, huge tractors, some developing 170 horsepower. An important new tillage tool was the Glencoe "Soil Saver," which promises to reduce soil losses from wind and water erosion. The tool mixes crop remains with the soil, and leaves corduroy-like ridges on the surface.

The Tax Reform Act, which came into effect in 1970, brought changes. The new tax rules limited the amount of losses city people could deduct from their nonfarm income. Many thus became less interested in investing in farming.

Farmers planned to chip in money from their pork and beef sales to promote these products. Farmers, and dairymen especially, took a more active part in the effort to sell their products at retail.

Cowmen from all over the country were excited about a whole new program of cross-breeding. It seemed probable, by crossing

The Glencoe "Soil Saver," a new tillage machine, can chew up cornstalks and root clumps and then mix them in with the surface soil. This timesaving machine also creates surface ridges which prevent soil from blowing away.

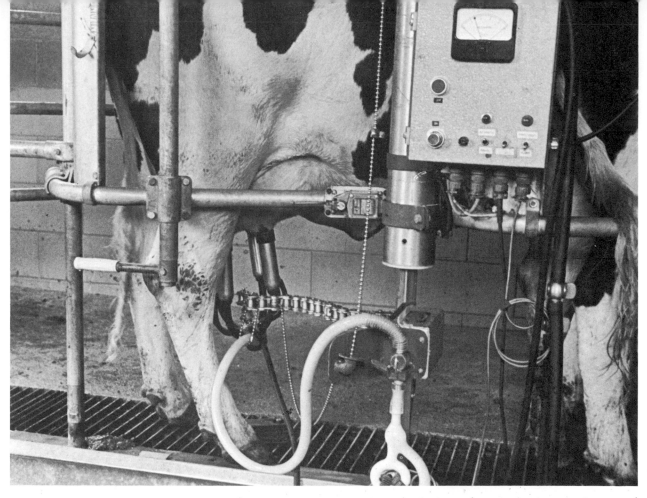

A fast milker can handle 4 cows an hour. But with new automated equipment, one man can milk as many as 120 cows an hour. In the unit above, an electronic "brain" senses when the cow is completely milked; it then automatically disengages. Below: An automatic machine milks 8 cows at once.

Engineer Robert Choate tells a Senate subcommittee that most dry cereals provide little nutrition. Cereal manufacturers termed Choate's report "untrue."

Angus and Hereford cows with big European breeds (Charolais, Simmental, Limousin, and others), to produce faster-growing calves.

Dairymen were discussing two big developments: automated milking and huge regional marketing co-ops. Some of the new milking equipment senses when the cow has given all her milk and removes the milker units. By hand a man can milk four cows an hour, at most. With new equipment and milking-building design, one may be able to milk 120 cows an hour.

▶ THE PLANTING SEASON

As May rolled around, rains flooded fields across much of the Corn Belt. Farmers couldn't plant on time. Finally the weather cleared. And as farmers struggled to get their crops into the soil, people in cities held giant rallies on Earth Day (April 22) to protest the pollution of our air, water, and general environment. Amid the talk of industrial pollution, there were charges that farm pesticides and fertilizer are a threat to the environment. From the scientific community came the reply: No case of human injury has ever been traced to proper use of approved farm chemicals. However, the United States Department of Agriculture (USDA) stepped up its program of checking soil and water for traces of pesticide.

Before a pesticide can be sold in interstate commerce, it must be proved safe and effective and registered with USDA. More than 45,000 pesticides are registered, made from combinations of 900 chemicals. USDA grew increasingly concerned that residues (remains) of DDT and other long-lasting pesticides might harm some species of wildlife. By the end of 1970 the agency had canceled registration of DDT for all uses, except for special cases.

In 1971, USDA is slated to hand over many of its pesticide-regulating powers to the new Environmental Protection Agency. This agency will take over pollution-control functions now scattered among Federal departments.

Late in the spring a special Presidential Task Force recommended the countryside as a remedy for sick, overcrowded cities. About 70 per cent of all Americans are jammed into 2 per cent of the land. The results: concentrated pollution from smog and wastes, paralyzed transportation, slum housing and slum living, a crime epidemic. The Task Force recommended setting a national growth policy to spread people over more of our country.

▶ SUMMER

By July there was talk that the nation's economic slowdown had reached its lowest point and things would start to improve. Prices for farm products were holding up reasonably well. It looked as though history would repeat itself. In four previous recessions since World War II, farmers had pulled through better than the rest of the economy.

Also strengthening demand for farm products was an expanded food-stamp program and other efforts to feed the needy. The USDA food-stamp program allows the poor to buy food coupons at a low price and then turn in the coupons at stores for food. In May, President Nixon signed a law prom-

During 1970, corn blight struck from the South to the Midwest, causing big losses to farmers.

ising free school lunches for all needy children. Altogether about 12,000,000 Americans received food aid from the Federal Government during 1970.

An attack on the nutritional value of leading dry breakfast cereals came in July. Robert B. Choate, Jr., a former government consultant on hunger, told a Senate subcommittee that 40 of 60 cereals he studied "fatten but do little to prevent malnutrition." Major cereal companies answered his attack by quoting opposing views of other nutrition authorities.

Reports of interesting new crop research appeared:

Corn. Seedsmen experimented with an entire redesign of the corn plant. Corn normally produces 1 or 2 ears. Each ear has about 700 kernels, or seeds, and is located halfway up the stalk. By a change in the plant's genes, it can be made to set seed on top, in an open tassel shape with about 2,000 small kernels. This change would simplify harvest by modern combines.

Wheat. Several new varieties yielded over 100 bushels an acre in Nebraska—well above average.

Soybeans. A whole series of new varieties was released, tailored to specific areas and markets.

Triticale. A cross between rye and barley, Triticale has shown amazing progress in recent years. University researchers see more years of development work before it is ready for widespread planting as a feed grain. Private seedsmen claim they have better seed than the universities do and that Triticale is almost ready for planting by farmers.

In the United States there are surpluses of farm products (larger amounts than can be sold or used). There are farm surpluses in Western Europe too. But in heavily populated, underdeveloped parts of the world, shortages, rather than surpluses, are the problem.

In 1969, for the first time in 12 years, there was no gain in the total amount of food produced throughout the world. The report was made by the Food and Agriculture Organization of the United Nations. World food experts say that the gap between the amount of food produced and the number of people in the world is growing larger.

▶ LATE SUMMER: THE BLIGHT

By mid-August, corn had grown big, solid ears, and farmers were expecting a near-record crop. But suddenly an alarm went up. A new type of virus disease called Race-T of Southern leaf blight was sweeping up from the South into the Midwest. The disease caused dark spots on the husk,

Cesar Chavez continued to organize farm workers. His United Farm Workers Organizing Committee signed contracts in 1970 with most major grape growers.

dead leaves at the lower part of the stalk, and a soft, easily broken cob. Estimates of loss ranged from 6 per cent to 15 per cent of the crop.

Many of the seed-corn companies' fields were blight-damaged. The companies scrambled to obtain enough blight-resistant seed for next year's crop. One company loaded equipment and seed onto a jet and produced a crop in Hawaii. However, not enough resistant seed will be available in 1971. So the blight will certainly be back—probably worse than in 1970.

The blight brought home a lesson. Many people thought that farming had become as sure and predictable as a chemical factory. 1970 was a stunning reminder that crops are still subject to whims of nature.

▶ FALL

In California, Cesar Chavez and his United Farm Workers Organizing Committee signed contracts with most major table grape growers. Chavez turned quickly to organize vegetable growers in the Salinas Valley. Then he sent organizers to the Midwest and East. Unionization of farm workers everywhere now seems only a matter of time—perhaps a short time.

With the fall came a new twist in another political struggle—the journey of the 1970 Farm Bill through Congress. The journey was marked by debate in the House and by Senate infighting. The details changed almost daily. But it became generally clear that there would continue to be some kind of support prices for basic grain crops. (The Government would make up the difference to farmers if prices for their crops went below a certain level.) It also became clear that there would continue to be payments to farmers for taking a certain amount of land out of production. The aim of this government policy is to keep farm prices up and prevent huge surpluses of certain crops.

The final farm bill, signed by President Nixon in November, limits the total government support payment for any one crop to a $55,000 maximum.

JERRY CARLSON
Managing Editor, *Farm Journal*

FARM CLUBS

A major goal of the Future Farmers of America (FFA) is to interest young people in farming. FFA members study farming in high school.

Water is one of the rancher's most precious natural resources. FFA members learn to conserve water and make the best use of it in irrigating land.

Electricity is a vital source of power on the farm. FFA students of vocational agriculture devote many hours of classroom study to the principles of electricity.

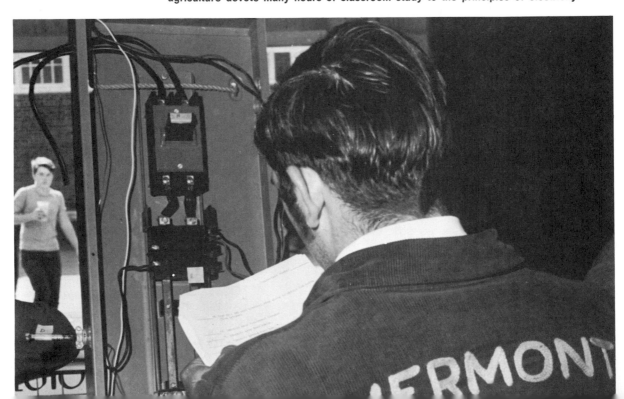

Above: FFA members at a dairy-products judging contest select the best milk samples. Below: members of a 4-H dairy club in Michigan. 4-H is the largest farm organization for young people. More than 3,500,000 young people take an active part in 4-H programs in the United States.

THE ARTS

IN 1970 the fine arts were noted for a blend of the old and the new; old masters were as popular as contemporary artists.

Big events in 1970 were the 100th-birthday celebrations of New York's Metropolitan Museum of Art and Boston's Museum of Fine Arts. Nearly every school of painting, from abstract expressionism to realism, was included in these shows. Other exhibitions during the year ranged from the 15th-century masterpieces of Rembrandt to the graceful, modern sculptures of Brancusi.

One of the most interesting photographic exhibitions was USSR Photo 70, representing some 400 Russian photographers. Bruce Davidson's book *East 100th Street* was a masterful collection of portraits of people living on a slum street.

Architects had a creative year, too, using new materials and inventive shapes. The St. Thomas Aquinas Church, shown on the opposite page, is but one example.

**A portrait from Bruce Davidson's "East 100th St,"
a "family photograph album" for East Harlemites.**

The graceful lines and smoothness of Brancusi's marble "White Seal" present the essence, rather than the actual image, of a seal.

The altar in St. Thomas Aquinas Church in Indianapolis. Function is stressed in its simple design.

Willem de Kooning's "Bill Lee's Delight," shown during the Metropolitan Museum of Art's 100th-birthday celebrations.

PHOTOGRAPHY

The 1970 business slump was bad for photography. For established photographers, there were fewer assignments. For young professionals, there were fewer opportunities to "make it." And for professionals and amateurs alike, there were rising costs and less money available for cameras, film, and equipment. Even teenagers, just starting out with photography as a hobby, had to think twice before spending allowance money for a camera or film.

But those who were interested enough in photography gave up other pleasures so they could continue "doing their own thing": creating pictures. For this reason, 1970 saw the continued display of outstanding photographs. Photography annuals continued to publish beautifully creative photos. And publishers continued to release high-quality photography books.

▶ PHOTOGRAPHY BOOKS AND MAGAZINES

The two most interesting and photographically important books of 1970 were *Sequences* by Duane Michals and *East 100th Street* by Bruce Davidson.

In his book, Michals shows how to tell picture stories in an interesting way with a sequence of only six or seven photographs. The stories are told so clearly that they do not need text to explain them. Furthermore, they deal with subjects that are of special interest to young photographers.

Many young photographers have made motion pictures, but have found that this can be very expensive. They might now find some satisfaction in following Michals' lead. Creative picture sequences can be like short, meaningful movies, and they are much less expensive to do.

Bruce Davidson's book is about people living in poverty on East 100th Street in the East Harlem section of New York City. The book is filled with large, quite formal photographs of people who have obviously posed for the camera. In fact, this was just the technique used by Davidson. He told his subjects to pose in whatever way they

would prefer. The result is a very powerful and moving group of photographs. The people of East 100th Street themselves see Davidson's book as a kind of family album of their street.

▶ NEW PHOTOGRAPHY MAGAZINES

Two new photography magazines were published in 1970. *Focus,* published in England, is very well written. The photographs and the printing are excellent. The young editors of *Focus* would like to help restore English photography's reputation, which has not been good in recent years. The high quality of their magazine suggests that they may indeed be able to accomplish their goal.

The outlook for *Creative Photography,* published in California, is less bright. Of all the American photography magazines, it comes closest to meeting the needs of beginners in photography. All other magazines are too technical or too sophisticated for beginners. However, in its first issue *Creative Photography* got off on the wrong foot. Its lead picture story was a group of nudes of a type that do not belong in a serious photography magazine.

▶ NEW PHOTOGRAPHY-BOOK CATALOGUES

Getting good, easy-to-understand information on photography can be a problem for amateur photographers. Material that is available, including the camera magazines, is mostly for very advanced amateurs. For beginners, the information is just too technical. And it often deals with picture subjects that are not very interesting to teen-agers.

This problem of making easy-to-understand information available to amateurs is being overcome. A New York book store and the Eastman Kodak Company now have catalogues that list about one thousand books, brochures, pamphlets and instruction sheets. Some are very technical and are for advanced amateurs and professionals. But there are also hundreds of publications for the beginner. With the catalogues, you can order the information you need by mail—and usually at a reasonable price.

Dan Budnick's striking photograph of a gone-to-seed dandelion appeared in Popular Photography Magazine's 1971 Photography Annual.

The Laurel Book Center, 1286 Broadway, New York, N.Y. 10001 will send you their catalogue on request. It lists books from all the American, English, and European publishers who have printed even one or two books on photography. It also lists the big publishers, such as Amphoto and Morgan and Morgan. The catalogue lists books on hundreds of photographic subjects.

Eastman Kodak now publishes two excellent catalogues. To get catalogue L-5, *"1971 Index to Kodak Technical Information,* write to Department 454, Eastman Kodak Company, Rochester, New York 14650. A second Eastman Kodak list should be of great value. Write to Department 841 at the same address and they will send you their list of amateur-photography publications.

▶ LIFE LIBRARY OF PHOTOGRAPHY

In 1970, Time-Life Books began publishing its eight-volume Life Library of Photography. The books are carefully researched, well-written, and beautifully illustrated. They contain a fund of information for the amateur and professional photographer.

The first two volumes issued in 1970 were *The Camera* and *Light and Film.* In *The Camera,* the four basic types of cameras —the viewfinder, the single-lens reflex, the twin-lens reflex, and the view camera—are studied in detail. Different types of lenses are also studied. There are magnificent color photographs of antique cameras. *Light and Film* deals with the nature of light and its photographic effects, and with the advantages and uses of different types of black-and-white and color films.

In 1970, too, *Life* magazine announced a unique photography contest for both amateurs and professionals. It will no doubt draw thousands of entrants. The contest prizes total $75,000. First prize is a one-year, $15,000 contract as a *Life* photographer. A contract photographer guarantees that he will make a certain amount of his time available for *Life* assignments. He gets paid the full amount of the contract even if he is not called on to work. Most photo-

journalists love to work for *Life* on this basis. It can be assumed that an amateur would find it a great thrill.

▶ USSR PHOTO 70 EXHIBITION

The most imposing photography exhibition in 1970 was USSR Photo 70, which toured many major American cities. It had 1,200 prints in color and black and white and represented the work of some 400 Russian photographers. Some critics did not like the show. They felt it was merely a rehash of American photography from the 1930's and 1940's. Other critics found it exciting, an indication that photography as an art is thriving in the Soviet Union. I see it as a very important exhibition, which indicates strongly that Americans and Russians share many of the same ideals.

In 1970 Time-Life Books published the first volumes of its Life Library of Photography. With "Leopard at Sunset," John Dominis shows effective use of the 1,000mm lens. Ben Rose uses strobe lights to create movement.

▶ INEXPENSIVE CAMERAS

Most professional photographers spend hundreds of dollars for a single camera. For most amateurs, especially teen-agers, such cameras are out of reach. This was especially true in 1970, because of the poor economic situation. However, many beginning photographers solved this problem with the Diana camera. The Diana is a plastic box-camera that looks expensive, but it costs only from $.89 to $1.89, depending on where you buy it. Its plastic lens gives a rather sharp picture on 120 film.

Actually, students in several college departments of photography are *required* to use Dianas in their basic photography courses. These students have created very handsome exhibits, with prints enlarged to as much as 8 × 10 and 11 × 14.

At Ohio University, photography students use very cheap film with the Diana. By buying in quantity, the Photography Department can sell the film to the students for about 10 cents a roll. This is much less than the cost of regular film. Usually, the speed of very cheap film is not as fast as advertised. Nor are the recommended developing times quite right. But at Ohio University, the teachers and advanced students figured out the correct speeds and times.

In some basic courses, students are required to shoot at least 12 rolls of film each week. They are taught that film is cheap, and through lots of shooting they will be able to express themselves very well—even with cheap film and a $1.00 camera.

RALPH HATTERSLEY
Popular Photography Magazine

SCHOLASTIC PHOTOGRAPHY AWARDS

The beautiful color photographs on these and the following two pages were taken not by professional photographers but by five teen-agers. These photographs were among the thousands of black-and-white prints and color transparencies entered in the 1970 Scholastic Photography Awards program. They all won awards in the "Wildlife and Pets" category.

Each year, for more than 40 years, Scholastic Magazines, Inc., has conducted this photography-awards program for students in grades 7 through 12. The Eastman Kodak Company is the sponsor. The judges, who must choose the best photographs, include Walter Chandoha, famous for his magnificent photographs of animals; Tom Hollyman, president of the American Society of Magazine Photographers; and David Vestal, associate editor of *Travel & Camera* magazine.

The results of the program clearly show the originality and creativity of many American and Canadian teen-age photographers.

"Everyone Loves a Parade" (below), by 13-year-old Eden Steiger of Churchill Junior High School, East Brunswick, New Jersey, was the winner of a First Award. Kenneth Valastro, 15, a student at George Washington High School, Ridgewood, New Jersey, won a Second Award for his "Dog's World" (right).

Tom Schneider, 16, a student at Ann Arbor Pioneer High School, Ann Arbor, Michigan, won an Honor Award for "Wild Wonder" (left). An Honor Award also went to Doug Crockett for his cow. Doug, 16, is a student at Oak Hills High School, Cincinnati, Ohio.

Tom Schneider won a second Honor Award for his "Late Fall Arrivals" (right). Laurie Baker's cat seems well camouflaged in a pile of fall leaves. For her photograph, 16-year-old Laurie won an Honor Award. She is a student at Rochester Adams High School, Rochester, Michigan.

PAINTING

In 1970 the Metropolitan Museum of Art in New York City and the Boston Museum of Fine Arts celebrated their 100th birthdays. As part of its birthday celebration, the Metropolitan held several major exhibitions. One was called "19th-Century America." It included paintings, sculptures, and room furnishings of that period.

Another exhibition was a big, brash, and ambitious show called "New York Painting and Sculpture, 1940–1970." In it appeared the works of many artists who have given shape and meaning to contemporary American painting.

In the past thirty years, the New York school of painting emerged as an art of bold primary colors and forms, which represent the artist's responses to the world and to his own personal experiences. The show had Kenneth Noland's velvety paintings which look like targets. There were the lonely glimpses of city life by Edward Hopper. And there were Frank Stella's hard-edged, precisely-lined, zigzag designs.

Ellsworth Kelly shows the effectiveness of simple form with deep color contrasts. The paintings of Adolph Gottlieb and Hans Hofmann assert power with their enormous canvases and bold designs. And Joseph Cornell's delicately detailed "shadow boxes" take on magical qualities with the placement of ordinary objects in unusual arrangements.

▶ BOSTON MUSEUM OF FINE ARTS

To commemorate its 100th birthday, the Boston Museum of Fine Arts assembled 130 acquisitions. Each one was either a recent gift or purchase. They ranged from a beautiful, small Correggio painting to a stainless-steel sculpture by David Smith.

Connected with the birthday celebrations was an archeological highlight. The museum

"Kee-O-Kuk, Chief of the Sauk and Foxes," by George Catlin (1796–1872), was part of the Metropolitan Museum of Art's "19th-Century America" exhibition. The painting was on loan from the Smithsonian Institution's National Collection of Fine Arts.

came up with a 4,000-year-old gold hoard: a treasure trove of jewelry from the tomb of an ancient princess. The museum's refusal to reveal the exact location of the tomb stirred up an international controversy.

▶ EARLY AMERICAN ART

The early American painting collection of Edgar William and Bernice Chrysler Garbisch ended a 2-year, 13-city tour on 3 continents. Some 35,000 French viewers turned out for the collection in Paris. And 15,000 Berliners saw it at Amerika Haus. Most Europeans were looking at this period of American painting for the first time. In 1970 the collection appeared in Houston, West Point, and Tokyo.

▶ THE OLD MASTERS

Possibly the most beautiful event of the year was a showing of fifty drawings by Rembrandt, the Dutch master. The drawings were seen at the Art Institute of Chicago, the Minneapolis College of Art and Design, and Detroit Art Institute. With just a few strokes Rembrandt was able to create explosions of light and dark in a crosshatch of pen lines. These exquisite and dramatic works have been regarded as a high point of Western art for three hundred years. They are even more intense than Rembrandt's paintings. The foremost setting for Rembrandt's paintings in 1970 was Amsterdam's Rijksmuseum. Besides the museum's usual pictures, there were loans from Rembrandt owners throughout the world. These included Leningrad's museum, The Hermitage, the British royal family, and the American millionaire Norton Simon.

The 400th anniversary of the death of Pieter Breughel was marked by small exhibitions. Breughel's paintings, with their crowded, lusty scenes of peasant life and haunting landscapes, capture the mood of the Middle Ages. The six paintings shown in Brussels, and the ones shown in Vienna and Prague, occupy a place of their own in art history.

The French honored their twentieth-century master painter Henri Matisse with a big exhibition at the Grand Palais in Paris.

Does the man on the left look happy? Or dazed? Perhaps both, because he—Alec Wildenstein of the Wildenstein Gallery in New York—had just bid $5,544,000 for the Velazquez portrait at Christie's Auction Gallery in London. The bidding took just 2 minutes to reach $5,544,000—the highest price ever paid for a painting at an auction. Said Mr. Wildenstein: "It's a painting that my great-grandfather wanted 80 years ago . . . he said it was the greatest picture he had ever seen."

Born in Seville, Spain, Diego Velazquez was one of the great seventeenth-century masters. He finished this portrait of his assistant and servant, Juan de Pareja, in 1649. Its correct title is "The Slave of Velazquez." De Pareja, a mulatto of Moorish descent, was himself a painter. A few of his paintings are still in existence. The portrait was first sold in 1801 for about $200. The Earl of Radnor bought it in 1811; his family kept it until the November 1970 auction.

Helium-filled polyethylene balloons snake their way past the Washington Monument in rhythmic "sky ballet." Artist Otto Piene calls his sky ballets a bringing together of "art, nature, and technology in a relaxed environment."

Matisse has been taken more or less for granted in his native country. This is because his pictures are lush, bright, and decorative rather than an expression of complicated theories. Many visitors, however, found that Matisse as a painter is still ahead of his times.

And there was further proof that the old masters were as popular as the moderns. Velazquez's portrait of his assistant, Juan de Pareja, brought a record price of $5,544,-000 at a London auction.

ENVIRONMENTAL ART

American painters in 1970 were not easel painters. At least not in the old way. A painter today may apply pigments to canvas. But he may also work with other media. Many "painters" work with earth, air, fire, and water to create an environment.

A fascinating show took place at New York's Museum of Contemporary Crafts. One exhibit was a hut made out of yarn by Ted Hallman. Another was an oak capsule, by Wendell Castle, in which one could recline. There was even an exhibit by Neke Carson where the spectator found himself surrounded by a fountain of water.

Dan Flavin created environment using lights. Robert Whitman used mirrors, and Walter de Maria used earthworks. The Smithsonian Institution in Washington, D.C., asked Otto Piene to stage a "sky ballet." He filled six huge polyethylene balloons, each one over 250 feet long, with helium. He tied all the ends to the ground. Slowly the balloons rose to the sky, in a snakelike, swirling pattern. Piene said the sky ballet was designed to "bring together art, nature, and technology in a relaxed environment."

CONTEMPORARY REALISTS

In 1970, one of the most vivid shows of the season was called "22 Realists." Held at the Whitney Museum in New York, it indicated a return to a style of painting that has been out of fashion. The realistic style shuns the elaborate abstract images that have for so long set the American pace.

The artists of "22 Realists" painted the world as they saw it, rather than as they imagined it. Malcolm Morley's and Howard Kanowitz's paintings told stories, just like American paintings did 100 years ago. Sidney Tillim and Philip Pearlstein worked from living models. And John Clem Clarke produced meticulous copies of Old Master paintings from slide reproductions.

ROBERT TAYLOR
Art Editor
Boston Globe Magazine

SCULPTURE

Augustus Saint-Gaudens, who died in 1907, is well-known for such large three-dimensional statues as his *Lincoln* and *The Puritan.* Saint-Gaudens also created magnificent bronze relief sculptures. In early 1970 the National Portrait Gallery in Washington, D.C., housed a brilliant collection of portrait-relief pieces by Saint-Gaudens. On the pieces, Saint-Gaudens had depicted both celebrities and obscure men and women whose faces interested him. Among the celebrities were the authors Robert Louis Stevenson and William Dean Howells. The modeling of the pieces, ranging in size from an inch-and-a-half to nearly six feet, showed the sculptor's technical skill and his sensitive feeling for character.

▶ BRANCUSI EXHIBITION

In the largest show ever devoted to him, some eighty sculptures by Constantin Brancusi were shown at New York's Guggenheim Museum. One problem that bothered sculptors before Brancusi was that of depicting motion in a nonmoving sculpture. Brancusi solved the problem by presenting the essence of his subjects. That is, rather than trying to show a bird in flight in terms of actual movement, he gave the viewer the idea of movement. His *Bird in Space* is a curved, polished metal arc, swift as a propeller blade. Brancusi worked with limestone, marble, and wood as well as bronze. He always presented the idea of a thing—the smoothness of the Alaskan seal and the roundness of an egg—rather than the actual thing itself.

▶ CONTEMPORARY SCULPTURE

In 1970, English sculptor Anthony Caro gave a superb New York exhibition of direct metal constructions. In such sculptures as *Orangerie, Deep North,* and *Sun Feast,* he demonstrated how important open space is to a sculptor. In a Caro work, this space is vital in the actual construction of his design.

American sculptor Robert Morris gave a show in Detroit, and later another one at

A bronze relief sculpture of Mildred and William Dean Howells by Saint-Gaudens.

Painted steel sculpture, "Orangerie," by English sculptor Anthony Caro.

Constantin Brancusi's "Flying Turtle," sculptured in marble, depicts motion in a nonmoving sculpture.

The Solomon R. Guggenheim Museum

the Whitney Museum in New York. The Whitney show included a 96-foot concrete, timber, and steel work—a savage and overwhelming construction.

Certainly among the most graceful sculptural exhibitions to tour the northeastern United States was that of James Rosati. His geometric sculptures of zinc, copper, and brass are abstract, but have a strong feeling of human presence.

▶ LIGHT AND SOUND SCULPTURE

As if to state that there can be other forms of sculpture too, a group of Yale University artists called Pulsa aimed stroboscopic lights and electronic sound devices at the Sculpture Garden of The Museum of Modern Art in New York City. The works in the garden blossomed into odd, strange, and new light and sound patterns.

ROBERT TAYLOR
Art Editor, *Boston Globe Magazine*

ARCHITECTURE

Nonresidential building continued at a rapid rate in 1970, in spite of the pressures of inflation. Some of the most talked-about new buildings are important because of their inventive, but practical, forms and shapes, and because of the unusual use of building materials. The buildings are also interesting for the contribution they make to the community in which they are built.

Housing—the other major area of design —was in a slump in 1970. There was a shortage of mortgage money to finance building. As a result, the most widely discussed program in this area was the Federal Government's Operation Breakthrough. This is an attempt to stimulate housing production by inviting firms and individuals to experiment with new ways to build.

▶ FRESH FORM AND SHAPE

Three buildings completed in 1970—one on the East Coast, one in the Middle West, and one in California—attracted wide attention for their fresh form and shape.

Perhaps most striking is architect Benjamin Thompson's Design Research Building in Cambridge, Massachusetts. Design Research is a retail store, selling fabrics, dresses, furniture, and household goods. Built very simply of concrete slab floors resting on concrete columns, the building is interesting because of its unusual use of glass. The glass wraps around the building without any upright posts (called mullions) between the sheets of glass. As a result, the building glistens with light. The color and movement of people inside the building are a major part of the design. Some feel that this building suggests a new kind of transparent building that might bring color, light, and warmth back to city streets.

Another strong break with usual forms is the Northwestern University Library at Evanston, Illinois. It was designed by Walter Netsch of Skidmore, Owings & Merrill. Because of its size, the building was broken into units. Each unit is developed in a form that looks almost like a crystal. All of the spaces radiate outwards from a center point.

But the unusual shape is not just a whim. The building is designed to make the search for books easy and organized. Reading carrels (individual study rooms) and other quiet spaces are tucked in private alcoves along the outer walls.

The Oakland (California) Museum, designed by architect Kevin Roche, is perhaps the year's most unusual building. Indeed, it does not look like a building, but like a terraced park. The museum is set on a sloping site, and the architect designed the gallery spaces as a series of steps down the hill. He used the roofs of the building spaces to plant trees and shrubs. Thus, while some people tour the exhibits, others can enjoy the lushly planted outdoor spaces. The museum is, in fact, a large new public park in the heart of the city's downtown area.

▶ THREE NEW TOWERS

Three important towers were completed in 1970. Again, one was in the East, one in the Middle West, and one in the West.

The 23-story building for the Knights of Columbus in New Haven, Connecticut, is a bold new landmark at the entrance to that city. Four round towers at the corners of the building are its structural support. The towers house fire stairs, air-conditioning ducts, and service rooms. Steel beams extend between these towers and to a central core for elevators. The floor space is entirely open and free of columns.

The 100-story John Hancock Center in Chicago is now the world's third-tallest building. (Tallest is the World Trade Center under construction in New York City. When it is completed the building will be 110 stories high. In October, 1970, it reached a height of 1,254 feet above street level.) New York's Empire State Building, which since 1931 had been the world's tallest building, lost its title by 4 feet.

"Big John," as the Hancock building is called in Chicago, is 1,107 feet tall. Its television antennas reach up to 1,449 feet. The building, designed by Skidmore, Owings & Merrill, is unusual in several respects. First, the sides taper. This device helps structurally and looks handsome. It is also practical, since the lower and larger floors are used for

One of the most interesting buildings erected in 1970 was the Design Research Building in Cambridge, Massachusetts. Designed by architect Benjamin Thompson, the building is noteworthy for its unusual use of glass. The movement of people inside and the color of the various displays become part of a design which adds light and warmth to the surrounding area.

The 23-story Knights of Columbus Building in New Haven, Connecticut, was designed by architect Kevin Roche. Four towers support the structure.

office space, while the smaller upper floors work well for the layout of apartments. A second unusual feature of the building is that it is multipurpose. On the lowest floors are shops and commercial space. Floors 6 through 12 are used for parking. Then come more offices, and apartments reaching up to the 92d floor. And above these are restaurants, places to observe the superb view, and television equipment. The third unusual feature is the diagonal or X-bracing. Steel beams arranged in the shape of huge X's help brace the building against the great wind forces of the Windy City.

The Bank of America tower in San Francisco was designed by two firms working together—Wurster, Bernardi & Emmons and Skidmore, Owings & Merrill—with Pietro Belluschi as consulting architect. The tower's most striking features are its color (it is made of dark red granite) and its shape. The walls are not smooth as they are in most skyscrapers. Rather, they are built in a zigzag or sawtooth shape. Thus, as one approaches the building, the light bouncing off the various flat surfaces gives a constantly changing appearance to the building.

▶ ON A SMALLER SCALE

There are of course hundreds of buildings completed each year that are worthy of note. Perhaps three will suggest in different ways the current trends in design. One is the Westyard Building designed for a site in a run-down part of New York City, near the mainline railroad tracks to New Jersey.

The building, designed by Davis, Brody & Associates, makes several points. It is in large part a warehouse building with small offices. Yet it received from the architect the same kind of attention given to much more prominent buildings. Its sloping walls seem particularly well suited to a building that spans 220 feet over railroad tracks. The complex engineering involved makes it possible to use a seemingly unusable site. As land in the central cities becomes scarcer and scarcer, many buildings are being designed to use the air rights above railroads and highways.

The architect's attention to function and purpose is evident again in St. Thomas

The Westyard Building in New York City, designed by Davis, Brody & Associates, is built over railroad tracks (bottom of photograph). Such use of airspace above railroads and highways in crowded cities is becoming more common.

A model of the headquarters building of the American Institute of Architects in Washington, D.C. The curved structure had to be designed to harmonize with the historic Octagon House (in foreground). The building was designed by The Architects Collaborative.

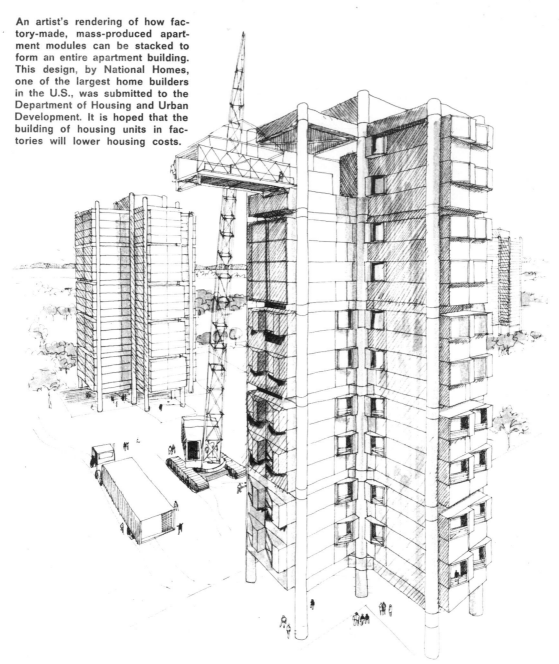

Aquinas Church in Indianapolis, designed by Woollen Associates. The church is one of the first designed in response to the new and simplified Roman Catholic church services. In sharp contrast to the familiar statues, banks of candles, and stained-glass windows are the modern features of this church. The architect has used an almost stylized cross, stainless steel altar furnishings, and an exposed truss roof. The roof is left open in places to let natural light filter down onto the altar.

The Architects Collaborative solved another kind of problem in its design for a new headquarters building for the American Institute of Architects (A.I.A.). The design had to meet three conditions. It had to serve as the "image" in Washington, D.C., for the architects' professional society. It had to be approved by the Fine Arts Commission, which has control over all design in areas near the Capitol and White House. And it had to be in harmony with the historic Octagon House, once the home of President James Madison, and now owned by the A.I.A. The design, approved by both the Fine Arts Commission and the annual convention of the A.I.A., is an elegant building. Its curved shape wraps around the Octagon House so that the two buildings complement, rather than compete with, each other. The building will soon be under construction.

▶ A.I.A. AWARDS

The A.I.A. gave its 1970 honor awards for excellence of design to 14 buildings, selected from 478 entries. One of the winners was the four-year-old Whitney Museum of American Art in New York City, designed by Marcel Breuer and Hamilton Smith. Another winner was The Cannery, a San Francisco landmark converted by Joseph Esherick & Associates into a shopping and entertaining area. The Milwaukee Center for the Performing Arts; Lake Point Tower, a 70-story apartment house in Chicago; and the Bancroft Elementary School in Andover, Massachusetts, were also among the award winners.

▶ FOCUS ON JAPAN

Attention was focused in 1970 on Japan. Its World's Fair, EXPO'70, is a striking example of the skill and ability of many brilliant Japanese architects, and of other architects around the world.

Perhaps the most notable building was the Theme Pavilion, designed by Kenzo Tange. It was a vast space covered by a great steel space-frame weighing 6,000 tons, supported by only six columns, and covered by an inflated plastic roof.

The United States Pavilion, designed by architects Lewis Davis, Samuel Brody, and Alan Schwartzman, and graphic designers Ivan Chermayeff, Thomas Geismar, and Rudolph De Harak, was different from all the others. It was built in the shape of a shallow saucer carved out of the earth. The building was covered by a fabric roof measuring 274 by 465 feet—the size of two football fields. The roof was supported entirely by air. (Huge blowers built up a pressure inside the building just a bit higher than normal atmospheric pressure.)

Another event in Japan was the opening of the new 17-story Imperial Hotel in Tokyo. The hotel was built on the site of the Imperial Hotel designed by the American architect Frank Lloyd Wright and completed in 1922. There was great disagreement over the tearing down of the Wright building in 1967. The hotel management said the building was unsafe. Many felt it should be left standing as a work of art.

▶ MORE HOUSING FOR CITIES

In the face of a severe shortage of housing in cities, George W. Romney, Secretary of the Department of Housing and Urban Development, devised Operation Breakthrough. He invited corporations and individuals to propose new ways of building houses by mass production. It is the Government's hope that building housing units in factories, or with other new methods, will lower the cost of housing. Hundreds of proposals were received and judged. The Government selected 22 for actual test production. Sites were obtained around the country, and construction of the original models was scheduled to begin early in 1971.

Many of the proposals involve stacking "modules," or units. Modules include complete bathrooms and kitchens, with heating and wiring ducts already in place.

Another approach to creating more housing at lower cost is the renovation of old buildings. One of the most interesting examples of this approach was worked out by architect Richard Meier in New York City. He turned a square block of old buildings into 384 apartments. Formerly, the buildings had been used as electrical laboratories and warehouses. Almost no work was done on the outside. But inside, the factory-like spaces were changed into a variety of single-floor and duplex apartments. The idea of developing apartments from commercial space would appear to apply to many cities.

WALTER F. WAGNER, JR.
Editor, *Architectural Record*

ASIA

IN Asia, nature caused more suffering than man in 1970. In November a killer cyclone accompanied by twenty-foot tidal waves took perhaps half a million lives on East Pakistan's Bay of Bengal. It was the costliest natural disaster in the twentieth century.

Earlier in the year, Asia and the world had been startled by the entry of U.S. troops into Cambodia. U.S. and South Vietnamese soldiers crossed into Cambodia in April to destroy secret Vietcong supply bases. President Nixon thought this action would protect U.S. troops and make it possible to send more of them home. But the attack also expanded the war into Cambodia and led to a communist counterattack in Laos. Still, by the fall of 1970 the North Vietnamese and U.S. leaders were offering cease-fire plans to each other. Though neither side accepted, the United States managed to withdraw about 135,000 troops during the year.

Communist China put its first space satellite into orbit in 1970. It also drafted a new constitution, making Mao Tse-tung's power permanent and complete. Japan continued to grow strong. Some people thought Japan would be the world's leading economic power by the end of the century.

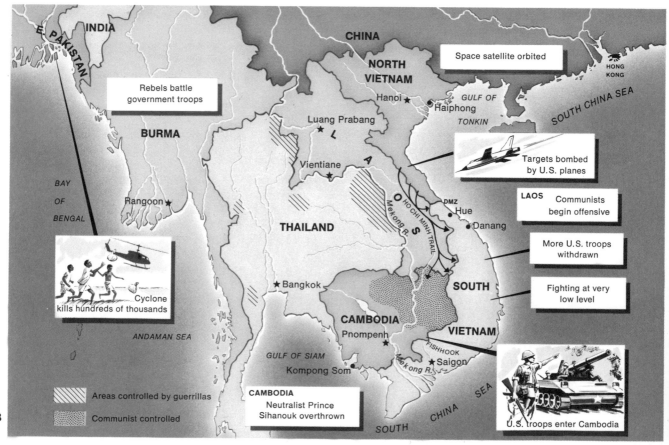

Tragedy is reflected in the face of this East Pakistani woman, whose village was destroyed by the November cyclone. In addition to the destruction and death caused by the storm and tidal wave, there was the prospect of hunger and disease. Below: An American helicopter drops bags of rice to a hungry survivor.

In 1970, the Vietnam war was widened into a war involving Cambodia. At right American troops leave Cambodia after a campaign to destroy communist bases and supplies. Below: Communist Pathet Lao troops in Laos, the third Indochinese nation racked by war.

In Paris, a North Vietnamese spokesman accuses the U.S. of resuming bombing of his country. At year's end, President Nixon said the U.S. would bomb North Vietnam if necessary. One bombing raid was used to divert North Vietnamese attention from a U.S. commando raid designed to free American prisoners held near Hanoi. Below: The President cites four of the commandos for bravery during the unsuccessful raid.

▶ SOUTHEAST ASIA

In 1970 the Vietnam war still cast its shadow over Southeast Asia. So Southeast Asia's most important events took place in the war zone—Vietnam, Cambodia, Laos.

In Cambodia, on March 18, the Government of Prince Sihanouk was overthrown. A new Government, led by General Lon Nol, came to power.

Prince Sihanouk had been a neutralist. This means he did not side with either the United States or the Vietnamese Communists in the Vietnam war. But the Vietnamese Communists had ignored his neutralism. They built secret supply bases and rest camps for their soldiers inside Cambodia, which shares a border with South Vietnam. Sihanouk tried to get the Communists out, but they would not leave. While Sihanouk was visiting Europe, the Parliament voted him out of office. His successor, General Lon Nol, declared he also wanted to be neutral. But he ordered the Cambodian Army to attack the Vietnamese Communists in his country. He also asked the United States for help.

On April 30, President Nixon ordered U.S. troops to attack the communist camps inside the Cambodian border. This act made many people fear the war in Southeast Asia would grow bigger. But Mr. Nixon said that the U.S. Army would not advance more than 21 miles into Cambodia. He also promised to take the U.S. troops out of Cambodia by June 30. Mr. Nixon explained that by destroying communist supplies inside Cambodia he hoped to weaken the Communists and thus shorten the war in South Vietnam. On June 29 the President announced that all U.S. forces had left Cambodia. He also described the military operation as a success.

The Cambodian Army, which had only 30,000 troops at the beginning of the year, grew to 200,000 men. The Cambodians continued to fight the Vietnamese Communists who had tried to build new secret bases in the northern part of the country. South Vietnamese troops stayed in Cambodia to fight the Communists too. As the year ended, the 1,168-year-old monarchy of Cambodia proclaimed itself a republic.

The expanding war in Indochina: U.S. troops fire at enemy positions in Cambodia. Cambodian recruits prepare to join the war which has engulfed their nation.

The Vietnamese Communists tried to regain lost ground by opening new attacks in neighboring Laos. They and the Laotian Leftists seized many towns and villages in a plan to make southern Laos a large supply area. The Laos Government announced an emergency, and U.S. bombers attacked the Communists from the air.

Although Cambodia and Laos attracted attention in 1970, the main conflict continued to center in South Vietnam. Compared with other years since 1965, however, the fighting in 1970 was low scale. Casualty rates on both sides dropped to their lowest in more than four years. But by late 1970 the United States had lost a total of 44,000 men in all the years of the war; the South Vietnamese had lost 115,000; and the Vietcong and North Vietnamese had lost more than 675,000.

On September 17 the Communists announced that they would agree to stop the shooting if all the U.S. troops left South Vietnam by June 30, 1971. On October 7 the United States replied by proposing that everyone stop shooting in Vietnam, Cambodia, and Laos. At the same time, the different armies would remain in the positions they held. This is called a "cease-fire in place." Although each side turned down the other's plan, some people thought that the war was slowly ending without an official cease-fire or a political agreement. Mr. Nixon was eager to end the war because more and more U.S. citizens thought the war should be ended.

Far to the south of the war zone, the island nation of Indonesia remained "non-aligned" in 1970. This means that, under the Government of President Suharto, Indonesia did not take sides in disputes between the communist countries and the Western democracies. Still, it was clear that Indonesia leaned toward the West. All its foreign aid in 1970 came from the United States and Japan. Western nations to which Indonesia owes large sums of money decided in 1970 to permit a longer period for repayment of the debt. Also, investments by Western nations in Indonesian lumber and minerals (mainly oil) increased greatly in 1970.

U.S. Secretary of Defense Melvin Laird describes a commando raid, deep inside North Vietnam, designed to free American prisoners of war.

Former President Sukarno, the architect of Indonesian independence, died in Jakarta on June 21. One of the leading figures in the Asian independence movement after World War II, Sukarno was elected president of the United States of Indonesia in 1949. A popular leader, Sukarno nonetheless ran his country into debt. In the 1960's he leaned so far toward Peking that he planned to let the Peking-dominated Indonesian Communists take over his Government. The Army found out about the plan and turned his Government out of office. The Army killed or arrested many thousands of Indonesian Communists. Gradu-

ally Sukarno's powers were removed, and during the last year of his life he was under house arrest.

Nearby Malaysia was governed under emergency powers during 1970 by the National Operations Council (NOC). The council had assumed the reins of government after Malay-Chinese rioting shook the country in 1969. A return to parliamentary government is planned for 1971.

In spite of the unusual conditions, Prime Minister Tunku Abdul Rahman, Malaysia's founder, decided the country was stabilized enough for him to step down. He resigned in September and appealed for racial har-

Indonesian President Suharto addresses the opening session of the first congress of the Afro-Asian Islamic Organization. The goal of this new organization is to foster co-operation among all Muslims.

Tun Abdul Razak, new prime minister of Malaysia.

mony. He turned his post over to a hand-picked successor, Tun Abdul Razak.

September 1970 was the month when a new king took office in Malaysia too. Kings in Malaysia are elected to five-year terms from among the nine rulers of the former Malay states. The new king is Sultan Abdul Halim Muazzam, nephew of the outgoing Prime Minister.

Britain plans to withdraw most of its naval and air power from nearby Singapore in 1971. Both Malaysia and Singapore will then have less protection. So in 1970 Malaysia installed guided missiles and other modern equipment in its naval ships.

Communist China made important gains in its space program in 1970. It put a space satellite weighing 381 pounds into orbit around the earth on April 24. The successful launching showed that China is on the way to building a missile big enough to carry atom and hydrogen bombs. In 1970, China also held new atomic-bomb tests.

China's successes made the Soviet Union uneasy, and new tensions developed along the Soviet-Chinese border. The Chinese began to fear they might be without allies if the Soviets attacked them, so they began to renew diplomatic ties around the world. By the end of 1970, Peking had sent about 30 ambassadors back to missions closed during China's 1967–68 Cultural Revolution. Diplomatic relations were established for the first time with Canada and Italy.

Chinese leaders drafted a new national constitution in 1970. It makes Mao Tse-tung the permanent and supreme leader of China and clearly states that Lin Piao shall be Mao's successor. The most fundamental rights and duties of a Chinese citizen are stated to be the supporting of Chairman Mao and Lin Piao and the supporting of the Communist Party of China and the "socialist system." The revolutionary committees staffed by the military during the Cultural Revolution are made permanent. This will give the military a political role at every level of Chinese life.

Yukio Mishima, a famed Japanese novelist with his own right-wing army, believed that Japan should return to the martial Samurai tradition (below). On November 25, from a balcony in an Army building (left), Mishima tried to convince Japanese soldiers to overthrow their Government. When the soldiers heckled him, he committed suicide. His act had great impact in Japan. Many feared that the world would view Japan as a nation seeking a return to militaristic nationalism.

President Nixon and Japanese Prime Minister Eisaku Sato in the White House garden. The two leaders discussed trade problems.

Japan's worst problem in 1970 was the possibility of a trade war with the United States. Just 25 years after its World War II defeat, Japan has achieved third place among the world's economic giants. This success was highlighted in 1970 by the opening of the Osaka World's Fair. But Japan's economic strength has led to trouble with the United States. In a recent year, the United States bought $4,800,000,000 worth of Japanese goods while Japan bought only $3,600,000,000 worth from the United States. Japan can both undersell and out-produce the United States because Japanese workers earn less and work more hours than U.S. workers. Also, Japan imposes tariffs (taxes) on some imports. In 1970 the United States threatened to impose import quotas on textiles, which would hurt Japan. President Nixon and Japan's Premier Eisaku Sato opened talks seeking ways to even out the U.S.–Japan trade balance. Premier Sato was re-elected head of the Liberal-Democratic Party in October.

Relief planes deliver blankets and other supplies to storm-ravaged East Pakistan. Supplies were slow in reaching the survivors of the cyclone.

▶ SOUTH ASIA

In India the ancient bitterness between Hindus and Muslims erupted again in 1970. In almost fifty districts there was tension between members of the two religions. Sometimes riots occurred in which many people were killed. Much of the trouble was caused by the Rashtreeya Seve Sangham (RSS), an extremist Hindu organization. Mrs. Indira Gandhi, the prime minister of India, was angry with the RSS. She said, "People in India are being provoked to attack their neighbors in the name of religion." She called upon government officials and teachers to help educate people against religious and racial hatred.

The Naxalites, a growing group of Peking-oriented terrorists, also caused India trouble in 1970. The Naxalites staged murders, raids, and kidnapings not only in their home state of West Bengal but as far away as Andhra Pradesh and Bombay.

In neighboring Pakistan, the province of East Pakistan was hit in August by severe floods. The floods came only weeks after Pakistan had launched its Fourth Five-Year Plan, aimed at making Pakistan self-sufficient in food. Then, on November 13, came a devastating blow. East Pakistan was hit by the worst natural disaster in the twentieth century. A cyclone (hurricane) with tidal waves twenty feet high hit a wide area of the Bay of Bengal coast. Whole islands were washed away, and half a million people were feared drowned.

On December 7, Pakistanis went to the polls to elect a National Assembly. This Assembly will draft a new constitution under which Pakistan will return to civilian rule. Army General Yahya Khan has ruled since March 1969.

A majority of the Assembly seats were won by the Awami League. The head of the League, Sheik Mujibur Rahman, is leader of the East Pakistan autonomy movement. The vote signified a shift in power from West to East Pakistan.

In Burma the Government was plagued in 1970 by increased rebel activity in the northeast. Chinese-supported Shan and Kachin rebels battled Burmese Government troops. The encounters were fierce, and both sides lost heavily.

In Ceylon's May elections a left-wing coalition headed by Mrs. S. R. D. Bandaranaike scored a startling upset. The coalition captured more than two thirds of the seats in Ceylon's House of Representatives. Mrs. Bandaranaike at once set Ceylon on an anti-Western course. In July the House approved a resolution that Ceylon become a republic and leave the British Commonwealth.

ARNOLD C. BRACKMAN
Author, *The Communist Collapse in Indonesia*

AMERICAN INFLUENCE IN SOUTHEAST ASIA

For good or for bad, American soldiers have introduced American culture to Southeast Asia. Jazz bands in Cambodia and Coca Cola in Thailand are common sights.

Batman, Robin and other comic-book heroes have been adopted by young Asians.

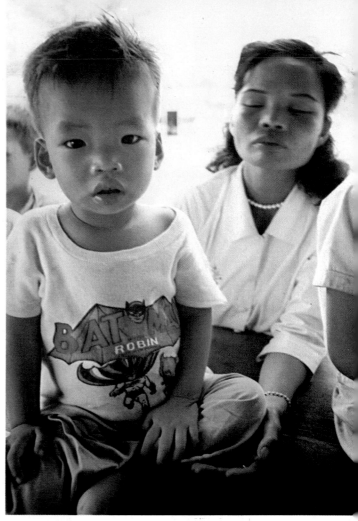

More and more teen-agers are wearing Western-style clothing. This trend actually began when the French ruled Indochina.

EXPO'70

In 1970, Japan played host to the first world's fair ever held in Asia. By all standards the fair—EXPO'70—was a great success. From March to September some 64,-220,000 people visited EXPO'70, which was located on the outskirts of Osaka, Japan's second-largest city.

The theme of EXPO'70 was "Progress and Harmony for Mankind." More than 110 national and private pavilions at the fair had exhibits and displays that reflected this theme. In addition to the pavilions, EXPO'70 featured a huge amusement park called Expoland. In Expoland were a glass castle, a space station, and a giant lizard which carried 500 passengers an hour on a thrilling ride.

There was so much to see at EXPO'70 that it took a full week for the average visitor to make even a quick tour of the fairgrounds.

The Swiss Pavilion, below, one of the most beautiful at EXPO'70, is a modernistic structure of glass and aluminum lit up by electric lights. At right, the Tower of the Sun looms high over the fair's Plaza of Harmony. The 198-foot-tall structure symbolizes man's dignity and progress. Within the hollow tower is the Tree of Life, which depicts the evolution of life.

Above: The Canadian Pavilion, which gives visitors the impression of being in a "palace of mirrors." Right: The Tower of Youth, near the Tower of the Sun, consists of six modern sculptures and depicts mankind's youthful energy. Below: Japanese schoolchildren at EXPO'70.

The exotic Burmese Pavilion was designed to look like an ancient "Royal Dragon Barge." The structure has twin dragon heads joined to a traditional Burmese structure. The building, with seven tiers, is set in a man-made pond. The pavilion at the left, which also has seven tiers, is a re-creation of a Japanese pagoda that was originally built in A.D. 730. This pavilion was built by a large Japanese industrial company.

This traditional Japanese structure was built by Japan's largest producer of electronics equipment and home appliances, the Matsushita Electrical Industrial Company. The pavilion, set in a pool, is surrounded by a thick grove of some 10,000 bamboo plants. The architectural style—one of combined elegance and simplicity—is from Japan's Tempyo period (A.D. 729–794).

AUSTRALIA, NEW ZEALAND

AND THE PACIFIC ISLANDS

FOR the widely scattered peoples of this vast area in the Pacific Ocean, 1970 was mainly a year of peaceful progress and development. Australians and New Zealanders enjoyed prospering economies. And two main Pacific island groups, Tonga and Fiji, attained independence from Great Britain.

A highlight of 1970 was provided by Great Britain's Queen Elizabeth and other members of the royal family. They toured the area, visiting Australia, New Zealand, Tonga, and Fiji. The commemoration of a historic event marked their visit to Australia. Two hundred years earlier, Captain James Cook, the great British explorer, became the first European to land on Australia's eastern coast. To celebrate this event, the landing was re-enacted from a ship built to look like Cook's ship, the *Endeavour*. It took place on the same beach, Botany Bay, where Cook had landed in 1770.

A scale model of Captain James Cook's ship the "Endeavour" sails through Sydney Harbor to mark Cook's landing in Australia in 1770. At right, Tongan schoolchildren welcome the British royal family. Tonga became independent in 1970.

AUSTRALIA

In 1970, Australians were concerned with their country's foreign policies and commitments. Many Australians opposed having their troops in South Vietnam. Because of this, the Government withdrew a battalion of 750 men in November. But it continued to give money and equipment to South Vietnam and Cambodia.

Australia is committed to the defense of Singapore and Malaysia in Southeast Asia.

It thus welcomed the decision of the new British Government to keep some armed forces in Singapore. Britain had planned to withdraw all forces east of Suez, by the end of 1971. And with the appearance of Russian naval ships in the Indian Ocean, Australia began to strengthen its west-coast naval defenses.

A small strain between Australia and the United States developed during 1970. This resulted from a 1963 contract for Australia

Four new submarines were added recently to the Australian Navy. Australia took steps to strengthen its naval forces because Great Britain plans to reduce its forces in Asia and because the Russians have been building up their forces.

A miner at work in Western Australia, where new deposits of nickel and iron ore were found in 1970. Other Australian mineral finds included silver and lead in Queensland, and rich uranium deposits in the Northern Territory.

to buy 24 F-111 swing-wing planes from the United States. Because of design problems, the planes were never delivered, and Australia wanted to cancel the order. However, the United States persuaded Australia to take Phantom aircraft until the defects of the F-111 could be worked out. The option was also given them to purchase a different plane.

Domestically, Australia was in a healthy financial position. Unemployment remained at a low level. The Government reduced the income tax of middle-income earners by 10 per cent. And pensions were slightly increased. But the Government's most im-

Helping the Australian economic boom were the thousands of immigrants from all over the world. The Nelsons moved to Australia from Arizona.

portant reform was the introduction of a new national health plan. Under this plan, people will pay less for medical and hospital services.

The strong economy was helped by Australia's vast mineral wealth. New deposits of nickel and iron ore were found in Western Australia. Silver and lead were discovered in Queensland. And what might be the world's richest source of uranium was found in the Northern Territory.

But economic progress created some social discontent. Most workers sought higher wages to meet rising living costs. Strikes and demonstrations by unions were common. And Australians found that their large industrial cities were being severely threatened by air and water pollution. In addition to this man-made threat, there was a natural threat to Australia's environment. It was discovered that the Great Barrier Reef was being destroyed by certain starfish, called crown of thorns, that feed on the reef's young coral. Hopefully, a solution will be found, and this unique and lovely tourist attraction will continue to exist.

New Zealand sheep outnumber New Zealand people by 25 to 1. And despite lower prices for wool in 1970, wool continued to earn millions of dollars for New Zealand. It accounts for about 20 per cent of the nation's export earnings.

Territory of Papua and New Guinea

The desire for independence caused problems in the Australian-administered Territory of Papua and New Guinea. Edward Whitlam, the opposition leader of Australia's Labor Party, visited the territory and demanded independence. This angered the natives in the Highland region of the territory who do not want early independence. Since the territory receives much money in aid from Australia, the Government would like to see it become self-sufficient. However, Prime Minister John Gorton feels that the territory is not yet ready for independence. Greater native participation in local affairs was granted. And the Australian Government improved health and education services. The newly formed University of Papua and New Guinea produced its first native graduate.

▶NEW ZEALAND

The National Party Government under Prime Minister Keith Holyoake remained secure in office. Many New Zealanders were pleased with its decision to withdraw half of its troops from South Vietnam. For defense and economic reasons, New Zealand continued to draw closer to Australia.

1970 brought damaging floods to Nelson on South Island. However, New Zealand's stable economy was not harmed. The highly successful limited free-trade agreement with Australia was further extended. And increased exports of forest products offset the lower prices for wool, butter, cheese. With little unemployment, more immigrants were allowed into the country. In 1970, for the first time in several years, the number of people entering New Zealand was greater than the number leaving it.

Great Britain's desire to join the European Economic Community (EEC) worried many New Zealanders. Now, New Zealand sells much of its dairy produce to Great Britain. This is very important to New Zealand's economy. If Britain becomes a member of the EEC, it might have to buy its dairy products from Common Market countries. The Minister of Overseas Trade made two trips to London to seek special treatment for New Zealand's products.

Promises of great mineral wealth came from an offshore oil strike near New Plymouth. High-grade silica was discovered in Southland and tin in south Westland.

In 1970 a dispute centered on Lake Manapouri, or lake of a hundred isles. It is set in a 3,000,000-acre national park. Conservation interests clashed with economic needs as to whether the water level of the lake should be raised. This would be done to supply electric power for an aluminum smelter at Bluff, a hundred miles away. But this would damage many of the lake's beautiful islands, which are inhabited by rare forms of animal life. The dispute remained unsettled at the end of the year.

▶THE PACIFIC ISLANDS

The southwestern Pacific Ocean is dotted with some thirty thousand islands. These islands are thought to be an earthly paradise because of their great beauty and leisurely way of life. In 1970 the Pacific islands seemed to be losing their romantic image. The search for mineral wealth and new tourist attractions was under way. No large island escaped the developers, and most natives welcomed the chance to earn money.

In 1970, Tonga and Fiji became the third and fourth independent Pacific-island nations. Western Samoa had become independent in 1962, and Nauru in 1968. Independence is now desired by almost all the other islanders. In the Solomon Islands, a new Governing Council was formed with most of its members being elected for the first time. The movement toward complete self-government gained speed in American Samoa and the Cook Islands. Even in the New Hebrides, jointly controlled by France and Britain, independence seemed a possible goal for the first time.

Only in French Polynesia was there no great desire for independence. However, these islanders were disturbed when the French Government exploded two atom bombs there. A ban-the-bomb movement started on Tahiti, the largest island in French Polynesia. Neighboring islands as well as New Zealand protested the French action.

E. J. TAPP
The University of New England (Australia)

FIJI AND TONGA BECOME INDEPENDENT

In 1970, Fiji and Tonga—two groups of Pacific islands—became independent. Fiji had been governed by Great Britain for 96 years, Tonga for 70 years.

Independence for the 533,000 Fijians came on October 10. Sir Kamisese Mara, Fijian prime minister, applied for and was granted UN membership for his country. Tonga became independent on June 4. Only 84,000 people live on the 150 Tongan islands, and the Government did not apply for UN membership.

Queen Elizabeth II of Great Britain and King Tauf'ahau Tupou IV of Tonga.

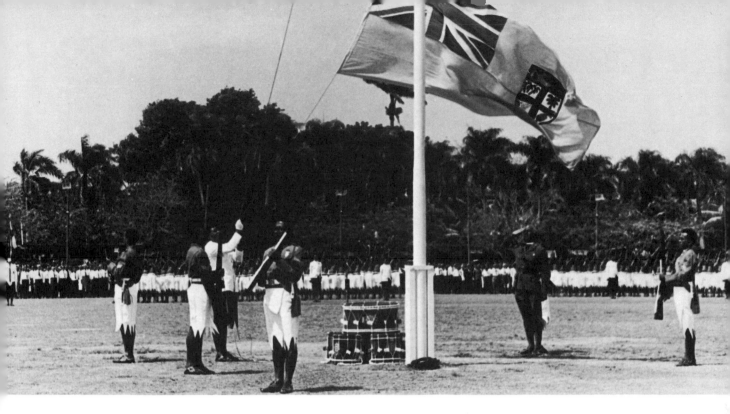

Fiji's new flag is raised at independence ceremonies on October 10. Fiji has a promising future as an independent country. Sugar, coconuts, mining, and tourism provide income. Fiji also has a medical school and a university.

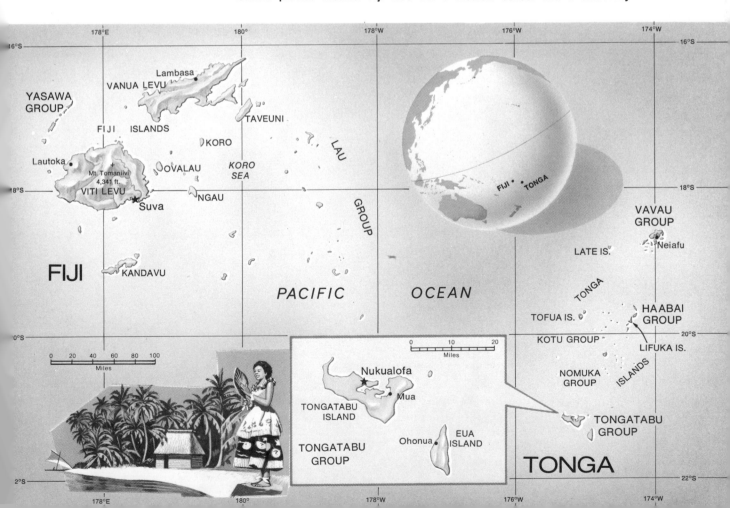

CANADA

IN 1970 the Canadian Government was winning its fight against inflation. The burdensome wheat surplus in Manitoba, Saskatchewan, and Alberta was being reduced to manageable proportions. Firm action was being taken against pollution of the environment. And Prime Minister Pierre Elliott Trudeau was enjoying great popularity. In general, it appeared that 1970 was going to be a good year for Canada.

Then, in early October, all of Canada was shocked when terrorists kidnaped and murdered a Quebec cabinet minister and abducted a British trade diplomat. The terrorists belong to an organization that is seeking the separation of French-speaking Quebec from the rest of Canada. To cope with the situation, Prime Minister Trudeau invoked the War Measures Act and ordered Federal troops into Ottawa, Montreal, and Quebec City to help find the kidnapers.

The tragic events of October 1970 seemed to draw all Canada closer together. English-speaking Canadians generally seemed more sympathetic toward Quebec's problems.

Prime Minister Pierre Trudeau speaks to the people of Canada shortly after hearing that Quebec Labor Minister Pierre Laporte had been murdered by the FLQ.

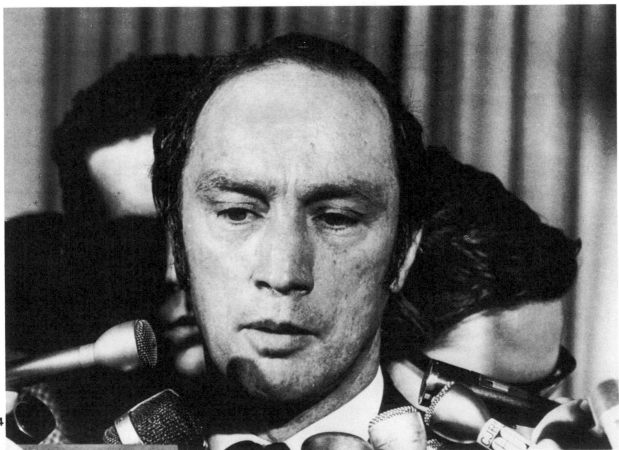

Following the kidnaping and murder of Pierre La-
porte (below right) and the kidnaping of James
Cross (right), Prime Minister Trudeau invoked the
War Measures Act and sent Federal troops into
Montreal and other Canadian cities.

Above left: A Quebec separatist. Most separatists believe in obtaining autonomy for Quebec by peaceful means. Right: Troops stand guard during funeral of Pierre Laporte.

▶ SEPARATIST TERRORISM

For most Canadians the year 1970 centered on two short weeks in October, when political terrorists kidnaped and murdered a Quebec cabinet minister and abducted a British trade diplomat.

The killing of Pierre Laporte, 49-year-old Quebec minister of labor and immigration, by members of the radical Front de Liberation du Quebec (FLQ), shocked all Canada. His death came after Quebec Premier Robert Bourassa refused a list of FLQ demands. These demands included the freeing and transportation into exile of 23 FLQ members held in prison or awaiting trial on charges of murder, bombing, and bank robbery. Laporte's body was found in the trunk of a stolen car. He had been strangled with the chain of a religious medal he wore around his neck.

Two days before Laporte's death, Prime Minister Trudeau had invoked the War Measures Act and called out the Army in an effort to track down the kidnapers. The order brought thousands of armed troops into Ottawa, Montreal, and Quebec City. The Act outlawed the FLQ and any similar or-

ganization advocating violent overthrow of the government. It gave peace officers or troops the power to arrest anyone they had "reason to suspect." And it placed the burden of proof of innocence on the person arrested—the exact opposite of ordinary court procedure.

In invoking the War Measures Act, Prime Minister Trudeau declared: "There are very few times in the history of any country when all persons must take a stand on critical issues. This is one of those times, this is one of those issues." Within hours after the War Measures order, more than 400 people were arrested, but 300 were released soon after. About 50 persons were charged with seditious conspiracy and with being members of the FLQ. Police issued warrants naming five persons in the kidnaping of Pierre Laporte, but only one man was arrested, and he denied being present when Laporte was murdered.

The events leading up to Laporte's death had all Canada on edge. The FLQ, founded in 1962, advocates the separation of French-speaking Quebec from the rest of Canada. Its terrorist activities have included bomb-

Robert Bourassa and his wife, Andrée, raise their hands in victory after he won Quebec's April provincial elections. He is Quebec's youngest premier since 1897.

ings in which three innocent persons died, bank robberies to supply the organization with money, and the theft of more than 2,000 pounds of dynamite. At most, its membership never exceeded 150.

Members of the group struck with sudden savagery on October 5. Two men invaded the home of James Cross, British trade commissioner in Montreal, and hustled him away in a stolen taxi. Then began a series of communiqués warning that Cross would be killed if the FLQ demands were not met. These included freeing the 23 prisoners, a ransom of $500,000 in gold, and political exile in Cuba or Algeria. A deadline of 6 P.M. October 10 was set by the terrorists. In a radio broadcast at 5:45, Quebec's Minister of Justice, Jerome Choquette, rejected the demands. His only offer was safe-conduct to a foreign country for Cross' kidnapers.

Minutes after Choquette's broadcast, Laporte was kidnaped on the street in front of his home.

As the hunt for the terrorists continued, a new anti-FLQ bill, to replace the War Measures Act, was introduced in Parliament.

It was to expire in 6 months. Cross was finally released by the terrorists on December 3. His kidnapers were allowed to fly to Cuba, where they were granted asylum.

On December 28, three suspects in the kidnaping and murder of Pierre Laporte were captured 25 miles south of Montreal.

▶ OTHER EVENTS IN QUEBEC

The year had started well for Quebec. Bourassa had been chosen leader of the provincial Liberal Party after the resignation of former premier Jean Lesage. The 36-year-old economist led his party to victory in an April election, defeating the government of Union Nationale leader Jean-Jacques Bertrand. The Liberals captured 72 of the 108 Legislative Assembly seats, compared with 17 seats for the Union Nationale, 12 for the Créditiste Party, and 7 for the separatist Parti Québecois, led by René Lévesque.

What surprised Canada and many Quebeckers was the strength of the separatists, who would like to see the province independent of the rest of Canada. Although Lévesque's party won only 7 seats, it captured 24 per cent of the popular vote.

Premier Bourassa promised a period of rapid economic growth and 100,000 new jobs in the province by the end of 1971. (Unemployment in Quebec was above 10 per cent in 1970.) He also brought Quebec into the Federal Medicare plan. The plan is compulsory for all Quebec residents and will cost an estimated $300,000,000 a year. Its introduction brought protests and a partial strike by the province's 3,600 medical specialists. They objected to a fee schedule that will keep their incomes below those of doctors in neighboring Ontario. But Bourassa called an emergency legislative session to pass a bill ordering the specialists to resume practice or face fines up to $500 a day or a month in jail.

▶ THE PROVINCES

Elections were held in three other provinces in 1970. In Prince Edward Island, the Liberal Party, headed by Alex Campbell, was returned to office in May. Campbell had ruled the legislature with 17 members, compared with 15 for the Progressive Conservative Party. When 1 Liberal bolted the party, Campbell was forced to call an election. The Liberals were returned with 26 seats to the Conservatives' 5 with one by-election still to be held.

In Nova Scotia, the Progressive Conservative Party, in power since 1956, was defeated by the Liberals, headed by Gerald Regan. The Liberals won 23 seats, Premier George ("Ike") Smith's Conservatives 21, and the socialist New Democratic Party 2.

After 10 years in office, New Brunswick's Liberal government, under Premier Louis Robichaud, lost to the Conservatives. Richard Hatfield, 39, led the Conservatives to victory with 31 seats to the Liberals' 27.

▶ THE PRIME MINISTER

After 30 months of his governing a country plagued by inflation, a static economy, and unemployment, the personal popularity of Prime Minister Pierre Elliott Trudeau remained high in all parts of Canada. And, during Trudeau's 19-day tour of Australia, New Zealand, Singapore, Malaysia, and Japan, many Canadians began to recognize the goodwill being created in other nations around the world by their Prime Minister.

In Australia, where newspapers called him "the Ever-Lovin' P.M.," Trudeau spoke to young people about the dangers of a growing drug culture. The Prime Minister ended his 27,000-mile trip at EXPO'70 in Osaka, Japan. Speaking to an overflow crowd at the fair's Canada Day celebration, Trudeau expressed the hope that his travels would mark a new beginning in Canada's awareness of its Pacific neighbors. Instead of the Far East, he said, Canadians should think of "our New West."

▶ FOREIGN RELATIONS

In October 1970, after 20 months of negotiations, Canada and Communist China established diplomatic relations. In recognizing Mao Tse-tung's regime, Canada joined several other Western nations in establishing ties with the world's most populous country. As a result of this decision, the Nationalist Chinese ambassador immediately left Canada, and the Embassy was closed down.

One of the purposes of Trudeau's Far East trip had been to sound out the reactions of leaders in that area to Canada's recognition of Communist China. Some voiced concern, but the Prime Minister explained, "We have an economic interest in trade with China, and political interest in preventing tension between China and its neighbors, but especially between China and the United States." (Canada has a very favorable trade with Communist China: over the past 10 years, annual exports have averaged over $100,000,000 while imports have been about $25,000,000.)

▶ ECONOMY

After a 2-year fight, Canada's war on inflation seemed to be nearing victory. The consumer price index showed prices rising at a rate of 3.2 per cent, compared with a 5 per cent average in 1968 and 1969. But tight money and a squeeze on credit slowed the economy. Profits in many businesses were down, and unemployment rose to almost 7 per cent. The gross national product, the total amount of goods and services produced, rose only 2.5 per cent.

During 1970, Prime Minister Trudeau toured Australia, New Zealand, and parts of Asia. He is shown here shoveling coal in Japan—with a shovel imported from Canada.

To help the static economy, the Bank of Canada reduced the prime lending rate. The Federal Government allocated some $100,000,000 for housing, to spur the construction industry, as well as $60,000,000 to help the jobless in hard-hit areas.

Most of the credit for the inflation victory went to the Government's Prices and Incomes Commission, headed by Dr. John M. Young. Business and labor were asked to follow voluntary wage and price guidelines set by the commission. In February 1970, more than 200 of Canada's leading business and professional men agreed to keep price increases to a minimum. Labor leaders, however, refused to go along with Young's 6 per cent wage-increase guideline.

When agreement above 6 per cent could not be reached, strikes were called or threatened. This caused wage settlements as high as 32 per cent, as well as a record number of man-days lost. The average wage settlement was 8 to 10 per cent.

The Government dropped its voluntary wage and price guidelines on January 1, 1971, because of complaints by business. Business leaders said that if labor refused to accept the guidelines, they too would refuse in the future.

On June 1, 1970, the Canadian dollar was freed from its fixed value. The result has been to make Canadian products more expensive in foreign markets, and imports cheaper. This in turn meant fewer sales and fewer jobs for Canadians. Finance Minister Edgar Benson said the dollar would not be stabilized until 1971.

▶ PRAIRIES: FARM ECONOMY

Things were beginning to improve for Canada's grain-growing provinces of Manitoba, Saskatchewan, and Alberta.

Concerned by a huge wheat surplus and lagging world sales, the Government introduced a program known as LIFT (Low Inventories for Tomorrow). Under the plan, farmers were paid to leave some land idle or for switching to other crops. As a result, only some 12,000,000 acres were seeded to wheat, a drop of 13,000,000 acres from 1969.

The benefits of LIFT are already apparent. The wheat surplus has been reduced to a manageable level. At the same time, poor crops in Europe, Argentina, and Australia created a more promising sales picture for the August 1970 to July 1971 crop year.

▶ PARLIAMENT

No piece of proposed legislation caused more controversy than the White Paper on Tax Reform presented by Finance Minister Benson. To create a more equitable tax structure, he proposed removing 750,000 low-income earners from the tax rolls. He also proposed that relief be provided for another 3,000,000 taxpayers. When critics, both in government and out, said some of these proposals would cripple the economy and retard business growth, Benson hinted he would make changes before presenting the bill to Parliament.

Parliament was also stirred by a wave of nationalism in 1970. This was brought on by the realization that most of Canada's raw-resources industries are foreign controlled—many by United States and British interests. This problem came to a head in March, when the Government intervened to prevent the sale of Denison Mines, Ltd.—the Western world's richest uranium mine—to an American-controlled company. The sale would have reduced Canada's control of its uranium resources to less than 10 per cent. Energy Minister Joe Greene explained that there was a growing conviction that Canadian ownership of its resources and industries is essential to the maintenance of a free Canada.

▶ POLLUTION

Canada has 25 per cent of the world's fresh-water supply, 17 per cent of the softwood trees, 6 per cent of the land, and only .5 per cent of the population. Yet the country faces a pollution problem out of all proportion to these statistics.

Mercury pollution far above permissible levels brought about a ban on commercial fishing in several parts of the Great Lakes. Beluga whales in Hudson Bay were found to be contaminated, too, apparently by industrial wastes carried by the South Saskatchewan River system. Oil spills did untold damage to fish and bird life. One of them, in Chedabucto Bay, New Brunswick, contaminated 75 miles of shoreline with heavy fuel.

Fearful of pollution in the Arctic, Prime Minister Trudeau announced that Canadian jurisdiction of shipping would extend 100 miles out from the Arctic Archipelago. The bill provided for fines up to $100,000 and forfeiture of ships (and cargoes) responsible for pollution. The United States tanker SS *Manhattan* agreed to abide by Canadian

Canada's grain surplus and lagging world sales and declining prices caused the Government to order wheat production cut by more than half in 1970.

An oil refinery in Alberta spews noxious gases into the air. Canadians became more concerned about pollution during 1970.

pollution-control measures before setting out on her second Northwest Passage voyage.

A joint effort to clean up the Great Lakes was launched by Ontario and the eight American states bordering on the lakes. Other measures introduced in 1970 include a joint Federal-provincial plan to cleanse inland waters of industrial waste and sewage; banning phosphates in detergents by the end of 1972; and an air-pollution alert system for Toronto, Montreal, and Hamilton.

▶ CITIES

Plans were introduced to control land use in a 90-mile arc from downtown Toronto— the fastest-growing area in North America in the last 10 years. The plan envisions an urbanized zone with an estimated population of 5,700,000 by the year 2000, hugging the Lake Ontario shore for 100 miles. Above this a 20-mile-wide belt of unspoiled land—with a population of no more than 300,000—would be preserved as a recreation area.

▶ YOUTH

By 1970 the drug culture had arrived in Canada in full force. Probably hundreds of thousands of young Canadians have used or are using marijuana or hashish. A commission appointed by Health Minister John Munro recommended that young drug offenders be treated with leniency. After six months of hearings in 23 cities and towns, the commission recommended increased controls on the production and prescription of amphetamine—the most dangerous drug after heroin. They also stated that education might help to cut down drug use.

The Cabinet and Parliament will decide whether the commission's recommendations will be implemented. An important opinion will be that of Prime Minister Trudeau, who has often said of drugs: "I feel the world is too exciting [for young people] to be using that kind of thing."

GUY BIRCH
News Editor, *Toronto Star*

ECONOMY

IN 1970, as every housewife knew, the cost of food, clothing, and just about everything else was going up month by month. In 1970, too, as every working man and woman knew, more and more people were losing their jobs. What was happening was that the American economy was experiencing both an inflation (rising prices) and a business slowdown (decreasing production and fewer jobs).

In early 1970 the rate of inflation was 6 per cent. This meant that in 1970 you had to pay $1.06 for the same product that cost you just $1.00 in 1969. There are two reasons for an inflation. First, if a manufacturer has to pay more for materials and for labor costs, he will charge more money for his product. Second, if the demand for goods is greater than the supply, prices will also go up. This often happens when people have a lot of money to spend.

To help stop the inflation, the Government took certain actions to decrease the amount of money people and companies would have on hand to spend. For one thing, it made it more costly to borrow money. The Government also cut its spendings, especially on space-exploration and defense projects. Many private companies also began to spend less. As a result, the inflation showed some signs of easing. Prices did not go up quite so fast. But another result was the business slowdown. And this caused thousands and thousands of people to lose their jobs.

Toward the end of 1970, the economy showed only a small improvement. Rising prices and unemployment continued to cause great concern.

President Nixon comments on the economy, explaining that the gross national product (GNP) has passed the one-trillion-dollar mark. GNP aside, it was a poor year for the economy.

ECONOMIC PARADOX

The United States economy was in poor shape in 1970. Millions of people were out of work, yet prices kept climbing. Usually, as more and more people lose their jobs and have little or no money to spend, prices start to decline. This was not the case in 1970. How does the Government hope to resolve this paradox?

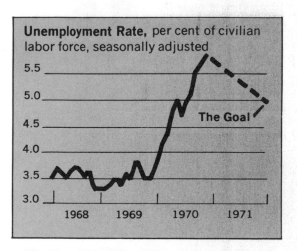

And slow the rise in wages . . .

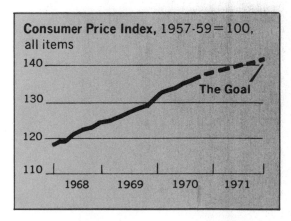

To put a rein on inflation . . .

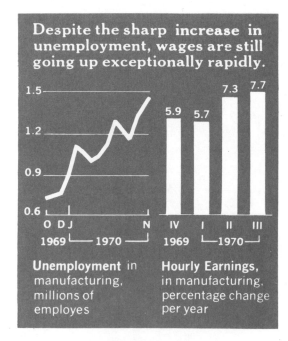

The President plans to spur economic growth . . .

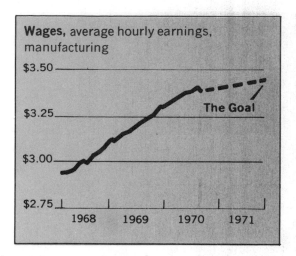

And drive down unemployment.

"Air Pollution? Nonsense! It's Just Gloom."

THE MINNEAPOLIS TRIBUNE '70

Gloom did invade the U.S. economic scene in 1970. As every housewife knew, shopping could be a trying experience, because prices for everything from food to clothing to cars were up—way up. Making matters worse was the growing unemployment. Joblessness hit usually stable industries, such as aerospace and advertising. As joblessness increased to 6 per cent in December, lines at state unemployment-compensation offices grew long.

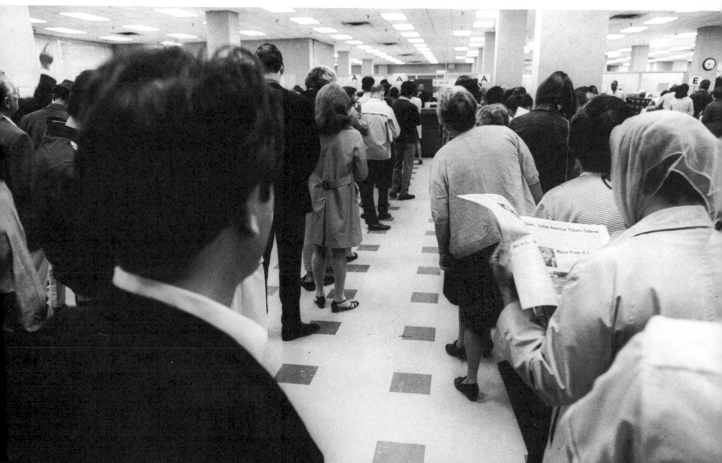

As 1970 began, inflation was the nation's most troublesome economic problem. But it was soon replaced as the No. 1 worry by the growing business slowdown and the accompanying unemployment. The unemployment rate climbed steadily. By May, 5 per cent of the labor force was out of work. By December, unemployment was 6 per cent.

For teen-agers the job situation was even worse. In June, as the summer began, unemployment among youths was about 15.7 per cent. It climbed to 15.9 per cent in August and 16.8 per cent in September. This was the highest figure in 5 years. Among Negro youths between the ages of 16 and 21, unemployment was 30.2 per cent. This was up sharply from 24.8 per cent for the same period in 1969.

There was increased unemployment, too, among factory, white-collar, and women workers. According to the Bureau of Labor Statistics, between July 1969 and August 1970, manufacturing workers lost 945,000 jobs.

Much of the increased unemployment was caused by Government cutbacks in defense spending. Because the United States withdrew more and more troops from Vietnam, less supplies were needed. Overall, in the pullback of troops and in the fight against inflation, the Government cut defense spending by about $4,500,000,000.

Thousands of people also lost jobs because the Government stopped spending so much money on the space program. Many people had argued that the Government should stop spending so much money on space. They felt that the money should be used to solve social and economic problems.

Despite these cuts, during the fiscal year of 1970 (which ended in July) the Government had a budget deficit of $2,900,000,-

000. That is, it spent that much more money than it collected in taxes and other forms of revenue.

Uneasiness over the economy was reflected in activity on the stock market. In the first three months of the year, corporation profits before taxes declined to $82,600,-000,000. It was not until the last months of 1970 that the profit picture brightened.

The number of shares being traded in the stock market dropped sharply in the first half of the year. But in midautumn, stock-market trading rebounded. On September 24, the New York Stock Exchange traded 21,300,000 shares of stock. On the following day 20,400,000 shares were traded. After that, market trading went through a Yo-Yo period of ups and downs.

Millions of people own shares of stock in the companies listed on the stock exchanges. Of the 30,492,000 shareowners of stocks re-

As "No work" signs appeared in more and more shopwindows, welfare rolls increased rapidly in almost every city in the country.

ported in a census by the New York Stock Exchange, young people under 21 numbered 2,221,000.

It was expected that prices would rise by 5.5 or 5.7 per cent in 1970. Still, many people were worried more about the growing unemployment than about inflation. They blamed the Government's "tight money" policies for causing the economic slowdown, which in turn caused the unemployment.

To help fight inflation, the Federal Reserve Board restricted the growth of the nation's supply of money in circulation. It also adopted regulations that at one point caused banks to charge 8.5 per cent interest, the amount you pay to borrow money.

When the business slowdown began to have a marked effect, this tight-money policy was eased somewhat. As the year ended its final quarter, the prime interest rate dropped to 6.75 per cent.

Higher interest rates and less money in circulation meant that it was harder to borrow money. Hard hit were people who wanted to buy a home with a long-term mortgage of 20 or more years. For the first half of the year, housing loans were very difficult to get.

The tight money and high interest rates also caused many corporations to run into financial trouble. The Penn Central Transportation Company, which operated the

The two-month strike by the United Automobile Workers at General Motors plants had a marked effect on many other industries. Thousands of workers at steel plants had to be laid off.

Penn Central Railroad, declared bankruptcy. This was the single biggest bankruptcy in the nation's history. Although the company had property and other assets valued at $7,000,-000,000, it did not have enough money on hand to pay its bills.

How the American economy looked in 1970 depended a great deal on where you lived. At one time during the year, 38 areas were classified as having "substantial" or "persistent" unemployment by the Bureau of Labor Statistics. This was the highest number in six years. These areas included Detroit and Grand Rapids, Michigan; New Orleans, Louisiana; Corpus Christi, Texas; Seattle and Tacoma, Washington; Atlanta,

Georgia; Racine, Wisconsin; Portland, Oregon; Los Angeles, Fresno, and Stockton, California; Springfield, Massachusetts; Jersey City and Newark, New Jersey; Cleveland, Ohio.

Because of high prices, workers demanded higher wages when it came time to negotiate new union contracts in 1970. Many of these demands were backed by strikes. For the first eight months of 1970, strike idleness was estimated at 31,700,000 man-days. The average union contract negotiated in the second quarter of the year averaged out to a 17.1 per cent increase for wages and benefits combined.

In the fall the biggest strike took place when the United Automobile Workers struck General Motors. About 400,000 people went out on strike. This strike had a marked effect on many industries. Even before the strike, U.S. steel production was down. The automobile industry normally uses 20 per cent of all domestic steel production. And General Motors uses half of that.

Taxes continued to play a big part in the economic picture. The Tax Foundation reported in 1970 that a representative worker earning $11,000 a year paid 32 per cent of his income in direct taxes.

On a total population basis, a person paid an average of $1,385 in Federal, state, and local taxes.

In spite of inflation and the business slowdown, the nation's economy was in fairly good shape. There was no danger of a very serious depression. It was estimated that in 1970 the 78,000,000 workers in the United States would earn $807,000,000,000. And commercial banks reported total deposits of $443,000,000,000 as of mid-September.

It was hoped that the magic trillion-dollar gross national product (GNP) would be reached in 1970. This hope was ended, however, with the business slowdown. Nevertheless, it was predicted that the GNP would be about $980,000,000,000.

WILBUR MARTIN
Managing Editor, *Nation's Business*

THE NEIGHBORHOOD YOUTH CORPS

For 414,000 teen-agers from low-income families, summer in 1970 meant a job through the Neighborhood Youth Corps Program. These were no make-work jobs just to keep young people off the streets. The teen-agers made valuable contributions in programs as varied as teaching and oceanography. They earned $1.45 an hour for up to 26 hours a week. The funds—$181,412,-000—were provided by the Congress.

Twenty thousand teen-agers in 121 cities worked in the Right-to-Read Program. They tutored youngsters who had reading and writing problems.

Some 5,000 were employed in a hundred cities, working as recreation aides with 6-to-13-year-olds. They took the smaller children on trips to zoos and museums. They also supervised play in public parks and playgrounds.

Over 1,000 teen-agers took part in Operation Clean Water in 11 cities, and in Puerto Rico and the Virgin Islands. Young people fanned out along rivers to clean up trash and debris, assisting the U.S. Army Corps of Engineers. In Washington, D.C., they removed about 10 tons of trash from the Potomac River.

Among the many jobs performed by teen-agers in the Neighborhood Youth Corps in 1970 was that of teachers aide. Here, a Corps member teaches a young girl to read.

Below: A Corpswoman helps out at a library, replacing books on shelves. This is good training for teen-agers who might want to become librarians. Right: A Corpsman works outdoors as a recreation aide.

EDUCATION

MORE people in the United States attended schools and colleges in 1970 than ever before. For most students and teachers it was an eventful year—a period of change and challenge. But it was also a year of too many tragedies and troubles, of too many unmet needs and unsolved problems.

Educators across the country, sometimes under pressure from their students, tried to give more meaning to school and college programs. New words, such as "ecology" and "environment," were heard in the classroom. Courses dealing with the histories and cultures of minority groups were added by many schools. At election time, some schools and colleges gave students time off to campaign for their chosen candidates.

In the spring, U.S. intervention in Cambodia touched off protest demonstrations on many campuses. On May 4 a protest at Ohio's Kent State University ended in the fatal shooting of four students by National Guard troops. A student protester and a passerby were killed by State Police at Jackson State College in Mississippi ten days later.

The tragedies cast a long shadow over the nation. But despite fears that there might be new troubles on campuses in the fall, most schools and colleges began the 1970–71 academic year in reasonably quiet fashion.

"I've never seen a class better prepared to meet the challenges of the present-day world."

A young girl screams in anguish after Ohio National Guardsmen shot into a crowd of demonstrating students at Kent State University. Four students were killed. The demonstration was in protest against President Nixon's decision to send U.S. troops into Cambodia.

In Lamar, South Carolina, highway patrolmen walk past a school bus over-turned by an angry group of whites trying to prevent integration of Lamar High School. Later, National Guardsmen were sent to protect Negro children (below). The Supreme Court ordered integration to proceed at a rapid pace.

To get around the Supreme Court integration order, some communities set up all-white private schools, such as this one in Canton, Mississippi. Below, Dr. James V. Allen, commissioner of education (left), and presidential-counsellor Daniel Moynihan brief newsmen about President Nixon's program to improve the quality of education.

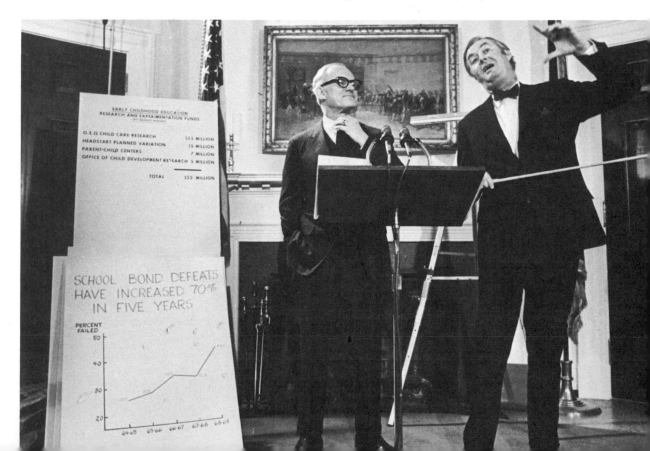

ENROLLMENT

For the 26th year in a row, enrollment in U.S. schools and colleges, both public and private, showed an increase. The United States Office of Education estimated that the total enrollment for 1970, from kindergarten through graduate school, was 59,400,000 students—800,000 more than in 1969. This meant that 3 of every 10 Americans were attending school or college.

Some people went to small schools, such as the one-room country school in Sparks, Nebraska, which had 15 pupils from kindergarten through eighth grade. All the pupils went to class under the same roof and were all taught by the same teacher. But most students went to much larger schools, some with many thousands of students. New York City's largest high school, De Witt Clinton in the Bronx, had 7,000 students—all boys.

Still, the enrollment increase was much smaller in 1970 than in previous years. Elementary schools, in fact, had fewer pupils than the year before. All told, there were 36,800,000 pupils in the elementary grades from kindergarten through eighth grade—100,000 less than in 1969.

Secondary schools enrolled 14,800,000 students in grades 9 through 12. This was an increase of 400,000 over the 1969 total. Colleges and universities had 7,800,000 students, a 1-year increase of 500,000

OPEN ADMISSIONS

In the fall of 1970, New York City's tuition-free City University started a program of "open admissions" that attracted nationwide attention. The new program is a variation of one that has been used in California for many years. The City University admitted every 1970 high-school graduate in the city who wanted to attend, regardless of his high-school grades or qualifications.

Some 35,000 freshman came, including about 9,000 who would not have been able to meet the university's normally high admissions requirements. Special help is being given to those students who need it. University officials are hoping that the program will succeed in bringing higher education to many young people who would not otherwise be able to have it.

The Carnegie Commission on Higher Education recommended in 1970 that college-level education be made available to more people all over the country. The commission was headed by Dr. Clark Kerr, former president of the University of California. He proposed that at least 230 new 2-year community colleges be opened within the next 10 years.

FINANCIAL TROUBLES

Many school systems and particularly many colleges and universities had a difficult time obtaining money. With operating costs soaring, even some of the nation's most famous universities—Yale, Harvard, Columbia, and Stanford—had money troubles.

Dr. Kerr's Carnegie Commission, shortly before the end of the year, warned that U.S. higher education was facing "the greatest financial crisis it has ever had." Two thirds of the country's colleges and universities, it said, were either in serious financial difficulty or headed that way.

PROTEST ON THE CAMPUS

Other problems also caused concern to students and teachers. The U.S. military intervention in Cambodia sent new shock waves through the academic world in the spring. The fatal shooting of 4 students by National Guardsmen during a demonstration at Kent State University in Ohio and, 10 days later, the fatal shooting of 2 youths by Highway Patrol troopers at Jackson State College in Mississippi touched off angry protests at hundreds of colleges and universities. Many shut down voluntarily for a while by joint decision of students, teachers, and administrators. Others were forced to close or curtail activities because of student strikes.

Concerned about the growing unrest among students, President Nixon appointed a special commission to look into the situation. The commission, headed by former Pennsylvania Governor William Scranton, made a number of recommendations for easing campus unrest and for preventing future demonstrations from leading to tragedy.

On May 21, Dr. James E. Allen, U.S. commissioner of education, said that he op-

Left: Students at graduation exercises at the University of Massachusetts display peace symbols. Right: Other students stage a "March for Victory" in Vietnam.

posed the U.S. entry into Cambodia and the continuation of the war in Vietnam. He said the war policy was having a disastrous effect on the young people in the United States. On June 10, Robert Finch, then secretary of health, education, and welfare, said he had been directed to ask for Dr. Allen's resignation. Dr. Allen at once stated he believed he was dismissed because his views on the war in Indochina and on school desegregation differed from those of the President. President Nixon countered that he was disappointed with the progress of Dr. Allen's "right to read" program. But Dr. Allen pointed out that the President had delayed nine months in setting up a planned National Council on Reading.

To give student activism an outlet, many colleges and universities, following the example of Princeton, closed for a two-week period in the fall of 1970 so that students could help in the election campaigns of their candidates. These institutions shortened their normal vacation periods later in the year to make up for the pre-election recess.

Elementary and high schools were also affected by the events in Southeast Asia and at Kent State and Jackson State. In New York City, all 900 public schools closed for a day on two occasions so that the system's 1,100,000 pupils could honor the memory of the slain college students. The pupils rededicated themselves to the principles of the United States, including the right to nonviolent dissent.

▶ STUDENT RIGHTS AND PARTICIPATION

Many high schools in the country took steps to meet growing student demands for a voice in school matters that affect them. A number of school systems, including Seattle and New York City, adopted statements spelling out the rights and responsibilities of students. The New York code acknowledges the personal and political freedoms of students, but it also stresses that no student has the right to interfere with the education of his fellow students.

Despite continued turmoil on college campuses and in secondary schools, the educational process was still going on, and pupils were learning the three R's and much more. Libby Childress, 14, won the 43d National Spelling Bee; Tom Moe, 14, was runner-up.

▶ **EXCITING EXPERIMENTS IN EDUCATION**

Even while student unrest attracted attention, efforts to make education more effective continued in 1970 in high gear.

In Portland, Oregon, the new John Adams High School ended its first year of operation amid high praise from many observers. At John Adams, the teen-age student were given great freedom to plan their own program of studies and to manage their own time. A study of U.S. schools commissioned by the Carnegie Corporation declared that John Adams High may well be the country's most important experiment in secondary education.

Informality and flexibility were also being stressed on the elementary-school level in several states, including North Dakota, where a systematic effort was under way to reform grade-school education. A number of reforms were based on the child-centered "open classroom" approach developed in Britain in recent years. This approach allows each child to work on his own at whatever he wishes during the school day. Children do not have to sit in one place all the time, starting and completing work at the direction of the teacher. Each may continue working on his own project until he thinks it is finished.

New ways of teaching reading and arithmetic were tried out by many schools. Some new programs used teaching machines, computers, and other modern equipment. Old-style basic reading books—such as those telling about Dick and Jane and their dog Spot—were replaced in many schools. The new books show more true-to-life boys and girls—both black and white—doing and saying more realistic things. One publishing company even brought out a beginning reader in hip language. Its leading character is a "cool cat."

Traditional marking systems—with their percentage or letter grades—came under attack in 1970 on both the college and high-school level. Some educators said that such grading systems tended to divide teachers and students into warring camps and encouraged students to strive not so much for knowledge as for high grades.

There was no widespread agreement on what would be a better grading method. Still, a number of schools and colleges were moving slowly toward a system that shows whether a student has passed, passed with honors, or failed.

▶ **DRUGS IN THE SCHOOLS**

The rising use of drugs by young people caused great concern in 1970. Almost every high school and many elementary and junior high schools offered courses or programs explaining the harm that drugs can cause. Un-

dercover policemen, posing as students, were sent into some schools to catch drug pushers. But this tactic often caused resentment among innocent students who felt they were being spied upon. In New York City high schools, groups of specially trained student leaders, operating on their own, are trying to curb drug abuse. But the task is a huge one. One New York City estimate held that about one out of every 14 high-school students was a drug addict.

▶ **SIGNS OF THE TIMES**

A number of high schools began offering draft counseling to students who face possible induction soon after graduation. The counselors advised students about all the options open to them, including possible conscientious-objector status.

Following a trend of recent years, many schools and colleges continued to introduce or expand programs in Afro-American, and Third World studies during 1970. But a new trend also emerged: many colleges were presenting "women's studies." These courses, which are partly an outgrowth of the Women's Liberation movement, are intended to show the proper role of women in society.

There was also widespread and growing student interest in environmental studies. Many students took part in antipollution campaigns in their communities in 1970.

▶ **SESAME STREET**

Of course, not all learning takes place in a classroom. A study of nearly 1,000 three-to-five-year-olds, made by the Educational Testing Service, found that the popular television program *Sesame Street* had an "excellent educational impact" on young viewers during its first year on the air. The study found, among other things, that: (1) All children learned a great deal from watching *Sesame Street*. The more regularly they watched, the more they learned. (2) Three-year-olds showed greater learning gains than five-year-olds. (3) Disadvantaged children who watched regularly made gains surpassing those of middle-class children who watched it infrequently.

LEONARD BUDER
The New York Times

ENTERTAINMENT

IN 1970 the lively arts reflected a mixture of traditional forms of entertainment with more-experimental styles. In the dance world, for example, both classical ballet and the avant-garde attracted large audiences.

The blend in music was also of the old and the new. There was a return to the simplicity of country and blues and old-time rock 'n' roll music. Still, The Who scored an impressive success with their modern rock opera *Tommy*.

In the theater, off-Broadway—always more experimental than Broadway—walked off with two major awards. Even in the movies, films on contemporary themes generated the most excitement. There were some old-time blockbuster movies, but these were on the wane.

One exciting sign in 1970 was that talented young people in some of the art media, especially the movies and television, were often in the spotlight.

Russia's superb Moiseyev Dance Company returned to the United States in 1970. Performing a Ukrainian folk dance, Aleksandr Strelkov leaps high in the air.

Right: Twelve-year-old Mitch Vogel captivated audiences in the movie comedy "The Reivers." Below: Scruffy, the dog in "The Ghost and Mrs. Muir," won a 1970 PATSY award as the best animal actor in a television series.

MOTION PICTURES

MANY of 1970's motion pictures reflected today's society. There was sorrow in the midst of gaiety, scarcity in the midst of plenty. And there was war in the midst of peace.

War movies were especially popular in 1970. In Robert Altman's *M*A*S*H* (Mobile Army Surgical Hospital), Donald Sutherland and Elliott Gould played young surgeons in Korea. Using black-comedy techniques, the film showed man's conditioned indifference to the horrors of war. In a similar vein was Mike Nichols' production of the Joseph Heller novel *Catch 22*. Its strong visual appeal left some critics less than satisfied. Others rated the movie excellent. Its many stars included Alan Arkin, Martin Balsam, Bob Newhart, Anthony Perkins, and Orson Welles.

The three-hour movie *Patton* dealt with the World War II activities of one of the most controversial generals of all time. The key role was played superbly by George C. Scott. He was ably assisted by Karl Malden as General Omar N. Bradley.

▶ CONTEMPORARY THEMES

Films about student activists were in great supply in 1970. *Getting Straight,* starring Elliott Gould and Candice Bergen, was a comedy-drama about an anti-Establishment hero in the middle of a campus rebellion. *The Strawberry Statement* was about Columbia University's student revolt in 1968. It hardly resembled the James Simon Kunen diary on which it was based. The film starred newcomer Bruce Davison, seen earlier in the Frank and Eleanor Perry production *Last Summer*.

A variation of this topical theme appeared in director John G. Avildsen's *Joe*. This film treated the generation conflict in a violent style. Director John Korty's *riverrun* handled the same problem, but in a soft, lyrical way.

Also appealing to the under-30 group was young director Michael Wadleigh's *Woodstock*. This picturization of the 1969 summer rock festival featured the musical groups

and the thousands of youths who had participated in one of the most orderly mass gatherings ever held. More than 400,000 young people had attended the festival.

The popularity of these contemporary themes brought foreign directors into the fold. Michelangelo Antonioni's first American-made film, *Zabriskie Point,* dealt with alienated youth. Greek director Costa-Gavras came through with *Z*. In this action thriller a political leader is assassinated by the authorities. Although the film took place in Greece, its scenes of rioting and protest were similar to actual American incidents. The movie starred Yves Montand, Irene Papas, and Jean-Louis Trintignant.

With startling visual effects, Federico Fellini presented *Fellini Satyricon*. It was a kind of costume epic dealing with the corruption of the Roman Empire during Nero's reign. Critics were quick to point out its parallels to modern society. Interestingly, the story centered on two young people and their bizarre adventures.

Films treating racial problems were also emphasized during 1970. The 20th Century-Fox production of *The Great White Hope* was about the first black heavyweight champion of the world, Jack Johnson. With a stunning performance by James Earl Jones, the film stressed the fighter's anguish in an antagonistic society. In a lighter style, Sidney Poitier re-created his role of police lieutenant Virgil Tibbs in the whodunit *They Call Me Mister Tibbs*. And Godfrey Cambridge romped through *Watermelon Man*. In this movie, a white suburbanite wakes up

George C. Scott stars as World War II General George S. Patton, Jr.

one morning to find himself black. Though the intended comic results didn't quite come off, the film's intent struck home.

▶ WESTERNS

Westerns, too, were in abundance. In 1970 they seemed grimmer and gorier than ever, with still more touches of realism. Among these was Abraham Polonsky's *Tell Them Willie Boy Is Here,* starring Robert Redford and newcomer Robert Blake. It was about a renegade Indian fighting in-justice. Paul Newman and Robert Redford glorified Old West outlaws in *Butch Cassidy and the Sundance Kid. A Man Called Horse,* starring Richard Harris, depicted Sioux Indian life with tribal warfare and many scalpings. Sam Peckinpah (*The Wild Bunch*) went comic this time with *The Ballad of Cable Hogue,* the story of the "true West." Clint Eastwood was back in the saddle with *Two Mules for Sister Sara.* The unlikely action-packed story also starred Shirley Mac-Laine.

▶ ROMANTIC DRAMA

Man-woman relationships were looked into in the light-romantic film *John and Mary,* starring Dustin Hoffman and Mia Farrow. Receiving much critical acclaim was the Frank and Eleanor Perry production *Diary of a Mad Housewife.* Carrie Snodgress and Richard Benjamin starred in this film of conflict and emotional crisis. United Artists had *Women in Love,* taken from D. H. Lawrence's novel of love in a provincial English mining town. Ingmar Bergman, using two of his favorite players, Max von Sydow and Liv Ullmann, offered *The Passion of Anna.* In this haunting drama, the characters stepped out of their roles to discuss the parts they were playing.

▶ LARGE-BUDGET MOVIES

Although blockbuster musicals were on the wane, large-budget films were represented by *Airport,* from the book of the same title. It featured an all-star cast including Burt Lancaster, Dean Martin, Jacqueline Bisset, Jean Seberg, Helen Hayes, and Van Heflin. Director Vittorio De Sica did *Sunflower* with Marcello Mastroianni and Sophia Loren. The two Italian stars played newlyweds who are separated by war, find each other, and then try to recapture the past.

A delightful bit of whimsy was *On a Clear Day You Can See Forever.* It starred Barbra Streisand, who, with her ESP powers, is transported to another century. On a more serious note was *They Shoot Horses, Don't They?* The Sydney Pollack film starred Jane Fonda, Michael Sarrazin, and Gig Young. Its theme, the way human beings were exploited in the dance marathons of the 1930's, appealed to old and young audiences alike.

▶ FILM FESTIVALS

The New York Film Festival was on and running again with 26 notable features. Included were two films which immediately went into commercial distribution. *Five Easy Pieces* had Jack Nicholson of *Easy Rider* fame playing an oil rigger in conflict with his "Establishment" family. Luis Buñuel's *Tristana* starred Catherine Deneuve and Fernando Rey destroying themselves as they destroy each other.

The National Student Association, in cooperation with Lincoln Center and the Motion Picture Association of America, held its fifth National Student Film Festival. Some 347 entries from 84 schools were received. The 5 grand-prize winners received $2,500 each. The prize money was put up by the Schlitz Brewing Company of Milwaukee.

HAIG P. MANOOGIAN
Institute of Film and Television
New York University

Disney's "The Aristocats"
premiered late in 1970.

DANCE

Dance companies, both large and small, tour cities throughout the world. It was on one such tour in 1970 that the Soviet Union lost a leading ballerina. Natalya Makarova, in London with the Kirov Ballet company, asked for and was granted asylum in Great Britain. She later announced that she would join the American Ballet Theater. Makarova will also team up with Rudolf Nureyev for international television and ballet guest appearances. Nureyev defected in 1961 from the same ballet troupe.

American dance companies traveled abroad with great success. Among them were Merce Cunningham, Paul Taylor, and The Alvin Ailey American Dance Theater. Ailey's troupe is an interracial group whose director and leading dancers are black. Its impact was smashing in Africa, the Soviet Union, and East Europe.

▶ BALLET AND MODERN DANCE

An interesting new work was one by Jerome Robbins. Having set ballets to Chopin's music, Robbins turned to Bach's music to create the ballet *Goldberg Variations*. The New York City Ballet premiered it at the Saratoga Performing Arts Center.

1970 saw two restagings of the Fokine-Stravinsky masterpiece, *Petrouchka*. (Michel Fokine was a great Russian choreographer.) One restaging was for the Joffrey Ballet, and the other for the American Ballet Theater. The 56-year-old ballet, although difficult to reconstruct, proved to be worth the trouble. Less successful was George Balanchine's new production of *The Firebird*. Stravinsky's music and Marc Chagall's decor were its main attractions. Another Balanchine work was the appealing *Who Cares?* It was danced to a medley of George Gershwin show tunes and captured the mood of the 1920's.

Brian Macdonald is the principal choreographer of Canada's Royal Winnipeg Ballet. The company offered three new Macdonald works in 1970: *5/13,* a study of the struggle for growth; *Ballet High,* a jazz ballet accompanied by an onstage rock group; and *The Shining People,* a *pas de deux* danced to the spoken love poems of Canadian poet Leonard Cohen. All were applauded abroad or at Ottawa's splendid new National Arts Center.

Not too long ago ballet and modern dance were ugly enemies. Now classic-ballet companies have discovered the creativity of modern-dance choreographers. These companies are including in their repertoires works that might otherwise rarely be seen. The American Ballet Theater presented modern-dance choreographer Jose Limon's *The Moor's Pavane* and *The Traitor*. Limon also staged three works for Stockholm's Royal Swedish Ballet.

▶ THE AVANT-GARDE

Ladies and gentlemen of the avant-garde, mostly in T-shirts, blue jeans, and sneakers, continued to shift, pull, gyrate, and jiggle, in expressing their dissatisfaction with the tradition of artificial dance movement. They disapprove of both ballet and of the traditional forms of modern dance. Movement-oriented Twyla Tharp and her dancers gave us *Dancing in the Streets of Paris and London, Continued in Stockholm and Sometimes Madrid*. It brought an unexpectedly large turnout at the Metropolitan Museum of Art. During the evening, performers cascaded down staircases, and around statues and audience. Meredith Monk resists the category of "dancer" and focused on a new kind of theater. She did a three-part, three-evening project titled *Juice*. It started at the Guggenheim Museum and changed locale at each performance.

▶ TERPSICHORE'S PROGRESS

To remind us of much earlier days, Lincoln Center's Library and Museum of the Performing Arts gave us a historical exhibition titled "Terpsichore's Progress." (Terpsichore was the Greek goddess of dance.) The exhibition traced the evolution of dancing from social pastime to theatrical art. Included were parchment-bound, fifteenth-century manuals of court dances. There were also engravings and drawings of country dances and royal pageants.

LYDIA JOEL
Dance Consultant

Edward Verso and Rebecca Wright as animated puppets in the Joffrey Ballet version of "Petrouchka."

MUSIC

Much of the musical excitement of 1970 stemmed from the celebration of a 200-year-old event: the birth of Ludwig van Beethoven on December 16, 1770. New biographies were published, and many recordings were issued. One record was titled *Happy Birthday, Ludwig.* Symphonic and operatic performances took place throughout the world. Leonard Bernstein directed Beethoven's opera, *Fidelio,* in New York and Vienna. Beethoven's Ninth Symphony was conducted by Leopold Stokowski in Carnegie Hall in New York, and by Zubin Mehta in the Mann Auditorium in Tel Aviv. Rarely heard songs of Beethoven's were revived at a Lincoln Center summer festival.

▶ THE OPERA WORLD

Carlisle Floyd's *Of Mice and Men* scored a success in its world premiere by the Seattle Opera Company. Floyd's musical setting of the John Steinbeck story emphasized its dramatic pathos while sticking to the traditional operatic forms. The San Francisco Opera performed Leos Janacek's seldom-heard *Jenufa.* It was a big year for the Czech composer, whose music seems to be attracting a cult of fans.

The 1969–70 season at the Metropolitan Opera in New York provided a new production of Mascagni's *Cavalleria Rusticana.* Considerable debate arose because of its deliberately slow pace. The Met's new staging of Bellini's *Norma* was more highly praised. Australian Joan Sutherland sang the title role, and New Jersey's Marilyn Horne made her debut as Adalgisa.

An unusual evening at the Met was provided by tenor Richard Tucker. He celebrated the 25th anniversary of his debut there by appearing in three acts from three operas. He sang with Joan Sutherland in Act I of *La Traviata,* Renata Tebaldi in Act II of *La Gioconda,* and Leontyne Price in Act III of *Aïda.*

At Lincoln Center's New York Opera, two of the most admired new productions were of Boito's *Mefistofele* and of Debussy's *Pelléas et Mélisande.*

Conductor Dean Dixon rehearses for the New York Philharmonic outdoor summer concert series.

In Rome, Metropolitan mezzo Grace Bumbry created something of a sensation when she appeared as a miniskirted Carmen.

▶ ORCHESTRAL MUSIC

Perhaps the most interesting new work was Dimitri Shostakovich's Symphony No. 13. It was presented, for the first time outside the Soviet Union, by the Philadelphia Orchestra led by Eugene Ormandy. Composed in 1962, the symphony was banned after a few performances in its home country, probably because of its denunciation of anti-Semitism. In the work, a chorus sings the poem *Babi Yar* by Yevgeny Yevtushenko. The poem describes the killing of thousands of Jews by the Germans during the World War II nazi occupation. Ormandy conducted the work both in Philadelphia and New York.

In contemporary music, composers continued to experiment with electronic devices. They also made "montages" consisting of different tape-recorded sounds. But such works failed to find a following among the musical public.

Among the rising new conductors was 25-year-old Michael Tilson Thomas. He took over many of the concerts of the Boston Symphony Orchestra when its Musical Director, William Steinberg, became ill.

The year was marked by a growing number of black musicians in the nation's symphony orchestras. The Philadelphia Orchestra engaged its first black regular, a violinist named Renard Edwards. Dean Dixon, who had been conducting European symphony orchestras, returned to the United States. He directed the New York Philharmonic in its summer concerts in New York

parks. And Henry Lewis, an extremely talented musician, became musical director of the New Jersey Symphony.

HERBERT KUPFERBERG
Music Critic, *The Atlantic*

GRAMMY AWARDS

Record of the Year: AQUARIUS/LET THE SUNSHINE IN (The 5th Dimension)
Album of the Year: BLOOD, SWEAT AND TEARS (Blood, Sweat and Tears)
Song: GAMES PEOPLE PLAY (Joe South)
Instrumental Theme: MIDNIGHT COWBOY (John Barry)
Contemporary Female Vocalist: PEGGY LEE (*Is That All There Is?*)
Contemporary Male Vocalist: NILSSON (*Everybody's Talkin'*)
Rhythm and Blues Female Vocalist: ARETHA FRANKLIN (*Share Your Love with Me*)
Rhythm and Blues Male Vocalist: JOE SIMON (*The Chokin' Kind*)
Folk Vocalist: JONI MITCHELL (*Clouds!*)
Country Female Vocalist: TAMMY WYNETTE (*Stand by Your Man*)
Country Male Vocalist: JOHNNY CASH (*A Boy Named Sue*)
Opera: WAGNER: SIEGFRIED (Herbert von Karajan)
Classical Album: SWITCHED-ON BACH (Walter Carlos)

POPULAR MUSIC

The big news of 1970 was the April breakup of The Beatles. Paul McCartney separated from the group because of "personal differences, business differences, musical differences." At the same time he released a new album (*McCartney*). He alone sang and wrote all the songs, and played all the instruments (including organ, guitar, and drums). McCartney's album, three Beatle albums (*Hey Jude, Let It Be,* and *Abbey Road*), and a John Lennon album (*Plastic Ono Band*) all proved very popular with fans during the year.

▶ ROCK MUSIC

Rock festivals were often in the headlines in 1970. In 1969, Woodstock had been hailed as the symbol of peacefulness, love, and brotherhood of a generation. However, many communities tried to ban these festivals because some turned violent and the use of drugs was widespread. The festival that received the most publicity in 1970 was the one scheduled to be held at Powder Ridge in Connecticut. Although a court injunction canceled the concert, more than thirty thousand young people arrived and created their own entertainment.

Rock music penetrated even movies and the theater. Arlo Guthrie starred in the movie version of *Alice's Restaurant*. Country Joe performed in the film *Zachariah*, and Mick Jagger of the Stones in *Ned Kelly*. *Hair,* the first hit rock musical, continued

A youth provides his own entertainment at one of 1970's many rock festivals.

playing around the world. And Broadway saw many more rock musicals open.

Rock's flirtation with the classics produced several startling developments. Working with the Mothers of Invention, the Los Angeles Philharmonic Symphony gave the world premiere of *22 Motels*. The work was composed by Frank Zappa of the Mothers. The Los Angeles Philharmonic also appeared with several rock groups on an NBC-TV spectacular, *The Switched-On Symphony*. The most surprising event was the appearance of The Who at the Metropolitan Opera House in two sold-out performances of their rock opera, *Tommy*.

Five rock groups climbed to the top in 1970. Crosby, Stills, Nash and Young, who came from the splintering of other groups, scored a million-dollar seller with their album, *Déjà Vu*. A San Francisco group, Creedence Clearwater Revival, did as well with three albums in the rock 'n' revival tradition. First popular as Bob Dylan's backup combo, The Band stepped out on its own with a blend of rock and country. Different influences flow through the music

of Blood, Sweat and Tears, but horns and a jazzy feeling are their special bag. The youngest and newest of the top groups is the Jackson 5, a product of the Motown sound. They made it on their first outing.

▶ **BACK TO THE '50'S**

The movement toward simplicity of music and lyrics continued. Phil Ochs, the writer and singer of antiwar and other protest songs, appeared at a Carnegie Hall concert. Dressed in a gold suit, patterned after early Presley, Ochs presented a program in which he went from "total rebel to total rock stylist." Bob Dylan, in a two-disc *Self-Portrait*, presented a low-keyed collection of country, blues, and bluegrass material. It included a surprise rendition of *Blue Moon*, the Rodgers and Hart pop ballad.

The revival of Rock 'n' Roll of the 1950's increased with reissues of such pioneer white and black rockers as Bill Haley and the Comets and Little Richard. Perhaps the most interesting anthology of records was a seven-volume *History of Rock and Roll Radio*. It even included the voices of the

Rock stars Jimi Hendrix and Janis Joplin. Their deaths in 1970 were attributed to drugs.

disc jockeys of the era. This revival of past rock brought popularity to a new group, Sha Na Na, which imitated the dress as well as the hits of yesteryear.

▶ COUNTRY MUSIC

Country music was *in*. Johnny Cash and Glen Campbell had their own prime-time network TV shows. Cash was also honored by being invited to perform at the White House. The President requested that he sing *Welfare Cadillac* and the hard-hatted *Okie from Muskogee*. These songs, which make fun of people on welfare and the hippies, are of a conservative, Establishment orientation. Cash did not sing either song. His program included his youth-oriented talking ballad *What Is Truth?*

▶ THE BLACK SOUND

Tom Jones' phenomenal popularity continued in 1970, and Diana Ross left The Supremes to make it on her own. The power of both rested on the continuing appeal of the black sound. The black sound was also responsible for the popularity of such white imitators of black as Johnny Winter, Lulu, Dusty Springfield, Delaney and Bonnie, and Joe Cocker. Even Elvis Presley went for the black sound in 1970.

▶ SONGWRITERS

Among songwriters, Laura Nyro became the madonna of soul in 1970. Her widely-recorded song *Stoned Soul Picnic* and two albums, *Eli and the 13th Confession* and *New York Tendaberry,* were very popular. Top honors also went to Burt Bacharach: he won Oscars for the song *Raindrops Keep Fallin' on My Head* and for the music from the movie *Butch Cassidy and the Sundance Kid.* Bacharach was named Music Man of 1970 on a *Newsweek* magazine cover, a rare spot for a songwriter.

ARNOLD SHAW
Author, *The Rock Revolution*

TELEVISION

In 1970, television continued to be the biggest in-home entertainer and informer. But the TV industry had little chance to bask in this glory. It was too busy fighting off attacks from all sides. TV journalists were accused of "liberal" bias in their news reporting. And the networks were accused of treating children as little consumers, as well as "polluting" the airwaves with too many commercials. The networks were also condemned for continuing to accept cigarette advertising, in spite of the link between cigarettes and cancer.

On top of all these troubles, speculation increased that over-the-air TV might not even have a future. The idea of manufacturing cartridge-TV playback machines for use in the home was becoming a reality. And cable TV was spreading from community to community. Some communications experts thought that between cables and cassettes, the present-day type of TV might disappear.

▶ POLITICS AND TELEVISION

A heated debate over political "fairness" on the airwaves was touched off in 1970. On five occasions, during prime time, President Nixon used the three networks to explain his Indochina policies. CBS, as part of a *Loyal Opposition* series, gave Democratic National Committee Chairman Lawrence O'Brien a half hour to speak out against Nixon's Vietnam war policies. The Federal Communications Commission (FCC) then ruled that CBS had to give the Republicans time to reply to O'Brien, because he had spoken about other issues. CBS then dropped the rest of its series. Along with their Republican-reply ruling, the FCC also ruled that antiwar spokesmen must be given uninterrupted prime time. The question of who should get free TV time to answer whom promised to be a political topic right down to the 1972 elections.

▶ REPORTING UNDER ATTACK

In 1968, TV viewers were angered over the networks' coverage of the Democratic convention in Chicago. Some people felt that the coverage had been biased against the police during antiwar demonstrations there. In late 1969, Vice-President Spiro Agnew renewed the controversy by bitterly attacking television's news coverage. He charged that the medium was projecting "a narrow and distorted picture of America." Many viewers were convinced that TV news was not reflecting the views of a so-called "silent majority" of Americans. Inside the networks, TV's proper role as an informer came in for wide questioning. On the air,

In 1970 several manufacturers were perfecting TV playback units, a major innovation in home entertainment. Below: the SONY Videocassette System.

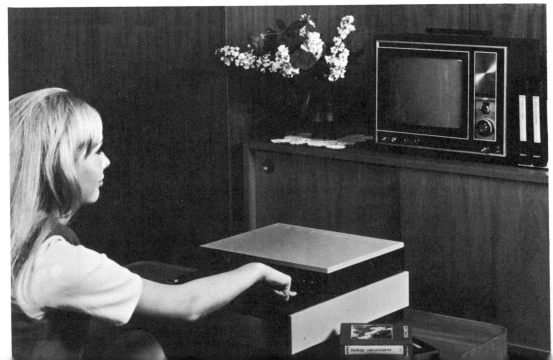

Popular carry-overs from the 1969 TV season were "Room 222," starring Lloyd Haynes (above) and "Mod Squad," starring Clarence Williams III, Michael Cole, Peggy Lipton, and Tige Andrews.

Among the new shows of 1970 were "The Young Rebels" (above) and "The Flip Wilson Show." Below: Flip sings a duet with guest Louis Armstrong, who celebrated his 70th birthday in 1970.

EMMY AWARDS

Dramatic Series: MARCUS WELBY, M.D., ABC

Comedy Series: MY WORLD AND WELCOME TO IT, NBC

Variety Series: THE DAVID FROST SHOW, Westinghouse

Variety Program (classical): CINDERELLA, NET

Variety Special: ANNIE, THE WOMEN IN THE LIFE OF A MAN, CBS

Dramatic Program: A STORM IN SUMMER, NBC

Children's Program: SESAME STREET, Children's Television Workshop

Actor in a Drama: PETER USTINOV (A Storm in Summer)

Actress in a Drama: PATTY DUKE (My Sweet Charlie, NBC)

Actor in a Dramatic Series: ROBERT YOUNG (Marcus Welby, M.D.)

Actress in a Dramatic Series: SUSAN HAMSPHIRE (The Forsyte Saga, NET)

Actor in a Comedy Series: WILLIAM WINDOM (My World and Welcome to It)

Actress in a Comedy Series: HOPE LANGE (The Ghost and Mrs. Muir, ABC)

News: AN INVESTIGATION OF TEEN-AGE DRUG ADDICTION-ODYSSEY HOUSE (The Huntley-Brinkley Report, NBC); CAN THE WORLD BE SAVED? (The CBS Evening News with Walter Cronkite)

News Documentaries: HOSPITAL, NET Journal; THE MAKING OF THE PRESIDENT, 1968, Metromedia Producers Corporation, CBS

Cultural Documentaries: ARTHUR RUBINSTEIN, NBC; THE JAPANESE, CBS; FATHERS AND SONS, CBS

less time was being devoted to public affairs. The trend in documentary programing swung away from hard-hitting exposés to travelogues and consumer-affairs reports.

▶ TV'S MONEY BIND

Powerful and rich as TV still was, forces were combining to pinch the broadcasters economically. Congress outlawed cigarette advertising on radio and TV as of January 2, 1971. This will deprive these media of about $236,000,000 a year. TV will be the bigger loser. Production costs on the big shows had risen to a point where there were often only small profits. And sponsors were cutting their TV budgets.

Added to all this, the FCC asked the TV industry and the public to comment on a proposal by a group of Boston-area mothers, calling themselves Action for Children's Television. It proposed that all commercials be eliminated from children's shows. Few observers really expected the FCC to pass such a rule. But it was clear that the networks were going to be under pressure to give young viewers more than a Saturday diet of slambang cartoons loaded with hard-sell toy, cereal, and candy commercials.

▶ THE ENTERTAINMENT SCENE

Viewers and critics alike found little to cheer about as the 1970 fall season opened. Possibly one exception was ABC's venturesome introduction of prime-time National Football League games on Monday nights. Otherwise, the new season was most notable for the shift by all the networks to new programs designed to appeal to "young adults." *The Young Lawyers* and *The Young Rebels* were among the new shows. *Marcus Welby, M.D., Room 222, The Johnny Cash Show,* and *The Mod Squad* were among popular carry-overs from the 1969 season. Comedian Flip Wilson looked like a quick hit in a new NBC variety hour.

In 1970, public television stations became part of an actual network, named the Public Broadcasting Service (PBS). PBS distributes programs to the country's nearly 200 noncommercial stations. In the fall, PBS launched its first prime-time lineup of unsponsored attractions. They ranged from a revival of *Kukla, Fran and Ollie* to "reports" by consumer activist Ralph Nader. Its most extraordinary offering was the British Broadcasting Corporation's *Civilisation* series. The 13 programs explored the history of Western man through paintings, architecture, sculpture, and music.

Sesame Street, public television's first big success, went into its second season. The program planned to take its preschool watchers beyond the first year's 1–2–3's and ABC's into some beginning arithmetic and reading. Many commercial stations wanted the series. And 2 big advertisers gladly paid the bill for Saturday reruns of *Sesame Street* in a number of cities.

RICHARD K. DOAN
Columnist, *TV Guide*

SESAME STREET

You have just turned on your TV set and find yourself at the front stoop of a small apartment house on a bright and cheerful street in New York City. On one side of the house is a candy store. On the other is a fence of colorful doors. You are watching *Sesame Street,* created by the Children's Television Workshop.

For one hour each day, five days a week, *Sesame Street* is trying to prepare preschool children (3 to 5 years old) for their formal schooling later on. It especially wants to reach underprivileged children, who often start school without any basic skills. The goals of the program are to teach these basic skills, such as the alphabet and counting; to develop a child's reasoning ability; and to teach simple concepts (around, up, down) and more-abstract ones (justice, fair play).

To hold a child's attention for a full hour seems almost impossible. And yet, through the use of cartoons, animals, live-action film, puppets, and lively jingles, *Sesame Street* is keeping children glued to their TV sets. The experimental show was an overnight hit with young people, as well as with adults and teachers. Tests revealed that children were indeed learning, and loving every minute of it. Some 20 countries will be seeing the original version of the show, and plans are under way for foreign-language versions to be filmed overseas. By 1971 the Workshop hopes to have a similar program to teach reading to 7 to 10 year-olds.

"Sesame Street" hosts (left to right): Bob (Bob McGrath), Gordon (Matt Robinson), Mr. Hooper (Will Lee), and Susan (Loretta Long). In 1970 the highly acclaimed educational program won three Emmy Awards and a Peabody Award. Currently the show is reaching some 7,000,000 preschoolers.

Famous celebrities, such as folk singer Pete Seeger (left), often drop in on "Sesame Street" to teach and entertain the children. Basic skills are taught by Jim Henson's Muppet puppets. Muppet Ernie (above) teaches the ABC's with the help of his "A-machine," a funny gadget designed to hold a child's attention. The Anything Muppets (below) sing "Five People in My Family," a song that teaches the number five while exploring the concept of family and the roles played by the family members.

An animated cartoon, showing a dime, a duck, and a dog, helps teach the letter D. Below, Big Bird and Susan explain the idea of relative size.

THEATER

In 1970, *Hello, Dolly!* closed after passing the record previously held by *My Fair Lady* to become the longest-running musical in Broadway history. It ended after 2,844 performances.

However, it was another statistic that concerned theater analysts. Sixty-two shows opened on Broadway during the 1969–70 season. Yet fewer than half of these were new dramas. To many, these figures pointed up the fact that Broadway is becoming a discouraging place for serious theater. It was off-Broadway, repertory companies, and regional theaters that continued to offer new theatrical life and excitement.

Off-Broadway's growing professionalism has made it something of a "little Broadway." This was clearly seen when two off-Broadway plays won major awards in 1970. *The Effect of Gamma Rays on Man-in-the-Moon Marigolds,* by new playwright Paul Zindel, was awarded the Drama Critics Circle Award for Best American Play. Charles Gordone's *No Place to Be Somebody,* a comedy-drama about the black experience, won the Pulitzer Prize.

▶ **DRAMA**

Successful in every way was *Child's Play* by Robert Marasco. This gripping chiller, set in a Jesuit boys' school, made some pointed comments about the growing violence among young people. *Borstal Boy* offered the rare joy of dramatic poetry. It was an adaptation of the autobiographical writings of Ireland's Brendan Behan. *Inquest* had great emotional impact in its treatment of the political trial of Julius and Ethel Rosenberg. (The Rosenbergs were American communists, executed in 1953 for having passed on information about the atomic bomb to the Soviet Union.) And Arthur Kopit's *Indians* was a brilliant study of the hypocrisy of the American liberal.

▶ **MUSICALS**

Company, with Stephen Sondheim's innovative music and lyrics, was a highlight of the season. This unusual show, directed by Harold Prince, was a musical examination of marriage, and the pressures that city living exerts on people. Another big hit was *Applause.* Lauren Bacall gave a dazzling performance in this old-fashioned, but wonderfully entertaining, musical version of *All about Eve.* Appearing in *Coco,* Katharine

A scene from "Purlie," starring Cleavon Little (right) and Melba Moore (center left).

Hepburn delighted the theater world in the singing/dancing role of Gabrielle Chanel, the famous Paris dress designer. Nevertheless, many were disappointed in the stage production. And audiences were charmed by *Purlie,* an appealing musical version of Ossie Davis' *Purlie Victorious.*

COMEDIES

Neil Simon's *Last of the Red Hot Lovers* was a witty but compassionate look at people who try to escape unhappiness through sexual adventures. *Butterflies Are Free,* about a spiritedly independent blind boy, was oversentimental but still managed to be funny. *Sheep on the Runway* was a zany political fantasy by the noted columnist Art Buchwald. But it proved again that political satire has a limited appeal to Broadway audiences.

REVIVALS

1969–70 was a season glittering with first-rate productions of classic shows, including a stunning production of Sir Noël Coward's *Private Lives* by Stephen Porter. Porter also directed a fine version of *Harvey,* which had memorable performances by James Stewart and Helen Hayes. Other revivals included *The Boy Friend, Our Town, The Front Page,* and *Oklahoma!*

OFF-BROADWAY

Musically speaking, off-Broadway did not offer very many good shows, despite the overpraise for such shows as *Salvation* and *The Last Sweet Days of Isaac.* However, *The Me Nobody Knows* was an irresistible musical in which the original poems and stories of ghetto youngsters were set to a vibrant rock score. Other treats were *The Golden Bat,* another rock musical, created by an appealing troupe of young Japanese students, and *Joy,* with its rich, jazz-based sounds of Oscar Brown, Jr.

In drama, off-Broadway made a good showing, especially with *Colette.* This autobiographical treatment of the famous French writer boasted a radiant performance by Zoe Caldwell. An interesting short-run play was *The White House Murder Case,* a funny antiwar, anti-governmental-hypocrisy satire by Jules Feiffer.

REPERTORY

The Repertory Theater of Lincoln Center reached excellence with its beautiful revivals of William Saroyan's *The Time of Your Life* and Tennessee Williams' *Camino Real.* The always-unpredictable New York Shakespeare Company premiered a mediocre play called *Mod Donna.* It was noteworthy only for being the first stage production dealing with the issue of Women's Liberation. The American National Theater and Academy brought a number of repertory companies from other states to its ANTA Theater. Especially good was William Ball's American Conservatory Theater of San Francisco.

As theater seasons go, the 1969–70 one was hardly revolutionary—except perhaps for the fact that many Broadway shows began offering half-price tickets to students. But neither was it the disaster which the critics always predict.

MARILYN STASIO
Drama Critic, *Cue* Magazine

ENVIRONMENT

"A commitment to make life better, not just bigger and faster . . ."

With these words, the youthful organizers of Earth Day summed up the spirit of what turned out to be a unique event in the world's history.

For the first time, on April 22, 1970, an entire nation paused in its usual activities to consider problems of its worsening physical environment. The United States Congress recessed for the occasion. More than 20,000,000 persons, according to estimates —especially young people in schools and colleges—took part in a wide variety of activities. All were focused on an "improved quality of life." These activities ranged from teach-in discussions to rubbish cleanups.

Earth Day set the theme for the entire year of 1970. It was a year of awakened public awareness of the need for greatly improved conservation of the planet's limited resources: air, water, land, space, and materials.

A blanket of air pollution hangs over New York City, all but hiding the sun.

Earth Day: A commitment to make life better, not just bigger and faster.

ENDANGERED SPECIES

Man is in the process of making his air un-breathable, his water undrinkable, his cities un-livable. If the trend continues, man could be added to the already-too-long list of "Endan-gered Species." This list now includes hundreds of species, including the animals shown here. Animals have been hunted for their pelts, shot for sport, and DDT'd because they happened to be in the wrong place at the wrong time. The problem is worldwide, too. In Africa, poachers invade game preserves to kill for profit. Whalers ply the oceans, decimating the once-plentiful schools of whales. In Canada, seal pups are slaughtered so that sealskin coats can be made.

Bald Eagle

Cheetah

Peregrine Falcon

Alligator

William D. Ruckelshaus, administrator of the Environmental Protection Agency.

President Richard M. Nixon's first official act of the decade was to sign the National Environmental Policy Act of 1969. He said, "The 1970's absolutely must be the years when America pays its debt to the past by reclaiming the purity of its air, its waters and our living environment. It is literally now or never."

The act established the three-member presidential Council on Environmental Quality. It provided that all Federal agencies submit advance reports to the Council before undertaking any projects that might affect the environment. The act also declared for the first time that it was national policy "that each person should enjoy a healthful environment."

The year brought a rapid and remarkable succession of developments in almost every field related to environment.

In the national election, the "quality of life" was high among voters' concerns. A number of candidates for Congressional, state, and local offices owed victories or defeats largely to their positions and voting records on environmental problems.

These problems also occupied much of Congress' time during the year. Some 2,000 environmental bills were introduced and 65 measures were made into law. In February President Nixon outlined a 37-point program. It listed legislative and administrative steps to speed efforts against water pollution, air pollution, and the solid-waste problem.

Oil spills from offshore oil rigs, such as this one burning in the Gulf of Mexico, kill sea life.

Polluted waters contaminate food. In 1970, tuna fish was found to contain high levels of mercury.

▶ WATER POLLUTION

A law was passed placing heavy penalties on shipowners or others responsible for ocean oil spills. One company was fined $1,000,000 for violation of offshore drilling regulations. The violation caused a month-long oil fire and oil slick off Louisiana.

Mercury is widely released into the environment by industry and in agricultural chemicals. Mercury was long considered inert. (An inert substance is one that does not combine easily with other substances.) However, in 1970 mercury was found to be forming highly poisonous compounds. Large numbers of fish, sea animals, and game birds were found to be contaminated. For two months the Government conducted a strong campaign to remedy the situation. Then Federal officials announced they had reduced mercury discharges by 86 per cent. The nationwide total was reduced to only about forty pounds a day.

Another new problem that gained attention was "thermal pollution." The term describes the harmful effects of hot water on fish and water plants. Industry discharges hot water at the rate of billions of gallons an hour after it cools boilers and other equipment. Federal officials began to place limits on such discharges.

Under pressure from Federal officials, the nation's big soap manufacturers began to reduce the amount of phosphates in detergents. (Phosphates are chemicals, made up mainly of phosphorus and oxygen, that improve the cleaning power of detergents.) The phosphates go unchanged down the drain through sewer lines and into lakes and rivers. There they stimulate weedy growths harmful to the waterways' plant-fish-insect life cycles.

Pollution of the seas was a subject of growing concern. During the year Thor Heyerdahl, the Norwegian explorer, completed a voyage by raft from Africa to America. He spoke of having seen "a continuous stretch of at least 1,400 miles of open Atlantic polluted by floating lumps of solidified, asphalt-like oil."

At present, ships dump their oily wastes on the high seas. United States Secretary of Transportation John A. Volpe proposed an international agreement to end the practice. He made the proposal at a Brussels meeting of the North Atlantic Treaty Organization.

▶ NOISE

Noise was another kind of pollution that moved to the forefront of public attention. There was debate throughout the year about the proposed supersonic transport (SST) plane. The SST would fly at speeds up to 1,800 miles an hour. It would produce a shock wave far more powerful than the familiar "sonic booms" of existing jet planes. According to many environmentalists the plane would be destructive to buildings and to people's hearing and nerves. A Federal development contract is being carried out by the Boeing Company in Seattle, Washington. But in December the Senate rejected the spending of additional funds on the SST.

▶ AIR POLLUTION

Air pollution continued to plague cities in almost all industrialized countries. In the United States the National Air Pollution Control Administration reported that more than 200,000,000 tons of gaseous contaminants (pollutants in the form of gases) were now going into the nation's skies every year. In 1966 the total was only 142,000,000 tons. Roughly half of this pollution comes from automobiles and half from industry and other sources, such as burning dumps and forest fires.

Some states and cities made headway toward imposing limits on the fumes given off from stationary sources, such as factories. But progress was slow.

Federal officials moved ahead with a schedule of fume limits on automobiles that becomes tighter each year. The automobile industry said that constant improvement of exhaust controls should reduce car fumes to a minimum by about 1980. (It will take that long to replace all the old cars now in use.) Members of Congress urged that the deadline for "clean" cars be advanced to 1975. Congressmen also urged that engines powered by other means (such as electricity)

One of the entrants in the seven-day cross-country clean-car race, which was held to dramatize the possibilities of achieving fume-free automobiles.

be introduced, if gasoline engines couldn't be fully improved by 1975.

In the meantime, the oil industry's attack on the problem of pollution was the development of gasolines that contain very little lead or no lead at all.

Students from about 30 colleges took part in a "clean car" race to dramatize the possibilities of achieving fume-free automobiles. The students staged a seven-day cross-country race in August from Cambridge, Massachusetts, to Pasadena, California. Forty-one cars, modified to reduce their smog, took part. Some used natural gas for fuel, some, electric motors, and some had special mufflers for neutralizing exhaust gases. Federal air pollution officials were impressed enough to start a detailed study of some of the competing cars.

Early in the year the major U.S. airlines accepted a three-year deadline, proposed by government officials. By late 1972 the airlines expect to have solved the problem of smoke trails from jets.

▶ CONCERN FOR THE "QUALITY OF LIFE"

Public concern about the "quality of life" resulted in a number of citizen lawsuits. These were brought to block proposed projects considered harmful to the environment. The projects ranged from atomic power plants and highways to commercial developments in national forests. Citizens' rights to bring such suits are often challenged, and the ground rules are not clear. Michigan adopted a state law guaranteeing these rights, and Congress began studying proposals for a similar national law.

Homes, businesses, and factories produce about one million tons of solid waste every day in the United States. The total is increasing every year.

"Once upon a time there lived a little green elf in an old oak tree which had been condemned to make way for Interstate 95. The old oak tree stood by contaminated waters that ran along the edge of the strip mine just twenty-five miles from the heavily polluted air of the city. In spite of his emphysema he was a fairly happy elf . . . "

An international conference on the problems of the human environment is being planned. Delegates met in March at the United Nations to start preparing for the United Nations Environmental Conference, to be held in Sweden in 1972.

▶ SOLID WASTE

The year brought a flurry of campaigns across the country for the collection of old cans and bottles. Manufacturers paid small rebates or bounties. No one got rich on these salvage operations, and the total flow of glass and metals in industry was not changed greatly. But the movement was a very important development in the environmental picture.

Of all the pollutions, the one most familiar to everyone is the growing accumulation of trash, or solid waste. Homes, businesses, and factories produce about 1,000,000 tons of solid waste every day, and the total is increasing every year.

Solid waste is an eyesore. It is costly, and under present conditions it is unhealthy. The Federal Bureau of Solid Waste Management estimates that disposal costs the country about $4,500,000,000 a year. Most city waste is either burned or put in dumps. Recently there was a Federal study of 12,000 city dump sites and 300 municipal incinerators. The study found the great majority "unacceptable" from a health standpoint.

At the same time, many economists are concerned about the wastefulness of present disposal practices. There is a mistaken idea that the United States and the world are blessed with unlimited resources. People believe that nations can go on consuming indefinitely for no more than the cost of taking materials from the earth and processing them.

Actually, the source of all these materials is a thin layer of the earth's surface. The amount of materials that can be taken from this layer is quite limited. There is no limit on products that can be grown, and there is enough coal to last for centuries. But the known supplies of most of the earth's basic resources, such as oil and metals, are only enough to last perhaps another thirty years, if we continue to use these resources at the present rates.

It is obvious that the world, and particularly the United States, which is the biggest consumer, will have to "recycle" resources. We will have to use materials over and over again.

Thus, two needs are meeting: the need to deal with waste materials in a thrifty way, and the need to recycle many of the substances that go into solid waste. In the light of these needs, the bottle and can recovery programs are a helpful first step toward practices that someday will be universal and absolutely necessary.

GLADWIN HILL
The New York Times

LAND USE: REDISTRIBUTING THE POPULATION

There are some 200,000,000 people in the United States, and there are over 3,000,000 square miles of land—enough to give every man, woman, and child about 11 acres. Yet 75 per cent of the people live on less than 5 per cent of the land. The remaining land stands relatively unused. Only a small fraction of it is needed for agriculture. One third of the nation's land is still owned by the Federal Government. A small part of this is in national parks and forests. But, again, most of it is idle and unoccupied.

The reason for this imbalance, and the many discomforts it causes people, is that little thought has been given to the best use of all the nation's real estate. How the land is used—whether for homes, industry, farms, or parkland—is decided largely by 60,000 separate local governments. They do not look beyond their own immediate needs.

Two developments in 1970 marked noteworthy steps toward changing this situation. One was a report by the Public Land Law Review Commission, established by Congress, on a five-year study of better use of Federal land. The report contained hundreds of recommendations.

The second development was the introduction in Congress by Senator Henry Jackson of Washington of a National Land Use Planning bill. It calls for Federal grants and technical assistance to the states to develop land-use plans that could be co-ordinated at the Federal level. The bill could be the basis for gradual redistribution of the nation's economic resources and population to take best advantage of the space available.

There is enough land in the United States to give every person about 11 acres . . .

. . . Still, more than three out of every four people live on less
than 5 per cent of the country's 3,000,000 square miles of land.

EUROPE

IN 1970 an era—the De Gaulle era—came to an end in Europe. Charles de Gaulle, who has been called the greatest Frenchman since Napoleon, died of a heart attack on November 9. For a quarter of a century De Gaulle had one goal: To restore France, which had suffered a shattering defeat in World War II, to what he considered its rightful position as a leader among nations. In pursuit of this goal, De Gaulle not only changed France but left an indelible mark on Europe and, indeed, the entire world.

If one era ended in 1970, perhaps a new and, hopefully, more peaceful one began. Charles de Gaulle first gained prominence during World War II, as leader of the Free French forces. The same world war left Europe divided between communist and non-communist nations. As Winston Churchill said, "An iron curtain has descended across the Continent." In 1970, West German Chancellor Willy Brandt took steps to raise that curtain. He signed a historic nonaggression treaty with the Soviet Union. He signed a treaty with Poland, ending a border problem that had plagued both nations since the end of World War II. And he began talks with communist East Germany, in an effort to normalize relations between the two parts of the divided nation. Brandt's efforts gave hope that there would be reduced tensions in Europe.

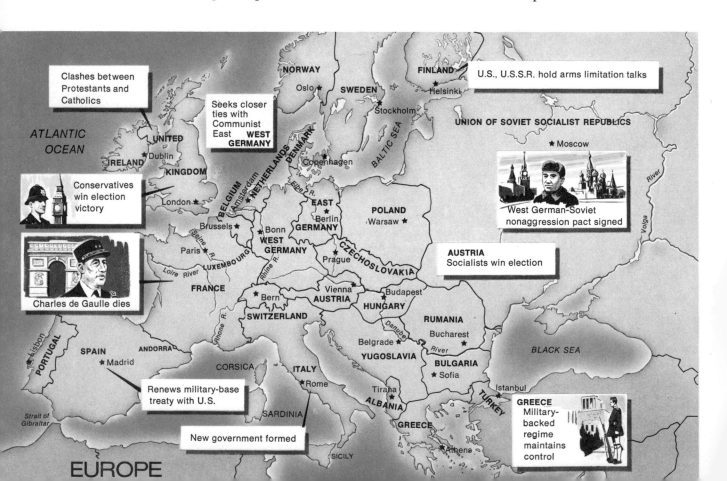

Clashes between Protestants and Catholics

Seeks closer ties with Communist East WEST GERMANY

U.S., U.S.S.R. hold arms limitation talks

ATLANTIC OCEAN

Conservatives win election victory

West German-Soviet nonaggression pact signed

Charles de Gaulle dies

AUSTRIA
Socialists win election

Renews military-base treaty with U.S.

New government formed

GREECE
Military-backed regime maintains control

EUROPE

In 1841, Scottish historian Thomas Carlyle wrote that "The history of the world is but the biography of great men." Certainly the history of the last quarter of a century is in no small part the biography of Charles de Gaulle. His death on November 9, 1970, ended a chapter in modern history. Whether the next quarter of a century of history will be in part a biography of West German Chancellor Willy Brandt (below right, with Soviet Premier Aleksei Kosygin) remains to be seen. Brandt's policy of seeking closer ties with the communist East could usher in a period of reduced tensions in the world. If it does, Brandt would rank with Charles de Gaulle as one of the molders of twentieth-century history.

Edward Heath, Great Britain's new prime minister, acknowledges the cheers of his supporters as he stands outside No. 10 Downing Street, his official residence.

Portuguese Prime Minister Marcelo Caetano (left) greets Francisco Franco, Spanish head of state. The leaders of the two Iberian nations faced several problems in 1970. Caetano sought to consolidate his power after the death of former Prime Minister Antonio Salazar. Franco coped with Basque political discontent.

In Moscow's Red Square, Russian schoolchildren pay tribute during the Soviet Union's celebration of the 100th anniversary of Lenin's birth. Lenin had led the 1917 revolution that established the communist state in Russia.

WESTERN EUROPE

Willy Brandt, a Socialist, became chancellor of West Germany on October 21, 1969. He immediately set out to improve relations with his country's communist neighbors to the east. In 1970, Brandt's efforts met with great success.

▶ WEST GERMANY LOOKS EASTWARD

On January 14, Chancellor Brandt proposed to East Germany that the two countries hold talks to "normalize" relations. West Germany would like to see the two German states eventually reunited. Brandt hoped that these talks might be a step in that direction. The leaders of communist East Germany hinted that they might be willing to talk with Brandt. But first they wanted West Germany to grant "internationally legal recognition" to East Germany. Brandt did not really do this, but he did say that if discussions were held, the two Germanys would talk as "equals." This seemed to satisfy the East Germans, and Brandt was then invited to East Germany.

On March 19 he traveled to Erfurt, East Germany, where he met with East German Premier Willi Stoph. This was the first time that the heads of government of divided Germany's two governments had ever met. The meeting was friendly, although no important decisions were made. The two leaders agreed, however, to meet again on May 21, this time in West Germany.

The second meeting between Brandt and Stoph, at Kassel, West Germany, was not so friendly as the first. Nothing was accomplished, and no further talks were held until late in the year. While matters were at a temporary standstill with East Germany, Brandt moved ahead with his diplomatic efforts in other areas.

In February, March, and May, West German State Secretary Egon Bahr held talks in Moscow with Soviet Foreign Minister Andrei Gromyko. The aim of these talks was to work out a nonaggression treaty. A draft treaty was agreed on in May, and, during the summer, Gromyko and Walter Scheel, the West German foreign minister, worked out the final details. Brandt flew to Moscow on August 12 to sign the treaty.

The pact is considered a historic landmark in East-West relations. Twenty-five years earlier the Soviet Union and Germany had fought each other in World War II, the most destructive war in history. Now, under the terms of the treaty, each pledged not to use force against the other. West Germany also agreed to accept the permanent annexation by Poland of the areas east of the Oder and Neisse rivers. Before World War II, this territory—more than 30,000 square miles—had belonged to Germany.

For its part, the Soviet Union dropped its demands that West Germany grant East Germany formal diplomatic recognition. It also agreed to accept from West Germany a letter reaffirming West Germany's right to work for the reunification of East and West Germany.

Mr. Brandt told the Soviets that he would not ask the West German Parliament to ratify the treaty until the Soviets and East Germans eased their stand on the Berlin question. Throughout the year, the East Germans had blocked or held up traffic between Berlin and West Germany.

The United States and other Western nations welcomed the Soviet-West German treaty. They cautioned, however, that only Soviet deeds (especially in Berlin) would demonstrate whether or not the Soviets acted in good faith when they signed the pact.

The West Germans also held talks during the year with Poland. In October the two nations signed a five-year trade and economic agreement. Then, in December, they signed a treaty in which the Germans again recognized Poland's right to keep the territory east of the Oder and Neisse rivers. (East Germany had already accepted Poland's annexation of this territory.)

Willy Brandt's diplomatic drive had its risks. The Soviet Union and the communist nations of Eastern Europe are not really anxious to see Germany reunited. Together, the two Germanys have a population of nearly 75,000,000. A reunited Germany would certainly be the most powerful nation in all of Europe.

The Russians were also slightly suspicious of West German motives. Some Russians thought that West Germany might be trying to weaken Soviet links to other members of the Soviet bloc. For their part, the nations of East Europe were afraid that if West Germany and the Soviet Union moved closer together, their interests would be hurt. Even the nations of the West were wary. They feared that if West Germany moved closer to the Soviet bloc, it would naturally move away from its Western European allies.

SALT TALKS

The Soviet-West German treaty is of great importance for the future peace in Europe. Still, many officials attach more importance to the Soviet-American talks on limiting long-range weapons of war. The Strategic Arms Limitation Talks (SALT) had opened in Helsinki, Finland, late in 1969. Further talks were held in Vienna, Austria, from April to August 1970. In November the negotiators moved back to Helsinki.

The United States proposed that the number of offensive missiles and strategic bombers be limited. It also said that antimissile systems should either be eliminated or limited in scope. The Soviets said that they would prefer a limited system instead of none.

NORTH ATLANTIC TREATY ORGANIZATION

In 1970 the United States began a review of its policy with regard to NATO. There are nearly 300,000 American troops stationed in Europe, and President Nixon would like to bring most of them home sometime in the future. If the troops are brought home, the United States would have to rely mostly on its nuclear weapons to defend Europe. In a message to the NATO foreign ministers meeting in Brussels in December, President Nixon said there would be no reduction of U.S. forces in Europe "unless there is reciprocal action from our adversaries."

Also, at that meeting, the ministers agreed to hold a European security conference with the communist bloc only if the four-power talks result in an agreement by the So-

'AHM ALL FER CALLIN' IT A DRAW, PARDNUH.'

viets to ease restrictions on West Berlin.

Earlier it had been reported that the United States had tried to get NATO to admit Spain. Great Britain and other nations said no to the idea. Nevertheless, in August, Spain and the United States signed a treaty that will permit the United States to keep its military bases in Spain for five more years.

The military-backed regime in Greece restored some constitutional rights in 1970. Still, the Council of Europe condemned Greece because of reports that political prisoners were being tortured there. After the Jordanian civil war, U.S. Defense Secretary Melvin Laird stated that Greece is very important to the NATO alliance. On September 22 it was announced that the United States had resumed full-scale arms shipments to Greece.

EUROPEAN ECONOMIC COMMUNITY

In the not-too-distant future, the six-member European Economic Community (EEC) may be joined by other nations. In March, probably because of pressure by the Soviet Union, Finland rejected the proposed Scandinavian Economic Union (NORDEK).

Londoners hold their noses as they walk past mounds of garbage that accumulated during a strike of garbage collectors. Edward Heath, Britain's new prime minister, had other labor problems: a slowdown by electrical workers caused power failures all over Britain.

As a result, Denmark and Norway let it be known that they would like to join the EEC. Great Britain and Ireland also began negotiating their entry into the EEC. This was made possible by France's shift in policy. When Charles de Gaulle was president of France, he vetoed British membership in the Common Market. In 1970, however, France's new President, Georges Pompidou, stated that he would not oppose the British on this issue. Negotiations were held throughout the year.

▶ THE DEATH OF CHARLES DE GAULLE

Until 1940, the year nazi Germany defeated France in World War II, Charles de Gaulle was a little-known Army officer. When the Germans overran his country, he fled to England. There he set himself up as leader of the Free French forces, and pledged to liberate his homeland. Four years later, in the summer of 1944, he kept his word. De Gaulle led French and Allied troops into Paris as the Germans fled eastward. After all of France was liberated, and Germany defeated, De Gaulle became president of France. He served until 1946 and then retired. But 12 years later, in 1958, his country called on him once again. In that year France was on the verge of a civil war between those Frenchmen who wanted to keep Algeria part of France and those who wanted to give it independence and end the long war there. De Gaulle was given wide powers, and he chose to end the war and give the Algerians their independence. He served as French premier and as president from 1958 until 1969, at which time a constitutional issue he supported was defeated in a national referendum and he retired once again. He was succeeded by Georges Pompidou.

In 1970 Pompidou continued, for the most part, to follow Gaullist policy. His policy differed in only one important way: He did not automatically reject British entry into the European Common Market.

▶ CONSERVATIVES WIN BRITISH ELECTION

On June 18, British voters gave the Conservative Party a surprising victory over Prime Minister Harold Wilson's Labor Party. The Labor Party had been favored to win by four out of five polls.

The Conservatives picked up 68 seats in the House of Commons, for a 31-seat margin. Edward Heath, Conservative Party leader, was sworn in as prime minister on June 22.

During the campaign, the ruling Labor Party was attacked for its handling of economic problems. In May, the month before the election, Britain had a trade deficit of $74,000,000. Prices went up month after month. Taxes were raised and there were many strikes and growing unemployment.

Upon taking office, Prime Minister Heath faced many of the same problems that Harold Wilson had faced. He fought hard to gain British entry into the EEC. He tried to find a solution to the Rhodesian problem. And he tried to come to some agreement with Britain's powerful trade unions. In September and October, 70,000 municipal workers went on strike. Among the strikers were garbage collectors, and in a short time Britain was facing a health hazard caused by uncollected mountains of garbage. Troops were called out to clean up one area of London.

Late in October it was announced that the Government would cut taxes as well as government spending in 1971. The Government also announced that it would keep a small military force in Southeast Asia, instead of withdrawing all troops by the end of 1971, as had been planned.

▶ SPAIN'S BASQUE CRISIS

For many years the Basques living in northern Spain have been seeking autonomy. In 1970 a trial of 15 Basques threatened a political crisis for Generalissimo Francisco Franco's regime. The Basques were charged with terrorism and the murder of a provincial police chief. The severe penalties being asked and the fact that they were being tried by court-martial outraged the Basques and other Spaniards. Strikes and protests occurred throughout Spain. In December, six of the Basque defendants were sentenced to death. Two days later, after clemency pleas from around the world, Franco commuted all the death sentences.

CONTINUED STRIFE IN NORTHERN IRELAND

During 1970, clashes continued between Catholics and Protestants in Northern Ireland. But they were not so serious or destructive as the fighting in 1969. In July, led by the militant Dr. Ian Paisley (above), 150,000 Protestants marched through Belfast to celebrate the victory by King William of Orange over the Catholic forces of James II in 1690.

Emilio Colombo, prime minister of Italy's 32d postwar Government.

▶ OTHER GOVERNMENT CHANGES

In Italy, for the 30th and 31st times since the end of World War II, governments fell.

On February 7, Mariano Rumor, the Christian Democratic Premier, resigned. He formed a new coalition Government on March 27, but resigned once again on July 6. Rumor resigned because the Socialist Party, one of the parties that made up his coalition Government, insisted on co-operating with the Communist Party.

A new coalition Government was formed a month later by the Christian Democratic Treasury Minister, Emilio Colombo. He agreed to let the Socialists co-operate with the Communists at the local level.

Two months after Colombo took office, Italy recognized Communist China.

Austrian elections, held on March 1, were won by the Socialists. Dr. Bruno Kreisky, head of the Socialist Party, became Austrian chancellor, replacing Dr. Josef Klaus.

Finland, too, received a new head of government in 1970. On July 14, Dr. Ahti Karjalainen became prime minister.

In Iceland, Johann Hafstein was named prime minister after a fire had killed Prime Minister Bjarni Benediktsson, his wife, and grandson.

Parliamentary elections were held in Sweden on September 20. Prime Minister Olof Palme's Social Democratic Party lost its absolute majority of seats, but Palme remained strong enough to keep his position.

J. J. MEEHAN
United Press International

SOVIET UNION AND EASTERN EUROPE

Communist Party General Secretary Leonid I. Brezhnev is the most important and most powerful man in the Soviet Union. During the early months of 1970, Brezhnev seemed to be reaching for even more power —at the expense of Soviet Premier Aleksei N. Kosygin. This effort began early in the year and reached a climax in April, when the 100th anniversary of Lenin's birth was celebrated.

Whenever he could, Brezhnev thrust himself into the spotlight. He appeared at public gatherings and seized every chance to deliver the most important speeches. Nevertheless, in the late spring and summer he seemed to suffer a setback. After he predicted that a new Communist Party congress would be held in 1970, the Communist Party Central Committee decided that the congress should be held in March 1971. Moreover, Premier Kosygin began to appear more in public and to show that he too held power. Still, Brezhnev seemed clearly to be the most important Soviet leader.

Brezhnev's seeming attempt to gain complete control was connected to the Soviet Union's disappointing economic showing in 1969. Farm production declined in that year, and industrial growth was slow. In December 1969 Brezhnev delivered a secret speech that apparently criticized those in charge of the Soviet economy. Since Premier Kosygin is normally in charge of economic matters, the speech was taken as a veiled attack on him.

Soviet economic performance in 1970 was much better than in 1969. Available evidence indicated that industrial production increased by about 8 per cent. Agricultural production also improved. This was due in part to good weather.

Charges of anti-Semitism again flared up in 1970. In December a Leningrad court found 11 defendants guilty of treason for planning to hijack a Soviet airliner. Nine of the defendants, including 2 who were sentenced to death, were Jewish. After Jews and others around the world appealed for leniency, the Russian Supreme Court commuted the death sentences to 15-year labor-camp terms.

▶ SOVIET-WEST GERMAN TREATY

On August 12, in Moscow, Soviet Premier Kosygin and West German Chancellor Willy Brandt signed a historic nonaggression pact. Both nations agreed not to use force against each other. West Germany also agreed to recognize the legality of Poland's post-World War II frontiers. At the end of World War II, Poland had incorporated some German territory.

Along with the treaty went talk of Soviet-West German economic and scientific cooperation. This would include West German loans and technical assistance to help the Soviet Union build the world's largest truck factory. However, Chancellor Brandt stated that he would not offer the treaty to the German Bundestag for ratification until the Soviets and East Germans made concessions on the Berlin question. Specifically, Brandt wanted guaranteed access routes from West Germany to West Berlin, which is surrounded by East German territory. By the end of 1970 no such concessions had been made by the Soviets or East Germans, and the treaty was not ratified.

▶ PRESIDENT NIXON VISITS YUGOSLAVIA

At the end of September, President Nixon visited Yugoslavia. He was received warmly by large crowds in Belgrade, the Yugoslav capital, and in Zagreb, the nation's second-largest city. Mr. Nixon and Yugoslav President Tito talked about many world problems, including the dangerous situation in the Middle East. Tito evidently attached great importance to the talks. This was indicated by the fact that he chose to receive Mr. Nixon rather than go to Cairo for the funeral of Egyptian President Nasser. Nasser and Tito had been very close friends.

As Russians celebrated the 100th anniversary of Lenin's birth, a power struggle was going on behind Kremlin walls.

President Richard Nixon waves to crowds of Yugoslavs as he rides with Yugoslav President Tito through the streets of Belgrade. Nixon and Tito discussed many world problems, including the tense situation in the Middle East.

In another interesting development in Yugoslavia, Tito announced that he would prepare for the succession to his power. (Tito, who has ruled Yugoslavia for 25 years, is nearly eighty years old.) He proposed that Yugoslavia have a sort of collective presidency. Under such a system, his powers would be exercised by a group of people rather than one man. The members of the collective presidency would represent the different Yugoslav regions as well as major social and political organizations. There has been a great deal of tension among Yugoslavia's half-dozen nationality groups. Tito's idea of a collective presidency

is apparently aimed at solidifying these groups, so that the nation does not fall apart after his death.

▶ CZECHOSLOVAK PURGES CONTINUE

Two years after the Soviet invasion of Czechoslovakia, liberals continued to be purged from the government, the Communist Party, and society in general. The aim was to remove everyone who had supported the liberal and democratic ideas of the Dubcek era in 1968. The prime victim of the purge was Alexander Dubcek himself. He was expelled from the Communist Party.

The hopelessness of the Czechoslovak people was shown on August 21, the second anniversary of the Soviet invasion. No effort was made to stage any public protest, such as had taken place a year earlier. The lack of any protests showed Gustav Husak, chief of the Czechoslovak Communist Party, that he was solidly in control. It also indicated that he was meeting Soviet demands for "normalization" of Czechoslovak political life. Husak thus felt confident enough to defy pro-Soviet extremists who demanded that Dubcek and other 1968 leaders be put on public trial for alleged treason and subversion. In late 1970 it was clear that Husak wanted no such trials. Nevertheless, a number of liberal intellectuals were put in jail.

▶ EAST GERMANY AND THE SOVIET-W. GERMAN PACT

The Soviet-West German nonaggression treaty placed Walter Ulbricht, the leader of communist East Germany, in a difficult position. For one thing, it weakened his propaganda that West Germany is still an evil imperialist country bent on "revenge" for the losses it suffered in World War II. Because East Germany is dependent on the Soviet Union, Ulbricht had to applaud the treaty. But he sought to sabotage it by hindering genuine improvement of the situation in Berlin.

East German-West German negotiations in the first half of 1970 foundered because of Ulbricht's demands that West Germans give East Germany complete and formal recognition as a sovereign state.

▶ HUNGARIAN ECONOMIC REFORM

In 1970, Hungary focused attention on trying to improve its economy and upon trying to ensure the success of its economic-reform plan. That reform—one of the most liberal in the Soviet bloc—gave a great deal of power to factory managers. The managers were allowed to run their own plants without much interference from central authorities. It was hoped that under such a plan, production and profits would increase.

Hungary also showed interest in increasing its economic links with West Europe. By doing so it would get the benefit of West-ern technology and, at the same time, be able to sell Hungarian products to the West.

▶ RUMANIAN INDEPENDENCE

Rumania remained under heavy Soviet pressure in 1970 to conform more closely to Moscow's line. The independent-minded Rumanians resisted. They refused, for example, to join the new Moscow-dominated Investment Bank initiated by the Soviet bloc's Council for Mutual Economic Assistance (Comecon). But the Rumanians did decrease their public expressions of disagreement with Moscow's foreign policy. They also agreed to enter into several economic projects with the Soviet Union of a type they had rejected earlier. Nevertheless, Rumania's insistence on managing its own affairs did not weaken. In the fall, Rumanian Communist Party leader Nicolac Ceausescu visited the United States.

▶ GOVERNMENT CRISIS IN POLAND

In Poland an economic crisis led to the purge of communist leader Wladyslaw Gomulka and several other members of the communist Politburo. In December the Polish Government announced that the prices of food, fuel, and clothing would sharply increase. Coming just before the Christmas season, this enraged the country's workers. Poland's worst rioting since 1956 broke out. Bloody clashes between civilians and the armed forces in Gdansk, Szczecin, and other urban areas left scores of people dead. On December 20, Gomulka, who had emerged as leader of the country after the 1956 riots, resigned. He was replaced by Edward Gierek as the leader of Poland's Communist Party.

Just several weeks earlier, the leaders of Poland and West Germany had signed a treaty establishing diplomatic relations between the two countries. For the Poles, the West German decision to accept the Oder-Neisse River as Poland's border was a triumph.

How Gomulka's fall from power would affect the Polish-West German treaty was left undecided as 1970 ended.

HARRY SCHWARTZ
The New York Times

HOBBIES

ALL hobbies continued their great popularity in 1970. Working with model trains and miniature cars was fun for people of all ages. For the professional or the hobbyist, stamp and coin collecting offered new excitement and interest. Many attractive commemorative stamps were issued. And the first of 36 "miniature" presidential medals were struck in 1970. The fun of handicrafts had people tie-dying, working with decoupage, making plastic-film flowers and sculpting with metals. Whether the finished product was to be worn or was for decoration, making something with one's hands was a most enjoyable task.

A model-railroad enthusiast uses a detailed diagram to assemble his set.

Model-car slot racing can provide hours of fun.

A youngster intently sculpts with "model-metal."

Stamp collecting as a hobby attracts more and more devotees every year.

ARTS AND HANDICRAFTS

In 1970, many people discovered a "new" craft: tie-dyeing. All over the world young people wore tie-dyed shirts, jeans, scarves, and neckties. And most of them had dyed the clothing themselves. Tie-dyeing is very simple. First, the material is tied in knots or bound with string or elastic. Then it is placed in a dyebath. Since the dye cannot reach the part of the material inside the knot, the material emerges from the dyebath partly dyed, partly undyed, creating beautifully colored patterns.

Tie-dyeing is actually an ancient craft. It originated hundreds of years ago in the Far East, and is still practiced in India, Indonesia, and parts of Africa. In these areas, the material is tied very precisely so that stripes, plaids, circles, polka dots, and other geometric patterns are created. Most young people today prefer to create freer patterns.

To create accessories for their tie-dyed shirts and jeans, boys and girls adopted another ancient craft: Indian beadwork. They discovered the fun of making necklaces, bracelets, rings, headbands, and anklets from the tiny colored beads that we associate with the American Indians. The beads are strung on wire or thread. With a little practice and patience, the strung beads can be looped or knotted to form many interesting designs.

Still another old craft that young people continued to enjoy in 1970 was decoupage. Decoupage, from a French word, means "the art of cutting." This craft was popular in eighteenth-century France. Today it has been rediscovered by hobbyists.

There are three basic steps to creating a piece of decoupage. First, a paper design from a magazine or book is carefully cut away from its background. Second, the design is glued onto a box, board, or other object. Finally, the item is given several coats of varnish. It should be sanded between coats until it is completely smooth to the touch. If you run your fingers over a good piece of decoupage, it is impossible to feel the edges of the design. Dedicated de-

A decoupage box purse with a beautiful strawberry design. Decoupage was a popular craft in 1970.

coupeurs (people who practice decoupage) will sometimes apply as many as thirty or forty coats of varnish to a single article, so that the design is completely embedded.

One of the most popular uses of decoupage is the making of box purses. A wooden box purse or a metal lunch box is decorated with cutouts, coats of varnish are applied, and the result is a one-of-a-kind handbag.

While some people were finding new ways to enjoy old crafts, others were creating flowers such as their grandparents never imagined. These are beautiful transparent "film flowers" made from liquid plastic. The outer edges of the petals are formed from wire. The wire form is then dipped into a special colored liquid plastic. The plastic remains suspended between the wire edges, forming a perfect glasslike petal. After several petals are made and have been allowed to dry, they are bound together with floral tape to form a complete flower. Bouquets of plastic flowers are dramatic and attractive proof that not all crafts are old ones.

SYBIL C. HARP
Editor
Creative Crafts Magazine

Indian beadwork was one of the popular crafts in 1970. The finished article could be a bag, belt, choker, or just about anything an inventive person could think of. The beads come in almost every color, and fringes can be added as decoration, as in the bag shown on the right.

Making "film flowers" from liquid plastic became a successful commercial enterprise, and many young people could be seen selling their creations. Tie-dying clothing, although messy, was really fun to do. By carefully knotting, twisting, or pleating, almost any color pattern can be formed.

STAMPS AND STAMP COLLECTING

The big stamp news in 1970 was the sale of one of the world's rarest stamps, the one-cent magenta. This stamp, issued in 1856 by the colony of British Guiana in South America, was sold at auction for $280,000. This was almost double the price ever before paid for a stamp.

For many people stamp collecting is not merely a hobby. In 1970, stocks and bonds declined in value. Many people turned to buying stamps, antiques, and other art objects as a form of business investment. So, the one-cent magenta was bought by a group of eight businessmen, each of whom paid an equal amount of money. Some years from now, when the stamp is sold, they will share the profits.

The British Guiana one-cent magenta is not the only one-of-a-kind stamp. (At least one sheet of this stamp was issued, but no

Two interesting commemoratives issued during 1970 were the UN's 25th-anniversary imperforate sheet and the United States "jumbo" Natural History Series. The UN sheet had as its theme "Peace and Progress." The Natural History Series pictured subjects on view at the American Museum of Natural History in New York City and the Peabody Museum in New Haven, Connecticut. Shown below is a copy of the British Guiana one-cent magenta, which was sold for $280,000 at an auction. It is one of the rarest stamps in the world.

AMERICAN BALD EAGLE

AFRICAN ELEPHANT HERD

HAIDA CEREMONIAL CANOE

THE AGE OF REPTILES

Canadian commemorative stamps honoring EXPO '70, Japan's World's Fair. Canada and its provinces of Quebec, Ontario, and British Columbia had pavilions at EXPO '70.

one knows what happened to the others.) But the one-cent magenta is the world's most legendary stamp. It was discovered by a schoolboy about twenty years after it was issued, and has brought higher prices every time it has come up for sale. The person who sold it in 1970 for $280,000 paid only about $40,000 for the stamp in 1940.

The United States, encouraged by the enthusiasm that its oversized "Moon Landing" stamp received in 1969, printed almost all of its 1970 commemoratives in the double size. One novelty of the "jumbo" stamp design was a Natural History Series of commemoratives. A block of four different stamps pictured popular subjects on view at the American Museum of Natural History in New York City and Yale's Peabody Museum in New Haven, Connecticut. An African elephant herd was shown in brilliant colors, as well as a prehistoric brontosaurus, a ceremonial war canoe, and an American bald eagle.

The United Nations also issued commemoratives on various subjects. To celebrate its 25th anniversary, the United Nations issued a small three-stamp imperforate sheet. The slogan on each stamp was Peace and Progress.

Both Canada and Great Britain continued their program of issuing stamps much more frequently than before. Canada's most unusual commemorative was its stamps honor-

ing EXPO'70, held in Japan. The four different stamps recurring on the sheet commemorated the participation in the fair of Canada and its provinces of British Columbia, Ontario, and Quebec. Great Britain, once a conservative issuer of commemorative stamps, now admittedly issues them for their revenue-producing value.

The 1970 international stamp exhibition opened in London on September 18 and ran through September 26. The British show, called Philympia, gathered hundreds of exhibitors from many nations and had on view some of the rarest stamps in the world. Included in the show were many of the designs presented in the 1839 British Treasury competition which led to the world's first postage stamp, the following year, the Penny Black. The United States issued a souvenir commemorative honoring Philympia. It was an engraved card that showed the designs of three 1920 stamps honoring the 300th anniversary of the landing of the Pilgrims at Plymouth Rock.

In August, President Nixon signed a bill replacing the U.S. Post Office Department with an independent government agency called the U.S. Postal Service. Stamp collectors can expect changes in postal operations including a price increase of first-class stamps.

HERMAN HERST, JR.
Columnist, Hobbies Magazine

COLLECTING STAMPS BY TOPICS

For many hobbyists, collecting stamps by country is old hat. Topical collections are the rage. A small sampling of two popular topics is shown here. With the growing concern about the destruction of wildlife and our environment, more and more philatelists are collecting stamps of wildlife and nature subjects. Stamps picturing cats and dogs appeal to many pet owners.

COINS AND COIN COLLECTING

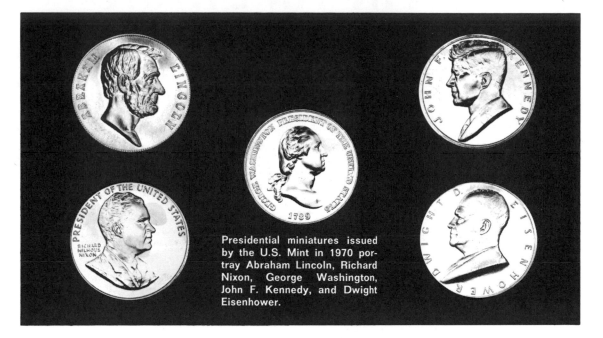

Presidential miniatures issued by the U.S. Mint in 1970 portray Abraham Lincoln, Richard Nixon, George Washington, John F. Kennedy, and Dwight Eisenhower.

In 1970, hobby organizations, professional collectors, and the Government continued to encourage young people's interest in the field of coin collecting.

An innovative change, with young people in mind, was provided by Mary Brooks, head of the U.S. Mint. She completely reorganized the tourist facilities at the Philadelphia and Denver mints. Most visitors to the mints (some 4,000 daily at each) are of elementary- and high-school age. To provide the public with greater knowledge of the history and manufacture of coins, she also launched the first government Numismatic Service, at the Philadelphia mint.

Young people will be attracted to a new series of "miniature" presidential medals produced in 1970. The medals, slightly smaller than the old silver dollar and larger than the half, sell for 50 cents at the mint. Nixon, Eisenhower, Kennedy, Truman, F. D. Roosevelt, Hoover, and Lincoln made up the first group. Medals for all 36 presidents are promised by the end of 1971.

In 1970, coin collecting as a hobby suffered from a completely silverless circulating coinage. Even a token circulation of the 40 per cent silver Kennedy half-dollars was missing. And the "sandwich" dimes and quarters introduced for circulation in 1965 had long ago replaced their silver counterparts previously in circulation.

Tied in with this problem was the extended debate over the issuing of a 40 per cent silver version of the proposed Eisenhower one-dollar coin for the collector, and/or a circulating copper-and-nickel clad version for the general public.

Although the move away from silver coins discouraged the professional and beginning collector, many attractive and scarce old coins have been up for sale in the past five years. Also, a small issue of 1970 Kennedy half-dollars was struck at the Denver mint. These 40 per cent silver coins were included in noncirculating collectors' sets.

Active participation by collectors of all ages was found at the national convention, held in St. Louis, Missouri, in August. Visitors witnessed the largest exhibition of coins, medals, and paper money ever put together by the American Numismatic Association.

CLIFFORD MISHLER
Coins Magazine and *Numismatic News*

LATIN AMERICA

IN 1970, for the first time in history, a Marxist was elected president of a Western nation. Dr. Salvador Allende Gossens, who had founded Chile's Socialist Party 38 years earlier, became president of Chile in November. Upon taking office, Dr. Allende said that he would move his nation away from capitalism and into socialism. He also re-established diplomatic relations with Communist Cuba. Presidential elections were also held in Colombia, Costa Rica, Guatemala, and Mexico. But the Chilean election was clearly the most important. It raised questions about whether other Latin-American nations might follow Chile's lead and elect Marxist presidents.

While most Latin Americans voted peacefully, some resorted to terrorism to obtain political aims. Several foreign diplomats were kidnaped during the year by Leftist terrorists in Guatemala, Brazil, and Uruguay. The terrorists then demanded the release of "political prisoners" as well as money. The Guatemalan and Uruguayan governments refused, and the terrorists killed two men they had kidnaped—the West German ambassador to Guatemala and an American AID official in Uruguay.

In 1970, President Nixon put into effect his plan to "lower the profile" of the United States in Latin America. The results were mixed. The United States was less of a ready target for Latin-American nationalists. But some Latin Americans were unhappy because the lower profile meant less United States aid.

Dr. Salvador Allende Gossens, president of Chile. Dr. Allende is the first Marxist ever to be elected president of a Western Hemisphere nation.

LATIN AMERICA

UNITED STATES

ATLANTIC OCEAN

GULF OF MEXICO

MEXICO

Luis Echeverria Alvarez elected president

Mexico City

Havana

CUBA

JAMAICA

HAITI
DOMINICAN REPUBLIC
Santo Domingo

PUERTO RICO

CARIBBEAN SEA

COLOMBIA
Misael Pastrana Borrero elected president

BARBADOS
TRINIDAD AND TOBAGO
Port of Spain

Caracas

Orinoco

GUYANA
Georgetown
SURINAM
Paramaribo
FRENCH GUIANA
Cayenne

VENEZUELA

CENTRAL AMERICA

Bogata
COLOMBIA

EQUATOR

ECUADOR
Quito

Amazon River

Amazon River

QUAKE EPICENTER

Rio Santa

Chimbote

Mt. Huascaran
Yungay

ANDES

Huaras

Earthquake kills 50,000

PERU

Chimbote

Lima

Kidnappings by terrorists

BRAZIL

Brasilia

BOLIVIA
General Juan Jose Torres takes over government

BOLIVIA
La Paz

Sucre

Lake Titicaca

São Paulo

Rio de Janeiro

PACIFIC OCEAN

Marxist president elected

ALLENDE

PARAGUAY

Asuncion

Parana River

Tupamaro guerrillas kill U.S. official

Valparaiso
Santiago

CHILE

Buenos Aires

URUGUAY
Montevideo

ARGENTINA

CENTRAL AMERICA (inset)

MEXICO

BRITISH HONDURAS
Belmopan

GUATEMALA
Carlos Arana Osorio elected president

GUATEMALA
Guerrillas kidnap and kill West German ambassador

GUATEMALA
Guatemala

HONDURAS
Tegucigalpa

San Salvador
EL SALVADOR

NICARAGUA
Managua

COSTA RICA
San Jose

PANAMA
CANAL ZONE
Panama

COLOMBIA

President Jose Figueres Ferrer reelected

CENTRAL AMERICA

General Roberto Marcelo Levingston takes over government

Strait of Magellan
TIERRA DEL FUEGO

A statue of Christ over-looks what was the city of Yungay, after a disastrous earthquake hit Peru's northern mountain region. The quake killed more than 50,000 people and left nearly 200,000 home-less. Several nations, in-cluding the United States, rushed food, clothing, and medical supplies to the stricken area.

Despite political problems, Brazilians found cause for rejoicing. Young people celebrate their soccer team's victory in the World Soccer Cup.

Foreign diplomats were kidnaped by urban guerrillas in several Latin-American nations. The guerrillas released the Japanese consul in Saõ Paulo, Brazil (above), only after the Brazilian Government agreed to release several political prisoners (below), who were then flown into exile in Mexico.

Dr. Salvador Allende holds a news conference after defeating two other candidates in Chile's presidential election. Allende won 36.3 per cent of the vote.

▶ CHILE ELECTS A MARXIST

Dr. Allende's victory in Chile came as a surprise to many. It was the fourth time he had sought the Chilean presidency. In 1964 he had been soundly defeated by Eduardo Frei Montalva, the leader of Chile's important Christian Democratic Party. But Dr. Allende came back to win in 1970.

There were three candidates in the 1970 Chilean elections. This divided the vote in a way that probably gave Dr. Allende his narrow victory margin.

The election was held on September 4. Dr. Allende won 36.3 per cent of the vote. His nearest rival was Jorge Alessandri Rodriguez, a former president now in his seventies. As candidate of the traditional Chilean conservatives, he polled 34.9 per cent. A margin of only 39,000 votes out of 3,000,000 separated the two. Radomiro Tomic Romero, candidate of President Frei's Christian Democratic Party, came in third. Because of his popularity, President Frei probably would have been re-elected. But the Chilean Constitution does not permit presidents to serve two terms in a row.

Many people had expected that Frei's popularity would help Mr. Tomic. This was not the case.

Neither Dr. Allende nor former President Alessandri had an absolute majority of votes. Thus it fell to Congress to decide the winner. In the past, Congress chose the candidate with the most votes. This time, because Dr. Allende is a Marxist, many people thought that Congress might choose Mr. Alessandri.

There was a great deal of political jockeying before the Congressional vote. The Christian Democrats indicated that they would vote for Allende. But first they wanted some guarantees. They wanted Allende to make sure that freedom of speech and the press would continue. They wanted a guarantee that opposition political parties would be allowed to exist. They wanted assurances of free elections in 1976, when Dr. Allende's six-year term will be up. And finally, they wanted guarantees that the armed forces and *carabineros*, Chile's elite national police force, would remain autonomous, nonpolitical units. With these guarantees given, the Christian Democratic bloc in Congress swung its vote to Dr. Allende. This bloc is the largest single political force in the legislature. After Congressional approval Allende was inaugurated on November 3.

Upon taking office, Dr. Allende said that he would nationalize certain foreign-owned holdings. An early target would be United States-owned copper mines. He also promised to break up "national monopolies" in private hands. Finally, he promised to restructure the national banking system. The exact details of Dr. Allende's proposals were not too clear. Still, his program was clearly Marxist, even though he said that non-Marxist political and economic ideas would be allowed to exist. Allende assured small businessmen that their enterprises would not be nationalized. But he indicated that government controls would determine some of their activities.

Chile already had a strongly socialized economy when Dr. Allende took power. State-owned mining, transportation, communication, and manufacture accounted for at least 40 per cent of the nation's economic activity. Chileans have become used to state economic controls. Thus many Chileans were less concerned about a Marxist-oriented economy than foreign observers were.

▶ **OTHER ELECTIONS**

In Colombia, Misael Pastrana Borrero, the candidate of the National Front coalition, narrowly won the presidency. He turned back a surprisingly strong bid by former dictator Gustavo Rojas Pinilla in the April elections.

In Costa Rica, former President Jose Figueres Ferrer easily won a new term in February. He promised major economic and social reform for his small Central American nation.

In Guatemala, Colonel Carlos Arana Osorio, who ran as a law-and-order candidate, edged out two opponents to be declared president after March elections. His early actions as president were less vigorous on the terrorism issue than many had expected.

Finally, in Mexico, the official candidate of the Partido Revolucionario Institucional, Luis Echeverria Alvarez, won an easy victory in July voting. He captured almost 90 per cent of the vote.

▶ **LEADERS OUSTED IN ARGENTINA, BOLIVIA**

Argentina's military strong man, General Juan Carlos Ongania, had served as president since 1966, when a civilian Government was ousted. In June 1970, Ongania himself was ousted by fellow military offi-

Misael Pastrana Borrero, winner of Colombia's April 19 presidential election. Pastrana defeated former Colombian leader Gustavo Rojas Pinilla by more than 63,000 votes.

Jose Figueres Ferrer promises a clean sweep of social and economic problems after winning Costa Rica's February 1 presidential election.

Carlos Arana Osorio, winner of Guatemala's March 1 presidential election. President Arana faced the problem of coping with political terrorism and the kidnapings.

cers. These officers were unhappy with the Government's economic performance and its failure to move Argentina at least somewhat on the road to civilian rule.

Ongania was replaced by General Roberto Marcelo Levingston. The new President encountered the same economic problems that had faced Ongania. At year's end, the Argentine peso appeared much less strong than it had at the start of 1970.

In Bolivia, one military strong man replaced another. General Alfredo Ovando Candia, who had led the military overthrow of civilian rule in September 1969, was himself ousted in October 1970. During his year as president, General Ovando had been buffeted by Rightist and Leftist elements in the armed forces. Shortly before his overthrow, the Rightists appeared to be gaining the upper hand. When they revolted, however, political jockeying among the military resulted in the emergence of General Juan Jose Torres as the new leader of the nation. Torres is a moderate Leftist.

Bolivia's unstable economy appeared worse than usual as the year ended. And there was a question about how long General Torres would be able to retain power.

▶ **POLITICAL PROBLEMS IN ECUADOR**

In 1970, Jose Maria Velasco Ibarra was serving his fifth term as president of Ecuador. During the year, he became involved in a political crisis that had stemmed from economic difficulties and student unrest. The President assumed broad dictatorial powers, and as the year wore on, his popularity seemed to wane. There were rumors of possible military action against him. Three of Velasco Ibarra's former four presidencies had been ended by military coups.

▶ **KIDNAPINGS AND TERRORISM**

The kidnapings of foreign diplomats and political leaders became a fairly common occurrence in some Latin-American nations. European and United States diplomats were

Luis Echeverria during a campaign stop at Queretaro, Mexico. Echeverria won 90 per cent of the vote in Mexico's July presidential election.

Uruguayan soldiers make a house-to-house search in an effort to find the Tupamaro guerrillas who kidnaped the Brazilian vice-consul. The Tupamaros kidnaped several people in 1970 and stole $6,000,000 from a bank.

the principal targets. The kidnapings took place in Guatemala, Brazil, and Uruguay. The kidnapers appeared to be Leftist-oriented urban terrorists.

In Guatemala there were several such kidnapings. Finally, in March, West German Ambassador Count Karl von Spreti was kidnaped. The terrorists demanded that the Guatemalan Government release political prisoners as well as pay a ransom. When the Government refused, the terrorists killed Von Spreti.

Von Spreti's death marked the end to the kidnapings in Guatemala—at least for the year. The terrorists turned to other activities. They bombed businesses, shot up police stations, and assassinated political leaders.

Similar kidnapings took place in Brazil. In June, terrorists kidnaped the West German ambassador to Brazil. He was released when the Brazilian Government released forty political prisoners who were then flown to Algeria. The Swiss ambassador was kidnaped in December.

In Uruguay, the urban-based Tupamaro guerrillas began a kidnaping spree in late July. They kidnaped the Brazilian vice-consul and an American AID official. The terrorists then picked up another American official, an agricultural specialist. The AID official, Dan A. Mitrione, was killed when the Uruguayan Government refused to release political prisoners as the Tupamaros demanded. At year's end, both the Brazilian vice-consul and the second American official were still in the hands of the Tupamaros.

In November the Tupamaros created a sensation when they stole $6,000,000 in cash and jewels from Uruguay's Bank of the Republic in Montevideo.

The Organization of American States tried to find a solution to the kidnaping problem. But the member nations could not agree on a common plan. Argentina and Brazil led the effort to find a solution. Chile and Mexico, however, were reluctant to go along with any of the proposals. One proposal would limit the right of asylum for prisoners released in exchange for diplomats. To Mexico and Chile, this seemed to interfere with the traditional practice of granting asylum to all exiles.

In Indiana, Mrs. Dan Mitrione comforts her youngest son. Her husband, Dan Mitrione, had been killed by Uruguayan guerrillas.

▶ LOWERING THE U.S. PROFILE

President Nixon's plan to "lower the profile" of the United States in Latin America went ahead in 1970. Washington cut back its embassy staffs. It reduced aid commitments. And it refused to be drawn into controversies over issues such as kidnapings and the Chilean election. Washington thus became less of a target for anti-American and nationalistic Latin Americans. But there was a great deal of unhappiness over the new American policy. Many Latin Americans complained that the United States was cutting Latin America adrift. They said that the United States was not living up to its commitments under the Alliance for Progress. Indeed, United States aid to Latin America was cut sharply during the year. And it seemed likely that aid would be further reduced in the coming years.

Latin Americans also protested United States trade policies. They want Latin-American goods to have easier access to the United States market.

JAMES NELSON GOODSELL
Latin America Editor
The Christian Science Monitor

LITERATURE

WITH the 1970 economic slowdown, the publishing industry did not fare well. Labor costs rose; paper prices went up; fewer new book titles appeared; and fewer picture books for children were published. As *Publishers' Weekly* noted, "Prices are up and editorial excitement is down."

In late 1970 some excitement was restored to the industry with the announcement that Time Inc. was going to serialize a manuscript of the reminiscences of Nikita S. Khrushchev, the former premier of the Soviet Union. The manuscript, made up of "material emanating from many sources," was issued by *Life* magazine as a four-part serial. And twenty other magazines and newspapers around the world serialized it. The book version, under the title *Khrushchev Remembers,* was published by Little, Brown and Co.

Many people questioned the authenticity of the manuscript. Time Inc. insisted it was genuine but refused to reveal from whom and how it was obtained. Khrushchev issued a statement denying that he had released any memoirs and dissociating himself from the publication.

Several books dominated the 1970 best-seller list. Among them were Mary Stewart's *The Crystal Cave,* Taylor Caldwell's *Great Lion of God,* the anonymous "J"'s *The Sensuous Woman,* Alvin Toffler's *Future Shock,* and Julius Fast's *Body Language.*

Former Soviet Premier Nikita Khrushchev made literary headlines with the serialized publication of his memoirs, "Khrushchev Remembers."

Henri Charrière was pardoned by the French Government on October 17, 1970, for the murder which led to his imprisonment in 1933. His international best-seller "Papillon" is based on his imprisonment and daring escapes from penal colonies in French Guiana.

George Jackson, still imprisoned, is the author of a socially significant book, "Soledad Brother: The Prison Letters of George Jackson."

The best fiction of 1970 was notable for its wit and humor. In *Bech: A Book,* John Updike wrote an affectionate satire about a New York Jewish novelist. Donald Barthelme's *City Life* contained elegant fables with a surrealistic feeling to them. Colin MacInnes, the British writer, produced both *Westward to Laughter,* an 18th-century adventure novel, and *Three Years to Play,* set in Shakespeare's London. Eudora Welty wrote her most ambitious novel, *Losing Battles,* about an uproarious Southern family reunion.

Possibly the most important novel of the year introduced a relatively new writer, Gabriel Garcia Marquez, with his *One Hundred Years of Solitude.* A mythical story set in South America, it was astonishing for its inventiveness. Another author famous for his imagination, Günter Grass, used *Local Anaesthetic* to show the limitations of escapism.

James Dickey, better-known as a poet, came out with a bow-and-arrow murder thriller, *Deliverance.* A sentimental best seller, made into a movie, was Erich Segal's *Love Story.*

Posthumously published was the open-air tale *Islands in the Stream,* by Ernest Hemingway. In a quite different mood, but in a style much influenced by Hemingway, was the brooding Hollywood novel *Play It As It Lays* by the confessional essayist and novelist Joan Didion. An even more introspective novel was Saul Bellow's *Mr. Sammler's Planet,* about the reflections of a seventy-year-old resident of Manhattan's upper West Side.

▶ **MEMOIRS, AUTOBIOGRAPHIES, AND BIOGRAPHIES**

A long-awaited book was Charles A. Lindbergh's *Wartime Journals.* In it he faithfully recorded his experiences as a leading isolationist before World War II, and then as a government aeronautic expert. Covering roughly the same period, but from an entirely opposite viewpoint, was James MacGregor Burns' second volume of his Roosevelt biography, *Roosevelt: The Soldier of Freedom.* Still another view of that period was Albert Speer's *Inside the Third Reich,* a memoir of his intimate association with Hitler.

The life of a Hitler purge victim was described by Eberhard Bethge in his biography of the theologian *Dietrich Bonhoeffer: Man of Vision, Man of Courage.* A famous prewar literary figure was portrayed by Nadezhda Mandelstam in *Hope against Hope: A Memoir,* describing the life of her husband, the poet Osip Mandelstam, during Stalin's purges.

Books on the presidency included Dumas Malone's fourth volume of his pioneer biography, *Jefferson the President: First Term, 1801–1805.* And Lady Bird Johnson came out with *A White House Diary,* a very personal account of her five years as First Lady.

Two giants in the field of economics were the subjects of biographies. *Andrew Carnegie,* a massive study by Joseph Frazier Wall, was based on recently made available U.S. Steel files. *Reuther* was based on interviews with the late leader of the United Auto Workers and his associates by the authors, Frank Cormier and William J. Eaton.

The lives of two nineteenth-century Englishmen were also portrayed. Elizabeth Longford wrote the first volume of two in *Wellington: The Years of the Sword,* about the victor of Waterloo. In the two-volume biography *Sir Walter Scott: The Great Unknown,* Edgar Johnson depicted the heroic career of the famous Romantic writer.

Cocteau, written by Francis Steegmuller, was a highly regarded biography of the elegant French artist, poet, and film maker. Nancy Milford's *Zelda* shed new light on the works of F. Scott Fitzgerald and established his wife, Zelda, as a memorable and tragic person in her own right. The distinguished pupil of Freud was the subject of an intellectual biography, *Erik H. Erikson: The Growth of His Work,* by Robert Coles.

Papillon, an autobiography by Henri Charrière, was about the author's years spent in French penal colonies and his daring escapes.

There were numerous works commemorating the centennial of Charles Dickens' death. An outstanding, beautifully illustrated study was *The World of Charles Dickens* by British novelist Angus Wilson.

Kenneth Clark's "Civilisation" is a magnificently illustrated survey of Western culture.

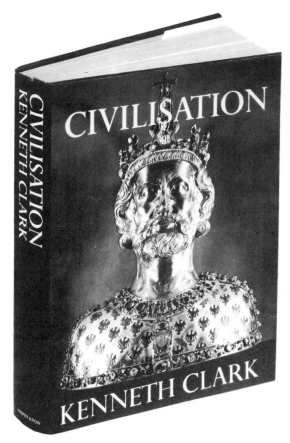

Charles A. Reich, a Yale law professor, analyzes today's youth culture in "The Greening of America."

The Greening of America

How the Youth Revolution is trying to make America livable

Charles A. Reich

227

In "Sexual Politics," Womens Lib expounder Kate Millett examines the relationship between the sexes.

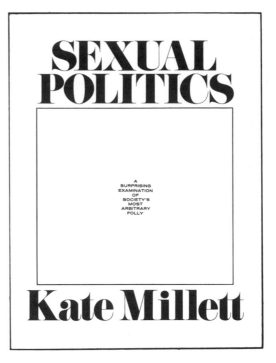

HISTORY

A fitting counterpart to his celebrated 1970 educational-TV series was (Lord) Kenneth Clark's aesthetic history *Civilisation,* a lavishly illustrated survey of Western culture. Geoffrey Bibby found what may be the very origin of Western civilization in the Persian Gulf. His *Looking for Dilmun* was a compelling archeological thriller. Another civilization was discussed in John Hemming's *The Conquest of the Incas.* The narrative included new archeological and manuscript findings.

Modern threats to Western civilization were described in two books. They were Heinz Höhne's monumental *The Order of the Death's-Head: The Story of Hitler's S. S.,* and John Toland's *The Rising Sun: The Decline and Fall of the Japanese Empire.* The second book was an account of the war in the Pacific from the Japanese point of view.

The Depression years were portrayed in the voices of a hundred Americans in *Hard Times: An Oral History of The Great Depression* by Studs Terkel.

POLITICS

President Nixon was the subject of ambitious studies. Jules Witcover's *The Resurrection of Richard Nixon* was a detailed reconstruction of the President's comeback to political power. Garry Wills' *Nixon Agonistes: The Crisis of the Self-made Man* explored the career of Richard Nixon, "the last liberal," as an example of modern American politics. A highly publicized book was *The Real Majority,* an analysis of Middle America, by Richard M. Scammon and Ben J. Wattenberg. Many political experts thought that the book influenced President Nixon's 1970 election campaign.

The Supreme Court during Earl Warren's years as Chief Justice was written about in two notable books. One, *The Supreme Court and the Idea of Progress,* by Alexander M. Bickel, concentrated on reapportionment and desegregation decisions. Fred Graham's *The Self-inflicted Wound* discussed the limited effects of those decisions relating to the rights of suspects.

A black who has been in California prisons for ten years wrote an angry, highly significant book: *Soledad Brother: The Prison Letters of George Jackson* was made up of letters written to his parents, Angela Davis, and others, and was reminiscent of Eldridge Cleaver's *Soul on Ice.*

SOCIAL COMMENT

Social criticism, covering varied topics, was the theme of many books in 1970.

Charles E. Silberman and the Carnegie Corporation came out with a massive documentation of the failures of American schools in *Crisis in the Classroom: The Remaking of American Education.*

Corporate organization was analyzed and reformed in a popular handbook by Robert Townshend, *Up the Organization.* Another attack on the "corporate state" came from Charles A. Reich in *The Greening of America.* In it he proposed adopting a new vision of the American ideal, based on his impressions of the American "counterculture."

The counterculture also held promise for Alvin W. Gouldner in his imposing and eloquent survey of the inadequacies and pitfalls of "objectivity" in Western social science in his *The Coming Crisis of Western Sociology.*

A plea for rational political and economic programs for the Third World countries was at the heart of Gunnar Myrdal's *The Challenge of World Poverty: A World Anti-Poverty Program in Outline.*

The military drew fire from several quarters, Vietnam often being the signal. Robert Sherrill's muckraking critique *Military Justice Is to Justice as Military Music Is to Music* argued for radical reform in military law. Mark Lane's controversial *Conversations with Americans* comprised graphic word-for-word accounts of American atrocities in Vietnam. Several books described an event that was in the headlines most of the year, the alleged Mylai massacre. One was *My Lai 4: A Report on the Massacre and Its Aftermath* by Seymour M. Hersh, who won a Pulitzer Prize for his investigation. Telford Taylor made important legal and moral comparisons in his *Nuremberg and Vietnam: An American Tragedy.*

The most notable book in behalf of Women's Liberation was a vigorous polemic by Kate Millett, *Sexual Politics.*

▶ POETRY

Novelist and poet Robert Penn Warren came out with *Audubon: A Vision.* It was a narrative poem with the famous naturalist-artist as the hero. Two collections of poems appeared in 1970. One, *City without Walls, and Other Poems,* was by the old master W.

Lillian Hellman

Winner of a 1970 National Book Award.

H. Auden. Another, by a younger poet, James Merrill, was titled *The Fire Screen.*

▶ CINEMA AND SPORTS

Two prominent film critics published selections of their work. Pauline Kael wrote *Going Steady,* and Andrew Sarris wrote *Confessions of a Cultist: On the Cinema, 1955–1969.*

Sports books as an industry grew as never before, but one title dominated: *Ball Four: My Life and Hard Times Throwing the Knuckleball in the Big Leagues* by Jim Bouton. It was an outspoken and funny memoir of the author's career.

ROGER JELLINEK
The New York Times Book Review

LITERATURE
FOR
YOUNG PEOPLE

A beautifully illustrated fantasy tale was "Alexander and the Wind-Up Mouse" by Leo Lionni.

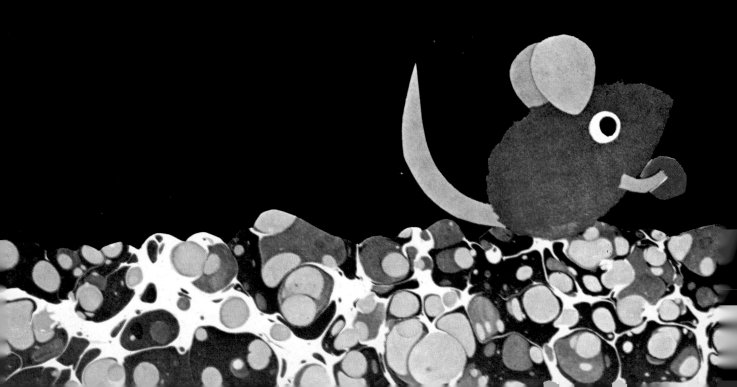

"The Judge" by Harve Zemach; humorously illustrated by Margot Zemach.

The slogan for the fifty-first Children's Book Week, November 1970, was "This Is the Age of the Book." Some publishers had their doubts as they watched costs go up and sales go down. More than one editor had orders to cut back expenses. It seemed to many people more like an age of the headache.

Books with pictures usually cost more than books without, so some houses began to publish fewer books with pictures and more books with no pictures. Color pictures cost more than those in black and white, which caused some publishers to use less color. Nearly every publisher had fewer young people's books on the market in 1970 than in previous years. Critics hoped that fewer books would mean better books, but by the end of the year no one was ready to say for sure that this was the case.

▶ PRIZEWINNERS

Good books, of course, continued to win awards. William Steig's *Sylvester and the*

Magic Pebble (Simon & Schuster) received the 1970 Caldecott Medal as a well-illustrated book from the year before. Protests resulted, because one picture showed two pigs in police uniforms. Was Mr. Steig saying policemen are pigs? Most critics thought not. More people seemed pleased with the choice of *Sounder* (Harper) for the 1970 Newbery Medal. In it, William H. Armstrong told a forceful tale of a black sharecropper's son who lost his father and dog, but won a chance for a better life.

On the lighter side was Lore Segal's *Tell Me a Mitzi* (Farrar), colorfully illustrated by Harriet Pincus. It contained three charming stories and won first place for picture books in the *Book World* Children's Spring Book Festival. Writing for somewhat-older youngsters, E. B. White won the Laura Ingalls Wilder Award and was a runner-up in the Spring Book Festival with *The Trumpet of the Swan* (Harper). His tall tale of a bird that played an instrument had suspense, humor, and honest nature lore. It lost out in the Spring Book Festival to *Sundiata: The Epic of the Lion King* (Crowell) by Roland Bertol.

Not aimed at any special age level, *A Day of Pleasure* (Farrar) won the 1970 National Book Award for Children's Literature. In it, Isaac Bashevis Singer told lightly-amusing and some sad episodes from his boyhood in Poland before and during World War I. Among teen-age books, Jill Paton Walsh's *Fireweed* (Farrar) placed first in the Spring Book Festival. About a boy and a girl in London during World War II, it gave a picture of young people who had to live through war and bombings.

For the quality of all his books, Maurice Sendak received the 1970 Hans Christian Andersen Award. It surprised no one that his *In the Night Kitchen* (Harper) delighted a large audience when it appeared late in the year.

▶ PICTURE BOOKS

A number of books for ages four to nine contained plenty of color and were well worth their prices. *The Beaver Pond* (Lothrop) told by Alvin Tresselt and illustrated by Roger Duvoisin was especially beautiful. It told of beavers and how their way of life affected a region. Also strikingly handsome, Gail E. Haley's *A Story, A Story* (Atheneum) brought Africa closer to American readers through folktales. Bright colors, splashed across the pages, made *The Tiny Seed* (Crowell) by Eric Carle a sure bet to capture any youngster's eye.

Outstanding books with little or no color included Robert Moery's *Kevin* (Bradbury), illustrated by Eros Keith. It showed that magic isn't always desirable. *All the Animals Were Angry* (Holt) offered one of William Wondriska's moral fables. Marguerita Rudolph mixed real people with fantasy ones in retelling the amusing Latvian yarn *The Brave Soldier and a Dozen Devils* (Seabury). On the realistic side, Joan M. Lexau told *Benjie on His Own* (Dial), in which a Negro lad helped his sick grandmother. Don Bolognese was the illustrator.

The most important new series of picture books was based on the *Sesame Street* television program. It included books of *Letters, Shapes,* and *Puzzlers* (Little).

Other picture books of special interest were *A & The* (Atheneum) by Ellen Raskin, *Finger Plays* (Holt) by Marianne Yamaguchi, *I'm Dan* (Scribner) by Ruth Orbach, *Timothy's Horse* (Pantheon) by Vladimir Mayakovsky, *Kulumi the Brave* (World) by Jenny Seed, and *The Angry Moon* (Little) by William Sleator. Imaginary animals figured in Bill Peet's *The Wumpworld* (Houghton), a timely tale of how pollution occurs. A real owl took center stage in Annette MacArthur-Onslow's *Uhu* (Knopf). And fairly real animals in highly imaginary

William H. Armstrong's "Sounder," about a sharecropper's family, won the Newbery Medal. Illustrations by James Barkely.

situations made a funny book of *Animals Should Definitely Not Wear Clothing* (Atheneum) by Judith Barrett, illustrated by Ron Barrett.

▶ FOR INTERMEDIATE AGES

Most books for ages 8 to 14 have black-and-white pictures, but one exception was the gorgeous *Jeanne d'Arc* (Crowell) by Aileen Fisher, illustrated by Ati Forberg. Earl Schenk Miers offered more detailed biography in *That Jefferson Boy* (World), about the growing up of America's third president. For youngsters wanting their history in fictional form, Scott O'Dell wrote about the Navaho Indians in *Sing Down the Moon* (Houghton).

The flood of books about black Americans continued. *Mumbet* (Dodd) by Harold W. Felton told of Elizabeth Freeman's court fight to win her freedom from slavery. Modern youngsters figured in *On and off the Street* (Viking) by Bob Adelman and Susan Hall, and writings by black and Puerto Rican boys and girls appeared in *The Voice of the Children* (Holt), collected by June Jordan and Terri Bush. *Rufus Gideon Grant* (Scribner) by Leigh Dean, another story about a sharecropper's son, had more humor than the prizewinning *Sounder*.

A far different book about a member of a minority, *Ox: The Story of a Kid on Top* (Little) by John Ney, stirred up controversy. Many people felt that its yarn of the foolish ways of a wealthy family had no place in today's world of serious problems. Such critics preferred the honesty of *Leo the Lioness* (Viking) by Constance C. Greene, in which a girl adjusts to change.

For animal lovers, Barbara Brenner produced *A Snake-Lover's Diary* (Scott), and Walt Morey wrote about a bear in *Gloomy Gus* (Dutton). *Runaway Ralph* (Morrow) gave further adventures of a mouse dreamed up by Beverly Cleary a few years ago.

Books based on fantasy have always had wide appeal. Particularly good among those

An exciting, fast-paced adventure story was "Journey Outside" by Mary Q. Steele. It was a runner-up for the Newbery Medal. The book was illustrated with striking, full-page woodcuts by Rocco Negri.

appearing in 1970 were (*George*) (Atheneum) by E. L. Konigsburg. The name appears in parentheses because he lives inside a boy. *The Marvelous Misadventures of Sebastian* (Dutton) was Lloyd Alexander's first book for intermediates since he won the Newbery Award for *The High King*. Brinton Turkle made use of a ghost and a witch in *Mooncoin Castle* (Viking), which had something to say about preserving old landmarks. And Zilpha Keatley Snyder mixed the real

with the fantastic worlds in *The Changeling* (Atheneum).

▶ **FOR TEEN-AGERS**

Books for older readers centered on today's problems. Many of these proved so serious, editors say they could not have published them ten years ago. An outstanding one was Elizabeth S. Helfman's *This Hungry World* (Lothrop). Whereas many writers say the world can feed its exploding popu-

lation, Mrs. Helfman took a different view. Arnold Madison looked at destruction and decided it wasn't without reason. Consequently, he called his book *Vandalism, the Not-So Senseless Crime* (Seabury), and considered it from the standpoints of yesterday, today, and tomorrow.

In *Students in Revolt* (McGraw-Hill), Janet Harris had something to say about twentieth-century wars and other serious events affecting young people today. J. J. McCoy worried about pollution, and his *Shadows over the Land* (Seabury) gave adults as well as teens things to think about. Two authors looked back to the atomic bombing of Hiroshima in 1945 and gave today's young adults a reason to worry about a modern nuclear war. Hiroko Nakamoto, who grew up in Hiroshima and went through the bombing, told her story in *My Japan 1930–1951* (McGraw-Hill). Betty Jean Lifton, who recently lived in Hiroshima, based much of her *Return to Hiroshima* (Atheneum) on interviews.

Fiction also reflected today's problems. Ivan Southall showed that a teen-ager in Australia faces much the same situations that confront America's youth. His *Walk a Mile and Get Nowhere* (Bradbury) offered more entertainment than the title might suggest. The Mexican-Americans in the Southwest are a minority group likely to receive more and more attention. Frank Bonham wrote a particularly good novel about a troubled Mexican-American boy in *Viva Chicano* (Dutton). School dropouts and the drug problem were explored in Paula Fox's *Blowfish Live in the Sea* (Bradbury), a story for girls.

After such serious books, *Brave His Soul* (Dodd) by Ellen Pugh seemed almost frivolous as it debated the issue of whether Prince Madog of Wales reached North America before Columbus. But teen-agers needed lighter works to balance the heavier ones, and could enjoy science fiction in *Alien from the Stars* (Putnam) by Jean and Jeff Sutton or humor in Betty Baker's *And One Was a Wooden Indian* (Macmillan).

CHARLES PAUL MAY
Author, *The Early Indians: Natural and Imaginary Worlds; Great Cities of Canada*

MEDICINE AND HEALTH

IN many ways, the work of a doctor is like that of a detective. They both work with clues to come up with the right answer to a problem. When a doctor solves his problem, he often benefits mankind. Let us look at such a case that started in New Mexico in December 1969. Three children who lived on a farm became very ill. They began to lose their eyesight. They could not co-ordinate their arm and leg movements. They lost consciousness, and two of the children even went into a coma. Their parents took them from doctor to doctor and hospital to hospital. At first, no one knew what was wrong with the children. Finally, after a careful investigation, it was learned that the family raised hogs. And these hogs had been fed grain seed treated with a certain fungicide that contains mercury. It was after the family killed and ate the hogs that they became sick. From this, the doctors discovered that the children were suffering from mercury poisoning. As a result of the case, the Department of Agriculture is trying to halt the sales of mercury fungicides.

During 1970, doctors worked on many such medical problems. They solved some and made progress on others. For example, medical researchers continued their search for the cause of arthritis, and worked on a possible cure for a deadly infant's disease. They established yet another link between cigarette smoking and lung cancer. They even discovered a new virus called Lassa fever. However, the mystery of the "rejection phenomenon" remained unsolved, and heart transplants were all but halted.

A new and deadly virus called Lassa fever was discovered recently. It was so dangerous, in fact, that medical researchers had to stop working on a cure for it. This photo shows the virus enlarged 69,000 times.

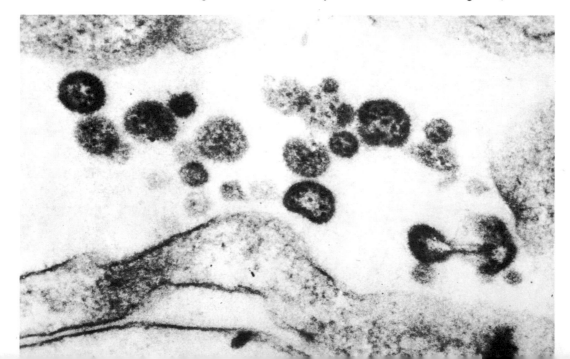

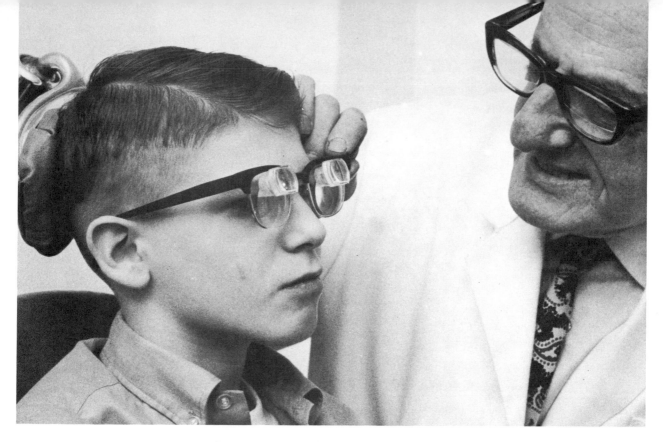

Drs. William Feinbloom (above) and Stanley Taub (below) are not so famous as the doctors who perform heart transplants. But to their patients they are the greatest doctors in the world. Dr. Feinbloom developed a special lens that let 11-year-old Russell Strayer see for the first time. Dr. Taub designed a plastic larynx that allowed his 76-year-old patient to speak again.

Only eight heart transplants were performed in 1970. Doctors stopped performing so many because few of the patients lived for any length of time. Louis B. Russell, Jr., a teacher, has lived the longest with his new heart. His operation was performed on December 3, 1967.

In 1970, heart transplant operations almost came to a standstill. Such operations were stopped because most of the patients did not survive for long afterward. This was because the body rejected the implanted heart. Many doctors feel that until the "rejection phenomenon" can be controlled, heart transplants should be stopped.

Kidney transplants, however, continued to save hundreds of lives. The major problem still is how to get enough of these organs. Each year more and more patients require kidney transplants to save their lives.

▶ NEW DEVELOPMENTS IN ARTHRITIS

Arthritis is a disease that has been known since biblical times. Even though we now have a much clearer understanding of it, we are not much closer to relieving the arthritis sufferers' pain and disability. In 1970, however, some important advances were made. Because of the efforts of the Arthritis Foundation, many clinical-research centers were set up throughout the country. At these centers are doctors who specialize in the treatment of arthritis and related diseases. The centers use the most recent therapeutic techniques and diagnostic tools. In this type of setting, patients will receive the greatest relief from their disability.

Two Canadian researchers, Dr. Morton A. Kapusta and Dr. Jack Mendelson, performed a series of experiments in this area of medical research. First they produced arthritis in a group of rats. They then took another group of rats, which had been treated with an antiviral agent (a substance that causes a resistance to viruses), and tried to produce arthritis. They found that they could not do it. This indicated that viruses may be a factor in the development of arthritis.

▶ THE FIGHT AGAINST CANCER

Immunology is the study of what makes people resist diseases. This science has once again contributed to the understanding of human cancers. A team of researchers at the National Cancer Institute worked with patients who had a very serious form of cancer. The researchers used an agent that increased the number of antibodies in the patient's blood. (An antibody is a protein in the blood that fights germs which cause

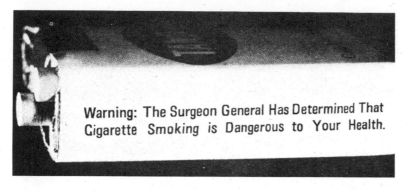

Warning: The Surgeon General Has Determined That Cigarette Smoking is Dangerous to Your Health.

The new, improved warning that appears on cigarette packs. It is hoped that this message will stop people from smoking cigarettes.

disease.) With this agent, a temporary improvement was noted in half the patients.

A series of experiments with animals established another link between cigarette smoking and lung cancer. Dr. Oscar Auerbach and Dr. E. Cuyler Hammond taught 86 beagle dogs to smoke cigarettes. Lung cancer developed in 12 dogs that had smoked 9 cigarettes a day for a 2-year period. This was the first time that malignant tumors developed in large animals that had been taught to smoke.

In 1970, Congress strengthened its warning on cigarette packages. It used to read: "Caution: Cigarette smoking may be hazardous to your health." It now reads: "Warning: The Surgeon General has determined that cigarette smoking is dangerous to your health." It is hoped that people will read and act on this important message.

▶A NEW VIRUS: LASSA FEVER

Two American missionary nurses working in Lassa, a remote village in Nigeria, died mysteriously in 1969. A third nurse, who had taken care of them, became very ill, but survived. Blood samples of all three nurses were sent to a research team at Yale Medical School. There, a new virus was identified. The disease was named Lassa fever. Then one of the doctors who was part of the research team became very ill. Since the disease was identified, the doctor was successfully treated with plasma taken from the nurse who had survived. The plasma was that part of her blood which contained the antibodies her body had made to fight the infection. These antibodies to Lassa fever saved the doctor's life. In 1970 a suspected outbreak of the same deadly virus occurred again in Nigeria.

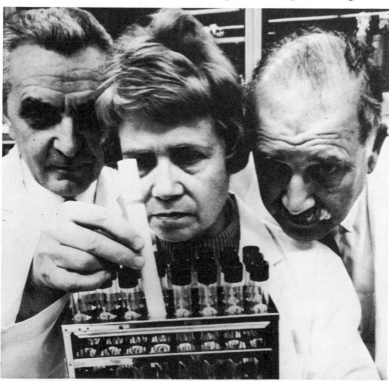

Three Yale University researchers, Dr. Jordi Casals (left), Dr. Sonja Buckley, and Dr. Wilbur Downs, discovered the Lassa fever virus. Dr. Casals became infected himself but was successfully treated.

HYALINE-MEMBRANE DISEASE

Hyaline-membrane disease, also called respiratory-distress syndrome, has caused the deaths of many newborn babies. The disease makes it very hard for the infant to breathe because it cannot get enough oxygen. The baby dies of exhaustion because it is striving too hard to breathe. In 1970 a newborn with this disease was given a transfusion of adult blood. The infant made a remarkable recovery. The next infant who had this disease was also treated in the same way. It too showed immediate improvement. Adult blood can carry oxygen more easily than can an infant's blood. It is now thought that the use of adult blood can help a newborn with the disease for a short period of time. This is all that is needed, because the disease usually disappears in the first week of life.

THE SPREAD OF CHOLERA

Cholera was once a deadly disease called the "scourge of the Middle Ages." It is still a serious and often fatal intestinal infection. It is spread through water or food that has been contaminated with certain bacteria. In 1970 a widespread outbreak of cholera led to many deaths in the Middle East, the Soviet Union, and parts of Africa. The disease was difficult to control because many countries did not report their cholera cases.

Research on many diseases is carried out at the National Communicable Disease Center in Atlanta, Georgia. The Lassa fever virus, described on the previous page, was sent here to be studied in specially sealed chambers.

A member of Phoenix House—a New York City-supported home for treatment of youthful drug users—tells young people about the dangers of drug use. The pre-teen-agers were contestants in an antinarcotics poster contest.

▶ **OTHER MEDICAL NEWS**

Dr. Kalyan Bagci, a nutritionist in India, estimated that 14,000 children in southeast and eastern India become blind each year as a result of an eye disease called keratomalacia (softening and ulceration of the cornea). The disease is brought about by poor nutrition.

In England an automatic blood analyzer was developed. It does 12 different tests on a blood sample and can test three hundred such samples each hour. This can be an important tool in screening large numbers of people. It might prove invaluable in preventive medicine.

In 1970 the use of heroin became the leading cause of death among teen-agers in New York City.

Frequently a disease that should be completely controlled by immunization still flares up. In San Antonio, Texas, for example, there was an outbreak of diphtheria in 1970. Diphtheria is a serious and contagious throat infection. About one hundred people were infected, and two children died. Once a diphtheria outbreak occurs, it takes about a year and a half to control.

There is an ever-growing need for more physicians and medical personnel. Because medical schools alone cannot fill this need, a new program called Medex has been introduced. It makes use of former military medical corpsmen. After receiving more medical training, the corpsmen can become physician assistants. They can help with surgery, take patient histories, perform some physical examinations and laboratory tests, and even make house calls. They relieve the busy doctor and permit him to use his time where it is really needed.

LEONARD I. GORDON, M.D.
Internist, New York City

MUSEUM OF MEDICAL SCIENCE

Houston, Texas, has a new and fascinating education center, the Museum of Medical Science. Anyone can visit this museum, but its exhibits are designed mostly for elementary-, junior-high-, and high-school students. The purpose of the museum is to improve people's health through knowledge.

Many exhibits, such as those shown here, are permanent. But the museum also plans to set up temporary exhibits dealing with subjects of current medical interest, such as organ transplants and drug abuse. A film library dealing with health hazards, such as cigarette smoking and air pollution, is also planned.

A volunteer worker at the museum shows a group of youngsters an exhibit on bones and muscles while one boy listens to a tape recording that explains the functions of different muscles and bones. Visitors are allowed to handle the skeleton.

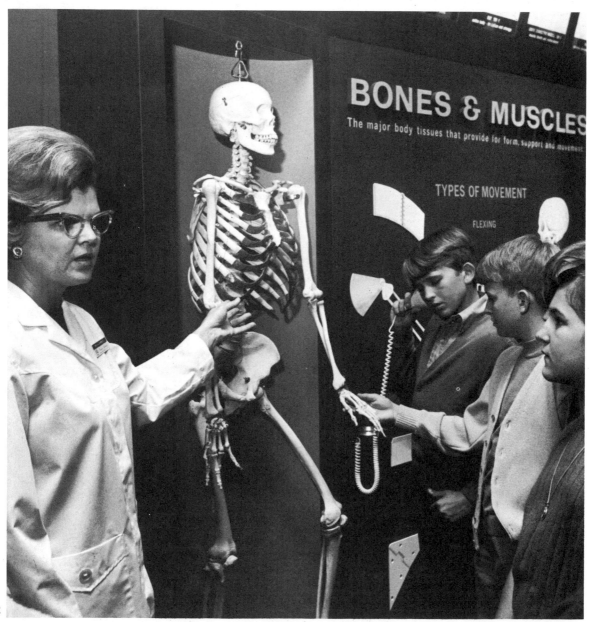

Above: Several visitors to the museum view the exhibit "Why and How
We Breathe" while a friend tests his lung capacity on a special machine.
Below: Dr. Eugene L. Slataper, a vice-president of the museum, talks
about the complicated workings of the heart and the circulatory system.

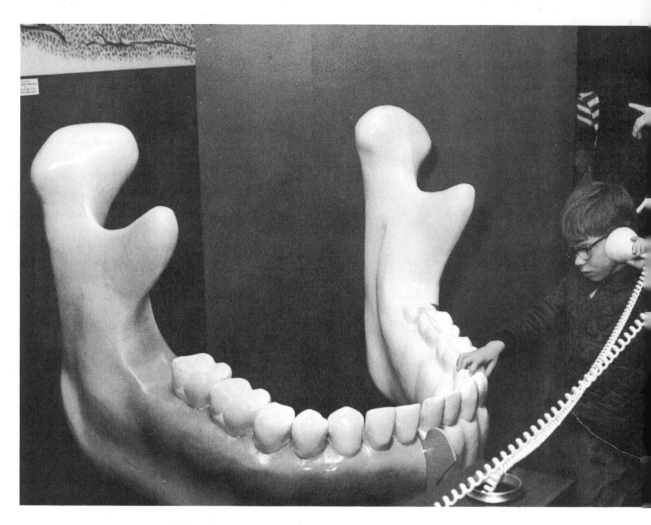

Below: A pupil checks the rhythm of her own heart by inserting her finger in a hole and watching electronic tracing on a round screen. The "Rhythm of Life" display also explains pulse, blood pressure, and heartbeat.

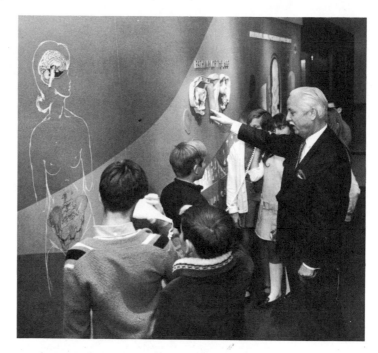

Dr. F. Scott Glover, president of the foundation that operates the museum, describes the pathway of the egg in human-reproduction.

While examining a large-scale model of the human jaw, students listen to a recording about how teeth function and how they are set in the jaw.

An exhibit on human reproduction teaches young pupils that the father determines the sex of children. It also describes how the sperm cell fertilizes the egg and how an embryo develops into a baby ready to be born.

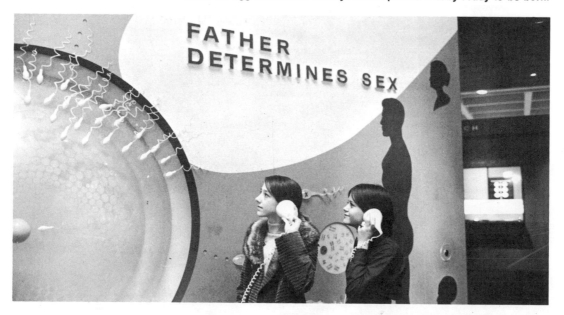

MIDDLE EAST

THE Middle East remained in a state of turmoil in 1970. Its problems continued to worry nations outside the area. There was still the possibility that the Arab-Israeli dispute would draw the Soviet Union and the United States into an unwanted war, with the Soviets on the Arabs' side, and the United States on the Israelis'.

In the Persian Gulf area, Britain's plan to withdraw all forces by the end of 1971 created a power vacuum. Friction between Iran and her Arab neighbors as well as between communist and Western interests was expected to increase in the area once the British were gone.

The arms race in the Middle East escalated during 1970. The Soviets and the United States were the chief suppliers of weapons and planes. Adding to the instability in the area was the growing strength of Arab Palestinian liberation movements.

Probably the most crucial event of all was the untimely death of President Gamal Abdel Nasser of the United Arab Republic (U.A.R.) on September 28. For 18 years Nasser had been the chief architect of Arab unity. His death left a frightening void in the leadership of the Arab world. Arabs everywhere were grief-stricken, and even the Israelis were dismayed. For in spite of Nasser's anti-Israel position, his forceful leadership had sometimes stayed the hand of more militant Arab factions.

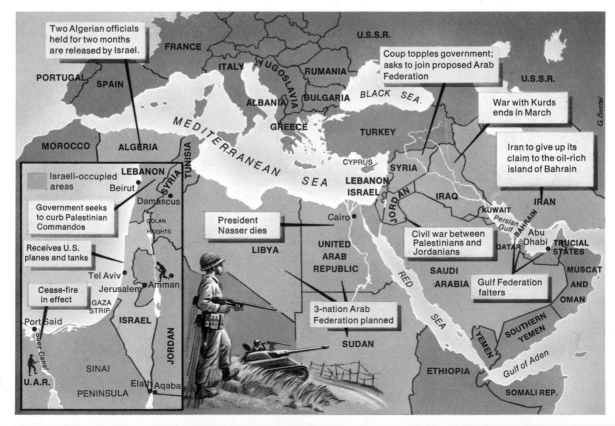

The funeral procession for Egyptian President Nasser. Nasser's death on September 28 left a void in the leadership of the Arab world. Another major event in the Middle East was the civil war (below) between Palestinian commandos and troops loyal to King Hussein in Jordan.

During 1970 the United States and the Soviet Union increased arms shipments to the Middle East. The Soviets supplied the United Arab Republic with jet fighters, artillery, and modern ground-to-air missiles. To counter the U.A.R. arms buildup, the United States gave Israel jets and tanks.

Israeli Defense Minister Moshe Dayan: In December he asked the U.S. for arms guarantees.

Three jetliners, belonging to the United States, Great Britain, and Switzerland, stand on a desert airstrip in Jordan after being hijacked by Palestine commandos.

An important development in the Middle East in 1970 was a cease-fire agreement reached in August between Israel, the U.A.R., and Jordan. In broad outline, the steps leading to the cease-fire were as follows. At the beginning of January, Israel decided upon a new response to Nasser's "war of attrition." Israel began bombing the U.A.R. heartland. The Israelis thought the bombings would make the Egyptians stop attacking along the Suez Canal front. They also thought the bombings would prevent a major Egyptian offensive across the Canal and would undermine Egyptian morale, possibly weakening President Nasser's political position.

The bombing strategy backfired, however. Egyptian morale did not collapse, and Nasser used his weakness to get more arms from the Soviet Union. At the end of January, in secret talks with the Russians, he got a promise for missiles, Soviet pilots, and additional military equipment and arms for the defense of the Aswan High Dam, Cairo, and Alexandria areas. As more Russian personnel and equipment entered the U.A.R., the Egyptians fought in the Canal zone with more daring and assurance than ever. By April, the Israelis halted their raids deep inside the U.A.R. in order to avoid conflict with the Soviet Union.

The Israeli Government announced it had proof that Soviet personnel were flying air missions. It also knew that a new anti-aircraft defense system had been installed in the heart of Egypt. In the meantime the fighting along the Canal increased in intensity. Casualties on both sides became high. With the Russians defending his interior and supplies, Nasser was able to place more men and artillery along the Canal front. To counter the U.A.R.'s new help from Russia, Israel demanded from the United States more jet aircraft, advanced electronic equipment, and other forms of military and economic assistance. The sharp escalation of the war and the prospect of air combats between Israeli and Russian pilots raised the specter of a direct confrontation between United States and Russian forces in the Middle East.

As the crisis worsened, a cease-fire was proposed by U.S. Secretary of State William P. Rogers and formally presented in the last week of June. The peace formula was for a cease-fire and peace talks to be supervised by UN mediator Dr. Gunnar V. Jarring of Sweden. The plan was accepted by the U.A.R. and Jordan in July and by Israel on August 7.

▶RESULTS OF THE CEASE-FIRE

On August 25, Israel announced that it had broken off the indirect Arab-Israeli peace talks because the U.A.R. had moved missiles into the Suez Canal region. This action violated the August 7 cease-fire accord. The U.A.R. denied the charges and accused Israel of not wanting the talks to

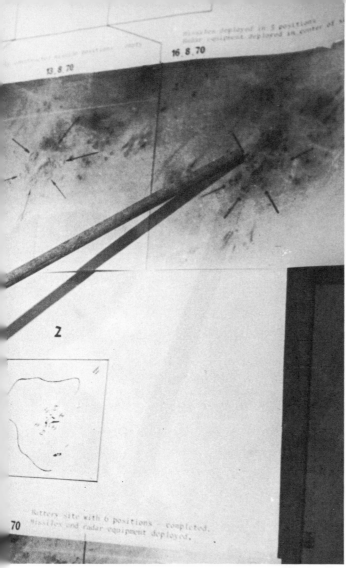

succeed. In September, the United States confirmed the Israeli charges and asked for the withdrawal of the missiles placed in the Canal zone after the August 7 cease-fire. Again, the U.A.R. denied the charges. It accused Israel of violating the cease-fire by reinforcing its defenses and by building new installations on the Israeli side of the Canal zone.

The Palestinian commandos showed their opposition to the cease-fire by attacks on Israel and a showdown with King Hussein of Jordan. To call attention to their cause, an extremist commando group hijacked four passenger planes over Europe on September 6 and diverted them to the Middle East— one to Cairo, and the other three to a desert airstrip in Jordan. In Cairo the passengers were released and their big 747 jet blown up seconds later. In Jordan the passengers were held hostage for about two weeks while a bloody civil war raged between the commando groups and King Hussein's fierce Bedouin Army. Hundreds, perhaps thousands, died in the fighting before Hussein, with great difficulty, regained control of much of the country. Still, the commandos remain a strong force in Jordan. The hijacked passengers were released after a two-

Left: An Israeli officer points to where Egyptians erected new missile sites in violation of the cease-fire. Below: Yasir Arafat (with glasses), the most powerful of the Palestine commando leaders.

Poverty and despair in Palestine refugee camps in Jordan and other Arab nations have turned them into training grounds for commando groups.

week ordeal on the desert and in Amman. They were exchanged for Palestinian commandos held in Europe.

Both before and during an Arab summit conference held in Cairo in mid-September, Nasser tried to persuade the Palestinian commandos to restrain themselves. Finally, toward the end of the conference, a Jordanian cease-fire was secured. Nasser received Hussein and commando leader Yasir Arafat, and the two foes clasped hands in at least a show of reconcilement. The next day, after escorting the last departing head of state (the Emir of Kuwait) to the Cairo airport, Nasser died suddenly of a massive heart attack.

▶ AFTER NASSER WHAT?

Former Vice-President of the U.A.R. Anwar al-Sadat was elected to succeed Nasser in a plebiscite held on October 15. Al-Sadat is reported to be more anti-Western than Nasser was. Even so, he joined with Jordan and Israel in early November in agreeing to a three-month extension of the cease-fire. The new extension was to expire February 5, 1971. Al-Sadat said the U.A.R. will not agree to any extensions past that date unless all parties have by then resumed the peace talks.

In order to get Israel to re-enter the peace talks, the United States had agreed in October to grant Israel $500,000,000 worth of military aid. Tanks, planes, artillery, and Shrike defensive air-to-ground missiles were included in the aid. This military aid was given in order to restore the "balance" lost by Israel when the U.A.R. built a strong antiaircraft system and installed Soviet-made missiles near the Suez Canal. These missiles are effective against low- and high-altitude attacks.

Anwar al-Sadat, the new president of the United Arab Republic. Al-Sadat agreed to extend the Middle East cease-fire for another three months, to February 5, 1971. But he warned of a new war if Israel did not rejoin the peace talks.

PROSPECTS OF THE PEACE TALKS

On December 28, Israel agreed to resume the indirect peace talks with the United Arab Republic and Jordan at the United Nations. However, the various Palestinian liberation groups have now become a factor in Middle Eastern politics, and they want to be considered in peace negotiations too. Their urgent demands for a homeland and their large and militant following in most Arab lands make them difficult and dangerous to ignore.

A NEW FEDERATION

As an aftermath of Nasser's death, the U.A.R., Libya, and Sudan announced in early November that they would work toward federation. Although plans for the federation may take several years to complete, all three proposed members think union will increase their strength and stability. The federation will bring together the oil of Libya, the great agricultural potential of Sudan, and the U.A.R.'s technology and surplus of labor.

Following a coup in Syria in mid-November that brought in a somewhat more moderate regime, Syria asked to be included in the federation. On November 27, Syria's acceptance by the three initial members was announced from Cairo.

THE CYPRUS DILEMMA

On Cyprus, negotiations between the Greek Cypriot majority (80 per cent) and the Turkish Cypriot minority (20 per cent) for a solution to the Cyprus problem remained deadlocked in 1970. Fear and suspicion on each side slowed progress in the talks. Neither side was willing to offer concessions. While both sides agree that Cyprus should remain an independent nation, they cannot agree on what should be its internal structure. The Turkish Cypriots insist on a federal state, made up of Greek and Turkish cantons (provinces), on the Swiss model. There would be local autonomy for the two communities and shared responsibility at the federal level. The Greek Cypriots view these demands as impractical. They think they would create a state within a state, and be the first step toward partition.

The Greek Cypriots insist on a unitary state. They want the two communities to be integrated, with minority rights for the Turkish Cypriots like those in force in most democratic nations and guaranteed by the UN. The Turkish Cypriots view the Greek Cypriot plans as one step closer to the notion of *enosis,* or union with Greece. They think the plans violate the 1959 London-Zurich Agreements, which created independent Cyprus.

IRAQ AND KURDISH NATIONALISM

The 8½-year struggle for self-government by the million and a half Kurds in Iraq ended in March of 1970 with concessions by the Iraqi regime. Still, the problems between the Kurds and the Government are far from over. The Kurdish tribesmen can be counted upon to retain most of their arms until the Iraqi regime shows it is prepared to keep its promises. The Kurds have learned from experience of the unreliability of promises announced from Baghdad.

The most important elements of the latest cease-fire were more local self-government in the Kurdish provinces where much of Iraq's oil is found, recognition of the Kurdish language, amnesty for the Kurds, the surrender of arms by the Kurds, and the rebuilding of Kurdish villages devastated in the fighting. The resettlement or re-establishment of the Kurdish refugees from neglected, war-torn areas was also promised. The Iraqi Kurds fear that the cease-fire may be merely a temporary effort by the Iraqi Government to improve its image in the eyes of the outside world.

DEVELOPMENTS IN THE PERSIAN GULF

Iran continued to play a leading role in the Persian Gulf area. It is Iran's policy to co-operate with the royal regimes of Saudi Arabia and Kuwait in keeping Arab revolutionary influences out of the Gulf. In May, Iran agreed to give up its claim to oil-rich Bahrain island, if a United Nations survey found this was what the islanders desired.

Mustafa al-Barzani, leader of Iraq's 1,500,000 Kurds. In 1970 the Kurds and the Iraqi Government ended, at least for the time being, their 8½-year civil war.

Said ibn Taimur, sultan of Oman, 1932 to 1970. In mid-1970 the 60-year-old ruler was ousted by his son in a bloodless coup d'état.

Yet Iran continued to meet Arab resistance to its claim on several small islands located inside the Gulf at the entrance to the Strait of Hormuz—the two Tumbs and Abu Musa. Iran considers these islands essential to its security and for control of the Persian Gulf.

An Iranian military buildup in the Persian Gulf is aimed at discouraging Iraq from renewing its claim to Kuwait. Iran also hoped to protect King Faisal's regime in Saudi Arabia. Should Arab revolutionary forces take over Saudi Arabia, the upheaval would be felt throughout the Arabian Peninsula—particularly in the small but wealthy Trucial States. These seven mainland sheikdoms, all British protectorates, have been trying for many months to form a federation with Qatar and the island protectorate

Qabus ibn Said, sultan of Oman, 1970–? After seizing power from his father, Qabus promised to improve conditions for his country's 800,000 people.

of Bahrain. Though the states had reached preliminary agreements, demands by Bahrain caused plans to collapse in October 1970.

One Gulf country where a potential Arab revolutionary thrust has been blunted is the Sultanate of Oman (formerly Muscat and Oman) at the southeastern end of the Arabian Peninsula. In a virtually bloodless palace coup on July 23, Sultan Said ibn Taimur, head of a benightedly old-fashioned regime, was overthrown by his 28-year-old son, Qabus. The new ruler at once began to improve conditions in the country and to remove a mass of restrictive laws.

HARRY J. PSOMIADES
Queens College of the
City University of New York

THE SOVIET UNION IN THE MIDDLE EAST

In 1970 the United States was still the most powerful force in the Middle East, but the Russians made major gains. After the Arab-Israeli war of June 1967, the Soviet Union replaced Britain as the region's second strongest power. It has set up a political and military presence on a scale larger than ever before.

The Soviet Union has a large Mediterranean fleet. Its ships use naval bases and ports in Algeria, Libya, the United Arab Republic (U.A.R.), and Syria. At its peak, the Soviet Mediterranean fleet had more than 60 naval vessels. These included a helicopter carrier, 4 cruisers, 8 guided-missile destroyers, 8 destroyers, and 10 submarines. Although the strength of the fleet changes continuously, it usually has between 30 and 40 ships. They cruise in all parts of the Mediterranean, but the main force usually stays close to the scene of the Arab-Israeli conflict.

The Russians have increased their naval presence in the Indian Ocean too. Parts of this smaller force have been active in the Red Sea, the Gulf of Aden, and the Persian Gulf.

The chance for massive Soviet penetration into the Middle East came when the U.A.R. and other Arab countries were defeated by Israel in the 1967 war. The Arabs felt a desperate need for new arms and equipment to counter what they thought was Israeli "expansion" supported by the United States. The Soviet Union quickly began or increased economic and military aid programs in most of the "revolutionary" Arab states—Algeria, Iraq, Libya, Southern Yemen, Sudan, Syria, the U.A.R., and Yemen. Over 20,000 Soviet economic and military advisers are busy today in the Arab world. Elements of the Soviet Air Force have visited Arab states. In the U.A.R., Soviet pilots have flown air missions against Israel.

A Soviet flotilla plies the waters of the Mediterranean Sea. At its peak, the Soviet fleet in the Mediterranean had more than sixty ships.

A U.S. Navy jet shadows a Russian-built bomber over the Mediterranean. The insignia on the plane is Egyptian, but the crew is Russian. Below, a Russian-made SAM-2 missile is fired at an attacking Israeli jet. The picture was taken from another Israeli jet. A second missile launch site is shown at the top center of the photo.

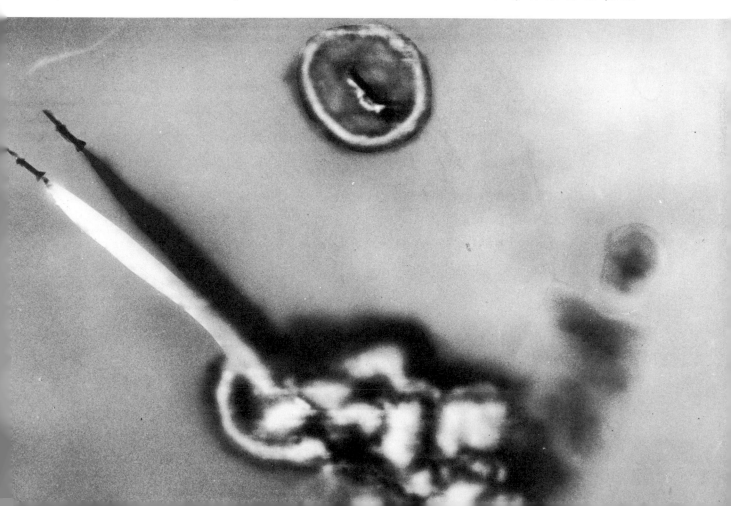

THE ISRAELI AIR FORCE

The importance of air power in the Middle East was dramatized by Israel's swift victory over the Arab states in the June 1967 war. The main part of this victory was achieved in the first day of the war, when air strikes by Israel knocked out the air forces of the United Arab Republic (U.A.R.), Iraq, Syria, and Jordan on the ground. In the three years since the war, air power has continued to be the decisive factor in the Middle East's balance of military power.

The Israeli Air Force consists of some 8,000 men and has a reserve of about 6,000 on constant alert. Its force of over 350 combat aircraft is a formidable fighting unit. It includes well over 100 Skyhawk light bombers and Phantom fighter-bombers procured from the United States since the 1967 war. It also has over 70 French-made Mystère fighter-bombers and the same number of French-built Mirage fighters.

By 1970 the strength of the Arab air forces had been renewed. Together they now outnumber the Israeli Air Force by at least 4 to 1. But Israel keeps its air superiority over the Arabs because of the high quality of both its pilots and aircraft and the amazing efficiency of its ground crews.

In 1970 the balance of air power began to change when the U.A.R. installed Russian-made SAM 2 and SAM 3 ground-to-air missiles in the Suez Canal zone. Soviet pilots arrived in the U.A.R. to train Egyptian pilots and fly air missions themselves.

These developments caused the Israelis grave concern. If Israel loses air superiority or even a large number of aircraft, the U.A.R. will be able to call its larger ground forces and artillery safely into play. The U.A.R. already has built defenses against the kind of air strike that gave Israel victory in 1967. In the fall of 1970, however, the United States committed itself to supplying Israel with enough aircraft to keep its air superiority.

The U.S.-built Phantom fighter-bomber has become one of the mainstays of the Israeli Air Force. In late 1970, after the U.A.R. moved Russian-built missiles close to the Suez Canal, the United States agreed to sell more Phantoms to Israel.

Young Israeli pilots attend a briefing. These men come from many countries and all must learn Hebrew before they can learn how to fly. Military analysts have called the Israeli Air Force the best in the world.

Although Israel buys all of its military planes from other countries (principally the United States), in 1970 it produced its first civilian plane. The Arava, a twin turboprop STOL (short take-off and landing) transport, can carry passengers as well as cargo. It is expected that someday the Israelis will make their own military airplanes.

MODERN LIVING

THE themes for contemporary living in 1970 were freedom, individualism, and awareness. These factors were certainly responsible for the mini-versus-midi battle that raged throughout the year. When the fashion industry pushed midis in the Year of Women's Lib, girls everywhere pushed back and either kept their minis or switched to pantsuits. Awareness—social awareness— was also responsible for the success of such instructive games as Generation Gap, Blacks & Whites, and Dirty Water, all designed to give people a better understanding of some major problems of contemporary life.

Mini-clad Phyllis Tweel (right), founder of GAMS (Girls Against More Skirt) leads her group in a demonstration against the maxi and the midi.

To many people, the modern-living scene seemed to be turned upside down in 1970. Some women wore bodysuits called Patternskins (above left), while others donned longuettes adorned with comic-strip characters. While fashion thus became more comical, games turned serious with such names as Ghetto (below) and Dirty Water.

FASHION

The big fashion controversy in 1970 was over skirt lengths. Was the mini dead? Many analysts of the *now* society said no. But the multi-billion-dollar fashion industry insisted on a longer skirt—the midi.

The first European collections of fall clothes were shown in Italy. Valentino was the first trend-setting *couturier* (high-fashion designer) to drop short skirts. Skinny, long-drawn-out silhouettes, and big planter hats were Valentino's decree. In Paris all the *couturiers* but one showed skirts longer than they had been. Chanel kept the below-knee length she had always shown. Fashion writers kept count of who was designing the midi; what stores were buying and selling the midi; and who were the first to wear the midi.

Then the battle began. Groups were formed to fight the midi. In Washington, D.C., it was FADD (Fight Against Designer Dictatorship). And in New York it was GAMS (Girls/Guys Against More Skirt). The 1970 economic slowdown did not help the industry's push for the midi either. Purse strings were tighter, and not many could afford the totally new wardrobe necessary for the midi-look. Disaster threatened for the stores that had heavily stocked the midi.

By late fall the battle was still not decided. But the odds seemed in favor of a change—to longer skirts.

▶ THE PANTS SCENE

The first reaction against the midi skirt was to jump into pants. The one thing that sold in every store that had them were jeans. And they sold in every fabric, shape, and color. Then people started tucking their jeans into their boots, and knickers took off as the hippiest look for pants. Knickers were worn not only for street and country, but in velvets for dressier outfits. Gauchos—open-end knickers—also attracted a large following.

▶ THE BODY LOOK

More-revolutionary changes in fashion created less controversy than the midi.

There was more of a sensuous "body look" in clothes. The new clothes looked right only when they were clinging to the body. For the middle-aged middle, this meant more exercising. Waistlines, hips, and legs that had been hiding under "constructed" clothes were once again on view. The first thing the customer had to get in 1970 was a young figure for these clothes.

Rudi Gernreich, the West Coast designer, named his summer swimwear collection "second skin." His basic unit was the body stocking. To this he added miniskirts, pants, and sweaters. Giorgio di Sant'Angelo, in New York, turned out colorful patterned tights and tops, which gave the impression of a brilliant tattoo.

▶ FANTASY CLOTHES

The fantasy outfit was popular with both youth and Establishment. Young people in feathers, leathers, brilliant colors, and funky hats filled the streets. For others there were tie-dyed velvet pantsuits, nailhead-studded felt midis, and fur- and fringe-trimmed Indian getups. Unimaginative clothes were out, and many people looked as if they were going to a masquerade party.

▶ HAIRSTYLES OF 1970

Hair hit the cutting-room floor. Skinheads appeared. Gernreich showed a man and woman with shaved heads in his second-skin clothes. Hair was still a form of protest. But the emphasis switched from lots of it to little of it. Vidal Sassoon, chopping away in New York, turned out 150 skinheads by the middle of June. A skinhead is really not a completely bald cut: it is an overall hairstyle about an inch long.

The Ape haircut emerged as the middle ground. The Ape is a scraggly, shaggy haircut that is short on top and long at the back of the neck. It started with rock groups—Mick Jagger—and moved into the hip Establishment group—Jane Fonda. Every hairdresser in New York learned to cut the Ape. And Leonard of London dyed the Ape fuchsia, navy blue, and grass green.

The mini-midi controversy left many girls pondering their skirt lengths in 1970.

Gaily colored head scarfs, butterfly-buckle belts, pouchy decorated bags, and every kind of choker were the popular accessories in 1970.

▶ MATCHING MAKEUP

Color came up strongly on the makeup front, too. At one extreme was Zandra Rhodes, a British fashion fantasist. With her Leonard hair-coloring, she wore makeup to match. The red, blue, green, and yellow circles and squiggles around her eyes even matched the squiggles printed on the fantastic clothes she wore.

Sant'Angelo showed a huge collection of clothes based on authentic American Indian costumes. He also added Indian makeup on his models. Soon his Indians were invading the most fashionable parties in town.

James Galanos of California presented his fall clothes with Chinese-style makeup: bright-red diamonds drawn around the eyes; eyebrows smudged with yellow; and two layers of eyelashes under the eye.

At the other extreme were the young people. For them the earth look was the most important. They wore no makeup at all, just clean skin, natural eyes, and barely-tinted lips.

▶ THE HANDMADE LOOK

For many people in 1970, the creative instinct became more important than the status-buying urge. Numerous handicraft magazines taught crocheting, beadwork, quilting, and embroidery. Whatever could be mastered was being made. Young people, especially, were serious about the handmade garment versus the manufactured. It was another way of attacking the commercial values of the Establishment. Basic, mass-produced garments, such as blue jeans, were the uniform. Some were styled with self-applied nailheads, studs, fringes, and appliqués.

▶ ACCESSORIES

Accessories became more important as a means of individualizing the uniform. Jew-

Boots and more boots: they were worn with midis, minis, gauchos, and knickers.

elry that had recognizable ethnic origins was the most popular: Indian beads, African beads and elephant hair, Byzantine and Persian metals. Seashells and leather were also popular accessories. Almost everybody got into the choker business, making them of ribbons, thongs, beads, and feathers.

And then came the rage for boots. Boots were the quickest way to the new look. The new long skirts practically demanded boots as an accessory. And last year's short skirts, let down as far as they could go, could be updated with a pair of knee-high, laced-up-the-front boots. Bootmakers had one of the few fashion success stories of 1970. The Chelsea Cobbler, a London boot shop that had been turning out intricately patch-worked on painted boots, opened a shop in New York. Boot salesmen in all the other stores in town showed signs of nervous breakdown from too much business. Price seemed to be no drawback. To an astonishing number of people, $75 to $100 was a reasonable investment in a pair of boots.

▶ **FASHION FURS AND CONSERVATION**

As the interest in conservation grew, concern about fur-bearing animals increased. During the week of the fur fashion openings, the Friends of the Earth took an ad in a special fur section of *Women's Wear Daily*. The headline read: "We Will No Longer Buy Anything Made from the Skins, Furs or Feathers of Wild or Endangered Animals." Under this appeared the names of some one hundred women. They ranged from Lauren Bacall to Mrs. Ernest Hemingway. Furriers made it clear that they were not using furs from endangered animals. The makers of fake-fur fabrics took ads in fashion magazines, describing the plight of the tiger and the snow leopard under the heading "Fur Coats Shouldn't Be Made of Fur." Fake furs, matching the skins of almost any animal, seemed to be the solution for many fashion-conscious conservationists.

Jo Ahern Segal
Fashion Editor
Look Magazine

GAMES FOR OUR TIMES

Playing games can be instructional as well as fun. They can help us solve problems by helping us understand them. "Generation Gap," for example, can help parents and teen-agers learn that by communicating—talking to each other—they can develop a relationship built on trust and respect. "Dirty Water" teaches us about an environmental problem. "Blacks & Whites" and "Ghetto" deal with related problems. In both games the players must cope with some of the frustrations felt by black Americans and by poor people. Perhaps this can lead to a greater understanding of blacks and poor people. Those who play "The Cities Game" face one urban crisis after another —as people in real cities do. The players will find that to make cities better places in which to live, they will have to co-operate with, not fight, each other. Only then will urban crises be avoided.

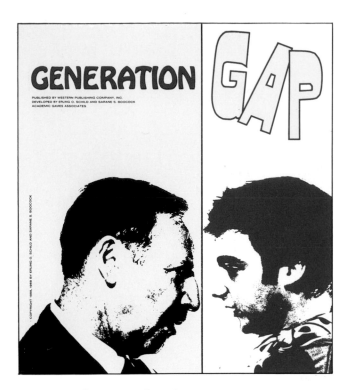

Generation Gap: Learning how to communicate.

Dirty Water: Learning about an environmental problem and how to help solve it.

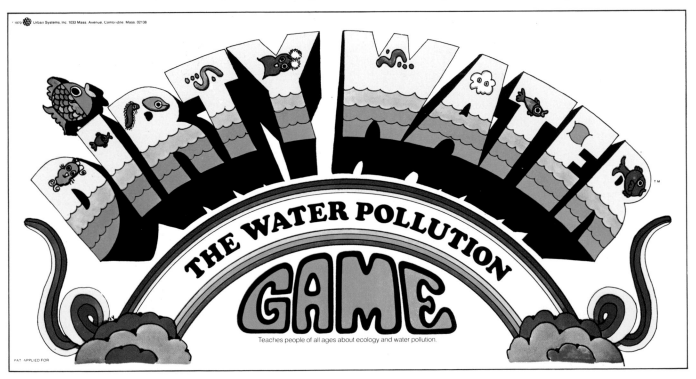

Blacks & Whites: Discovering what it means to be black in "White America."

The Cities Game: Learning about the problems involved in improving our cities.

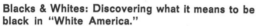

Ghetto: Finding out about the life of the poor in an inner-city neighborhood.

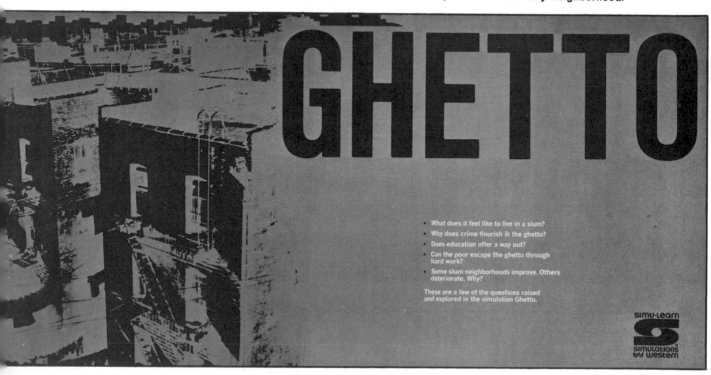

- What does it feel like to live in a slum?
- Why does crime flourish in the ghetto?
- Does education offer a way out?
- Can the poor escape the ghetto through hard work?
- Some slum neighborhoods improve. Others deteriorate. Why?

These are a few of the questions raised and explored in the simulation Ghetto.

SIMU-LEARN
SIMULATIONS BY WESTERN

DECORATING ROOMS FOR YOUNG PEOPLE

Very young people usually accept the surroundings provided by their mothers and fathers. But as they grow older they begin to develop their own tastes. Then, of course, they like to take an active part in planning their rooms.

Perhaps more than adults, young people take pleasure in decorating their rooms with things that reflect their own special interests. And unlike many adults, they do not like stiff or too-elegant rooms. Rather, young people prefer informal surroundings, where they can gather in comfort with their friends.

Following are some of the furnishings and decorations that young people liked most during 1970.

▶ **FURNITURE**

Built-ins were among the most popular pieces of furniture. These practical, multi-purpose units contain shelves for books, cabinets for clothes, and even storage bins that can hold games, toys, or hobby materials. Some of these units are made of plain, modern-looking wood. Others come painted in bright blues, reds, or yellows.

Plastic furniture was also a favorite in 1970. Some swivel chairs, for example, were made of molded plastic. These proved to be very comfortable. But what really caught on were inflatable plastic furniture and floor cushions. Inflatable chairs actually look like giant red, blue, or yellow sausage rolls assembled to look like a chair. Half the fun comes in blowing up the plastic pieces and then assembling them.

Despite the appeal of plastic, many young people still preferred the old stand-by: big, chunky couches and chairs made out of foam rubber.

This informal, comfortable room makes good use of multipurpose stack-units.

Conso Publishing

A boy's interests and hobbies are evident in the decoration of these two rooms. Scatter rugs and plastic pillows were popular accessories in 1970.

Conso Publishing

FLOORS

Because many teen-agers love to dance, and some enjoy doing messy experiments with chemistry sets, vinyl floors were being put down in more and more rooms. Vinyl is tough and hard to scuff. Anything that is spilled on it can be wiped up very easily—without leaving a trace. In 1970 many vinyl designs were on the market, often with gay patterns or bright solid colors. Many young people liked to add a little warmth by putting down a scatter rug or a shag rug. Each type of rug has its advantage. Scatter rugs are small and can easily be rolled up and put away. Shag rugs are soft and make ideal resting places—especially if you like to lie on the floor and watch TV.

Indoor-outdoor carpeting also gained in popularity during the year. This type of synthetic carpet is almost indestructible. It can be hosed down if it gets very dirty, and it will not show wear and tear.

WALLS

Most young people continued to live with plain, painted walls. But in 1970 many switched to vinyl wallpaper with big patterns and bright colors. There seemed to be no end to the designs available. Some had cartoon characters, others had pop art or the signs of the zodiac.

Whether the wall was painted or papered, inevitably it was partially covered by the ever-present bulletin boards and posters. Some of the bulletin boards were factory-made, but many young people made their own out of cork. On the bulletin boards went personal mementos, photos, clippings from magazines—almost anything that caught the teen-ager's eye.

And of course there were posters and more posters. In 1970 posters could be bought through the mail, from book stores, from card stores—even from poster stores. The variety of subjects was amazing, ranging from cartoons to beautiful scenics to rock stars to movie stars such as Humphrey Bogart.

Another wall treatment that became more popular in 1970 was pegboard. Indeed, sometimes an entire wall was covered with pegboard—and for a good reason. Pegboard walls are as good as huge storage bins because you can hang almost anything on them, including tennis rackets, skis, and skates.

Colorful dolls and flowers add warmth to this softly feminine girl's room.

Conso Publishing

WINDOWS

The most usual way to decorate windows is to hang curtains or louvered shutters. Of all the types of curtains, cafe curtains—especially those made in two sections—seem to appeal most to young people. With this type of curtain, the top section can be pulled back to let in air and light, while the bottom section can be kept drawn over the window for privacy.

FABRICS

Fabrics can really make a room interesting. If a room is furnished with stained-wood pieces or even more-modern-looking chrome, bright fabrics can add just the right touch of color.

Shiny chintz, printed canvas or sailcloth, and leather and imitation animal skins were popular in 1970. Vinyl and suede also appealed to some youths. Insofar as some teen-agers were concerned, the wilder and brighter the print, the more they liked it. Checks, plaids, geometric patterns and small abstract designs covered many a bed or couch in young people's rooms.

ACCESSORIES

For a young person, furniture, rugs, wallpaper, and curtains are all nice and necessary. But what gives his room its individuality is what he himself puts into it—the accessories.

Most young people are collectors. They collect rocks, minerals, and seashells. They collect and mount butterflies and insects. They collect miniature automobile models. They collect just about everything, and this is what makes their rooms so warm and so comfortable to work and play in.

Young people who have bulletin boards fill them with postcards from friends, photographs, theater programs, political-campaign buttons, and personal souvenirs. Displaying of these collections and personal items is what makes a room "lived in."

Of course, many youths also bought accessories, and in the department stores and specialty shops they had an enormously wide variety to choose from. Among the best-selling items in 1970 were paper lanterns, Japanese wind chimes and fans, Mexican paper flowers, peacock feathers, and straw flowers. Over-size plastic reproductions of Coke bottles, soup cans, and cereal boxes added a touch of humor to many rooms.

WILLIAM PAHLMANN
Fellow, American Institute
of Interior Designers

This girl's interest in horses is expressed in almost all her accessories.

Conso Publishing

PERSONALITIES

HAPPINESS IS . . .

. . . quintuplets. Mr. and Mrs. William Kienast of Liberty Corner, New Jersey, prepare to leave the hospital with their three daughters and two sons.

. . . $1,000,000. George Ashton, his wife, Genevieve, and their 16-year-old son, Glenn, seem quite pleased about winning New York State's super lottery.

THE ARMY . . .

. . . wants you. Curtis W. Tarr, the new Selective Service director, explains the new double-draw draft-lottery system.

. . . and Women's Lib. Mrs. Mamie Eisenhower poses with Anna Mae Hays (left) and Elizabeth P. Hoisington, the U.S. Army's first two lady generals.

THE ADVENTURERS

Thor Heyerdahl (with arms folded) poses with the crew of the "Ra II," a papy-
rus reed boat that carried them on an exciting 57-day transatlantic voyage.

Dean Caldwell (left) and Warren Harding toast their conquest of the nearly vertical 3,400-foot El Capitan in Yosemite National Park.

High-wire artist Karl Wallenda defies gravity by walking 1,000 feet across the 700-foot-deep Tallulah Gorge in Tallulah Falls, Georgia.

THE SPOKESMEN

Spiro T. Agnew watches and T-shirts became popular retail items in 1970 as the vocal Vice-President continued his role as administration gadfly.

Mrs. Martha Mitchell, wife of U.S. Attorney General John Mitchell, became in 1970 an unofficial spokeswoman for the Nixon administration, yielding not even to Spiro Agnew in outspokenness.

THE PEOPLE VS . . .

. . . Charles Manson. For his alleged role as mastermind in the 1969 murder of actress Sharon Tate and others, Charles Manson was indicted on seven counts of murder. The trial of Manson and three of his girl followers continued into 1971.

. . . Angela Davis. For allegedly supplying the weapons that were used in an attempted jailbreak and the murder of a judge, Miss Davis was placed on the FBI's Most Wanted List. She was captured in New York and extradited to California for trial.

DEATHS

Charles de Gaulle, 79, died on November 9. The World War II hero and former leader of France envisioned a France restored to a position of greatness. On his death, the French people were told: "General de Gaulle is dead. France is a widow."

Gamal Abdel Nasser, 52, leader of Egypt since 1952, died on September 28. The pragmatic leader of the Arab world sought to unite and strengthen the Arab countries.

280

Rube Goldberg, 87, cartoonist who satirized American life, died on December 7. His creation of a cartoon "inventor" resulted in a dictionary definition of the adjective "Rube Goldberg" as "accomplishing by extremely complex roundabout ‚means what . . . could be done simply." Above: Goldberg demonstrates how to take a picture of himself the hard way at a Smithsonian Institution exhibition of his gadgets.

Richard Cardinal Cushing, 75, died on November 2. Named a cardinal in 1958, he was archbishop of Boston from 1944 until his retirement in October 1970.

Versatile character actor Ed Begley died on April 28 at the age of 69. Movie, stage, and TV star, he won an Academy Award in 1963 for his portrayal of the tough political boss in "Sweet Bird of Youth." His greatest Broadway success was in "Inherit the Wind."

Vince Lombardi, 57, professional-football coach, died on September 3. He coached the Green Bay Packers from 1959 until the end of the 1967 season. However, his announced retirement did not last long. A year later he was back on the gridiron coaching the Washington Redskins. Under Lombardi, the Redskins had their first winning season in 14 years.

Above: Detective- and mystery-story writer Erle Stanley Gardner, 80, died on March 11. The prolific author created the character Perry Mason, on whom the popular TV series was based. Below: Outspoken labor leader Walter P. Reuther, 62, was killed in a plane crash in Michigan on May 9. He had been president of the United Automobile Workers since 1946.

AGNON, S. Y., 81, Israeli novelist. Shared the 1966 Nobel Prize for Literature. February 17.

BARBIROLLI, SIR JOHN, 70, British conductor. July 29.

BELYAYEV, PAVEL, 44, Soviet cosmonaut. Commander of the flight during which man first walked in space. January 10.

BENEDIKTSSON, BJARNI, 62, prime minister of Iceland since 1963. July 10.

BENZELL, MIMI, 47, American operatic soprano; stage and nightclub entertainer. December 23.

BORN, MAX, 87, German physicist. Winner of 1954 Nobel Prize in Physics. January 5.

BRÜNING, HEINRICH, 84, German chancellor (1930–32) under the Weimar Republic. March 30.

BURKE, BILLIE, 84, American stage and silent-screen comedienne. May 14.

CRUZEN, RICHARD L., 72, American Arctic and Antarctic explorer. Was second in command to Richard E. Byrd during historic Antarctic expedition in 1939. April 15.

DALADIER, EDOUARD, 86, French leader during the prewar Third Republic. October 10.

DAVIS, BENJAMIN O., SR., 93, first Negro to be named a general in the U.S. armed forces. November 26.

DIONNE, MARIE, 35, one of the famous Canadian Dionne quintuplets. February 27.

DOS PASSOS, JOHN, 74, American author. Novels include the trilogy *U.S.A.* September 28.

FORSTER, E. M., 91, British author. His writings include the novel *A Passage to India.* June 7.

FOSTER, PRESTON, 69, American movie and TV actor. July 14.

GROVES, LESLIE R., 73, American Army general. Director of the W.W. II Manhattan Project, which developed the atomic bomb. July 13.

GUNTHER, JOHN, 68, American journalist and author. Known for his "Inside" books, including *Inside Europe.* May 29.

HENDRIX, JIMI, 27, American rock star. The singer-guitarist's death was attributed to an overdose of drugs. September 18.

HOFSTADTER, RICHARD, 54, American historian. Winner of two Pulitzer Prizes (1956 and 1964) for his books *The Age of Reform* and *Anti-Intellectualism in American Life.* October 24.

HOPPER, WILLIAM, 54, American TV actor. Played Paul Drake in the *Perry Mason* series. March 6.

ISHAK, YUSOF IBN, 60, president of Singapore since 1964. November 23.

JACOBS, HIRSCH, 65, American Thoroughbred-racehorse trainer. His horses earned over $12,000,000 in purses. February 13.

JOPLIN, JANIS, 27, American rock singer. Her death was attributed to an overdose of drugs. October 4.

KERENSKY, ALEXANDER, 89, leader of first phase of Russian Revolution before Communists came to power. June 11.

KEYES, FRANCES PARKINSON, 84, American authoress. July 3.

KOENIG, PIERRE, 71, French W.W. II military leader. September 3.

KRUTCH, JOSEPH WOOD, 76, American drama critic, author, and conservationist. May 22.

LAPCHICK, JOE, 70, American basketball player (the original New York Celtics) and coach (St. John's University and New York Knickerbockers). August 10.

LEE, GYPSY ROSE, 56, American burlesque queen and actress. April 26.

LIPSCOMB, GLENARD P., 54, American politician. Republican representative from California since 1953. February 1.

LOUISE, ANITA, 53, American movie and TV actress. April 25.

MACLEOD, IAIN, 56, British chancellor of the exchequer since June 1970. July 21.

MARCH, HAL, 49, American actor, and TV emcee of the quiz show *$64,000 Question.* January 19.

MAURIAC, FRANÇOIS, 84, French author. Winner of 1952 Nobel Prize for Literature. September 1.

McKAY, DAVID O., 96, American Mormon leader. President of the Church of Jesus Christ of Latter-Day Saints since 1951. January 18.

MacMILLAN, DONALD B., 95, American Arctic explorer. Was on Robert E. Peary's historic North Pole expedition (1908–09). September 7.

MIKOYAN, ARTEM I., 65, Russian codesigner of the MiG jet fighter planes. December 9.

MORRIS, CHESTER, 69, American movie actor. Created role of Boston Blackie. September 11.

NEWMAN, BARNETT, 65, American painter and sculptor. July 3.

O'HARA, JOHN, 65, American author. Works include the novel *Butterfield 8* and the libretto *Pal Joey.* April 11.

RAMAN, SIR CHANDRASEKHARA V., 82, Indian physicist. Winner of 1930 Nobel Prize in Physics. November 21.

REED, CAROL, 44, American TV weather girl, whose sign-off, "Have a happy," became a popular expression. June 4.

REMARQUE, ERICH MARIA, 72, German-born author. Novels include *All Quiet on the Western Front.* September 25.

RIVERS, MENDEL L., 65, American politician. Democratic representative from South Carolina since 1941; chairman of the House Armed Services Committee since 1965. December 28.

ROSSITER, CLINTON L., 3d, 52, American historian, political scientist, and professor. His book *The American Presidency* became a classic on the presidency. July 11.

ROTHKO, MARK, 66, American abstract-expressionist painter. February 25.

ROUS, FRANCIS PEYTON, 90, American biologist. Winner of 1966 Nobel Prize in Medicine. February 16.

RUGGLES, CHARLES, 84, American stage, motion-picture, and television actor. December 23.

RUSSELL, BERTRAND, 97, British philosopher, mathematician, and author. Winner of Nobel Prize for Literature in 1950. February 2.

SACHS, NELLY, 78, German-born Jewish poetess. Shared the 1966 Nobel Prize for Literature. May 12.

SALAZAR, ANTONIO DE OLIVEIRA, 81, premier of Portugal (1932–68). July 27.

SCOPES, JOHN, 70, American schoolteacher. Taught Darwin's theory of evolution, which led to famous 1925 "monkey trial." October 21.

SHIELDS, ARTHUR, 74, Irish-born character actor. Films included *The Quiet Man.* April 27.

SHRINER, HERB, 51, American humorist, actor, and TV emcee. April 24.

SILVERA, FRANK, 55, Jamaican-born actor, director, and producer. June 11.

SKULNIK, MENASHA, 78, Polish-born comic actor. Starred in Yiddish comedy and on the Broadway stage. June 4.

SLIM, VISCOUNT, WILLIAM J., 79, British military W.W. II leader. Led the campaign that liberated Burma in 1945. December 14.

ST. ONGE, WILLIAM L., 55, American politician. Democratic representative from Connecticut since 1963. May 1.

STEVENS, INGER, 35, Swedish-born movie and TV actress. Star of TV series *The Farmer's Daughter* (1963–66). April 30.

SUKARNO, 69, president of Indonesia (1949–66). A dominant leader in Asia's postwar struggle for independence, he was stripped of his powers after he had unsuccessfully tried to bring the Communists to power in Indonesia. June 21.

SZELL, GEORGE, 73, Hungarian-born conductor of the Cleveland Orchestra since 1946. July 30.

TIMOSHENKO, SEMYON K., 75, Soviet W.W. II military leader. March 31.

TURNBULL, ANDREW, 48, American biographer. Wrote the lives of F. Scott Fitzgerald and Thomas Wolfe. January 10.

UTT, JAMES B., 70, American politician. Republican representative from California since 1953. March 1.

WARBURG, OTTO, 86, German biochemist. Winner of 1931 Nobel Prize in Medicine. August 1.

RELIGION

PERHAPS the most dramatic event of the year was the assassination attempt on Pope Paul VI in Manila, the Philippines. The Pope was unharmed.

In the United States during 1970, members and leaders of the three major religions became more involved with social and political problems. Many clergymen continued to oppose the war in Indochina. Indeed, two Roman Catholic priests, Fathers Daniel and Philip Berrigan, were sentenced to jail for burning draft records. Another antiwar priest, Father Robert Drinan, was elected to Congress.

While members of the Women's Liberation movement marched through the streets, the Lutheran Church ordained its first woman minister.

Many Jews feared that they were witnessing a rise in anti-Semitism in the United States and in the Soviet Union.

Elizabeth Platz, first woman to become a Lutheran minister, gives Communion to her mother. Miss Platz, a lay chaplain since 1965, was ordained on November 22.

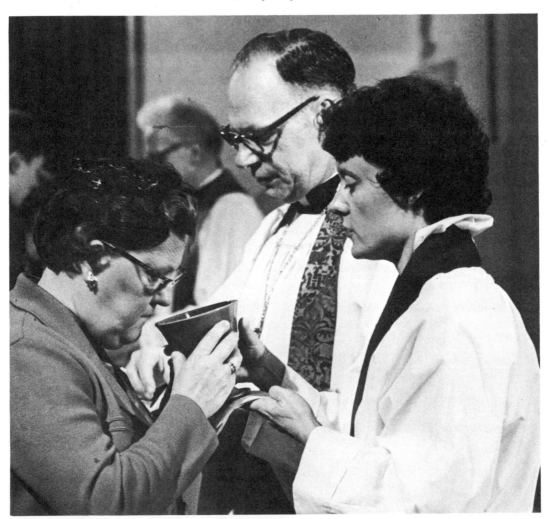

In Manila, Benjamin Mendoza y Amor Flores (right, with crew cut) is restrained after attempting to assassinate Pope Paul VI (left, with skullcap).

New York City Jews demonstrate against Soviet support of the Arab states. Other demonstrations protested discrimination against Jews in Russia.

PROTESTANTISM

America's Protestants numbered more than 70,000,000 in 1970. They continued to be faced with conflict over the question of what their faith required of them. Should Protestant bodies continue to take a stand on racial and political issues, even if it meant a loss in contributions?

One of the organizations most threatened by loss of financial support because of its stand on social issues was the National Council of the Churches of Christ in the U.S.A. The National Council is made up of 33 Protestant and Orthodox denominations. Four ways of changing the Council were under study. One method would open membership to all denominations and related bodies, such as the American Bible Society.

▶ A PLAN OF UNION

The future of the National Council and of Protestant church government will be strongly influenced by the work of the Consultation on Church Union (COCU). COCU, formed in 1962, is trying to unite nine American Protestant denominations. The proposed merger will have a total membership of 25,000,000. The new church will be named the Church of Christ Uniting (also COCU). In 1970, specific merger proposals were sent to the nine denominations for study. The target date for the union is 1980. Blacks, women, youth, and minorities are to be represented at every level.

▶ WOMEN, YOUTH, AND MINORITIES

Women, youth, and minorities were three central points of tension among Protestants during the year. The Women's Liberation movement began, in part, in the churches. It began over such questions as the place of women in the church, and personal-social-moral issues. (These include abortion and attitudes toward sexual relationships.)

At its convention in June, the Lutheran Church in America (the largest Lutheran denomination) approved the ordination of women (making women ministers). Only three other major Protestant bodies ordain women to the ministry.

Youth played a prominent part in church thinking, not only because of campus riots and student deaths, but because of the role of youth in the peace movement. The World Council of Churches appealed for contributions to support the Canadian pastoral work among "U.S. draft-age immigrants." There are between 25,000 and 75,000 United States draft resisters and servicemen "absent without official leave" in Canada, according to the World Council. The Church of the Brethren, a historic peace church, has revised its Statement on War. The church now places its support behind young men who refuse to co-operate with the draft, as well as with those who choose another kind of service than combat.

The United States Justice Department formally dropped conspiracy charges against the Rev. William Sloane Coffin, Jr., Yale chaplain and Presbyterian clergyman. He had been accused of counseling violation of Selective Service Acts.

The National Committee of Black Churchmen in New York City issued a document patterned on the United States Declaration of Independence. The document announced that "we shall be . . . free and independent from the injustices of white America, that unless we receive full redress and relief from these inhumanities we will move to renounce all allegiance to this nation."

▶ OTHER EVENTS

The complete New English Bible was published and quickly climbed to the best-seller list. Southern Baptists voted in their annual convention to change a commentary on Genesis which their publishing house had issued. The commentary caused great dispute.

Although some churches have voluntarily paid local taxes on their property, church property used for religious purposes has been tax exempt. Church officials were relieved when the United States Supreme Court upheld that such tax exemption is constitutional.

KENNETH L. WILSON
Editor
Christian Herald

ROMAN CATHOLICISM

The one event of 1970 most interesting to Roman Catholics was the Pacific journey of Pope Paul VI. During this trip, which took place in late November and early December, the Pope traveled about 30,000 miles. He visited Iran, Pakistan, the Philippines, the Samoan Islands, Australia, Indonesia, Hong Kong, and Ceylon. The biggest news of the journey was an incident at the airport in Manila, the Philippines. Soon after the papal airplane landed, a man who had disguised himself in a priest's clothing rushed up to the Pope and tried to kill him with a knife. The attacker, Benjamin Mendoza y Amor Flores, a Bolivian, was stopped by the people around the Pope, and no one was hurt. Later Mendoza told police he wanted to kill the Pope because he thought religion and the churches are nothing but superstition.

The Pope met many people and gave many speeches during his journey. In most of the speeches he talked about the need for peace among nations. He also talked about the duty of rich people and rich countries to help the poor and give them a chance to improve their way of living. He told young people who rebel against unfair conditions that they are right to criticize injustice, but that they should not give way to bitterness and hatred.

Two Bibles were published in 1970: The New American Bible and The New English Bible.

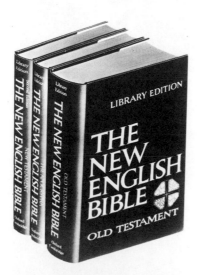

▶CONFLICTS WITHIN THE CHURCH

The Pope also reminded Catholics everywhere of their duty to stay united and loyal despite their many differences of opinion. For in 1970, as in the years just before, there was much conflict within the Catholic Church.

Basically, the many separate arguments were concerned with one question: How much should the Church change its rules and customs to meet new problems and new ways of thinking? For example, some people, including quite a large number of priests, believe that the rule of celibacy should be changed. (The rule forbids priests to marry.) Those who favor change feel that priests should be allowed to marry and still carry on their priestly work. But the Pope and almost all Catholic bishops could not agree. During 1970 many priests left the ministry because of this issue, or else because they thought they could do better work as lay persons.

There were disputes also over the rules of Catholic worship, the use of church money, the way new bishops are selected, the church's teaching about divorce, the rules governing the lives of priests, monks, and nuns, and over the way religion is taught in Catholic schools and parishes. Some Catholics (usually called "conservatives") thought all this conflict hurt the church, but "liberal" Catholics said it should be considered a normal part of Church life.

In the United States there were differences among Catholics (as there were among other Americans) over the war in Vietnam. Two famous priest-brothers, Father Daniel Berrigan and Father Philip Berrigan, were sent to prison for helping to burn draft records. The Berrigans said that burning the files was their way of obeying their consciences and of telling other Americans that the war was wrong. Another Catholic priest, Father Robert Drinan, chose a different way of opposing the war. He entered politics and became the first Catholic priest ever elected to Congress.

▶ OTHER CHURCH ACTIVITIES

During 1970 Catholic and Protestant churchmen continued to discuss ways of bringing their churches closer together.

In the United States the first steps were taken toward starting a National Pastoral Council. This is a new Catholic organization that will include representatives of the laity (nonclergy), as well as of the bishops and clergy. The American Catholic bishops asked their people to give money to a new fund which will help underprivileged people. The bishops want to collect $50,000,000 for this purpose.

▶ CHURCH LEADERS

Richard Cardinal Cushing, who had been archbishop of Boston and a close friend of the Kennedy family, died in 1970.

In Rome there were rumors that Pope Paul plans to retire when he reaches the age of 75. The Pope himself did not say this, but some of his actions seemed to suggest that he would do so. Late in the year, the Pontiff ruled that cardinals who had reached the age of 80 could not participate in the election of a new pope. And cardinals who were in charge of the Roman Curia—the Vatican's administrative body—were asked to resign voluntarily when they became 75 years old.

ROBERT G. HOYT
Editor, *The National Catholic Reporter*

Robert Drinan, who ran as an antiwar Democrat, won election to the House of Representatives in November 1970. He is the first Catholic priest ever elected to Congress.

JEWS AND JUDAISM

The major concern of Jews in 1970 was the continuing Arab-Israeli conflict. During the summer, Israel and the Arabs agreed to a cease-fire, but real peace seemed far away.

▶ ANTI-SEMITISM AND ANTI-ZIONISM

Another concern of Jews was Soviet anti-Semitism and anti-Zionism. Many Russian Jews would like to go to Israel, but the Soviet Government will not let them. Late in 1970 several Russian Jews were tried for allegedly trying to hijack a plane to leave the country. Two were sentenced to death, but a world outcry forced the Soviets to commute the sentences. The alleged hijackers were given long prison terms. Anti-Soviet demonstrations and activities by Jewish groups in the United States caused a minor crisis between the two nations.

Related to the anti-Semitism problem were the activities of the militant Jewish Defense League (JDL). Organized in New York City in 1968, the JDL has a membership of about seven thousand. The organization has branches in several cities, including Montreal. The JDL believes that dramatic or violent measures are sometimes necessary to prevent or counter anti-Semitic acts. The group has organized patrols in Jewish neigh-borhoods to help prevent robberies and muggings. But it has also sought confrontations with Arabs, black militants and others that it considers anti-Israeli or anti-Jewish. JDL activities have been condemned by traditional Jewish organizations.

▶ JEWISH ORGANIZATIONS

Two major conferences relating to Zionism brought Jewish leaders together in 1970. The 81st annual convention of the Central Conference of American Rabbis was held in March, meeting in Jerusalem for the first time. This organization represents the American rabbis of the Reform movement of Judaism. At one time, the Reform movement was anti-Zionist. Now it is seeking to show its identity with Israel. Rabbi Roland B. Gittelsohn, president of the Central Conference, said that Reform Jews see Israel's triumphs, ordeals, and fate as their own.

In May, thirteen American Zionist organizations and ten youth groups, with a combined membership of 700,000 Jews, united to form the American Zionist Federation. The Federation would like American Jews to accept the Zionist principle that the Jews are "one people, united by a common history, heritage, and destiny, with Israel as the center of Jewish life."

MEIR BEN-HORIN
Dropsie University

Young members of the Jewish Defense League (JDL). The JDL, with seven thousand members, militantly opposes anti-Israeli and anti-Jewish acts.

SCIENCE

THE world of science was filled with wondrous discoveries and accomplishments in 1970. For the first time ever, a biologist synthesized a gene. This important step on the road to "genetic engineering" may lead to cures for genetic diseases, diseases that are handed down from parent to child. Another important discovery was the finding of amino acids in a meteorite. Because amino acids are the building blocks of life, this could mean that there is some form of life in space.

Physicists, meanwhile, pushed forward with the creation of strange particles of antimatter and artificial elements that decay so rapidly that there is hardly time to study them.

In another area of research, oceanographers plumbed the depths of the seas to learn how the earth has evolved. And earth scientists discovered that an ancient South Pole is sitting in the middle of the hot Sahara.

A scientist examines a piece of a meteorite which contains amino acids, the building blocks of life. This find indicates there may be life in space.

On June 2, Dr. H. Gobind Khorana, shown here in his lab at the University of Wisconsin, announced that he had synthesized a gene.

In 1970, Dr. John Ostrom of Yale University discovered a fossil of an archaeopteryx. It is the earliest bird fossil ever identified and may help scientists discover why the first "bird" began to fly.

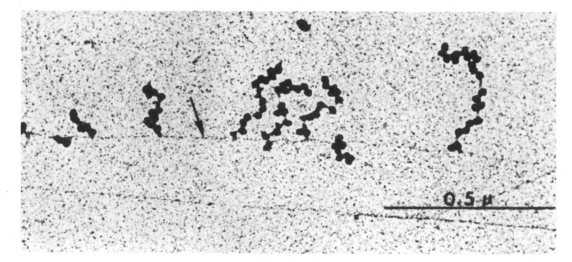

Scientists at the National Institutes of Health photographed protein synthesis, the process that determines the nature and behavior of all living cells. The arrow is pointing to a chromosome, which directs the protein synthesis.

The solar corona—the outermost part of the sun's atmosphere—as seen during the March 7 total solar eclipse.

Do we learn behavior patterns, or are we born with them? Can our behavior be changed in any significant way? In 1970, Dr. Peter N. Witt sought answers to these and other questions by studying how spiders spin their webs. Below: Dr. Witt holds a picture of a normal web. Right: Under the influence of drugs, a spider spins an erratic web.

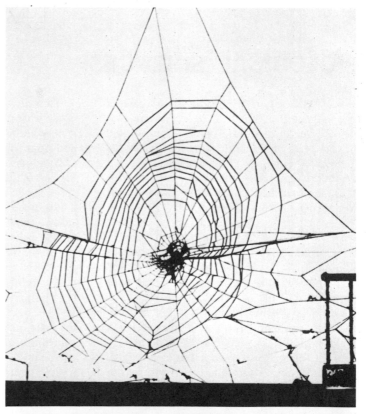

BIOLOGICAL SCIENCES

In 1970 important research was carried out in genetics, the branch of biology that deals with genes and heredity. A major goal of this type of research is to find cures for genetic diseases. While geneticists carried on their work, other scientists—called astrochemists—probed the universe in an effort to find out how life began.

▶ SYNTHESIS OF A GENE

In 1970 a major breakthrough in genetics was made by Dr. H. Gobind Khorana of the University of Wisconsin. Dr. Khorana, winner of the 1968 Nobel Prize in Medicine, synthesized (built) a gene.

Genes are made up of molecules of DNA (deoxyribonucleic acid), a type of nucleic acid. (Nucleic acids are basic chemical building blocks.) DNA is called the master chemical, or "code of life," because it dictates the hereditary characteristics of all living cells. DNA passes its hereditary information to another type of nucleic acid called RNA (ribonucleic acid), which then transfers the information to the cells.

▶ SEEKING CURES FOR DISEASES

Biologists have known for some time that certain cancers in animals are caused by viruses. Though it has not yet been proved, viruses may also cause cancer in human beings. In 1970, several experiments seemed to support this theory. Using the powerful electron microscope, scientists detected viruses in human tumors. Biochemical experiments with these tumors further indicated the presence of viruses.

In 1970 Dr. Howard Temin of the University of Wisconsin made a startling discovery. He found that with some viruses which cause cancer in animals, the RNA in the virus dictated that the animal cell make a special kind of DNA. The DNA then gave instructions that made the cell grow as a cancer cell instead of a normal cell. Usually DNA dictates hereditary instructions to RNA. In this case, just the opposite happened: the RNA dictated to the master chemical DNA.

This discovery may help biologists learn how viruses cause cancer. Once this is done it may be possible to devise ways to prevent and treat this disease.

Biologists at the University of Maryland School of Medicine experimented with viruses in the hope of curing genetic diseases. They successfully used an unusual virus to carry genetic information (DNA) into mouse cells. The biologists must now find out if the DNA will mix and function with the DNA already in the mouse cells.

A similar experiment—this time with human beings—was attempted in Germany in 1970. Two young girls were very ill because they did not have a certain enzyme. (Enzymes are catalysts that speed up the body chemistry.) Doctors infected the girls with a virus which contains the DNA that, hopefully, will dictate that their cells produce this enzyme. If the girls are cured, scientists will have a new tool to use against diseases that up to now have been untreatable.

▶ SEARCH FOR THE BEGINNINGS OF LIFE

The basic elements of life are hydrogen oxygen, carbon, and nitrogen. In 1970 several simple molecules containing some of these elements were found in clouds at the center of our galaxy, the Milky Way. Using radio telescopes and huge antennas, astrochemists are continuing their studies of these chemicals. Their aim is to discover whether the slow chemical evolution that gave rise to life on earth is also occurring in space.

Amino acids are the precursors of life. Many scientists believe that in the primeval past, solar and radioactive energy transformed amino acids into proteins. When these proteins combined with nucleic acids, such as DNA, life was created.

In 1970 scientists reported that they had found traces of amino acids in a meteorite which fell in Australia in 1969. This could mean that there is some form of life in space.

SUSAN ZOLLA
Assistant Professor
New York University Medical School

PHYSICAL SCIENCES

In 1970, researchers continued to investigate the structure of matter. Two important developments were the creation of antihelium nuclei and the synthesis of element 105. Research also continued into a new form of water called polywater.

▶ CREATION OF ANTIHELIUM NUCLEI

Scientists have long theorized that the universe is made up of both ordinary matter and antimatter. Everything that we know of on earth is composed of ordinary matter. Atoms of ordinary matter are composed of electrons, protons, and, sometimes, neutrons. An electron is a tiny particle with a negative charge. A proton has a positive charge, and a neutron has no charge.

Electrons in an atom of antimatter have a positive charge and are known as positrons. Antimatter atoms also have negatively charged protons (called antiprotons), and perhaps antineutrons.

Beginning in 1934, scientists have detected several antiparticles. In 1965, physicists at the Brookhaven National Laboratory combined antiprotons and antineutrons to form a single, larger particle called an antideuteron.

This work with antiparticles is important because many scientists believe that the universe is symmetrical, or that for every particle of matter there is a particle of antimatter with corresponding but opposite charges. If particles of matter and antimatter ever collided, they would annihilate each other, giving off great amounts of energy. This is something like adding 1 and −1 to get 0.

Some scientists have theorized that somewhere in the universe there are "antiworlds." These, however, cannot be detected with telescopes or radio telescopes.

In 1970, Soviet scientists added new weight to this theory when they created antihelium nuclei. In January, after examining some 200,000,000,000 negative nuclear particles, a team of Soviet scientists led by Professor Yuri Prokoshkin succeeded in creating and detecting five antihelium-3 particles. These are the heaviest antimatter particles yet observed.

▶ ELEMENT 105

In 1970, Albert Ghiorso and a team from the Lawrence Radiation Laboratory in Berkeley, California, reported the synthesis of element 105. Using a machine called the HILAC (heavy ion linear accelerator), they bombarded a tiny amount of californium 249 (a rare element) with nitrogen-15 ions. The reaction produced element 105. The Berkeley group suggested it be named hahnium, as a tribute to Otto Hahn, the German chemist who was a codiscoverer of nuclear fission in the 1930's. (Russian physicists claimed that they had synthesized element 105 two months earlier.)

▶ POLYWATER

Several years ago, Soviet scientists announced that they had discovered a fascinating substance called polywater, or water II. Polywater has the same chemical composition as ordinary water, but it is much more stable. It does not freeze, and it will not boil until it is heated to 900° F. It is also much more dense than ordinary water. In 1969, British and American scientists confirmed the existence of polywater.

In 1970, however, other scientists questioned the existence of this new substance. They said that what is thought to be polywater is really ordinary water with certain contaminants, such as carbon and salts. These contaminants would make ordinary water more dense, more stable, and less likely to freeze or boil.

In June 1970 a special conference of scientists was held at Lehigh University to try to determine if polywater actually exists. The results were inconclusive. It takes a very long time just to make a tiny amount of polywater. And it is very difficult to study and analyze these tiny drops. The answer to the question "Is polywater really a new form of water?" will have to wait until the substance can be manufactured in greater quantities.

LEWIS FRIEDMAN
Senior Chemist
Brookhaven National Laboratory

OCEANOGRAPHY

In recent years, scientists have developed interesting theories about how the ocean basins were formed and about how the earth has evolved. Now, evidence to support these theories is being provided by one of the most exciting and successful scientific projects of all time: the Deep Sea Drilling Project. Cores of sediment and rock from the ocean floor are being recovered by the project's deep-sea drilling ship, the *Glomar Challenger*.

Since the project began, in August 1968, scientists have recovered more than 30,000 feet of sediment and rock from the ocean floor. These samples have provided evidence that supports three related theories.

Continental drift. This theory suggests that all the continents were once joined together in one giant landmass. This landmass split apart. Its pieces—the continents of today—slowly drifted until they reached their present locations.

Sea-floor spreading. This theory suggests that the drift of the continents is due to the spread of the ocean floor. Scientists think the ocean floor is spreading outward from a worldwide chain of underwater ridges. The spreading occurs at different rates. The floor of the Pacific, for example, seems to be spreading at least six times as fast as the floor of the Atlantic.

Plate tectonics. This theory suggests that the earth's crust is divided into a group of large, slablike parts. Each part is called a tectonic plate. These plates consist of the continents and the ocean floor. It is the movement of these plates, toward or away from each other, that is thought to cause sea-floor spreading and continental drift.

By late 1970, the *Glomar Challenger* had completed 14 drilling missions. Some surprising and unexpected findings were made during a 56-day mission in the Mediterranean Sea. Studies of the 2,200 feet of core material from the Mediterranean floor seem to indicate that the sea is getting smaller. This would mean that the continents of Europe and Africa are slowly moving together.

The scientists also "found signs of many strange events in the history of the Mediterranean Sea." According to Dr. William B. F. Ryan of Columbia University, one of the leaders of the mission, "between 12,000,000 and about 5,000,000 years ago, the Mediterranean periodically dried up, forming a basin much like the Dead Sea or Death Valley in California. This happened many times." If man had existed millions of years ago, he "could have stood up on a continental shelf off [southern] France and looked out over a magnificent vista of a dry ocean floor," said Dr. Ryan.

What could have caused such periodic changes in this area? It is possible that upward movements of the tectonic plates could have closed the Strait of Gibraltar. This would have caused the Mediterranean to slowly dry up. As the newly-raised rock at the Strait was eroded, water would again enter the Mediterranean from the Atlantic. (Today, if water did not enter the Mediterranean from the Atlantic and from various rivers, evaporation would cause the level of the sea to drop about three feet each year.)

In the spring of 1970, the *Glomar Challenger* recovered the oldest sediments yet found from the ocean floor. They were recovered from the bottom of the Atlantic Ocean, 200 to 300 miles off the east coast of the United States. These sediments were about 150,000,000 to 160,000,000 years old. (In comparison, the oldest rocks found on the continents are 3,500,000,000 years old.)

It is believed that, at one time, North America and Europe were joined together. As the two continents separated and drifted apart, the Atlantic Ocean formed between them. Scientists once thought this had happened about 100,000,000 years ago. But the new findings indicate it must have occurred closer to 200,000,000 years ago.

In 1971, the *Glomar Challenger* will cruise the Pacific Ocean. She will drill into the deep-ocean bottom, and scientists will learn still more about the history of our planet.

JENNY E. TESAR
Senior Editor
The Book of Popular Science

ANCIENT SOUTH POLE IN THE SAHARA

The most amazing science story of 1970 was the discovery of a very ancient South Pole in the Sahara—at a point in southeastern Algeria, to be exact. The reason a South Pole was found in such an unexpected place is that about 450,000,000 years ago the landmasses of the earth were in different locations than they are today. Africa—the part where Morocco, Algeria, Libya, Mauritania, Niger, and Chad now are—was at the earth's South Pole. Scientists now know beyond a doubt that this whole region moved. The entire landmass drifted northward, as part of a continuous, though very slow, slippage of the earth's crust. What was once the rocky base beneath a polar ice cap slid 5,500 miles to become eventually a region of burning sands and baking sun.

Such sliding of huge regions is known as continental drift. The continents are almost like huge islands floating on melting rock—though that rock is about 100 miles underneath the surface.

The earth's north and south poles can move in another way too. The earth is a spinning globe kept fairly steady in its orbit by the gravitational pull of the sun. But the earth does not always spin quite true. The polar axis can drift. But the amount of drift that occurs is probably too slight to account for a pole's moving all the way to the Sahara.

How was the mysterious South Pole in the Sahara discovered, and how do scientists know their discovery is correct? About 1960 a group of French and Algerian geologists were in the central Sahara searching for oil. In some places they found deep grooves in the rocks. Some of the grooves were several hundred miles long. Scientists know these deep scratches can only be made by polar ice. The last North American polar Ice Age left behind many such grooves in Canada and the United States. The marks look as though some gigantic prehistoric bulldozer had scraped across the landscape.

The rocks in the Sahara with the deep grooves are known to be 450,000,000 years old because trilobite fossils were found in them. (Trilobites were crablike marine creatures that ceased to exist after that period.) After the grooves in the rocks were noticed, another important discovery was made. Scientists in Australia, South America, and Africa were studying ancient rocks of the same age as those in the Sahara and measuring their magnetism. They found that the tiny bits of iron in these ancient igneous rocks all point toward the Sahara. These bits of iron act like little magnets. They always point in the north-south direction that existed when the rocks were formed. This was further proof that a 450,000,000-year-old South Pole is in the Sahara.

In January 1970 a panel of earth scientists from 11 nations were invited by the Institut Algerien du Pétrole to go and see the Saharan South Pole for themselves. They spent most of January exploring the region by airplane, land rover, and on foot. At the end of their explorations, the scientists held a meeting in Algiers. They agreed that an ancient South Pole did exist in the Sahara.

RHODES W. FAIRBRIDGE
Columbia University

These deep grooves found in rocks in the Sahara were made millions of years ago by polar ice.

DIGGING UP OUR PAST

Archeologists and students examine the wreck of an eighteenth-century Dutch merchant ship. The ship had been submerged in quicksand for more than two hundred years.

The end section of a tomb found at Paestum, Italy. This tomb, one of 180 uncovered, was built by an ancient tribe called the Lucanians between 340 and 310 B.C. Before the discovery of the artistically decorated tombs, archeologists had thought the Lucanians to be unsophisticated barbarians. Archeologists now believe the Lucanians were an artistic people with a distinctive civilization.

Visitors to the British Museum study a battered marble head which American archeologist Iris Love claims is the long-lost head of the Aphrodite of Cnidus by Praxiteles, a fourth-century-B.C. work. Miss Love discovered the head in the basement of the British Museum. Other authorities agreed that the head was sculptured In the fourth century B.C. but disputed Miss Love's claim that it is the head sculptured by Praxiteles.

PHOTOGRAPHING THE HEAVENS

A sequence of photographs taken from a jetliner 39,000 feet over the Massachusetts coast shows the progression of the March 7 total eclipse of the sun by the moon.

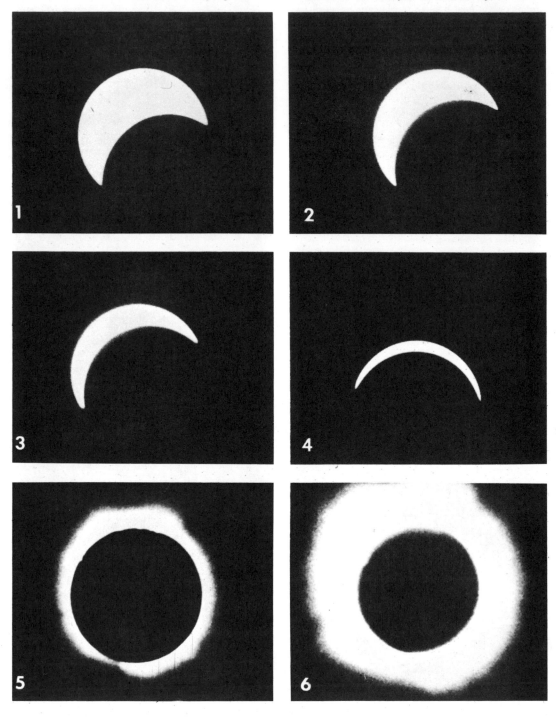

The Tago-Sato-Kisaka comet (above), discovered by Japanese astronomers in October 1969, was photographed from a U.S. Air Force plane in February 1970. Another comet, code-named 1970–F, was discovered on May 20 by Chilean astronomers. Venus can be seen at the top of the picture.

A photograph of the planet Uranus, taken by a 36-inch telescope hoisted 80,000 feet by a balloon, is 5 times sharper than the best photo taken by ground-based telescopes.

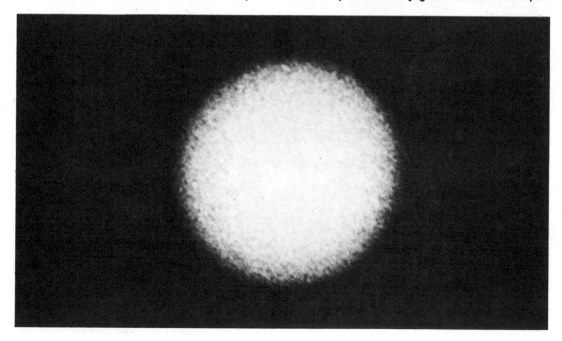

ON THE TRAIL OF THE DINOSAUR

The prehistoric dinosaur has always been of fairy-tale interest to young people. Even among adults, the sheer size of the beast creates a sense of wonder.

In 1970, hundreds of children took part in a festive day marking the dedication of Dinosaur Trailside Park in New York City. For the youngsters, the most fun was digging up fossils from two large sandboxes. Eventually, the park will contain 52 dino-saur tracks, cast from originals found near Glen Rose, Texas.

With the help of two teen-agers, the dino-saur also had his day in New Jersey. There the two boys found scientifically important dinosaur tracks and other fossils in a deso-late quarry, and began petitioning to pre-serve the site. After two years, the owner donated 19 fossil-bearing acres for a park, and the dinosaur triumphed.

The festivities dedicating Dinosaur Trailside Park in New York City included puppet shows, clowns, and fossil-digging for the youngsters. Below: A young boy is learning how to shape a dinosaur from clay.

Paul Olsen (left) and Tony Lessa, who plan to be paleontologists, display a dinosaur footprint they discovered in a New Jersey quarry. Below: Paul uses pieces of the imprint to make a fiber-glass mold.

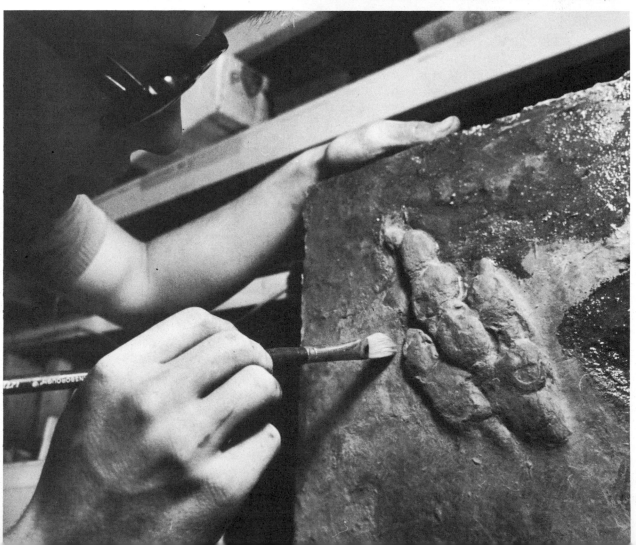

SPACE

THE exploration of outer space entered a new decade in 1970. Landing a man on the moon had been a successful goal of the 1960's. Now many space experts were considering the use of unmanned spacecraft to explore the universe.

This became an especially important decision after the serious setbacks suffered by the United States space program in 1970. The Apollo 13 flight nearly ended in disaster, and the public became aware of the hazards of manned space exploration. On top of this, Congress cut so much money from NASA's budget that some Apollo flights had to be canceled.

The Soviet Union, on the other hand, made impressive strides forward in their space-exploration program. Instead of concentrating on manned space flight, the Soviets launched many unmanned, remote-controlled spacecraft. In 1970 two unmanned Luna crafts achieved "space firsts." Luna 16 traveled to the moon, landed, and then successfully lifted itself off the lunar surface and returned to earth. Luna 17's performance was even more remarkable. It landed an eight-wheeled "robot" vehicle on the moon, capable of propelling itself.

The importance of international co-operation was stressed by all space experts in 1970. New countries became full-fledged members of the space club by launching satellites with their own boosters. The signing of a co-operative space treaty by the United States and the Soviet Union in 1970 might be a step toward international space co-operation that will benefit mankind.

Three lucky astronauts aboard the Apollo 13 space capsule await recovery in the Pacific on April 17 after their planned lunar landing nearly ended in disaster.

While the United States suffered a major setback with the failure of Apollo 13, the Soviet Union made great strides forward in its space program. Luna 16, shown at right in an artist's conception, traveled to the moon, retrieved soil from the lunar surface, and returned to earth. Earlier in the year, aboard Soyuz 9, Soviet cosmonauts Vitaly Sevastyanov (below, at left) and Andrian Ni-kolayev set a manned space-flight record of 17 days 16 hours 59 minutes.

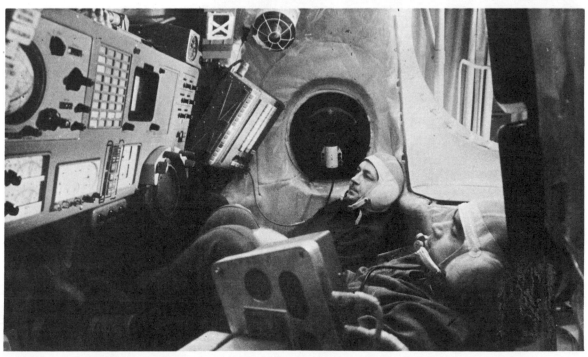

In 1970 the Soviet Union landed an unmanned robot vehicle on the moon. This vehicle, Lunokhod 1, was carried to the moon atop the Luna 17 spacecraft (above). After Luna 17 landed, Lunokhod rolled down a ramp to the lunar surface (below).

On the lunar surface (above), Lunokhod rolled along, picking up and analyzing lunar soil. This information was then transmitted back to earth. The United States will use a manned lunar rover (below) to explore the moon's surface.

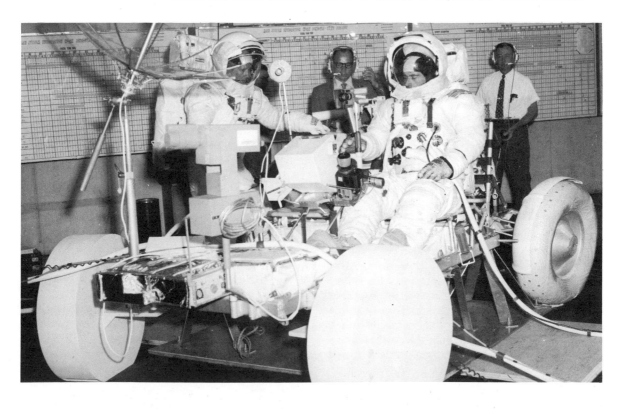

In Honolulu, Hawaii, President Nixon praises astronauts John L. Swigert, Jr. (left), Fred W. Haise, Jr. (center), and James A. Lovell, Jr., for their great courage aboard the ill-fated Apollo 13 spacecraft.

▶ THE APOLLO PROGRAM

The Apollo 13 flight to the moon was a failure which nearly ended in the death of three astronauts. For that reason, the drama of the flight equaled that of Apollo 11, man's first moon landing.

Apollo 13 was successfully launched on April 11. Aboard were James A. Lovell, Jr., Fred W. Haise, Jr., and John L. Swigert, Jr. It was to have achieved man's third lunar landing. On April 13, however, one of the two oxygen storage tanks in the service module exploded. The other tank was damaged by the blast. The oxygen was vital for breathing, pressurization, and to provide electrical power for the spacecraft. The service module was now useless.

The command module's battery power and reserve oxygen tank had to be saved for the craft's re-entry into earth's atmosphere and landing. So the small lunar module, with its separate oxygen and power supplies, was the only hope for the three astronauts.

The astronauts crawled into the lunar module. All power systems were reduced to essential uses to save the small quantity of oxygen. For 3½ days the spaceship made its way back to earth while the world tensely waited. On April 17 the astronauts returned to the command module. They then jettisoned the lunar module and landed safely in the Pacific.

This near-tragedy led to the postponement of the Apollo 14 flight which was to have been launched on December 3, 1970. President Nixon's budgetary cuts added to this setback by forcing NASA to cancel 2 of the remaining 6 lunar landings. (Only 2 moon landings are planned for 1971, and 2 for 1972.) And in October, four senators urged ending all manned space flights, in favor of automatic spacecraft.

▶ SOVIET SPACE FLIGHTS

1970 was a very good year for the Soviet Union's space programs. They set three world space records with Soyuz 9, Luna 16, and Luna 17.

Soyuz 9 was launched into earth orbit on June 1 with Andrian G. Nikolayev and Vitaly I. Sevastyanov aboard. By the time it returned to earth on June 19, it had set a manned space-flight endurance record of 17 days 16 hours 59 minutes.

The Soviet unmanned Luna 16 left earth on September 12. Five days later it went into lunar orbit. Guided by signals from earth, the craft landed on the moon for a stay of about a day and then successfully returned to earth. Luna 16 was the first unmanned spacecraft ever to land on the moon, lift itself off, and return to earth. It brought back soil dug out of the moon's surface by an automatic shovel-device.

Then, in November, the Soviet Union announced that an unmanned craft, Luna 17, had transported an eight-wheeled, self-propelled vehicle onto the moon. It had been carried on top of Luna 17 and, on command, slid down a track to the moon's surface. Lunokhod 1, which means Moon Rover, was automatically controlled from the earth. Its wheels were powered by solar energy. Lunokhod rolled along, picked up and analyzed lunar material, and transmitted the information back to earth. Russia later announced that neither Luna 17 nor the Lunokhod would return to earth.

Venera 7 was launched in August. It sent back data after landing on the planet Venus. Zond 8, a reconnaissance spacecraft, was launched on October 10. It circled the moon, took pictures, and returned to earth.

▶ SPACE CO-OPERATION

As Zond 8 splashed down in the Indian Ocean, Russian and American space experts were completing two days of talks. On October 29 it was announced that the two nations had agreed to standardize the equipment used to link one manned spacecraft to another. This means that the linkup systems of their manned spacecraft will be the same. Thus, if an emergency occurs in outer space, one nation's spacecraft will be able to rescue astronauts trapped in the other nation's spacecraft.

The Soviet Union and the United States will not totally dominate space for long. Great Britain and Italy have launched satellites with American-made booster rockets. France has launched six satellites with its own booster. And in 1970, Japan and Red China launched satellites with their own boosters. Israel, India, and Germany are other possible entries into the space club.

With so many countries exploring outer space, international co-operation is becoming more and more important.

There were many examples of Soviet-American co-operation during 1970. In October, Soviet cosmonaut Andrian Nikolayev (seated) visited the Marshall Space Flight Center in Alabama. Astronaut Russell Schweickart is at the left.

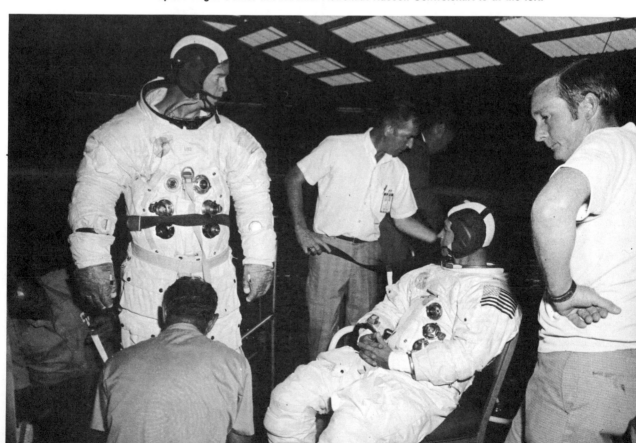

SPACE STATIONS

Both the United States and the Soviet Union are expected to put space stations in orbit in the mid-1970's. In October, representatives to the 21st Congress of the International Astronautical Federation called for the orbiting of an international space station under UN auspices. Such a station might house a crew of a hundred engineering and scientific specialists from many different nations. They would include flight controllers, doctors, astronomers, physicists, and meteorologists.

EARTH-RESOURCE MEASUREMENTS

U.S. space experts have been exploring the possibility of using manned spacecraft to make earth-resource measurements. This means that observations would be made from outer space that would be useful in agriculture, meteorology, cartography, forestry, pollution monitoring, and in surveying natural disasters.

In 1970 the United States continued its work on an experimental automatic spacecraft that would be able to make these earth-resource measurements. The 1,800-lb. Earth Resources Technology Satellite (ERTS) will be placed in a near-polar orbit in 1972. Using a special television system, the satellite will be able to detect even the beginnings of disease in crops.

WEATHER AND COMMUNICATIONS SATELLITES

Networks of satellites already provide weather and communication services glob-

A drawing showing how a wild elk was tracked by Nimbus 3, a meteorological satellite. The collar contains batteries, a transmitter, and sensors to indicate the animal's condition.

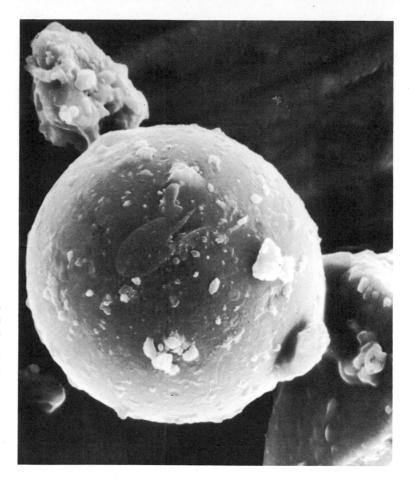

This glassy spherule, enlarged 6,600 times, was found among the rocks brought back by Apollo 11. The spherule may have been created when a meteorite crashed into the moon, causing lunar material to melt. The photo was taken with a scanning electron microscope.

ally. Both the Soviet Union and the United States improved these systems during 1970.

Between April 1969 and April 1970, Nimbus 3, a U.S. meteorological satellite, sent back over 150,000 weather pictures. Equipped with an infrared sensing detector, it can monitor weather day and night. Its instruments include radio-tracking equipment. During 1970 it "tracked" a wild elk wandering around Jackson Hole, Wyoming. The elk had been fitted with a collar carrying batteries, a transmitter, and sensors to indicate the animal's physical condition.

The same kind of system could be fitted to anything that moves—icebergs, animals, or balloons. Nimbus 4, launched April 8, 1970, tracked balloons floating around the world at altitudes up to 79,000 feet. The tracking was part of a system to measure winds and temperatures in the atmosphere.

The Intelsat commercial communication-satellite network is managed by Comsat in the United States. During 1970 it added new satellites to the Intelsat 3 series. In 1971 the first satellite of Intelsat 4 series will be launched.

In 1970 the Soviet Union launched four more Meteor satellites. This weather-reporting network started in 1969, and now has six satellites in operation.

Russia added five more satellites to its communication-satellite network with the launchings of Molniya 13 through 17.

▶ LUNAR ROCKS

Analysis of lunar rocks continued in 1970. On May 26, Gerald J. Wasserberg of the California Institute of Technology reported that his analysis of a rock from the moon's Ocean of Storms (Apollo 12) indicated that it is 4,600,000,000 years old. He noted: "It now appears that we have on the surface of the moon—and in our laboratories—materials that date back to the formation of the solar system."

JOHN NEWBAUER
Editor in Chief
Astronautics & Aeronautics

SKYLAB: A SPACE LABORATORY

The United States plans to launch its first space station late in 1972. Called Skylab, this 6.5-ton laboratory will orbit the earth at an altitude of 220 miles. Skylab will be lofted into space by a Saturn 5 rocket. Three astronauts will be sent into space the following day in an Apollo spacecraft. After docking with the Skylab the astronauts will enter the workshop. They will stay in orbit for about a month, performing scientific experiments. Later Skylab missions will last for longer periods of time. Skylab will help NASA plan long missions, such as a flight to Mars. It will tell NASA, for example, whether astronauts can stay in space and work there for a long period of time without suffering physical damage. If they cannot, the answer may be to orbit automated equipment.

A model of the work station in the interior of Skylab's Multiple Docking Adapter (MDA). The MDA sits between the Apollo Telescope Mount (ATM), the command and service module, and the Saturn workshop (see diagram at right). From the MDA, astronauts will control solar experiments and earth-resource experiments. The control and display panel at the left monitors the telescope mount.

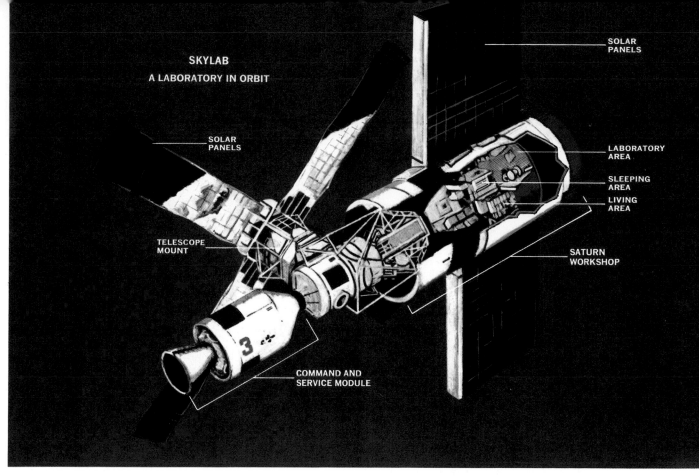

SKYLAB
A LABORATORY IN ORBIT

SOLAR PANELS

SOLAR PANELS

LABORATORY AREA

SLEEPING AREA

LIVING AREA

TELESCOPE MOUNT

SATURN WORKSHOP

COMMAND AND SERVICE MODULE

Skylab, a three-man earth-orbit station, is scheduled to be launched in late 1972.

Three test engineers prepare a meal in a model of the wardroom section of the Skylab workshop. Skylab will be able to accommodate three astronauts.

An engineer takes a nap in the sleep section of the model Skylab workshop. In the weightlessness of space, astronauts will not need "horizontal" beds.

SPORTS

THE year 1970 was one of the most exciting in sports history. Many individual athletes helped make that excitement. George Blanda of Oakland, for example, gave heart to the over-40 set by kicking and passing the Raiders into the NFL play-offs; he won or tied several games single-handedly with but a few seconds left on the clock. Baltimore's Brooks Robinson thrilled World Series fans with his magic glove. Bobby Orr led the Boston Bruins to victory in the Stanley Cup play-offs and collected four trophies on the way. And towering Willis Reed led the New York Knicks to a 4–3 win over Los Angeles in the NBA play-offs; Reed was named League and play-off MVP.

Nonteam efforts were as exciting: Willy Shoemaker rode his 6,033d mount to victory to set a new record; Margaret Court scored a tennis grand slam; and Christos Papanicolaou of Greece became the first man to pole vault 18 feet.

Muhammad Ali, alias Cassius Clay, made his ring comeback in 1970. He KO'd Jerry Quarry in 3, but took 15 to down Argentinian Oscar Bonavena.

Mrs. Margaret Court won the Australian, French, American, and Wimbledon tennis championships in 1970, the first grand slam since 1953.

Skippered by William Ficker, the "Intrepid" sails toward the finish line to defeat "Gretel II" of Australia 4-1 in the America's Cup race.

WORLD SOCCER CUP

The most popular sport in the world is one that gets very little attention in the United States. This sport is soccer. Symbolic of world supremacy in soccer is the Jules Rimet Trophy, better known as the World Cup.

Every four years a tournament is held to determine the winner of the World Cup. The championship team is permitted to retain the trophy only until the next tournament, when it must give it up if another team wins. The only time a country can keep the cup permanently is after it has won the world championship three times. This feat had never been achieved—until 1970.

In June 1970, in Mexico City's Aztec Stadium, the Brazilian national team defeated the Italians, 4–1, for its third world title. This triumphant occasion was witnessed by a crowd of more than 112,500 and a worldwide television audience of 1,000,000,000 fans.

The Brazilians won the cup in 1958 and again in 1962. In 1966 it looked as though they would win it again. But they were upset by a tough, defense-minded team from Great Britain. The major reason for that upset was an injury to Brazil's best player, who also happens to be the greatest soccer player who ever lived. His name is Edson Arantes do Nascimiento, but soccer fans the world over know him as Pele.

Pele is only 5'8" tall. Nevertheless, he can do things on a soccer field that no one else has ever done. He shoots and passes brilliantly with either foot. His quickness and agility make it almost impossible for any single opponent to stay with him. His leaping ability and body control in midair are nothing short of phenomenal. They allow him to make head shots and head passes above the crowds of players. Some of his shots cannot be believed—even when they are seen. At the age of 30, Pele has scored more than 1,000 goals.

Despite his small stature, Pele is very strong. It is this strength that has enabled him to survive in soccer. Soccer, like American football, is a hard-played sport that can sometimes be cruel.

Pele stayed healthy in the 1970 tournament, and the Brazilians swept through undefeated. Indeed, they had only one tough match—with the British. Only the British had the defense to stop Pele and his fast-moving, quick-passing teammates. Only the British had the offensive strength to keep the ball away from the Brazilians and take advantage of their relatively weak defense. But the Brazilians were not to be denied. Fourteen minutes into the second half, Pele made a beautiful pass to an unguarded teammate to the right of the British goal. He scored easily, and the Brazilians won 1–0. They had clear sailing after that, winning five more games to take permanent possession of the World Cup.

Brazil's dynamic Pele drives the ball toward yet another goal. Pele, the greatest soccer player in the world, has scored an unbelievable 1,000 goals in his career.

AUTO RACING

Auto-racing fans around the world were saddened by the deaths in 1970 of three prominent drivers. New Zealander Bruce McLaren, who designed and built his own cars, was killed during a test run. Piers Courage, a Britisher, was killed in the Dutch Grand Prix. This race, in June, was won by Jochen Rindt of Austria, who covered the 208.8-mile course at an average speed of 113.08 miles per hour. In addition to the Dutch Grand Prix, Rindt won the 1970 French, Monaco, British, and German Grand Prixes. His amazing skill won him the World Road-Racing Championship. But the award had to be presented posthumously, for Rindt was killed during trials for the Italian GP—which was to have been one of his last races before retirement.

Jochen Rindt, the 1970 world racing champion. The 28-year-old racer was killed when his car crashed during trials for the Italian Grand Prix.

Grand Prix	Driver
South African GP	Jack Brabham, Australia
Spanish GP	Jackie Stewart, Scotland
Monaco GP	Jochen Rindt, Austria
Belgian GP	Pedro Rodriguez, Mexico
Dutch GP	Jochen Rindt
French GP	Jochen Rindt
British GP	Jochen Rindt
German GP	Jochen Rindt
Austrian GP	Jackie Ickx, Belgium
Italian GP	Clay Regazzoni, Switz.
Canadian GP	Jackie Ickx
U.S. GP	Emerson Fittipaldi, Brazil
Mexican GP	Jackie Ickx

World Road-Racing Champion: JOCHEN RINDT (named posthumously)
USAC National Champion: AL UNSER, U.S.
NASCAR Grand National Champion: BOBBY ISAAC, U.S.
SCCA Canadian-American Challenge Cup: DENIS HULME, NEW ZEALAND
SCCA Trans-American Title: PARNELLI JONES, U.S.
Indianapolis 500: AL UNSER, U.S.

BASEBALL

1970 was the year that the Mets did not win the pennant, or the World Series, or even their division (the National League East). It was the year that their victims of the 1969 Series, the Baltimore Orioles, won it all.

In 1970, the Orioles were the best-balanced team in baseball. In Mike Cuellar, Jim Palmer, and Dave McNally, they had three starting pitchers who each won twenty games or more. In Dick Hall, they had an excellent man in the bullpen. Frank Robinson and Boog Powell, the American League's Most Valuable Player, supplied the power. Outfielders Paul Blair and Don Buford provided speed. Second baseman Davey Johnson, shortstop Mark Belanger, and third baseman Brooks Robinson gave the Orioles an airtight infield.

Baltimore, as expected, took an early lead in the American League's Eastern Division and coasted through the rest of the season. In the American League West, the Minnesota Twins also had an easy time. They were sparked by the hitting of Harmon Killebrew and Tony Oliva, and the pitching of Jim Perry. But the Twins were no match for Baltimore in the pennant playoffs. The Orioles won three games to none.

The National League West featured baseball's most publicized team in 1970, the

Baltimore pitcher Mike Cuellar raises his arms in victory as he rushes to meet third-baseman Brooks Robinson after Orioles won fifth and final game of the World Series. Robinson (below) made several spectacular catches and was named series MVP.

Oriole first baseman Boog Powell, whose big bat helped beat "The Big Red Machine," was named the American League's Most Valuable Player in 1970. During regular-season play, Powell batted .297 while collecting 156 hits including 35 home runs.

Cincinnati Reds. The Reds were explosive. Tony Perez, Johnny Bench, and Lee May had tremendous power. Pete Rose, Bobby Tolan, and Bernie Carbo could also hit the long ball. The Reds did not just defeat their opponents, they destroyed them. And for that reason, they were given the nickname "The Big Red Machine."

The only close race was in the National League East. Going into the final weeks of the season, the Mets, the Chicago Cubs, and the Pittsburgh Pirates each had a chance for the division title. The Pirates, with fine hitting and defense, and adequate pitching, finally won the exciting struggle and the right to face the Reds in the championship series for the National League Pennant. It was no contest. The Reds swept all three games to set up the confrontation with the Orioles.

The Series was a shocking experience for the Reds. Led by Brooks Robinson's timely hitting and brilliant fielding, the Orioles won the Series in five games. Robinson was the 1970 choice for the Series' most valuable player. Late in the fifth and final game, Brooks came to bat and took a called third strike. The Baltimore fans, realizing that his hitting and fielding had won the Series, gave him a standing ovation anyway.

BASEBALL

FINAL MAJOR-LEAGUE STANDINGS

AMERICAN LEAGUE

Eastern Division

	W	L	Pct.	GB
*Baltimore	108	54	.667	
New York	93	69	.574	15
Boston	87	75	.537	21
Detroit	79	83	.488	29
Cleveland	76	86	.469	32
Washington	70	92	.432	38

Western Division

	W	L	Pct.	GB
Minnesota	98	64	.605	
Oakland	89	73	.549	9
California	86	76	.531	12
Milwaukee	65	97	.401	33
Kansas City	65	97	.401	33
Chicago	56	106	.346	42

NATIONAL LEAGUE

Eastern Division

	W	L	Pct.	GB
Pittsburgh	89	73	.549	
Chicago	84	78	.519	5
New York	83	79	.512	6
St. Louis	76	86	.469	13
Philadelphia	73	88	.453	15½
Montreal	73	89	.451	16

Western Division

	W	L	Pct.	GB
*Cincinnati	102	60	.630	
Los Angeles	87	74	.540	14½
San Francisco	86	76	.531	16
Houston	79	83	.488	23
Atlanta	76	86	.469	26
San Diego	63	99	.389	39

*Pennant Winner

LEADING BATTERS (400 or more at bats)

American League

	G	AB	H	Pct.
Johnson, California	155	614	202	.3289
Yastrzemski, Boston	161	566	186	.3286
Oliva, Minnesota	157	628	204	.325
Aparicio, Chicago	145	552	173	.313
Fosse, Cleveland	120	450	138	.307
F. Robinson, Baltimore	132	471	144	.306
Smith, Boston	147	580	176	.303
Munson, New York	131	450	137	.302
Piniella, Kansas City	144	542	163	.301
Cater, New York	155	582	175	.301

National League

	G	AB	H	Pct.
Carty, Atlanta	136	478	175	.366
Clemente, Pittsburgh	108	412	145	.352
Sanguillen, Pittsburgh	127	486	159	.327
Torre, St. Louis	161	624	202	.324
Williams, Chicago	161	636	205	.322
Parker, Los Angeles	161	614	196	.319
Gaston, San Diego	146	584	186	.318
Perez, Cincinnati	158	587	186	.317
Rose, Cincinnati	159	649	205	.316
Tolan, Cincinnati	152	589	186	.316

WINNING PITCHERS (20 or more wins)

	W	L
Cuellar, Baltimore, AL	24	8
McNally, Baltimore, AL	24	9
Perry, Minnesota, AL	24	12
Gibson, St. Louis, NL	23	7
Palmer, Baltimore, AL	20	10

HOME-RUN LEADERS (40 or more runs)

	HR
Bench, Cincinnati, NL	45
Howard, Washington, AL	44
Killebrew, Minnesota, AL	41
Williams, Chicago, NL	41
Yastrzemski, Boston, AL	40
Perez, Cincinnati, NL	40

1970 WORLD-SERIES RESULTS

	R	H	E	Winning/Losing Pitcher
1. Baltimore	4	7	2	Palmer
Cincinnati	3	5	0	Nolan
2. Baltimore	6	10	2	Phoebus
Cincinnati	5	7	0	Wilcox
3. Baltimore	9	10	1	McNally
Cincinnati	3	9	0	Cloninger
4. Cincinnati	6	8	3	Carroll
Baltimore	5	8	0	Watt
5. Baltimore	9	15	0	Cuellar
Cincinnati	3	6	0	Merritt

Atlanta's Hank Aaron begins the swing that will bring him the 3,000th hit of his career. In the 101 years of baseball history, only eight other batters have joined the ranks of the exclusive 3,000 club.

In the fifth and final game of the World Series, Baltimore's Mike Cuellar pitches his team to a 9–3 win over Cincinnati. During regular season play Cuellar had an impressive 24–8 win-loss record.

BASKETBALL

Few teams have ever played the game of basketball better than the New York Knickerbockers played it during the 1969–70 season. Executing coach Red Holzman's theories to perfection, the Knicks went on a record-breaking 18-game winning streak early in the campaign. They easily captured the National Basketball Association's Eastern Division title, with a win-loss record of 60–22.

The Knicks should have won the World Championship just as easily, but it took them the full seven games to do it. Willis Reed, their great center and the NBA's Most Valuable Player, injured his leg in the fifth game of the final series with the Los Angeles Lakers. Without Reed, the Knicks were forced to play seven games. Reed returned for the final game, and New York defeated the Lakers 113–99.

The American Basketball Association championship was won by the Indiana Pacers, the only team in that league capable of competing with the better NBA clubs.

For the fourth year in a row, and for the sixth time in the last seven years, UCLA won the NCAA basketball championship. Many experts had predicted that the Bruins could not continue as champions without Lew Alcindor, who joined the Milwaukee Bucks in the NBA. But after losing only two games during the regular season, coach Johnny Wooden's team swept through the NCAA tournament and handily defeated Jacksonville in the finals, 80–69.

Coach Red Holzman of the New York Knicks.

FINAL NBA STANDINGS
Eastern Division

	W	L	Pct.
New York	60	22	.732
Milwaukee	56	26	.683
Baltimore	50	32	.610
Philadelphia	42	40	.512
Cincinnati	36	46	.439
Boston	34	48	.415
Detroit	31	51	.378

Western Division

	W	L	Pct.
Atlanta	48	34	.585
Los Angeles	46	36	.561
Chicago	39	43	.476
Phoenix	39	43	.476
Seattle	36	46	.439
San Francisco	30	52	.366
San Diego	27	55	.329

NBA Championship: New York

FINAL ABA STANDINGS
Eastern Division

	W	L	Pct.
Indiana	59	25	.702
Kentucky	45	39	.536
Carolina	42	42	.500
New York	39	45	.464
Pittsburgh	29	55	.345
Miami	23	61	.274

Western Division

	W	L	Pct.
Denver	51	33	.607
Dallas	45	39	.536
Washington	44	40	.524
Los Angeles	43	41	.512
New Orleans	42	42	.500

ABA Championship: Indiana

COLLEGE BASKETBALL

NCAA: UCLA
National Invitation: MARQUETTE
Atlantic Coast Conference: SOUTH CAROLINA
Big Eight: KANSAS STATE
Big Sky: WEBER STATE
Big Ten: IOWA
Ivy League: PENNSYLVANIA
Mid-American: OHIO
Missouri Valley: DRAKE
Pacific Eight: UCLA
Southeastern: KENTUCKY
Southern: DAVIDSON
Southwest: RICE
West Coast Athletic: SANTA CLARA
Western Athletic: TEXAS (El Paso)

"Pistol" Pete Maravich, LSU's 1969–70 star, joined the Atlanta Hawks in 1970.

FOOTBALL

Oakland quarterback George Blanda, hero of the football season, gets a pass off in the 3d quarter of the AFC title game, but the Colts downed the Raiders 27–17.

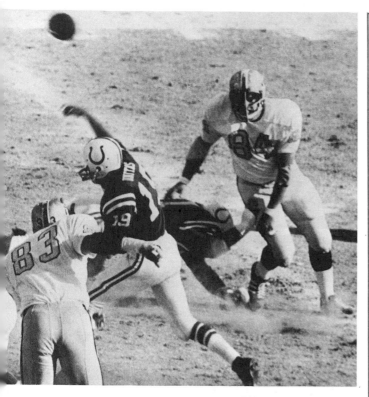

Johnny Unitas passes the Colts to victory in the AFC championship game. Below: The Cowboys celebrate their 17–10 NFC title victory over the 49ers.

FINAL NFL STANDINGS

NATIONAL CONFERENCE

Eastern Division

	W	L	T	Pct.	PF	PA
Dallas*	10	4	0	.714	299	221
N.Y. Giants	9	5	0	.643	301	270
St. Louis	8	5	1	.615	325	228
Washington	6	8	0	.429	297	314
Philadelphia	3	10	1	.231	241	332

Central Division

	W	L	T	Pct.	PF	PA
Minnesota	12	2	0	.857	335	143
Detroit	10	4	0	.714	347	202
Chicago	6	8	0	.429	256	261
Green Bay	6	8	0	.429	196	293

Western Division

	W	L	T	Pct.	PF	PA
San Francisco	10	3	1	.769	352	267
Los Angeles	9	4	1	.692	325	202
Atlanta	4	8	2	.333	206	261
New Orleans	2	11	1	.154	172	347

AMERICAN CONFERENCE

Eastern Division

	W	L	T	Pct.	PF	PA
Baltimore*	11	2	1	.846	321	234
Miami	10	4	0	.714	297	228
N.Y. Jets	4	10	0	.286	255	286
Buffalo	3	10	1	.231	204	337
Boston	2	12	0	.143	149	361

Central Division

	W	L	T	Pct.	PF	PA
Cincinnati	8	6	0	.571	312	255
Cleveland	7	7	0	.500	286	265
Pittsburgh	5	9	0	.357	210	272
Houston	3	10	1	.231	217	352

Western Division

	W	L	T	Pct.	PF	PA
Oakland	8	4	2	.667	300	293
Kansas City	7	5	2	.583	272	244
San Diego	5	6	3	.455	282	278
Denver	5	8	1	.385	253	264

* Conference Champions
1971 Super Bowl Winner: Baltimore

COLLEGE FOOTBALL

Heisman Trophy: JIM PLUNKETT, Stanford
Lambert Trophy: DARTMOUTH
Atlantic Coast: WAKE FOREST
Big Eight: NEBRASKA
Big Ten: OHIO STATE
Ivy: DARTMOUTH
Mid-American: TOLEDO
Pacific Eight: STANFORD
Southeast: LSU
Southern: WILLIAM AND MARY
Southwest: TEXAS
Western Athletic: ARIZONA STATE
Yankee: CONNECTICUT

DOGS AND DOG SHOWS

WESTMINSTER KENNEL CLUB

Best in Show: CH. ARRIBA'S PRIMA DONNA
Hound: CH. VIN-MELCA'S VAGABOND, Norwegian Elk-
hound
Nonsporting: CH. STAR Q'S BRASS BUTTONS, Boston
terrier
Sporting: CH. COUNTERPOINT'S LORD ASHLEY,
pointer
Terrier: HOLMWIRE TUDOR RELIANT, wire fox terrier
Toy: CH. BEAUPRE'S TOMSJOY LEA-CHIM, Pekingese
Working: CH. ARRIBA'S PRIMA DONNA, boxer

Arriba's Prima Donna—better known as
Suzy—was named Best in Show at the
Westminster Kennel Club Show. Suzy
is a reddish- and fawn-colored boxer.

Handler Peter Green displays Special Edition, the
Lakeland Terrier that won Best in Show at the
International Kennel Club Show in Chicago.

This beautiful, 180-pound St. Bernard was named Dog Hero of the Year and awarded the Ken-L Ration Gold Medal for saving his owner from a grizzly bear. Surprisingly, the dog had always been called "Grizzly Bear."

TRACK AND FIELD

WORLD TRACK AND FIELD RECORDS SET IN 1970		
Event	Holder	Time or Distance
Men		
600-yard dash	Marty McGrady, U.S.	1:07.6
3,000-meter steeplechase	Kerry O'Brien, Australia	8:22.0
440-yard hurdles	Ralph Mann, U.S.	0:48.8
Pole vault	Christos Papanicolaou, Greece	18' ¼"
Triple jump	Viktor Saneyev, U.S.S.R.	55' 7¼"
Women		
100-yard dash	Chi Cheng, Taiwan	0:10.0
220-yard dash	Chi Cheng	0:22.6
500-yard dash	Kathy Hammond, U.S.	1:06.3
200-meter dash	Chi Cheng	0:22.4
400-meter dash	Marilyn Neufville, Jamaica	0:51.0
50-yard hurdles	Chi Cheng	0:06.5
70-yard hurdles	Mamie Rallins, U.S.	0:08.8
Long jump	Heidi Rosendahl, West Germany	22' 5¼"

Chi Cheng, the fastest woman in the world, set records in the 100-yard, 220-yard and 200-meter dashes as well as in the 50-yard hurdles.

Marty McGrady races across the finish line during the 82d AAU Indoor Track Championship 600-yard run. McGrady's 1:07.6 bettered his own world record. He became the first runner in 35 years to collect three consecutive titles in the 600-yard run.

BOXING

WORLD BOXING ASSOCIATION CHAMPIONS

Heavyweight: JOE FRAZIER, U.S.
Light Heavyweight: BOB FOSTER, U.S.
Middleweight: CARLOS MONZON, Argentina
Jr. Middleweight: CARMELO BOSSI, Italy
Welterweight: BILLY BACKUS, U.S.
Jr. Welterweight: NICOLINO LOCHE, Argentina
Lightweight: KEN BUCHANAN, Scotland
Jr. Lightweight: HIROSHI KOBAYASHI, Japan
Featherweight: SHOZO SAIJYO, Japan
Bantamweight: CHUCHO CASTILLO, Mexico
Flyweight: MASAO OHBA, Japan

HORSE RACING

HARNESS STAKES WINNERS

Race	Horse
International Trot	Fresh Yankee
Dexter Cup Trot	Marlu Pride
Hambletonian	Timothy T.
Kentucky Futurity	Timothy T.
Yonkers Futurity	Victory Star
United Nations Trot	Fresh Yankee
Realization Trot	Pridewood
Little Brown Jug	Most Happy Fella
Messenger Stakes	Most Happy Fella
Cane Futurity	Most Happy Fella
Realization Pace	Bye Bye Sam

THOROUGHBRED STAKES WINNERS

Race	Horse
Arlington Classic	Corn Off The Cob
Belmont Futurity	Salem
Belmont Stakes	High Echelon
Brooklyn Hdcp	Dewan
Flamingo Stakes	My Dad George
Jockey Club Gold Cup	Shuvee
Kentucky Derby	Dust Commander
Metropolitan Hdcp	Nodouble
Preakness	Personality
Suburban Hdcp	Barometer
United Nations Hdcp	Fort Marcy
Wood Memorial	Personality

ICE SKATING

FIGURE SKATING

United States Championships

Men: TIM WOOD
Women: JANET LYNN
Pairs: JO-JO STARBUCK-KEN SHELLEY
Dance: JUDY SCHWOMEYER-JAMES SLADKY

World Championships

Men: TIM WOOD, U.S.
Women: GABRIELE SEYFERT, East Germany
Pairs: IRINA RODNINA-ALEKSEI ULANOV, U.S.S.R.
Dance: LUDMILLA PAKHOMOVA-ALEKSANDR GORSHKOV, U.S.S.R.

SPEED SKATING

World Championships

Men: ARD SCHENK, Netherlands
Women: ATJE KEULEN-DEELSTRA, Netherlands

A field of 14 horses heads for the first turn in the 95th running of the Preakness Stakes. Personality (partially hidden by No. 2) was the winner.

HOCKEY

FINAL NHL STANDINGS

East Division

	W	L	T	Pts.	GF	GA
Chicago	45	22	9	99	250	170
Boston	40	17	19	99	277	216
Detroit	40	21	15	95	246	199
New York	38	22	16	92	246	189
Montreal	38	22	16	92	244	201
Toronto	29	34	13	71	222	242

West Division

	W	L	T	Pts.	GF	GA
St. Louis	37	27	12	86	224	179
Pittsburgh	26	38	12	64	182	238
Minnesota	19	35	22	60	224	257
Oakland	22	40	14	58	169	243
Philadelphia	17	35	24	58	197	225
Los Angeles	14	52	10	38	168	290

Stanley Cup: Boston

HOCKEY AWARDS

Art Ross Trophy: Bobby Orr, Boston
Calder Trophy: Tony Esposito, Chicago
Georges Vezina Trophy: Tony Esposito
Hart Trophy: Bobby Orr
Lady Byng Trophy: Phil Goyette, St. Louis
Norris Trophy: Bobby Orr

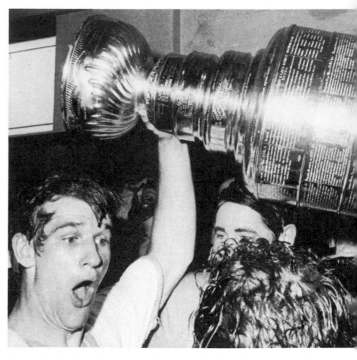

Boston's Bobby Orr raises high the Stanley Cup after scoring the winning goal in overtime to give the Bruins a 4–3 victory over the St. Louis Blues.

Citation, the first racehorse to win $1,000,000 in purses, died in 1970 at the age of 25.

SWIMMING

WORLD SWIMMING RECORDS SET IN 1970

Event	Holder	Time
Men		
100-meter backstroke	Roland Matthes, E. Germany	0:56.9
200-meter backstroke	Roland Matthes	2:06.1
200-meter breaststroke	Brian Job, U.S.	2:23.5
200-meter butterfly	Gary Hall, U.S.	2:05.4
	Mark Spitz, U.S.	
100-meter freestyle	Mark Spitz	0:51.9
400-meter freestyle	Gunnar Larsson, Sweden	4:02.6
1,500-meter freestyle	John Kinsella, U.S.	15:57.1
200-meter indiv'l medley	Gunnar Larsson	2:09.3
400-meter indiv'l medley	Gary Hall	4:31.0
Women		
100-meter butterfly	Alice Jones, U.S.	1:04.1
200-meter butterfly	Alice Jones	2:19.3
400-meter freestyle	Debbie Meyer, U.S.	4:24.3
800-meter freestyle	Karen Moras, Australia	9:02.4

Gary Hall set a world record in the men's 200-meter butterfly. Karen Moe broke the world record in the women's 200-meter butterfly, but her record was later shattered by Alice Jones.

GOLF

Although there are other tournaments that offer more money in prizes, there are four annual tournaments which golfers want to win more than the others. They are the Masters, the most prestigious of all; the PGA; and the United States and British Opens.

Early in 1970, Billy Casper became the second golfer (the first was Arnold Palmer) to reach earnings of $1,000,000 from professional play. In April, Casper went on to capture the Masters crown. After six years as a professional golfer, Dave Stockton won his first major victory by capturing the Professional Golfers' Association (PGA) championship.

The U.S. Open was won by a Briton, and the British Open was won by an American. Twenty-five-year-old Tony Jacklin became the first Englishman to win the U.S. Open in fifty years. And in the seventy years of U.S. Open play, Jacklin was only the fourth golfer to lead the tournament from start to finish. The United States' great Jack Nicklaus won the British Open. It was the eighth major professional championship that Nick-

laus has won in his outstanding career. Nicklaus also captured the World Series of Golf, the game's most exclusive tournament. Only the "big-four" winners of the year are permitted to compete.

Billy Casper's caddy seems unhappy about a putt that would not drop. But Casper recovered and went on to win the Masters, adding handsomely to his $1,000,000 in golf earnings.

TENNIS

TOURNAMENT TENNIS

	U.S. Open	Wimbledon	Australian Open	French Open
Men's Singles	Ken Rosewall, Australia	John Newcombe, Australia	Arthur Ashe, United States	Jan Kodes, Czechoslovakia
Women's Singles	Margaret Smith Court, Australia	Margaret Smith Court	Margaret Smith Court	Margaret Smith Court
Men's Doubles	Pierre Barthes, France-Nicki Pilic, Yugoslavia	John Newcombe-Tony Roche, Australia	Bob Lutz, U.S.-Stan Smith, U.S.	Ilie Nastase, Rumania-Ion Tiriac, Rumania
Women's Doubles	Margaret Smith Court-Judy Tegart Dalton, Australia	Billie Jean King, U.S.-Rosemary Casals, U.S.	Margaret Smith Court-Judy Tegart Dalton	Françoise Durr, France-Gail Chanfreau, France

Australian Ken Rosewall really stretches to return a shot by Tony Roche in the U.S. Open Tennis Championships. Rosewall won the Men's Singles title.

SKIING

UNITED STATES ALPINE CHAMPIONSHIPS

Men

Slalom: BOB COCHRAN
Giant Slalom: TYLER PALMER
Downhill: ROD TAYLOR
Combined: BILL MCKAY

Women

Slalom: PATTY BOYDSTUN
Giant Slalom: SUSAN CORROCK
Downhill: ANN BLACK
Combined: ROSI FORTNA

WORLD CUP

Men: KARL SCHRANZ, Austria
Women: MICHELE JACOT, France

NCAA CHAMPIONSHIPS

Slalom: MICHAEL PORCARELLI, University of Colorado
Giant Slalom: OTTO TSCHUDI, University of Denver
Cross-Country: OLE HANSEN, University of Denver
Jumping: JAY RAND, University of Colorado
Team: UNIVERSITY OF DENVER

Billy Kidd shows championship form in the 1970 Alpine World Ski Championships. He was the first American male skier to win a gold medal in the combined standings.

SPORTS FOR YOUNG PEOPLE

Eight teams played in the 1970 Little League World Series. Above: The Wayne, New Jersey, team rejoices after beating Highland, Indiana, 4-0. Below: Wayne's player just misses stealing second base against Campbell, California. But the New Jersey team won the game and captured the Series title, the first for a U.S. team since 1966.

Over 60,000 boys from North America spent part of their summer learning how to play hockey. Right: A ten-year-old tries to master the difficult sport. Below: Hollis Stacy successfully defends her title as United States Golf Association junior girls champion.

TRANSPORTATION

THE biggest news in transportation in 1970 was bad news for the United States financial community. The country's biggest railroad—the Penn Central—was forced to file for reorganization in bankruptcy. A mid-December nationwide rail strike, which could have seriously damaged the economy, was called off after 18 hours. The threat of huge fines forced the union workers to return to their jobs.

Financial worries plagued the airlines, too. For the scheduled airlines it was a year of higher costs and vanishing profits. Airline analysts were predicting that United States airlines would lose as much as $200,000,000 in 1970.

In shipping, one more superliner left the United States passenger fleet. The once-glorious liner *United States* was placed in dead storage. However, the shipbuilding program of the Nixon administration promised to restore strength to the nation's merchant fleet.

In the automobile industry, a two-month strike at General Motors halted production. The settlement, raising wages about 30 per cent, cast a shadow of things to come at Ford and Chrysler.

Transportation Secretary John Volpe explains how the new National Passenger Corporation's network will link together the major cities of the United States.

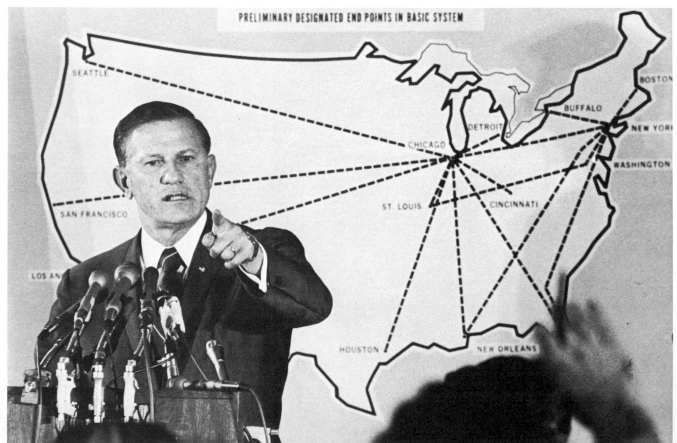

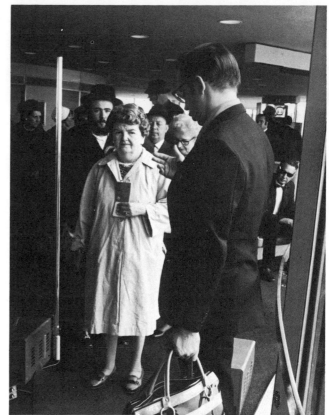

Airlines were plagued by many problems in 1970. The much-heralded Boeing 747 took off one day late on its first commercial flight (below), and later flights had many empty seats. Hijackings forced airlines to check passengers before they boarded planes (above right). Even the Soviets had hijacking problems. A Turkish soldier (above left) guards a Soviet plane hijacked to Turkey.

FIRST COMMERCIAL PASSENGER FLIGHT of BOEING 747
PAN AMERICAN WORLD AIRWAYS · JANUARY 21, 1970

One bright note in the transportation scene was President Nixon's decision to build 300 American merchant ships during the next 10 years. American shipyards now build only 10 ships a year, and in recent years the American merchant fleet has been a second-rate one.

In an effort to cut air pollution, auto manufacturers moved forward in two areas. They increased efforts to develop engines and exhaust systems that will reduce emissions. And they continued work on experimental battery-driven cars, such as General Motors' XEP, shown here.

▶ RAILROADS

The Penn Central Transportation Company, the nation's biggest railroad, was formed by the merger of the New York Central and Pennsylvania railroads. Only a little more than two years after the merger, Penn Central was losing about $700,000 a day on railroad operations. In the face of the nationwide recession, the railroad could not pay its bills and still have enough left over to satisfy its bond-holders and other creditors.

For most investors the first news that Penn Central was in really serious financial trouble came at the annual meeting in May. At that time chairman of the board Stuart T. Saunders announced that annual dividends would have to end.

Penn Central was already having trouble raising the necessary cash to pay its bills and debts. As a result, Penn Central took its problems to the Government. From late 1969 on, Saunders and his key officers had been meeting with Transportation Secretary John A. Volpe and other officials of his department.

Penn Central was seeking loan guarantees, a form of federal aid that had been used in the past. The administration was willing to make an emergency loan. Both the Federal Government and the financial community were worried about the crisis in confidence that the collapse of a large company like the Penn Central might create in the rest of the economy.

The Penn Central's hopes for a $200,000,000 loan ran into the firm opposition of Congressman Wright Patman, chairman of the House Banking and Currency Committee. Patman argued that the public should not be asked to pay for the mistakes of the railroad's management. On June 21 the line filed for a reorganization in bankruptcy. In reorganization, the Penn Central began a twofold program of tightening its belt, and, at the same time, improving railroad service. The railroad seemed likely to continue running at least until 1971.

Two important transportation bills were signed into law as 1970 drew to a close. One was the Rail Passenger Service Act. The other was a $3,100,000,000 program

of grants to urban mass transit systems.

The Rail Passenger Service Act will provide $340,000,000 to establish a new National Railroad Passenger Corporation to take over rail passenger service. This is of prime importance to Penn Central, which operates about a third of all long-haul passenger service. The Rail Passenger Service Act may preserve up to 85 per cent of the 375 intercity passenger trains still operating. (Commuter trains are not included

Commuters await a slow train—and speedy help from the new Mass Transportation Act.

under this act, but will benefit from the Mass Transportation Act.) No decisions have yet been reached on what routes will be used and what kind of service will be provided.

New trains, which may be added under the program, will not be provided immediately. But the best of existing equipment will be repaired and new equipment will be added gradually. The act also gives the Transportation Department power to set

the standards of service on intercity trains.

The new $3,100,000,000 mass transit program should improve the dismal lot of commuters, who make up the bulk of rail passengers today. But that improvement will not be immediately evident, either. The first order of business for the Urban Mass Transportation Administration is the improvement of existing bus and rail transit systems, rather than the building of new systems.

The Nixon administration could point with pride to the passage in 1970 of its maritime program. The program is an attempt to reverse past policies that have seen the United States merchant fleet dwindle in importance, compared to foreign fleets.

The new law, signed in October, calls for the building of 300 merchant ships over the next 10 years. This shipbuilding program will triple the present output of 10 ships a year from American shipyards. The new law also calls for the extending of subsidies (financial aid) to almost the entire United States merchant fleet.

The year also saw the defeat of oil interests in their effort to break certain provisions of a 50-year-old law. The Jones Act prohibits the moving of cargo between ports in the United States on foreign-built or foreign-flag ships. Union Oil Company of California had asked the Treasury Department if the Jones Act provisions might be set aside in a particular case. Union Oil wanted to re-register the 70,000-dwt tanker *Sansinena* under the United States flag. (Dwt is the abbreviation for deadweight tonnage, or the total weight a ship can carry.) The tanker had been built in the United States in 1958, but had then been registered under the Liberian flag and operated with a foreign crew. Union Oil would very much like to have the ship to serve new oil developments on the North Slope of Alaska.

The Treasury Department at first granted Union Oil's request. Then it reversed its position while further study went on. Faced with the united opposition of Congressmen, shipbuilding companies, American-flag tanker operators, and some major shipbuilding unions, Treasury Secretary David Kennedy finally upheld the full provisions of the Jones Act.

Humble Oil reported on the 1969 test of its ice-breaking tanker *Manhattan*. The *Manhattan* was the first commercial vessel to go through the ice-clogged Northwest Passage between Alaskan oil camps and the East Coast of the United States. However, the *Manhattan* test proved to Humble engineers that ice-breaking tankers would be too costly to operate in commercial service. A pipeline seemed a more likely way to transport oil.

A land-locked Oklahoma city became the nation's newest port. The United States Corps of Engineers completed a waterway up the Arkansas and Verdigris rivers to Catoosa, Oklahoma. Catoosa is a Tulsa suburb that is now set for a boom as a port. Because the Arkansas flows into the Mississippi River, Tulsa-Catoosa will become a "gateway to the sea" for the plains states. The Federally-funded $1,200,000,000 Arkansas River Navigation Project is the most expensive waterway project in the world.

▶AVIATION

By any measurement, 1970 was a disappointing year for the aviation industry. A cost squeeze gripped the airlines. In the United States, National Airlines and Northwest Airlines went through major strikes. In Great Britain pilots demanded higher pay for flying jumbo jets.

The annual rate of increase in air traffic dropped from the usual 15 per cent to about 6 per cent during 1970. Airlines depend on the yearly increase in traffic to meet higher costs and pay for new equipment.

In the United States the Civil Aeronautics Board began early in 1970 an investigation that resulted in increases for certain domestic fares. The increases will give the airlines $100,000,000 a year. International air fares were also increased slightly during the year.

Passengers generally showed considerable enthusiasm for the jumbo 747's, but the plane had its full share of troubles at the start. Pan American World Airway's inaugural flight of the 747, scheduled for January 21, did not get off the ground until early on January 22. Before takeoff an engine overheated, forcing the pilot to go back to the starting gate. A backup plane made the flight instead.

By October, 747's had flown over 5,000,-000,000 passenger miles. But there were several other incidents of trouble with its JT9D jet engines, manufactured by United

The McDonnell Douglas DC-10 tests its wings during its August 29, 1970, maiden flight. The new jumbo jet will accommodate 255 to 345 passengers.

Aircraft Corporation. An associate of safety crusader Ralph Nader charged that the FAA was keeping from the public vital information about "defects and failures" in the engines. The FAA denied that there was anything unsafe about the 747.

The public found that the roomy cabins of the big jets offered a substantial improvement in the quality of service. But even this was a mixed blessing. With a growing number of 747's already in service, the airlines found it harder and harder to sell seats on the older generation of long-haul jets. (This problem will increase in 1971, when the wide-bodied McDonnell DC-10 and Lockheed L-1011 go into commercial service.) On the moneymaking United States transcontinental routes, a "seat war" developed. The major lines competed with one another to find new ways of changing interior arrangements to give each passenger more room. The new seating patterns were popular, but cut each plane's earning capacity severely.

On the horizon was the shadow of the SST (supersonic transport). The British-French, and Russian models had already flown at twice the speed of sound. In January 1971 the 91st Congress extended the funding for the American version of the SST for three months. But the 92d Congress will have to decide whether to continue Federal financing after that.

Hijackings assumed a new degree of seriousness. Over the September Labor Day weekend members of the Popular Front for the Liberation of Palestine seized control of three airliners bound for New York from Europe. A Pan American World Airways 747 jumbo jet was switched to Cairo. The plane was blown up within seconds after landing. (The passengers and crew had made a wild exit through escape chutes.) And a Trans World Airlines Boeing 707 and a Swissair DC-8 were forced to land in the Jordanian desert. These two were later joined by a BOAC VC-10. Passengers were held hostage while negotiations went on for the release of Palestinians held in various Western jails. After a week the hostages were released and the airliners destroyed. A similar attempt on an El Al 707 failed when armed Israeli guards killed one hijacker and wounded the woman working with him.

These hijackings resulted in greatly increased security measures at most international airports. The United States FAA increased airport ground detection measures and recruited a force of "sky marshals" as armed guards for flights thought likely to be hijacked. In Europe thorough baggage searches and passport checking became routine.

RODERICK CRAIB
Contributing Editor, *Business Week*

THE AUTO INDUSTRY: BIG STRIKE, SMALL CARS

A strike that stopped all production at General Motors for two months ended just before Thanksgiving. The United Automobile Workers (UAW) and the company worked out a contract calling for an estimated rise of 30 per cent in wages and fringe benefits over the next three years.

The strike was led by Leonard Woodcock, UAW president. He replaced the veteran UAW leader, Walter P. Reuther, who was killed in an airplane crash in May.

Higher costs of labor and materials are expected to be reflected in price increases. As early as September, General Motors announced there would be an average increase of 6.2 per cent on its 1971 cars.

American manufacturers decided to give the makers of low-priced foreign cars a run for their money by entering the small-car field. It is estimated that small cars (both American and foreign) will account for 25 to 30 per cent of all car sales in 1971. The Ford Pinto ($1,919), Chevrolet Vega ($2,069), and American Motors' Gremlin ($1,999) are the domestic answers to Japan's Datsuns ($1,736) and Toyotas ($1,798) and Germany's Volkswagens ($1,780).

Members of the United Automobile Workers picket General Motors. The two-month strike resulted in higher wages for the auto workers. But it also contributed to the nation's growing inflation and joblessness.

Chevrolet Vega

American Motors Gremlin

Ford Pinto

UNITED NATIONS

ON October 24, 1970, the United Nations was 25 years old. The formation of the world organization in 1945 was the second effort in this century to commit nations to settle their differences at the conference table instead of on the battlefield. The first such effort —the League of Nations—had been destroyed by World War II.

Many plans were made to mark the UN anniversary. In June, ceremonies were held in San Francisco to observe the signing of the UN Charter 25 years earlier. In July, a special World Youth Assembly was held at UN headquarters in New York City. And in October, a part of the 25th General Assembly was devoted to the UN's anniversary.

During the anniversary celebrations, many people applauded the UN's accomplishments. Many more declared support for the future. But the world organization was also criticized. For above the words of praise could be heard the sounds of war. Like the League of Nations, the UN, at 25, was struggling with the problems created by man's use of force as a way to deal with relations between nations.

UN Secretary-General U Thant welcomes a Bolivian delegate to the World Youth Assembly, which was held as part of the UN's 25th-anniversary celebrations.

New York City Mayor John V. Lindsay presents a birthday cake to the United Nations. Standing in the background are Secretary-General U Thant and Dr. and Mrs. Edvard Hambro. Dr. Hambro is the new president of the General Assembly.

United States ambassador to the United Nations Charles Yost (left) during the counting of ballots for the election of the president of the 25th General Assembly. In December, George Bush, a Texas congressman, was named to replace Yost.

Miss Angie Brooks of Liberia, president of the 24th UN General Assembly, presents a gavel to her successor, Edvard Hambro of Norway. Dr. Hambro's father had been president of the final session of the League of Nations Assembly.

President Nixon addresses the General Assembly. He asked the Soviet Union to join with the United States in ending the arms race. More than forty heads of state and government attended the UN's 25th-anniversary commemorative sessions.

During 1970 many world leaders visited the UN headquarters. French President Georges Pompidou met with U Thant on March 2. He was accompanied by the French ambassador to the UN (left) and French Foreign Minister Maurice Schumann.

United Nations headquarters has become a kind of international art gallery. Paintings, sculpture, priceless tapestries, and historical objects adorn its halls and lounges. One interesting historical object hangs near the entrance to the Security Council chamber. Given to the UN by Turkey, it is a replica of the world's oldest surviving peace treaty. The original, a small clay tablet, is in the Archeological Museum in Istanbul, Turkey. The treaty was made in 1269 B.C. by the king of the Hittites and Rameses II, king of the Egyptians. Under the terms of the treaty, both leaders pledged eternal friendship, lasting peace, nonaggression, and mutual help.

The provisions of this ancient treaty are very much like the principles of the UN Charter. When UN Secretary-General U Thant received the gift from Turkey, he was moved to recall that "the road to peace is long and arduous. It has been trod by men since the dawn of history."

The principles of the UN Charter had special meaning in 1970. For this was the 25th year in which the world organization would try to walk that "road to peace."

▶ANNIVERSARY CELEBRATIONS

In June many officials traveled to San Francisco to mark the 25th anniversary of the signing of the UN Charter. There was some disappointment that President Nixon, head of the host Government, could not attend. However, Mr. Nixon did address the General Assembly in October.

The 25th General Assembly convened on September 15. Edvard Hambro of Norway was elected president. (Dr. Hambro's father, Carl, had been president of the final session of the League of Nations Assembly.)

On October 14 the Assembly began a ten-day period of speeches and ceremonies in honor of the UN's anniversary. Ironically, on that same day, the United States, the Soviet Union, and Communist China all tested nuclear weapons. Previous sessions of the General Assembly had called for an end to all nuclear testing.

Indonesian President Suharto arrives at the United Nations with his wife and daughter Ave Ave. Earlier, Suharto had flown to Washington, D.C., where he met with President Nixon to discuss U.S. military actions in Cambodia.

Soviet Premier Aleksei Kosygin was not among the 42 heads of state and government who attended the 25th-anniversary commemorative sessions. Secretary-General Thant had hoped that many world leaders would attend and that they would hold private talks aimed at easing world tensions. This did not happen. President Nixon, however, did address the Assembly on October 23. He stated that there were deep differences between the United States and the Soviet Union. He hoped, however, that the competition would remain peaceful. Talking to the assembled delegates and world leaders, President Nixon said "Let us resolve together that the second quarter century of the United Nations shall offer the world what its people yearn for and what they deserve: a world without any war, a full generation of peace."

The commemorative Assembly reaffirmed its dedication to the UN Charter. It adopted a declaration of friendly relations among states. And it issued a statement of strategy for the Second Development Decade. During the Second Development Decade, which was to begin on January 1, 1971, the nations agreed to promote a more just world economic and social order. A major goal would be an average annual growth rate of at least 6 per cent in the gross national product of the developing countries. Earlier, a special committee of the UN Conference on Trade and Development had worked out an agreement whereby the industrialized nations of the world would give preferential treatment to the exports of underdeveloped countries.

The commemorative Assembly also adopted a controversial resolution on colonialism. The resolution said that colonialism is a crime and a violation of the UN Charter. It reaffirmed the "right of colonial people to struggle by all means necessary against colonial powers which suppress their aspiration for freedom and independence." And it called on governments to aid liberation movements. Eighty-six nations voted in favor of this resolution. But because the

Giant Jigsaw

UN peace envoy Gunnar Jarring talks with Israel's representative to the UN, Josef Tekoah (far right), and with the Jordanian Ambassador to the United States, Abdul Hamid Sharaf (right), in an effort to find a peaceful solution to the Middle East crisis. Jarring's efforts were complicated by many factors, as the cartoon (left) suggests.

Peb in "The Philadelphia Inquirer"

wording was so harsh, the United States, Great Britain, Australia, New Zealand, and others voted against it.

▶ SEARCH FOR PEACE IN THE MIDDLE EAST

1970 opened with the usual military clashes between Israel and its Arab neighbors. Secretary-General Thant's special Middle East representative, Gunnar Jarring, had returned to his post as Sweden's ambassador to the Soviet Union. He had traveled for months in the Middle East in search of a settlement. His efforts were fruitless. It thus became clear that there would be no progress toward peace until the United States and the Soviet Union found some area for agreement. So the UN ambassadors of the two superpowers, and the ambassadors of Great Britain and France, began meeting privately. They discussed ways to help Jarring, but had little success.

Meanwhile, increased fighting along the Suez Canal raised the possibility of yet another Middle East war.

On August 7, however, there was a dramatic diplomatic development. Secretary-General Thant announced that the Jarring mission had been reactivated because Israel, Jordan, and Egypt had agreed to a three-month cease-fire and to talk with Jarring. Ambassador Jarring began talks with representatives from the three nations. But then Israel's delegate, Josef Tekoah, left for Israel to get further instructions from his Government. Soon after, Israel accused the Egyptians of violating the cease-fire agreement by moving missiles closer to the Suez Canal. Israel refused to resume peace talks until the missiles were withdrawn.

On November 4 the General Assembly adopted a resolution recommending that the cease-fire be extended from November 5 for

another three months. Israel and the Arab states accepted the extension. The Israelis eased their stand in December, and it was expected that they would return to the peace talks before the cease-fire ran out on February 5, 1971.

▶ THE ARMS RACE

Because of the Egyptian missile buildup, the United States sent new arms and planes to Israel. The Russians continued to send weapons to the Arab states. This was all part of the general emphasis on military power, to which all nations seemed to be returning with increased vigor.

The treaty to ban the spread of nuclear weapons did come into effect in 1970. And the General Assembly approved by a vote of 91–2 a treaty to ban the placing of nuclear and other mass-destruction weapons on the seabed. But no efforts were made to ban all nuclear tests. No efforts were made to ban the use of chemical and biological weapons. And no efforts were made to reduce the production and stockpiles of weapons.

▶ OTHER UN ACTIONS

The General Assembly passed a resolution condemning airplane hijackings and called on governments to punish or extradite hijackers.

The General Assembly approved a U.S. plan to protect prisoners of war.

The Security Council condemned Portugal after a UN fact-finding mission reported that Portuguese-trained and -led troops had invaded Guinea.

Communist China received a majority of Assembly votes but not the two thirds necessary for UN membership.

PAULINE FREDERICK
United Nations Correspondent, NBC News

WORLD YOUTH ASSEMBLY

In 1970 the United Nations was 25 years old. In 1970, too, more than half the people in the world were younger than the UN. Secretary-General U Thant accordingly suggested that a World Youth Assembly be held so that these young people could become involved in the UN's activities.

The World Youth Assembly was held at UN headquarters in New York City from July 9 to July 17. More than 600 people from over 100 nations, areas, and groups took part.

The Assembly was divided into four commissions to take up the following topics: world peace, development, education, man and environment. Unfortunately the hostility in the adult world was reflected in debate in the youths' Peace Commission. Such topics as the war in Southeast Asia, the Middle East, colonialism, racism, and militarism were discussed.

Finally, on July 17, the Youth Assembly was able to approve a message to the 25th UN General Assembly. The message called for the immediate withdrawal of American troops from Indochina, Israeli troops from occupied Arab territories, and Soviet troops from Czechoslovakia.

The message also called for the following:

1. Admission of Communist China and East and West Germany to the UN.

2. Abolition of racial discrimination.

3. Abolition of colonialism.

4. Abolition of the veto in the UN Security Council.

5. Progress toward general disarmament and against hunger.

6. Recognition of the right of young people to have an active role in the UN.

The World Youth Assembly also suggested that it be convened every two years.·

Delegates to the United Nations World Youth Assembly gather for an informal meeting. More than 600 young people took part in the Assembly.

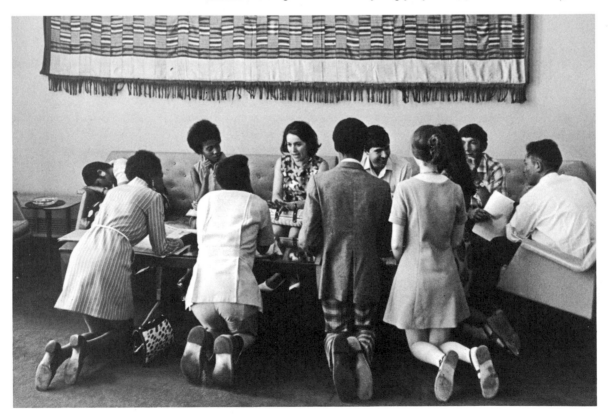

UN Secretary-General U Thant addresses the opening session of the World Youth Assembly on July 9. He is flanked by Richard Akwei of Ghana (left), chairman of the Committee for the Twenty-Fifth Anniversary of the United Nations, and François Pouliot of Canada, chairman of the Planning Committee for the Youth Assembly.

World Youth Assembly delegates dance on the UN lawn during a reception held for them by U Thant. The statue portrays the Biblical passage "They shall beat their swords into plowshares, and their spears into pruninghooks: nation shall not lift up sword against nation, neither shall they learn war any more."

UNITED STATES

AS the new decade—the 1970's—began, the United States faced many problems. In Vietnam, thousands of miles from American shores, American soldiers were still fighting and dying. In the Middle East, the continuing Arab-Israeli conflict threatened, at times, to explode into a war that would pit the United States against the Soviet Union. Problems at home were as serious. Antiwar students held demonstrations on hundreds of campuses. Many of these ended in violence, and in one case four students were shot and killed by National Guardsmen. Bombings by white militants and confrontations between police and black militants were on the rise. As if this were not enough, the nation's air and water were becoming increasingly polluted. Prices were rising month by month. And more and more people were losing their jobs, as the nation's economy went into a slump.

In 1970 there seemed to be a new sense of urgency about curing the nation's ills. But even this positive attitude led to problems. For when people became more concerned, they became more vocal. And this led to conflicts between groups that had differing ideas about how to solve the problems. Many people feared that the nation was becoming polarized. They feared that conflicts would further increase between blacks and whites, young and old, Left and Right.

President Richard M. Nixon

Vice-President Spiro T. Agnew

"Hard-hats" demonstrate in
support of President Nixon.

"...Son...!"   "...Dad...!"

The continuing war in Vietnam and the extension of the war into Cambodia in mid-1970 fueled domestic turmoil in the United States. Conflicts increased between supporters of President Nixon's policies and antiwar demonstrators.

Against this background the American people went to the polls in November. They voted for congressmen, senators, governors, and many local representatives. As midterm elections go, this one was fairly important because of the conflicts within American society. President Richard Nixon and Vice-President Spiro Agnew campaigned very hard for candidates who would support the President's policies. Still, the results of the elections were mixed. The Republicans gained 1 Senate seat. But the Democrats gained 8 seats in the House of Representatives and 11 governorships. Many political analysts felt that the gains made by the Democrats would put them in a stronger position for the 1972 presidential election.

In 1970 President Nixon campaigned for candidates who support his policies. He is shown here in Texas with the Republican gubernatorial and senatorial candidates.

WOMEN OF THE WORLD UNITE!

1970 was a year of demonstrations for equal rights. A new force on the scene was Women's Liberation. Dozens of different groups, attracting women of all ages, were organized to gain "first-class citizenship" for women. Their rallying cry was "Women of the world unite," and their demands ranged from "equal pay for equal work" to free day-care centers.

Other groups that demonstrated for equal rights in 1970 were the Black Panthers, and the American Indians, who "liberated" Alcatraz Island in May.

Rising prices and lack of jobs were major American concerns during 1970. Indeed, it was clear to many that the Republicans did not fare better in the elections because of the nation's economic problems. Many people blamed the Republican administration for the inflation.

Economic Problems

The rise in the cost of living forced many Americans to tighten their belts. Because fewer goods were bought, fewer workers were needed, and many employees were fired. By November 1970, 5.8 per cent of the labor force was out of work. This means that 4,600,000 Americans had no jobs.

Even as people lost their jobs, they found that they had to pay more money for food, rent, clothing, and other items. To stop this inflation, President Nixon began pressuring manufacturers to keep their prices down. He also tried to get labor unions to keep their wage demands at a reasonable level. It seemed likely that in 1971 President Nixon would have to take further steps to improve the economy. (For further details, see the article ECONOMY, which begins on page 144.)

Unrest on the Campus

On April 30, President Nixon announced that he was sending American troops to fight in Cambodia. Immediately, thousands of students across the nation began holding antiwar demonstrations. At Kent State University in Ohio, demonstrators burned down a building on campus, and National Guard troops were called in. On May 4, the Guardsmen fired into a group of students,

Chairman Arthur Burns poses with other members of the Federal Reserve Board. In 1970 Burns eased credit in an effort to stimulate economic growth.

William Scranton, chairman of the President's Commission on Campus Unrest, presents the commission's report to President Nixon. It called on the President to use his prestige to create a climate of understanding. Nixon later attacked the report.

killing four. Ten days later, police fired on students at Jackson State College in Mississippi, killing two. These shootings caused a wave of indignation. Students held rallies and forced confrontations with the authorities. They seized some buildings and burned others. Such events took place on more than three hundred college and university campuses. Again, in many instances police and National Guardsmen were called in. There were many injuries, but no further deaths.

President Nixon appointed a commission to investigate the causes of the Kent State and Jackson State deaths. William Scranton, former governor of Pennsylvania, headed the commission.

The National Guard had defended its action at Kent State by saying that a sniper had fired at the troops, and that they just returned the fire. However, the Scranton Commission could find no evidence of a sniper. The commission deplored the use of firearms by the National Guard. It called on President Nixon to use his prestige and position of leadership to create a climate of understanding in the nation. The commission also warned that the crisis on the campuses threatened the nation's survival.

In October, a grand jury in Portage County, Ohio, indicted 25 persons, including several Kent State students. It virtually cleared the National Guardsmen of any responsibility in the deaths of the four students. Robert I. White, president of Kent State, called the grand-jury report inaccurate and frightening. He said that it would only add to the tensions on that campus and others throughout the nation.

Civil Rights

In the South, the Supreme Court ordered that the bussing of students be enforced so that there would be a better balance of black and white students in the schools. The state of Mississippi had been slow in carrying out this policy. It now began to comply because of pressure by the Federal Government.

Nevertheless, 21 civil-rights leaders expressed their disappointment with the Nixon administration. They were particularly upset by a "secret" memorandum written by White House aide Daniel P. Moynihan. In his memorandum, Moynihan had said that the issue of race would benefit from a period of "benign neglect."

Closely allied with civil rights in 1970 was the growing Women's Liberation movement. The purpose of this movement is to ensure equal rights for women in all areas of American life. Citing statistics, supporters of Women's Lib showed that women are discriminated against in medicine, law, and other professions.

The 1970 Elections

Most public-opinion polls in 1970 showed that the majority of Americans approved of President Nixon's actions. Mr. Nixon was cheered by these reports—and anxious to increase the number of Republicans in Congress. As a result, he campaigned harder in an off-year election than any other president in American history. When the President's tour began in October, Vice-President Agnew had already been campaigning for several weeks. Both men urged voters to vote Republican. Their theme was that by voting for men who would support the President, they would be voting against "radicals" who wished to destroy the structure of American life.

The President visited Vermont, New Jersey, Ohio, North Dakota, California, and other states. Special targets of the President were incumbent liberal senators. Some of these men—Tennessee Democrat Albert Gore, Maryland Democrat Joseph Tydings, and New York liberal Republican Charles

Presidential adviser Daniel Moynihan created a storm by saying that the issue of race would benefit from a period of "benign neglect." Moynihan resigned at the end of 1970.

New York Conservative James L. Buckley claims victory in the U.S. Senate race. He became the first U.S. senator from a third party in thirty years.

Goodell—were defeated in the election. But others—New Jersey Democrat Harrison Williams, North Dakota's Quentin Burdick, and Utah's Frank Moss—held their seats.

The Democrats' chief issue in the campaign was the economy. Figures released a few weeks before the election showed that prices were still rising and that inflation was a serious problem. At the same time, the rate of unemployment was much higher than the administration had expected. Most Democratic campaigners did not criticize the President's handling of the Vietnam war.

When the election returns were in, both parties claimed victory. The Republicans picked up one seat in the Senate. In addition, they could expect the support of James Buckley of New York, who ran as a Conservative. Because of this, the President believed that the new Senate would give greater support to his programs. However, most observers agreed that the President would get added support only in so far as foreign policy is concerned.

In the House of Representatives, the Democrats increased their majority by eight seats. They also gained eleven governorships. These included such key states as Pennsylvania, Ohio, Florida, Wisconsin, and Minnesota.

Senator Edmund Muskie of Maine easily won re-election. He emerged from the election as a strong national spokesman for the Democrats.

Congress

Several major proposals of the Nixon administration were approved by the first session of the 91st Congress. These included the major part of the President's anticrime program and legislation establishing operation of the U.S. postal system by an independent Federal agency.

Another important legislative development was the approval of a measure to lower the voting age to 18. President Nixon signed the bill only after calling for a court test of its constitutionality.

MAJOR CONGRESSIONAL LEGISLATION IN 1970

CIGARETTES

Public Health Cigarette Smoking Act (April 1) * bans cigarette commercials on radio and televison, effective January 2, 1971. The Act also places a stronger warning on cigarette packages: "Warning: The Surgeon General has determined that cigarette smoking is dangerous to your health."

CONGRESSIONAL REFORM

Legislative Reorganization Act of 1970 (October 26) revises Congressional committee procedures. Committee hearings, except for those of the Appropriations Committee, will be open, if national security is not involved.

CRIME

Organized Crime Control Act (October 15) strengthens Federal crime laws and legal procedures relating to organized crime.

DRUGS

Comprehensive Drug Abuse Prevention and Control Act (October 27) revises Federal drug and narcotics laws. The Act provides for the classification of drugs into five categories, according to the degree of possible danger. The "no-knock" provision allows the police, with permission of a judge, to enter a private home without notice, in order to seize drugs.

ENVIRONMENT

Clean Air Act of 1970 (December 31) sets a six-year deadline for the auto industry to develop an engine that will cut auto fumes by 90 per cent.

Federal Water Pollution Control Act Amendment (April 3) provides measures dealing with pollution of waters by oil spills, sewage from ships, and discharges from mines. The Act also establishes controls of thermal pollution from atomic power plants.

POST OFFICE

Postal Reorganization Act (August 12) turns over the postal system to an independent Federal agency, the United States Postal Service. The Act also increases salaries of postal workers.

INDIANS

Taos Pueblo Indians Act (December 15) gives Taos Pueblo Indians title to 48,000 acres of Carson National Forest in New Mexico, including Blue Lake, sacred to the Taos.

VOTING RIGHTS

Voting Rights Act Amendments of 1970 (June 22) bans voter literacy tests and lowers the voting age to 18.

WASHINGTON, D.C.

District of Columbia Self-Government Act (September 22) provides for a nonvoting delegate from Washington, D.C., to the House of Representatives. The Act also establishes a Commission on the Organization of the District of Columbia.

* the date on which President Nixon signed the bill into law

The U.S. Supreme Court (left to right): Thurgood Marshall, John M. Harlan, Potter Stewart, Hugo L. Black, Byron R. White, Chief Justice Warren E. Burger, Harry A. Blackmun, William O. Douglas, and William J. Brennan, Jr.

The Cabinet

The first change in the Nixon Cabinet took place in June. Robert H. Finch resigned as secretary of health, education, and welfare. He joined the White House staff as a counselor to the President. Many analysts agreed that Finch's administration of HEW had been too politically liberal to suit conservative Republicans in the Congress and the administration. The President appointed Undersecretary of State Elliot L. Richardson to succeed Finch. A few days later, the President announced that Labor Secretary George P. Shultz would become director of a new Office of Management and the Budget. James D. Hodgson became new secretary of labor.

In December another—not unexpected—change took place. President Nixon dismissed Interior Secretary Walter J. Hickel. Earlier in the year, Secretary Hickel had written a letter to the President, urging him to establish better communications with the nations' youth. Mr. Hickel also said that the President should consult more with his Cabinet, and urged that Vice-President Agnew stop his attacks on young people. The President was reportedly angered when the letter was leaked to the press. So Mr. Hickel's ouster came as no surprise. He was replaced by Rogers C. B. Morton, chairman of the Republican National Committee.

In December it was announced that former Texas Gov. John Connally would replace David Kennedy as Treasury secretary.

The Supreme Court

As had been the case in 1969, most interest in the Supreme Court involved the appointment of an associate justice to succeed Abe Fortas, who had resigned in 1969.

In November 1969 the Senate refused to confirm the appointment of Clement Haynsworth of South Carolina. In January 1970,

MAJOR DECISIONS OF THE SUPREME COURT IN 1970

CHURCH AND STATE

Walz. v. New York (May 4) ruled 7–1 that laws that exempt church property from taxation do not violate the Constitution's provision for separation of church and state.

DEFENDANT'S RIGHTS

Allen v. Illinois (March 31) ruled unanimously that during trials a judge can have a disruptive defendant bound, gagged, cited for contempt, or expelled from the courtroom so as to maintain order.

JUVENILES

Winship v. New York State (March 31) ruled 5–3 that juvenile defendants must have the same constitutional safeguards as adults have. The Court ruled that juvenile courts may convict a child only if he is found guilty "beyond a reasonable doubt," and not by a "preponderance of the evidence."

LABOR

Boys Markets, Inc. v. Retail Clerk's Union (June 1) ruled 5–2 that a Federal judge may bar workers from striking if they violate no-strike clauses of collective-bargaining contracts.

SELECTIVE SERVICE

Breen v. Selective Service, Local Board No. 16, Bridgeport, Connecticut (January 26) ruled unanimously that students who lose their draft deferments after turning in their draft cards may challenge their reclassification in court before induction.

Toussie v. United States (March 2) ruled 5–3 that young men who do not register with their draft boards at age 18 cannot be prosecuted after five years have elapsed.

SCHOOL DESEGREGATION

Carter v. West Feliciana Parish School Board (January 14) overruled 6–2 a U.S. Court of Appeals decision setting a September 1970 deadline for public-school desegregation in six Southern states. The Court ruled that the schools be integrated by February 1970.

WELFARE

Wheeler v. Montgomery; Goldberg v. Kelly (March 23) ruled 5–3 that people receiving welfare have a constitutional right to formal hearings including "due process of law," before welfare officials may cut off their benefits.

Williams v. Maryland (April 6) ruled 5–3 that states may set limits on the amount of welfare benefits a family may receive.

VOTING RIGHTS

Oregon v. Mitchell (December 21) upheld 5–4 the right of an 18-year-old to vote in Federal elections. The Court also ruled that Congress had acted unconstitutionally when it lowered the voting age to 18 for state and local elections.

U.S. v. Arizona; U.S. v. Idaho (December 21) upheld 5–4 the 1970 amendments to the Voting Rights Act that abolished long-residency requirements and literacy tests for voting.

President Nixon nominated another Southerner, G. Harrold Carswell of Florida. Carswell was opposed by political liberals and by civil-rights advocates, who condemned his record as a judge in Florida. In April, the Senate rejected Carswell by a vote of 51–45.

A week later, President Nixon submitted a third nominee: Judge Harry A. Blackmun of Minnesota. He was confirmed on May 12 as the 99th justice of the United States Supreme Court.

A significant decision of the Supreme Court in 1970 was the order to speed the pace of school desegregation in the South. The Court refused to consider a challenge to the constitutionality of the Vietnam war from the Massachusetts legislature.

▶ FOREIGN AFFAIRS

During 1970, United States concern was focused on three areas: Southeast Asia, the Middle East, and Latin America. In Southeast Asia, American soldiers were still fighting in Vietnam. For a short period, they also fought in Cambodia. Still, President Nixon, as he had promised, brought more American soldiers home.

In the Middle East, the United States took the initiative. It proposed a cease-fire that was accepted by the Israelis and the Arabs. For the last half of the year, fighting was at a standstill as efforts went forward to arrange a permanent peace.

For the most part, the United States stayed out of Latin-American affairs as much as possible. Still, the election of a Marxist as president of Chile caused great concern in Washington.

Though concerned by these events, the United States tried very hard to improve its relations with the Soviet Union. The major thrust was toward working out a plan to limit strategic nuclear weapons.

The Indochina War

In 1970 the Vietnam war became the Indochina war, as fighting spilled over into Cambodia.

As the year began, the suspension of bombing raids over North Vietnam continued. President Nixon also promised to gradually withdraw all American troops from the war. In February, in a message entitled "United States Foreign Policy for the 1970's: A New Strategy for Peace," the

U.S. Defense Secretary Melvin Laird (left) watches an Army colonel pinpoint North Vietnamese and Vietcong sanctuaries inside Cambodia. U.S. troops entered Cambodia in April and May.

President reaffirmed the "Nixon Doctrine" of 1969. This doctrine states that the United States will stick to its worldwide treaty commitments. However, more emphasis will be placed on U.S. co-operation and partnership with the nations involved. Further, greater care will be used in determining where U.S. interests lie.

Referring to South Vietnam, the President said that "tangible progress" had been made in the Vietnamization program. This program is an effort to let the South Vietnamese themselves conduct the war and do more of the fighting. Toward this end, the South Vietnamese armed forces have been greatly strengthened. The President also said that the pacification program is succeeding. This program is an effort to protect Vietnamese citizens from guerrilla Vietcong attacks.

There was a general lull in the fighting from September 1969 to April 1970. In that month, however, the Communists began attacking and shelling American bases. Then, on April 30, President Nixon announced that he was sending American and South Vietnamese troops into Cambodia. The President called the invasion a temporary one and said that it would last only six or eight weeks. He said the invasion had a limited goal: to destroy communist supplies and hiding places just over the Cambodia border.

The President's announcement was met by immediate and widespread protest. He saw the Cambodian invasion as a short-term effort to help shorten the war. But his critics saw it as an escalation of the Vietnam conflict.

Thousands of students demonstrated on hundreds of campuses. In many places, there was violence. In Washington, D.C., nearly 100,000 people protested on May 9. A few days later the administration announced the first troop withdrawals from Cambodia. The President also said all troops would be taken out of Cambodia by June 30. The last troops actually left on June 29. This was the same day the Senate by a vote of 58–37 enacted the Church-Cooper amendment. This amendment prohibits the President from spending money for future

Captain Ernest Medina: accused of killing Vietnamese civilians. Reports of atrocities by U.S. soldiers in Vietnam continued to mount in 1970.

Cambodian operations without Congressional approval. The same Senate, in September, defeated the McGovern-Hatfield "end the war" amendment.

Meanwhile, the Paris peace talks went on. But little or no progress was made. In August, David K. Bruce replaced Henry Cabot Lodge as the chief U.S. delegate.

In early September, 14 senators urged President Nixon to propose a standstill cease-fire in Vietnam. Later in the month, at Paris, the Vietcong presented an eight-point plan to end the war. The plan called for the withdrawal of all U.S. troops by June 30, 1971, and for talks about releasing prisoners of war. But the Vietcong said they would agree to a cease-fire only after all other points in their proposal were agreed to.

The United States did not like the Vietcong proposals, and on October 7 President Nixon presented his own plan. It called for an immediate cease-fire, and an extended peace conference that would deal with Laos and Cambodia as well as Vietnam. The President also called for the immediate release of all prisoners of war. The plan was given to the Vietcong on October 8 in Paris. But they immediately denounced it. No progress was made at the peace talks for the rest of the year.

The Middle East

During the first half of 1970, tensions continued to build in the Middle East. For a time it seemed that there would be a new war. But in July the United States proposed, and Israel and the Arabs agreed to, a three-month cease-fire. The plan went into effect in early August, but there was little movement toward a genuine peace. Almost immediately, Israel accused Egypt of violating the cease-fire and broke off talks.

Other events complicated matters. First, Egyptian President Gamal Abdel Nasser died suddenly on September 28. This happened shortly after Palestine commandos had hijacked several Western planes and forced them to land in Jordan. The hijackings led to a civil war between the Palestinians and the Jordanian Army.

During all this turmoil, President Nixon was visiting Europe and the U.S. Sixth Fleet in the Mediterranean. He planned to stage a show of force in the Mediterranean, but canceled the military show when Nasser died.

The cease-fire ran out in November, without any serious talks taking place. Both sides agreed to extend the cease-fire for another three months. The United States put pressure on Israel to resume talks.

Israeli Foreign Minister Abba Eban (left) meets with U.S. Secretary of State William Rogers to discuss the continuing crisis in the Middle East.

Galo Plaza, secretary-general of the Organization of American States (left), meets with U.S. Secretary of State Rogers (center) and Fernando Amiama Tio of the Dominican Republic to discuss the wave of diplomatic kidnapings in Latin America.

The United States also stepped up arms deliveries to Israel. This was done because the Soviet Union had supplied Egypt with very modern weapons, including ground-to-air missiles.

At year's end, Israel still held Arab land it had seized during the 1967 war. The Arabs still demanded the return of this territory. Peace seemed a long way off.

Latin America

The United States tried as much as possible in 1970 not to become involved in Latin-American affairs. Still, American diplomats were disturbed by the trend toward authoritarian regimes of the far Right and the far Left. In October it was estimated that 12 Latin-American nations with over 62 per cent of the area's 270,000,000 people were ruled by far-Right and far-Left regimes. The United States seemed unable to halt this trend.

The situation in Chile illustrated the problem. Dr. Salvador Allende Gossens, a Marxist, was elected president by the Chilean Congress after he had polled 36 per cent of the popular vote in a three-way race. The United States feared that a Marxist Chile might have even greater influence than communist Cuba in the hemisphere. Still, Washington realized that any attempt to interfere would not succeed. Rather, it would only decrease the United States' already low prestige in Latin America. Ralph Dungan, a former U.S. ambassador to Chile, urged Americans to "adopt an attitude of studied neu-

THE THREAT

ESTIMATED DATE
AS OF FEB. 70

CHINESE ICBM FIRST TEST 1970
CHINESE ICBM EARLIEST OPERATIONAL DATE ... 1973
SOVIET ICBM's OPERATIONAL .... OVER 1100
SOVIET SS-9's OPERATIONAL OR
UNDER CONSTRUCTION .... OVER 275
SOVIET Y CLASS SUBMARINES WITH SLBM's OVER 9

FY 71 RECOMMENDATION

UPPER
NORTHWEST   MALMSTROM
AFB

CENTRAL
CALIFORNIA

WARREN AFB

SOUTHERN
CALIFORNIA   WHITEMAN

PHASE I -
CONTINUE   CENTRAL TEXAS

AUTHORIZE
NEW SITE

AUTHORIZE ADVANCED PREPARATION

At a Pentagon press conference, Defense Secretary Melvin Laird explains why
the Government wants to build a new antiballistic-missile installation. Laird
cited the nuclear threat from both the Soviet Union and Communist China.

trality toward South America and let them
work things out for themselves."

U.S.–Soviet Relations

Because the United States and the Soviet
Union were on opposing sides in the Vietnam and Middle East conflicts, relations between the two superpowers remained cool
during the year. President Nixon admitted
that these relations were "far from satisfac-
tory." And Leonid Brezhnev, head of the
Soviet Communist Party, said there were
deep differences between the two nations.

Still, both sides made an effort to resolve
their differences. In January, President
Nixon said he would like to enter "an era of
negotiation" with the Soviets. And Brezhnev
said he would not rule out peaceful settlement of the issues that divide the two countries.

One positive step was the signing in February of another cultural exchange program.
But of greater importance for the peace of
the world were the continuing talks on limiting strategic weapons.

Talks were held early in the year in Vienna, Austria. The negotiators then moved
back to Helsinki, Finland, for a third round
of talks. United States and Soviet negotiators were optimistic that they could work
out a plan to limit the production and deployment of offensive weapons as well as
antimissile systems.

JOHN B. DUFF
Professor of History
Seton Hall University

THE 1970 CENSUS

Every ten years, the Federal Government makes a count of the country's population. 1970 was such a year. In every household throughout the United States, busy people took time to fill out a form provided by the Census Bureau.

Many interesting facts were revealed by the census. The population of the United States, for example, stood at 204,765,770. This was an increase of 13.3 per cent, or 24,000,000 people over the year 1960.

The census also showed that for the first time people living in suburban areas outnumber those living in large cities. But cities are still growing. More than 75 per cent of the entire population growth took place in large metropolitan areas.

According to the census, California has more people than any other state. Nearly 20,000,000 people live there. New York is second with 18,000,000 people. New Jersey is one of the smallest states (46th in size). But it has most people per square mile.

President Nixon holds up a sign showing the population of the U.S., as determined by the census.

	1970	CHANGE 1960 TO 1970	
		NUMBER	PER CENT
United States	*203,184,772	+23,861,597	+13.3
Alabama	3,444,165	+ 177,425	+ 5.4
Alaska	302,173	+ 76,006	+33.6
Arizona	1,772,482	+ 470,321	+36.1
Arkansas	1,923,295	+ 137,023	+ 7.7
California	19,953,134	+ 4,235,930	+27.0
Colorado	2,207,259	+ 453,312	+25.8
Connecticut	3,032,217	+ 496,983	+19.6
Delaware	548,104	+ 101,812	+22.8
Dist. of Columbia	756,510	− 7,446	− 1.0
Florida	6,789,443	+ 1,837,883	+37.1
Georgia	4,589,575	+ 646,459	+16.4
Hawaii	769,913	+ 137,141	+21.7
Idaho	713,008	+ 45,817	+ 6.9
Illinois	11,113,976	+ 1,032,818	+10.2
Indiana	5,193,669	+ 531,171	+11.4
Iowa	2,825,041	+ 67,504	+ 2.4
Kansas	2,249,071	+ 70,460	+ 3.2
Kentucky	3,219,311	+ 181,155	+ 6.0
Louisiana	3,643,180	+ 386,158	+11.9
Maine	993,663	+ 24,398	+ 2.5
Maryland	3,922,399	+ 821,710	+26.5
Massachusetts	5,689,170	+ 540,592	+10.5
Michigan	8,875,083	+ 1,051,889	+13.4
Minnesota	3,805,069	+ 391,205	+11.5
Mississippi	2,216,912	+ 38,771	+ 1.8

* not including overseas personnel

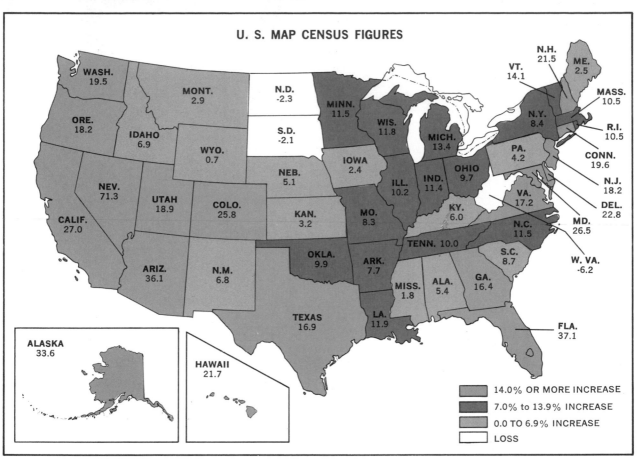

U. S. MAP CENSUS FIGURES

WASH. 19.5
MONT. 2.9
N.D. -2.3
MINN. 11.5
VT. 14.1
N.H. 21.5
ME. 2.5
ORE. 18.2
IDAHO 6.9
S.D. -2.1
WIS. 11.8
MICH. 13.4
MASS. 10.5
N.Y. 8.4
R.I. 10.5
NEV. 71.3
WYO. 0.7
IOWA 2.4
PA. 4.2
CONN. 19.6
UTAH 18.9
COLO. 25.8
NEB. 5.1
ILL. 10.2
IND. 11.4
OHIO 9.7
N.J. 18.2
DEL. 22.8
CALIF. 27.0
KAN. 3.2
MO. 8.3
KY. 6.0
VA. 17.2
MD. 26.5
ARIZ. 36.1
N.M. 6.8
OKLA. 9.9
ARK. 7.7
TENN. 10.0
N.C. 11.5
W. VA. -6.2
S.C. 8.7
MISS. 1.8
ALA. 5.4
GA. 16.4
TEXAS 16.9
LA. 11.9
FLA. 37.1

ALASKA 33.6

HAWAII 21.7

	14.0% OR MORE INCREASE
	7.0% to 13.9% INCREASE
	0.0 TO 6.9% INCREASE
	LOSS

	1970	CHANGE 1960 TO 1970	
		NUMBER	PER CENT
Missouri	4,677,399	+ 357,586	+ 8.3
Montana	694,409	+ 19,642	+ 2.9
Nebraska	1,483,791	+ 72,461	+ 5.1
Nevada	488,738	+ 203,460	+71.3
New Hampshire	737,681	+ 130,760	+21.5
New Jersey	7,168,164	+ 1,101,382	+18.2
New Mexico	1,016,000	+ 64,977	+ 6.8
New York	18,190,740	+ 1,408,436	+ 8.4
North Carolina	5,082,059	+ 525,904	+11.5
North Dakota	617,761	− 14,685	− 2.3
Ohio	10,652,017	+ 945,620	+ 9.7
Oklahoma	2,559,253	+ 230,969	+ 9.9
Oregon	2,091,385	+ 322,698	+18.2
Pennsylvania	11,793,909	+ 474,543	+ 4.2
Rhode Island	949,723	+ 90,235	+10.5
South Carolina	2,590,516	+ 207,922	+ 8.7
South Dakota	666,257	− 14,257	− 2.1
Tennessee	3,924,164	+ 357,075	+10.0
Texas	11,196,730	+ 1,617,053	+16.9
Utah	1,059,273	+ 168,646	+18.9
Vermont	444,732	+ 54,851	+14.1
Virginia	4,648,494	+ 681,545	+17.2
Washington	3,409,169	+ 555,955	+19.5
West Virginia	1,744,237	− 116,184	− 6.2
Wisconsin	4,417,933	+ 466,156	+11.8
Wyoming	332,416	+ 2,350	+ 0.7

381

WEST INDIES

THE islands of the Caribbean Sea are separated not only by stretches of water, but by the different languages and cultures. But whether the inhabitants speak English, Spanish, French, or Dutch, each island seeks its own identity. At the same time, common needs are beginning to stimulate regional co-operation.

There are 51 inhabited islands in the Caribbean archipelago. Four large islands make up the northern half. They are Cuba, Hispaniola (shared by Haiti and the Dominican Republic), Jamaica, and Puerto Rico. They have over 80,000 square miles of land. The remaining 47 islands share the rest of the land, about 8,000 square miles. Many of the difficulties and problems the islands face spring from the smallness of the land.

On many of the islands, people of African descent are in a large majority. East Indians are an important segment of the population, particularly on Trinidad and Tobago. Race has always been an important factor in the West Indies. There is now a strong black-power movement in the Caribbean. It is both an affirmation of black dignity, merit, and equality, and a claim that a country should control its resources.

Soldiers in Port of Spain, Trinidad, stand guard after some Army troops rebelled against the Government. The uprising was instigated by black-power militants.

Unrest in the West Indies has been caused by lack of jobs, lack of educational opportunities, and high birth rates. The various island governments have been trying to remedy this situation. In Jamaica, for example, the Government has begun a family-planning service (left). And the University of the West Indies now has campuses on Jamaica, Trinidad (below), and Barbados.

REGIONAL DEVELOPMENTS

The English-speaking countries, now called the Commonwealth Caribbean, have taken two important steps toward co-operative effort in economic development. In 1968 they established a Caribbean Free Trade Area (CARIFTA), and there are already signs that the larger market is stimulating trade and industrial production. In January 1970, the Caribbean Development Bank began to function. Founded under United Nations leadership, this bank hopes to promote economic co-operation with particular regard to the needs of the less-developed countries. Its headquarters are in Bridgetown, Barbados. In July the mainland country of Colombia joined the bank.

In higher education, the University of the West Indies represents one of the most important regional undertakings of the Commonwealth Caribbean. Founded in 1948, it has three centers, one on Jamaica, one on Trinidad, and the newest on Barbados. Described as a university with a campus two thousand miles across, it shows how small countries can share the high cost of university education.

TRINIDAD AND TOBAGO

In April, the Government of Trinidad and Tobago put down a mutiny by a rebellious portion of the Army. The rebellion followed a series of demonstrations by black-power militants, the unemployed, and student groups. The loyalty of the police and the coast guard enabled the Government to regain control.

There have been many grievances expressed by the islanders. The rate of unemployment is high, and many of the young cannot find work. There are charges that American, British, and Canadian interests dominate the island's economy and that the Government, led by Prime Minister Eric Williams, has done little to reform this state of affairs.

The black-power movement added the spark to the unrest which had been building up. There were demonstrations and marches, demands for employment, attacks on foreign-owned places of business, and then the mutiny.

A state of emergency was declared with many arrests made. By the end of the year, all political prisoners were released, and the situation was apparently quiet. The Government has been making efforts to encourage Trinidadian-owned businesses.

JAMAICA

The Government in 1970 focused its attention on the state of the economy. A major concern was the prospect of Britain's entry into the European Economic Community (Common Market). There is a question of whether or not Britain would be allowed to continue the trade concessions to the Commonwealth Caribbean. Jamaica, along with the other Commonwealth nations, has much to lose if these preferences are not retained, and the West Indian sugar, bananas, and other agricultural products could not find a profitable market in Britain.

Another cause for anxiety was the continuing trade deficit. Jamaica must import heavy machinery and transport equipment in an effort to become industrialized. These imports are an investment in the future. On the other hand, the importation of food continued to increase, partly as a result of higher wages and greater demand.

BARBADOS

Traditionally, Barbados is a sugar island, with nine out of every ten tons of exports being sugar, molasses, or rum. The Barbados Government continued to diversify the economy in 1970 by investing in tourism and by developing a number of small industries. There was a boom in the construction industry, some of it as a result of increased tourism. The island's deep-water harbor, opened in 1961, is now too small to cope with the cargo that comes in.

CUBA

Fidel Castro, in a speech made in the summer of 1970, disclosed that Cuba's economy had failed. Castro took full responsibility for the bleak picture and offered to resign. The sugar crop, on which Castro

Cuban Premier Fidel Castro helps harvest sugar, but the 1970 crop was poor.

Joaquin Balaguer is congratulated by one of his supporters after being re-elected president of the Dominican Republic in May 16 balloting.

had placed much of his hope, was a million and a half tons short of the goal. With practically no exceptions, food, drinks, tobacco, consumer and industrial goods were in short supply, and many items will have to be rationed even more strictly.

Chile resumed full relations with Cuba in 1970. Six years earlier the Organization of American States had decided to isolate Cuba by severing diplomatic, commercial, and transportation ties.

The United States reported some sort of construction at Cienfuegos on the southern coast of Cuba and speculated that the Soviet Union was building a submarine base. It was learned that the Russians had removed equipment from Cienfuegos, and the whole incident was played down.

▶ DOMINICAN REPUBLIC

President Joaquin Balaguer was re-elected to a second term as president of the Dominican Republic. The Dominican Revolutionary Party, led by Juan Bosch, boycotted the election, claiming that it would not be an honest one.

Even though the Dominican Republic received grants and loans from the United States, and President Balaguer tried to keep government expenses down, the economy of this country showed only slight improvement in 1970. Unemployment was very high. Land reform and irrigation must be expanded to improve agriculture.

Many Dominicans complained that the Balaguer Government represses any opposition to the regime.

▶ HAITI

Three coast guard cutters attempted to shell the presidential palace of François Duvalier, but failed to make any direct hit. All but one of the rebels asked for and received asylum in the United States. The boats were returned to Haiti.

Reports from Port-au-Prince indicated that political prisoners and some members of the rebels' families had been executed.

▶ PUERTO RICO

The small island of Culebra, a municipality of Puerto Rico, was the subject of much controversy in 1970. The United States Navy has been using the uninhabited part of this island of 900 people for target practice. Reports on the subject were made for the governor of Puerto Rico and for the United States Navy, and it appears certain that the Navy will stop the practice in the next few years.

▶ VIRGIN ISLANDS

Melvin H. Evans became the first popularly elected governor of the American Virgin Islands. He had also been the last governor appointed by the president of the United States.

SIR PHILIP SHERLOCK
Secretary-General
Association of Caribbean Universities

Youth Organizations

THE major youth organizations in the United States accepted new challenges in the opening year of the 1970's. A new awareness of opportunities for service marked the programs of the Boy Scouts of America, Boys' Clubs of America, Camp Fire Girls, 4-H Clubs, Future Farmers of America, and Girl Scouts of the U.S.A. Expansion was the order of the day in each organization. Membership drives were carried on in such a way that ghetto dwellers and minority-group members everywhere might learn of the organizations and wish to join them. Many social-service programs were added to the roster of regular activities. The urgency of the needs these programs filled lent a special zest to the work involved in executing them.

In all the organizations, outdoor and recreational activities remained important—but they were now almost always coupled with efforts to conserve the environment. Several of the organizations gave training in how to fight pollution, and many actual cleanup projects were undertaken.

Internationalism flourished. Most of the organizations in the United States sent some members to visit foreign countries, where they usually lived and worked with families. Overseas counterparts of the U.S. organizations in turn sent youngsters to visit the U.S.

All the youth organizations geared themselves to the new trends of the new times. They refashioned themselves as channels for youth's vigorous determination to make the world a better place.

President Nixon presents a plaque to James Heath, 17, who was named Boy of the Year by the Boys' Clubs of America. Heath was cited as typifying juvenile decency in action.

A Girl Scout helps young children from an inner-city ghetto learn how to read.

Boy Scouts collect aluminum cans for recycling.

A young Future Farmer of America works on a farm in West Germany.

GIRL SCOUTS OF THE U.S.A.

In 1970 the Girl Scouts continued to serve their communities in imaginative and useful ways. Among their many service projects were day camps for children of migrant workers, remedial-reading classes for problem readers, and special-training sessions for mentally retarded youngsters. The Girl Scouts' longtime interest in conservation work spurred other community groups to join them in carrying out such projects as the "Hackensack River Cleanup."

A nationwide effort called ACTION 70 was mounted by all 3,922,000 members of the Girl Scouts. Its aim was to combat prejudice and foster understanding among people everywhere. One of its goals was to extend Scouting activities to minority-group youngsters and adults.

During the summer months thousands of "camperships" were awarded to minority-group boys and girls and to other youngsters of limited means. Family Camp Weekends were found to be a good way to involve parents of campers in Girl Scout programs. Under ACTION 70, Girl Scout membership drives were mounted in poverty areas. And Girl Scout troops everywhere were encouraged to explore the cultures, arts, and crafts

A Girl Scout learns how to ride bareback during a field trip to Rhode Island.

of all ethnic and racial groups in the United States.

Nationally sponsored Girl Scout events in 1970 included a "Wyoming Trek" to Girl Scouting's National Center West. The Center is a 13,000-acre property owned by the Girl Scouts in a wildly beautiful part of northern Wyoming. From 34 states and 4 foreign nations came 1,750 girls to stay one or two weeks in this unspoiled, mountainous region. Girls could choose among such varied activities as archeological digs, backpacking trips into the wilderness, geological explorations, horseback riding, and trips to nearby places of interest. Visits were arranged to Big Horn National Forest and other areas rich in American lore.

Another exciting event of 1970 was the visit of 131 Senior Scouts to Cape Kennedy,

Florida, to see the Apollo 12 moon shot. The Scouts were guests of the National Aeronautics and Space Administration.

A Girl Scout-governed community named Panorama City, U.S.A., was set up at a Girl Scout residence camp in Elkhorn, Wisconsin. The "citizens" (264) elected a "city council" and "mayor." "Speakouts" on the major concerns facing youth today were held in "coffeehouses."

On the international scene during 1970, more than 100 U.S.A. Girl Scouts took part in overseas "exploration" trips and home visits. Forty-eight Girl Guides and Scouts from member countries of the World Association of Girl Guides and Girl Scouts attended events in the United States. Twenty-four Girl Guides from 12 nations joined 24 U.S.A. Girl Scouts in a 3-week workshop in Community Service through Folk Songs and Folk Games. After the workshop ended, each Girl Guide accompanied a U.S.A. Girl Scout to her home community to teach the games and folk songs they had learned to underprivileged and ethnic-group youngsters. They visited these youngsters at Head Start centers, day camps, ghetto park projects, and on Indian reservations.

Twenty-four girls, including 8 from the United States, attended a study session on hunger at the International Girl Guide/Girl Scout Center at Sangam, India. Forty-two girls made international "explorations" to Austria, Brazil, Spain, and the Philippines. Twenty-three girls made "home visits" to families in Chile, Peru, Finland, and Iceland. Four U.S. girls attended a "Guide Caravan" in England.

Girl Scout national headquarters in New York City welcomed two important visitors in 1970. In February, Mrs. Richard M. Nixon, a former Girl Scout volunteer, flew to New York for her investiture as Honorary President of the Girl Scouts of the U.S.A. In July, Lady Olave Baden-Powell, World Chief Guide and widow of the founder of the Boy Scouts, also visited the New York headquarters. She then made a brief trip to the national organization's Edith Macy Training Center in Briarcliff Manor, New York.

RICHARD KNOX
Girl Scouts of the U.S.A.

BOY SCOUTS OF AMERICA

During 1970 the Boy Scouts of America increased its efforts to reach its goals for BOYPOWER '76. This is an 8-year program to improve the quality of Scouting and to bring it to more boys. BOYPOWER '76 began in January 1969. It aims to make Scouting available to at least one third of all American boys from 8 to 17 years old, by the end of 1976.

As part of the campaign, the recruiting of new Scouts was stepped up in urban ghettos and rural poverty pockets. Tens of thousands of needy children, both Scouts and non-Scouts, in these areas went to Scout camps during the summer.

About 2,500,000 Cub Scouts (boys 8 to 10 years old) enjoyed weekly den meetings and monthly pack meetings during 1970. Their programs of work and play focused on such themes as nature, sports competitions (called Cub Scout Olympics), and magic.

Boy Scouts, who are from 11 to 17 years old, spent their time mastering the skills of Scouting (such as setting up camps and building fires) and having fun outdoors with their patrols and troops. Many troops took part in community-service projects.

The highlight of the year for the Explorers (young people from 14 to 17) was the First National Explorer Olympics. The event, held in co-operation with the United States Olympic Committee, took place at Colorado State University, Fort Collins, Colorado, between August 24 and August 28. The Olympics brought together 1,500 Explorers from nearly every state to compete in track and field, swimming and other sports.

During 1970, thousands of young women joined Explorer posts as "Explorer participants" and took part in many activities.

Membership in the Boy Scouts of America continued to increase in 1970. At year's end, the total number of members was nearly 5,000,000, and the number of adult leaders was 1,750,000. Continued steady growth is expected during the remaining 6 years of BOYPOWER '76.

ALDEN G. BARBER
Chief Scout Executive
Boy Scouts of America

4-H CLUBS

"We Care" was the theme of National 4-H Week, which was observed from October 4 to October 10, 1970. And throughout 1970, 4-H'ers everywhere showed real concern for the problems of their communities and country. With the "4 H's" (Head-Heart-Hands-Health), members helped to fight air and water pollution, poverty, hunger, and drug abuse. They also gave help to the mentally and physically handicapped. They tried to improve their neighborhoods, equip themselves for future jobs, and understand people of other cultures.

The number of youths taking part in the 4-H program in all fifty states, Washington, D.C., Puerto Rico, and the Virgin Islands rose to nearly four million in 1970. Most undertook "learn by doing" projects in such areas as family living, personal development, conservation, money management, agricultural production, and engineering.

From April 19 to 24 the National 4-H Conference was held in Washington, D.C. A highlight of the conference was groundbreaking for the expanded National 4-H Center on the outskirts of Washington, D.C.

Conference delegates spent much time in work-study or discussion groups. Among topics explored were: big-city nutrition, world hunger, human environment, and intergroup and interrace relations.

All 4-H members who attended the National 4-H Congress in Chicago were state, regional, or national winners of awards. More than 200 of these 4-H'ers received college scholarships valued at $500 to $1,600.

During 1970, 153 young men and women were International Farm Youth Exchangees. These youths traveled to other countries to live and work on farms, usually for about 6 months. Eighty young people from 40 U.S. states lived in other countries in 1970, and 71 youths from other countries visited the United States. Thirty-two countries participated in the plan.

E. DEAN VAUGHAN
4-H Programs

CAMP FIRE GIRLS

In 1970 the Camp Fire Girls' slogan, "Give Service," took on added meaning. With the help of a grant from the Sears Roebuck Foundation, the Camp Fire Girls opened several inner-city workshops.

In Birmingham, Alabama, Camp Fire was determined to offer its programs to all the youth: black and white, boys and girls. Camp Fire's local council ran a 3-week day camp for 6-to-14-year-olds from Birmingham's mostly black South Side. The main purpose was to show the South Side children the world beyond their local neighborhood.

The Smithville Youth Program, for boys and girls age 14 to 19, was held in an all-black neighborhood in Birmingham. The members met one evening a week to talk about topics of current concern.

In Kansas City, Missouri, interns in the National Teachers Corps enlisted the aid of Camp Fire in setting up a program of activities for inner-city girls. Camp Fire recognized that the children's interest had to be aroused before they would have a real wish to join Camp Fire. So a different kind of duty was provided each girl each week, on a try-and-see basis. One week a girl might plan the menu and buy the food for the group's midday meal. Another week she might write letters and arrange for guest speakers. Or she might write a poem or a song on a Camp Fire theme. Gradually, as the girls gained a sense of belonging to the group, they asked to join the Camp Fire Girls.

In 1970, Camp Fire members were hard at work planning for the third Horizon Club Conference. (Horizon Club is for girls 14 through about 18 years old.) The conference is to be called Aware '71 and will take place in June and July 1971 on five college campuses. About 2,500 teen-agers and adults are expected to attend. The conference will concern itself with such problems as conservation and ecology, war and peace, drugs and escapism, crime and justice.

AUDREY M. HUDSON
Camp Fire Girls, Inc.

BOYS' CLUBS OF AMERICA

In 1970 the Boys' Clubs of America made great efforts to bring their services to "every needy boy." One way they did this was by expanding inner-city programs. Another way was to establish more clubs. In 1970 the total number of Boys' Clubs grew to 880. The total membership grew to 875,000.

In December 1969 a 5-year "Drive for Decency" was ushered in at a White House dinner hosted by President Richard Nixon. At the dinner, which honored the Boys' Clubs' national board of directors, the Drive for Decency's goal of reaching 3,000,000 more boys during the first half of the 1970's was announced.

Recognizing that each community's needs are different, the Boys' Clubs plan to find out what help is most needed in each town or city they serve. Then, often through the activities of the Keystone Clubs (organizations of mid-teen-age youths), Boys' Club members will use their imagination and skills to help solve community problems.

Boys' Club scholarships and grants helped dozens of deserving boys go to college in 1970. Many of the boys would not have been able to continue their education without this financial aid. Boys with talent in music and art also received money to continue their studies from funds such as the Epstein Memorial Foundation. Boys' Club members without college ambitions were offered basic training in trades such as printing, radio and television repair, carpentry, and automotive mechanics. One Club ran a radio station, and another offered training in operating TV stations.

National Boys' Club Week was celebrated in hundreds of cities and towns from March 15 to March 21. The climax of the week was a White House ceremony at which the President installed James Heath of the Catskill, New York, Boys' Club as "Boy of the Year" and the nation's leading example of "Juvenile Decency." James received a $4,000 scholarship from the Reader's Digest Foundation. He was described by President Richard Nixon, a past Boys' Clubs of America board chairman, as "symbolizing the very best we produce in America."

E. J. STAPLETON
Boys' Clubs of America

In Gainesville, Florida, as well as in other American cities, members of the Boys' Clubs helped clean up their community and thus improve their environment.

FUTURE FARMERS OF AMERICA

The Future Farmers of America (FFA), the national organization for students of agriculture, grew to more than 430,000 members in 1970. FFA chapters were active in 8,000 high schools in 49 of the 50 U.S. states and in Puerto Rico, the Virgin Islands, and Guam.

A new nationwide community action program called "Building Our American Communities" was begun in 1970. Its purpose is to get FFA members involved in community activities. The new program will give over 5,000 awards to FFA chapters that carry out major projects aimed at making their communities better places in which to live and work.

In October more than 15,000 FFA members and guests attended the 1970 National FFA Convention in Kansas City, Missouri. The Star Farmer of America award was given to Merrill Kelsay, a 21-year-old dairy-and-crop farmer from Whiteland, Indiana. This is the nation's top honor for a young farmer. Earl M. Weaver, 21, of Middletown, Pennsylvania, was named Star Agribusinessman of America. This is the top award to an FFA member working in an agriculture-related business. Both Kelsay and Weaver received $1,000 cash awards.

Kevin Hall, of Gaithersburg, Maryland, won the National Public Speaking contest, another highlight of the convention. The title of his winning speech was "A Thing Called Leadership." A prize of $300 accompanied the honor.

At the convention's final business meeting, new national officers were elected to serve for the 1970–71 term. J. Dan Lehmann, 20, of Pleasant Plains, Illinois, was elected national president.

The FFA continued its exchange program with other nations in 1970. It sent 25 members to 9 European countries on a 3-month "work experience" program. The FFA also arranged for visits by 15 European students to U.S. farms.

Dave Dietz, National FFA vice-president of the Pacific Region, was sent to Vietnam during 1970 to help the South Vietnamese set up their own Future Farmers organization. Dietz visited schools where agriculture was taught and helped the students learn about the Future Farmer program. He urged them to work actively in the new Future Farmers of Vietnam (FFVN) organization.

A. D. REUWEE
Director of Information
Future Farmers of America

Merrill Kelsay, 21, from Whiteland, Indiana, accepts his award as Star Farmer of America.

Earl Weaver of Middletown, Pennsylvania, the FFA's Star Agribusinessman of America.

YOUNG PEOPLE IN THE NEWS

In May, 21-year-old Robin Lee Graham docked his 33-foot sloop, "Return of the Dove," at Long Beach, California. In doing so, he became the youngest person to have sailed alone around the world. He started out when he was 16, and acquired a wife, whom he met in Fiji, and four cats along the way.

Petite and pretty as a picture, nine-year-old Taryn Thomas was crowned Little Miss America.

The World Youth Orchestra, conducted by Erich Leinsdorf, made its debut in Copenhagen.

A Los Angeles lass, Rewa C. Walsh, was named Miss Teenage America in 1970.

Kenneth Robinson: named Outstanding Teenager of America for his work with a retarded child.

STATISTICAL SUPPLEMENT

NATIONS OF THE WORLD

NATION	CAPITAL	AREA (in sq. mi.)	POPULATION (in millions)	HEAD OF STATE AND/OR GOVERNMENT
AFGHANISTAN	Kabul	250,000	17.0	Mohammad Zahir Shah—king Noor Ahmad Etemadi—prime minister
ALBANIA	Tirana	11,100	2.2	Enver Hoxha—communist party secretary Mehmet Shehu—premier
ALGERIA	Algiers	919,593	14.0	Houari Boumedienne—president
ARGENTINA	Buenos Aires	1,072,158	24.3	Roberto Marcelo Levingston—president
AUSTRALIA	Canberra	2,967,909	12.5	John G. Gorton—prime minister Sir Paul Hasluck—governor-general
AUSTRIA	Vienna	32,374	7.4	Bruno Kreisky—chancellor Franz Jonas—president
BARBADOS	Bridgetown	166	.3	Errol W. Barrow—prime minister Sir Winston Scott—governor-general
BELGIUM	Brussels	11,781	9.7	Baudouin I—king Gaston Eyskens—prime minister
BOLIVIA	La Paz	424,163	4.6	Juan Jose Torres Gonzales—president
BOTSWANA	Gaberones	231,804	.6	Sir Seretse Khama—president
BRAZIL	Brasilia	3,286,478	93.0	Emilio Garrastazu Medici—president
BULGARIA	Sofia	42,823	8.5	Todor Zhivkov—communist party secretary Georgi Traikov—president of the presidium
BURMA	Rangoon	261,789	27.7	Ne Win—chairman of the revolutionary council
BURUNDI	Usumbura	10,747	3.6	Michel Micombero—president
CAMBODIA	Pnompenh	69,898	7.1	Lon Nol—premier Chen Heng—head of state
CAMEROUN	Yaoundé	183,569	5.8	Ahmadou Ahidjo—president
CANADA	Ottawa	3,851,809	21.4	Pierre Elliott Trudeau—prime minister Roland Michener—governor-general
CENTRAL AFRICAN REP.	Bangui	240,535	1.5	Jean Bedel Bokassa—president
CEYLON	Colombo	25,332	12.6	Sirimavo Bandaranaike—prime minister Sir William Gopallawa—governor-general
CHAD	Fort-Lamy	495,754	3.7	François Tombalbaye—president

NATION	CAPITAL	AREA (in sq. mi.)	POPULATION (in millions)	HEAD OF STATE AND/OR GOVERNMENT
CHILE	Santiago	292,259	9.8	Salvador Allende Gossens—president
CHINA (COMMUNIST)	Peking	3,691,512	759.6	Mao Tse-tung—chairman Chou En-lai—premier
CHINA (NATIONALIST)	Taipei	13,885	14.0	Chiang Kai-shek—president C. K. Yen—premier
COLOMBIA	Bogota	439,736	21.4	Misael Pastrana Borrero—president
CONGO (Brazzaville)	Brazzaville	132,047	.9	Marien Ngouabi—president
CONGO (Kinshasa)	Kinshasa	905,565	17.4	Joseph Mobutu—president
COSTA RICA	San Jose	19,575	1.8	Jose Figueres Ferrer—president
CUBA	Havana	44,218	8.5	Fidel Castro—prime minister Osvaldo Dorticos Torrado—president
CYPRUS	Nicosia	3,572	.6	Archbishop Makarios II—president
CZECHOSLOVAKIA	Prague	49,370	14.7	Gustav Husak—communist party secretary Ludvik Svoboda—president Lubomir Strougal—premier
DAHOMEY	Porto-Novo	43,483	2.7	Hubert Maga—president
DENMARK	Copenhagen	16,629	4.9	Frederik IX—king Hilmar Baunsgaard—prime minister
DOMINICAN REP.	Santo Domingo	18,816	4.3	Joaquin Balaguer—president
ECUADOR	Quito	109,483	6.1	Jose Maria Velasco Ibarra—president
EL SALVADOR	San Salvador	8,260	3.4	Fidel Sanchez Hernandez—president
EQUATORIAL GUINEA	Santa Isabel	10,830	.3	Francisco Macias Nguema—president
ETHIOPIA	Addis Ababa	471,777	25.0	Haile Selassie I—emperor
FIJI	Suva	7,055	.533	Ratu Kamisese Mara—prime minister
FINLAND	Helsinki	130,120	4.7	Urho K. Kekkonen—president Ahti Karjalainen—prime minister
FRANCE	Paris	211,207	51.1	Georges Pompidou—president Jacques Chaban-Delmas—premier
GABON	Libreville	103,346	.5	Albert B. Bongo—president
GAMBIA	Bathurst	4,361	.4	Sir Dauda K. Jawara—president
GERMANY (East)	East Berlin	41,610	16.2	Walter Ulbricht—chairman of the council of state Willi Stoph—premier
GERMANY (West)	Bonn	95,743	58.6	Willy Brandt—chancellor Gustav Heinemann—president

NATION	CAPITAL	AREA (in sq. mi.)	POPULATION (in millions)	HEAD OF STATE AND/OR GOVERNMENT
GHANA	Accra	92,099	9.0	Kofi A. Busia—prime minister Edward Akufo Addo—president
GREECE	Athens	50,944	8.9	Constantine II—king (in exile) George Papadopoulos—premier
GUATEMALA	Guatemala City	42,042	5.1	Carlos Arana Osorio—president
GUINEA	Conakry	94,926	3.9	Sékou Touré—president
GULF EMIRATES, FEDERATION OF	Abu Dhabi	36,531	.5	Zayed ibn Sultan al-Mihayan—president
GUYANA	Georgetown	83,000	.7	Forbes Burnham—prime minister Arthur Chung—president
HAITI	Port-au-Prince	10,714	5.2	François Duvalier—president
HONDURAS	Tegucigalpa	43,277	2.7	Oswaldo Lopez Arellano—president
HUNGARY	Budapest	35,919	10.3	Janos Kadar—communist party secretary Jeno Fock—premier
ICELAND	Reykjavik	39,768	.2	Kristjan Eldjarn—president Johann Hafstein—prime minister
INDIA	New Delhi	1,261,813	554.6	Indira Gandhi—prime minister V. V. Giri—president
INDONESIA	Jakarta	575,894	121.2	Suharto—president
IRAN	Tehran	636,294	28.4	Mohammad Riza Pahlevi—shah Amir Abbas Hoveida—premier
IRAQ	Baghdad	167,925	9.7	Ahmad Hassan al-Bakr—president
IRELAND	Dublin	27,136	3.0	Eamon de Valera—president John M. Lynch—prime minister
ISRAEL	Jerusalem	7,992	3.0	Golda Meir—prime minister Schneor Zalman Shazar—president
ITALY	Rome	116,303	53.7	Emilio Colombo—premier Giuseppe Saragat—president
IVORY COAST	Abidjan	124,503	4.3	Felix Houphouet-Boigny—president
JAMAICA	Kingston	4,232	2.0	Hugh Shearer—prime minister Sir Clifford Campbell—governor-general
JAPAN	Tokyo	142,811	103.5	Hirohito—emperor Eisaku Sâto—prime minister
JORDAN	Amman	37,738	2.3	Hussein I—king Wasfi al-Tal—premier
KENYA	Nairobi	224,959	10.9	Jomo Kenyatta—president
KOREA (North)	Pyongyang	46,540	13.9	Kim Il Sung—premier
KOREA (South)	Seoul	38,922	32.1	Chung Hee Park—president Paik Too Chin—premier

NATION	CAPITAL	AREA (in sq. mi.)	POPULATION (in millions)	HEAD OF STATE AND/OR GOVERNMENT
KUWAIT	Kuwait	6,178	.7	Sabah al-Salim al-Sabah—head of state
LAOS	Vientiane	91,429	3.0	Savang Vatthana—king Souvanna Phouma—premier
LEBANON	Beirut	4,015	2.8	Suleiman Franjieh—president Saeb Salaam—premier
LESOTHO	Maseru	11,720	1.0	Leabua Jonathan—prime minister
LIBERIA	Monrovia	43,000	1.2	William Tubman—president
LIBYA	Tripoli	679,360	1.9	Muammar al-Qaddafi—head of the revolutionary council, and premier
LIECHTENSTEIN	Vaduz	61	.023	Francis Joseph II—prince
LUXEMBOURG	Luxembourg	999	.4	Jean—grand duke Pierre Werner—premier
MALAGASY REP.	Tananarive	226,657	6.9	Philibert Tsiranana—president
MALAWI	Zomba	45,747	4.4	Hastings K. Banda—president
MALAYSIA	Kuala Lumpur	128,430	10.8	Abdul Halim Muazzam—head of state Tun Abdul Razak—prime minister
MALDIVE ISLANDS	Male	115	.108	Ibrahim Nasir—president
MALI	Bamako	478,765	5.1	Moussa Traore—president
MALTA	Valletta	122	.3	Giorgio B. Olivier—prime minister
MAURITANIA	Nouakchott	397,954	1.2	Moktar O. Daddah—president
MAURITIUS	Port Louis	720	.9	Sir Seewoosagur Ramgoolam—prime minister Sir Arthur Leonard Williams—governor-general
MEXICO	Mexico City	761,602	50.7	Luis Echeverria Alvarez—president
MONACO	Monaco	0.4	.023	Rainier III—prince
MONGOLIA	Ulan Bator	604,248	1.3	Zhamsarangin Sambu—head of state
MOROCCO	Rabat	172,997	15.7	Hassan II—king Ahmad Laraki—prime minister
NAURU		8	.007	Hammer DeRoburt—head of state
NEPAL	Katmandu	54,362	11.2	Mahendra Bir Bikram Shah Deva—king
NETHERLANDS	Amsterdam	12,978	13.0	Juliana—queen Petrus J. S. de Jong—prime minister
NEW ZEALAND	Wellington	103,736	2.9	Keith J. Holyoake—prime minister Sir Arthur Porritt—governor-general

NATION	CAPITAL	AREA (in sq. mi.)	POPULATION (in millions)	HEAD OF STATE AND/OR GOVERNMENT
NICARAGUA	Managua	50,193	2.0	Anastasio Somoza Debayle, Jr.—president
NIGER	Niamey	489,190	3.8	Hamani Diori—president
NIGERIA	Lagos	356,668	55.1	Yakubu Gowon—head of state
NORWAY	Oslo	125,181	3.9	Olav V—king Per Borten—prime minister
OMAN	Muscat	82,030	.8	Qabus ibn Said—sultan
PAKISTAN	Islamabad	365,528	136.9	Agha Mohammad Yahya Kahn—president
PANAMA	Panama	29,205	1.5	Demetrio Lakas Bahas—president
PARAGUAY	Asuncion	157,047	2.4	Alfredo Stroessner—president
PERU	Lima	496,223	13.6	Juan Velasco Alvarado—president
PHILIPPINES	Quezon City	115,830	38.1	Ferdinand E. Marcos—president
POLAND	Warsaw	120,664	33.0	Edward Gierek—communist party secretary Piotr Jaroszewicz—premier Jozef Cyrankiewicz—president of the council of state
PORTUGAL	Lisbon	35,553	9.6	Americo Thomaz—president Marcelo Caetano—premier
RHODESIA	Salisbury	150,333	5.0	Ian D. Smith—prime minister
RUMANIA	Bucharest	91,699	20.3	Nicolae Ceausescu—communist party secretary Ion Maurer—premier
RWANDA	Kigali	10,169	3.6	Gregoire Kayibanda—president
SAUDI ARABIA	Riyadh	829,997	7.7	Faisal ibn Abdul Aziz—king
SENEGAL	Dakar	75,750	3.9	Léopold Senghor—president Abdou Diouf—prime minister
SIERRA LEONE	Freetown	27,699	2.6	Siaka Stevens—prime minister
SINGAPORE	Singapore	224	2.1	Lee Kuan Yew—prime minister
SOMALIA	Mogadishu	246,200	2.8	Mohammad Siad Barre—president of the supreme revolutionary council
SOUTH AFRICA	Pretoria Cape Town	471,444	20.1	Balthazar J. Vorster—prime minister J. J. Fouche—president
SOUTHERN YEMEN	Medina al-Shaab	112,000	1.3	Salmin Rubaya—president Mohammad Ali Haitham—prime minister
SPAIN	Madrid	194,884	33.2	Francisco Franco—head of state
SUDAN	Khartoum	967,497	15.8	Gaafar al-Nimeiry—president of the revolutionary council
SWAZILAND	Mbabane	6,704	.4	Sobhuza II—king Makhosini Dlamini—prime minister

NATION	CAPITAL	AREA (in sq. mi.)	POPULATION (in millions)	HEAD OF STATE AND/OR GOVERNMENT
SWEDEN	Stockholm	173,649	8.0	Gustaf VI Adolf—king Olof Palme—prime minister
SWITZERLAND	Bern	15,941	6.5	Rudolf Gnaegi—president
SYRIA	Damascus	71,498	6.2	Hafez al-Assad—premier Ahmad al-Khatib—head of state
TANZANIA	Dar es Salaam	362,820	13.2	Julius K. Nyerere—president
THAILAND	Bangkok	198,456	36.2	Bhumibol Adulyadej—king Thanom Kittikachorn—prime minister
TOGO	Lomé	21,622	1.9	Etienne Eyadema—president
TONGA	Nuku'alofa	270	.084	Taufa'ahau Tupou IV—king
TRINIDAD & TOBAGO	Port of Spain	1,980	1.1	Eric Williams—prime minister Sir Solomon Hochoy—governor-general
TUNISIA	Tunis	63,378	5.1	Habib Bourguiba—president Hedi Nouira—prime minister
TURKEY	Ankara	301,381	35.6	Suleyman Demirel—prime minister Cevdet Sunay—president
UGANDA	Kampala	91,134	8.6	Milton Obote—president
U.S.S.R.	Moscow	8,649,512	240.0	Leonid I. Brezhnev—communist party secretary Aleksei N. Kosygin—premier Nikolai V. Podgorny—president of the presidium
UNITED ARAB REP.	Cairo	386,660	33.9	Anwar al-Sadat—president Mahmoud Fawzi—premier
UNITED KINGDOM	London	94,212	56.0	Elizabeth II—queen Edward Heath—prime minister
UNITED STATES	Washington, D.C.	3,615,123	204.8	Richard M. Nixon—president Spiro T. Agnew—vice-president
UPPER VOLTA	Ouagadougou	105,869	5.4	Sangoule Lamizana—president
URUGUAY	Montevideo	72,172	2.9	Jorge Pacheco Areco—president
VENEZUELA	Caracas	352,143	10.8	Rafael Caldera Rodriguez—president
VIETNAM (North)	Hanoi	61,294	20.0	Le Duan—communist party secretary Ton Duc Thang—president Pham Van Dong—premier
VIETNAM (South)	Saigon	67,108	18.0	Nguyen Van Thieu—president Nguyen Cao Ky—vice-president Tran Thien Khiem—premier
WESTERN SAMOA	Apia	1,097	.143	Malietoa Tanumafili II—head of state
YEMEN	Sana	75,290	5.7	Abdul Rahman al-Iryani—president Moshen al-Aini—premier
YUGOSLAVIA	Belgrade	98,766	20.6	Josip Broz Tito—president Mitja Ribicic—premier
ZAMBIA	Lusaka	290,585	4.3	Kenneth D. Kaunda—president

THE UNITED NATIONS 25th SESSION

THE SECRETARIAT
Secretary-General: U Thant

THE GENERAL ASSEMBLY
President: Edvard Hambro (Norway)

MEMBER NATIONS AND CHIEF REPRESENTATIVES

Nation	Representative
Afghanistan	Abdur-Rahman Pazhwak
Albania	Sami Baholli
Algeria	Amar Dahmouche
Argentina	Carlos Ortiz de Rozas
Australia	Laurence McIntyre
Austria	Kurt Waldheim
Barbados	Oliver H. Jackman
Belgium	Edouard Longerstaey
Bolivia	Walter Guevara Arze
Botswana	T. J. Molefhe
Brazil	João A. de Araujo Castro
Bulgaria	Milko Tarabanov
Burma	U Soe Tin
Burundi	Nsanze Terence
Byelorussian S.S.R.	Vitaly S. Smirnov
Cambodia	Khim Tit
Cameroun	Michel Njine
Canada	Yvon Beaulne
Central African Rep.	Michel Adama-Tamboux
Ceylon	Hamilton S. Amerasinghe
Chad	Bruno Bohiadi
Chile	Jose Piñera
China	Liu Chieh
Colombia	Augusto Espinosa Valderrama
Congo (Brazzaville)	Nicolas Mondjo
Congo (Kinshasa)	Theodore Idzumbuir
Costa Rica	Jose L. Molina
Cuba	Ricardo Alarcon Quesada
Cyprus	Zenon Rossides
Czechoslovakia	Zdenek Cernik
Dahomey	Wilfrid de Souza
Denmark	Otto R. Borch
Dominican Rep.	Fernando Amiama-Tio
Ecuador	Leopoldo Benites
El Salvador	Reynaldo Galindo Pohl
Equatorial Guinea	Eduardo Ondomba
Ethiopia	Yohannes Tseghe
Fiji	Semesa K. Sikivou
Finland	Max Jakobson
France	Jacques Kosciusko-Morizet
Gabon	Jean Davin
Gambia	vacant
Ghana	Richard M. Akwei
Greece	Dimitri S. Bitsios
Guatemala	Rafael E. Castillo-Valdes
Guinea	El Hadj Abdoulaye Touré
Guyana	P. A. Thompson
Haiti	Marcel Antoine
Honduras	Salomon Jimenez Munguia
Hungary	Károly Szarka
Iceland	Hannes Kjartansson
India	Samar Sen
Indonesia	Hadji Roeslan Abdulgani
Iran	Mehdi Vakil
Iraq	Talib El-Shibib
Ireland	Cornelius C. Cremin
Israel	Yosef Tekoah
Italy	Piero Vinci
Ivory Coast	Siméon Ake
Jamaica	Keith Johnson
Japan	Senjin Tsuruoka
Jordan	Muhammad H. El-Farra
Kenya	Joseth Odero Jowi
Kuwait	Muhalhel Mohamed Al-Mudhaf
Laos	Platthana Chounramany
Lebanon	Edouard A. Ghorra
Lesotho	M. T. Mashologu
Liberia	Nathan Barnes
Libya	Mohamed Maki Abuzeid
Luxembourg	André Philippe
Malagasy Rep.	Blaise Rabetafika
Malawi	Nyemba W. Mbekeani
Malaysia	H. M. A. Zakaria
Maldive Islands	vacant
Mali	Seydou Traore
Malta	Arvid Pardo
Mauritania	Sid'Ahmed Ould Taya
Mauritius	Radha Krishna Ramphul
Mexico	Alfonso Garcia Robles
Mongolia	Mangalyn Dugersuren
Morocco	Ahmed Taibi Benhima
Nepal	Padma B. Khatri
Netherlands	Robbert Fack
New Zealand	John V. Scott
Nicaragua	Guillermo Sevilla-Sacasa
Niger	George M. Condat
Nigeria	E. O. Ogbu
Norway	Edvard Hambro
Pakistan	Agha Shahi
Panama	Aquilino E. Boyd
Paraguay	Miguel Solano Lopez
Peru	Jose Guzman
Philippines	Privado G. Jimenez
Poland	Eugeniusz Kulaga
Portugal	Antonio de Medeiros Patricio
Rumania	Gheorghe Diaconescu
Rwanda	Fidèle Nkundabagenzi
Saudia Arabia	Jamil M. Baroody
Senegal	Ibrahima Boye
Sierra Leone	Davidson S. H. W. Nicol
Singapore	T. T. B. Koh
Somalia	Abdulrahim Abby Farah
South Africa	C. F. G. von Hirschberg
Southern Yemen	Abdul Malek Ismail
Spain	Jaime de Pinies
Sudan	Fakhreddine Mohamed
Swaziland	Mboni Naph Dlamini
Sweden	Olof Rydbeck
Syria	George J. Tomeh
Tanzania	Salim A. Salim
Thailand	Anand Panyarachun
Togo	Alexandre J. Ohin
Trinidad and Tobago	P. V. J. Solomon
Tunisia	Rachid Driss
Turkey	Umit Haluk Bayulken
Uganda	E. Otema Allimadi
Ukrainian S.S.R.	Mikhail D. Polyanichko
U.S.S.R.	Yakov A. Malik
United Arab Rep.	Mohammed Hassan El-Zayyat
United Kingdom	Colin Crowe
United States	George Bush
Upper Volta	Tensoré Paul Rouamba
Uruguay	Augusto Legnani
Venezuela	Andres Aguilar M.
Yemen	Mohamed Said Al-Attar
Yugoslavia	Lazar Mojsov
Zambia	V. J. Mwaanga

THE CONGRESS OF  THE UNITED STATES

92d Congress First Session

UNITED STATES SENATE

ALABAMA
John J. Sparkman (D)
James B. Allen (D)

ALASKA
Ted F. Stevens (R) *
Mike Gravel (D)

ARIZONA
Paul J. Fannin (R) *
Barry M. Gold-
water (R)

ARKANSAS
John L. McClellan (D)
J. William Ful-
bright (D)

CALIFORNIA
Alan Cranston (D)
John V. Tunney (D) **

COLORADO
Gordon L. Allott (R)
Peter H. Dominick (R)

CONNECTICUT
Abraham A. Ribi-
coff (D)
Lowell P.
Weicker, Jr. (R) **

DELAWARE
J. Caleb Boggs (R)
William V.
Roth, Jr. (R) **

FLORIDA
Edward J. Gurney (R)
Lawton Chiles (D) **

GEORGIA
David H. Gambrell (D)†
Herman E. Tal-
madge (D)

HAWAII
Hiram L. Fong (R) *
Daniel K. Inouye (D)

IDAHO
Frank Church (D)
Len B. Jordan (R)

ILLINOIS
Charles H. Percy (R)
Adlai E. Steven-
son 3d (D) **

INDIANA
Vance Hartke (D) *
Birch Bayh (D)

IOWA
Jack R. Miller (R)
Harold E. Hughes (D)

KANSAS
James B. Pearson (R)
Robert J. Dole (R)

KENTUCKY
John S. Cooper (R)
Marlow W. Cook (R)

LOUISIANA
Allen J. Ellender (D)
Russell B. Long (D)

MAINE
Margaret Chase
Smith (R)
Edmund S.
Muskie (D) *

MARYLAND
Charles Mathias,
Jr. (R)
J. Glenn
Beall, Jr. (R) **

MASSACHUSETTS
Edward M.
Kennedy (D) *
Edward W. Brooke (R)

MICHIGAN
Philip A. Hart (D) *
Robert P. Griffin (R)

MINNESOTA
Walter F. Mondale (D)
Hubert H.
Humphrey (D) **

MISSISSIPPI
James O. Eastland (D)
John C. Stennis (D) *

MISSOURI
Stuart Syming-
ton (D) *
Thomas F. Eagle-
ton (D)

MONTANA
Mike Mansfield (D) *
Lee Metcalf (D)

NEBRASKA
Roman L.
Hruska (R) *
Carl T. Curtis (R)

NEVADA
Alan Bible (D)
Howard W. Can-
non (D) *

NEW HAMPSHIRE
Norris Cotton (R)
Thomas J. McIn-
tyre (D)

NEW JERSEY
Clifford P. Case (R)
Harrison A. Wil-
liams, Jr. (D) *

NEW MEXICO
Clinton P. Ander-
son (D)
Joseph M. Mon-
toya (D) *

NEW YORK
Jacob K. Javits (R)
James L.
Buckley (C) **

NORTH CAROLINA
Samuel J.
Ervin, Jr. (D)
B. Everett Jordan (D)

NORTH DAKOTA
Milton R. Young (R)
Quentin N. Bur-
dick (D) *

OHIO
William B. Saxbe (R)
Robert Taft, Jr. (R) **

OKLAHOMA
Fred R. Harris (D)
Henry L. Bellmon (R)

OREGON
Mark O. Hatfield (R)
Robert W. Pack-
wood (R)

PENNSYLVANIA
Hugh Scott (R) *
R. S. Schweiker (R)

RHODE ISLAND
John O. Pastore (D) *
Claiborne Pell (D)

SOUTH CAROLINA
Strom Thurmond (R)
Ernest F. Hollings (D)

SOUTH DAKOTA
Karl E. Mundt (R)
George S.
McGovern (D)

TENNESSEE
Howard H.
Baker, Jr. (R)
William E.
Brock 3d (R) **

TEXAS
John G. Tower (R)
Lloyd M. Bent-
sen, Jr. (D) **

UTAH
Wallace F. Bennett (R)
Frank E. Moss (D) *

VERMONT
George D. Aiken (R)
Winston L.
Prouty (R) *

VIRGINIA
Harry F. Byrd, Jr. (I) *
William B.
Spong, Jr. (D)

WASHINGTON
Warren G.
Magnuson (D)
Henry M.
Jackson (D) *

WEST VIRGINIA
Jennings Randolph (D)
Robert C. Byrd (D) *

WISCONSIN
William Proxmire (D) *
Gaylord Nelson (D)

WYOMING
Gale W. McGee (D) *
Clifford P. Hansen (R)

* incumbent returned to office 1970   (R) Republican (D) Democrat (C) Conservative (I) Independent
** elected 1970
† appointed to complete term of Richard Russell, who died Jan. 21, 1971

UNITED STATES HOUSE OF REPRESENTATIVES

ALABAMA
1. J. Edwards (R)
2. W. L. Dickinson (R)
3. G. W. Andrews (D)
4. W. Nichols (D)
5. W. Flowers (D)
6. J. H. Buchanan, Jr. (R)
7. T. Bevill (D)
8. R. E. Jones (D)

ALASKA
 N. J. Begich (D)*

ARIZONA
1. J. J. Rhodes (R)
2. M. K. Udall (D)
3. S. Steiger (R)

ARKANSAS
1. W. V. Alexander, Jr. (D)
2. W. D. Mills (D)
3. J. P. Hammerschmidt (R)
4. D. Pryor (D)

CALIFORNIA
1. D. H. Clausen (R)
2. H. T. Johnson (D)
3. J. E. Moss (D)
4. R. L. Leggett (D)
5. P. Burton (D)
6. W. S. Mailliard (R)
7. R. V. Dellums (D)*
8. G. P. Miller (D)
9. D. Edwards (D)
10. C. S. Gubser (R)
11. P. N. McCloskey, Jr. (R)
12. B. L. Talcott (R)
13. C. M. Teague (R)
14. J. R. Waldie (D)
15. J. J. McFall (D)
16. B. F. Sisk (D)
17. G. M. Anderson (D)
18. R. B. Mathias (R)
19. C. Holifield (D)
20. H. A. Smith (R)
21. A. F. Hawkins (D)
22. J. C. Corman (D)
23. D. Clawson (R)
24. J. H. Rousselot (R)
25. C. E. Wiggins (R)
26. T. M. Rees (D)
27. B. M. Goldwater, Jr. (R)
28. A. Bell (R)
29. G. E. Danielson (D)*
30. E. R. Roybal (D)
31. C. H. Wilson (D)
32. C. Hosmer (R)
33. J. L. Pettis (R)
34. R. T. Hanna (D)
35. J. G. Schmitz (R)
36. B. Wilson (R)
37. L. Van Deerlin (D)
38. V. V. Veysey (R)*

COLORADO
1. J. D. McKevitt (R)*
2. D. G. Brotzman (R)

3. F. E. Evans (D)
4. W. N. Aspinall (D)

CONNECTICUT
1. W. R. Cotter (D)*
2. R. Steele (R)*
3. R. N. Giaimo (D)
4. S. McKinney (R)*
5. J. S. Monagan (D)
6. Ella T. Grasso (D)*

DELAWARE
 P. S. duPont 4th (R)*

FLORIDA
1. R. L. F. Sikes (D)
2. D. Fuqua (D)
3. C. E. Bennett (D)
4. W. V. Chappell, Jr. (D)
5. L. Frey, Jr. (R)
6. S. M. Gibbons (D)
7. J. A. Haley (D)
8. C. W. Young (R)*
9. P. G. Rogers (D)
10. J. H. Burke (R)
11. C. D. Pepper (D)
12. D. B. Fascell (D)

GEORGIA
1. G. E. Hagan (D)
2. D. Mathis (D)*
3. J. T. Brinkley (D)
4. B. B. Blackburn (R)
5. F. Thompson (R)
6. J. J. Flynt, Jr. (D)
7. J. W. Davis (D)
8. W. S. Stuckey, Jr. (D)
9. P. M. Landrum (D)
10. R. G. Stephens, Jr. (D)

HAWAII
 S. M. Matsunaga (D)
 Patsy T. Mink (D)

IDAHO
1. J. A. McClure (R)
2. O. Hansen (R)

ILLINOIS
1. R. Metcalfe (D)*
2. A. J. Mikva (D)
3. M. F. Murphy (D)*
4. E. J. Derwinski (R)
5. J. C. Kluczynski (D)
6. G. W. Collins (D)*
7. F. Annunzio (D)
8. D. Rostenkowski (D)
9. S. R. Yates (D)
10. H. R. Collier (R)
11. R. C. Pucinski (D)
12. R. McClory (R)
13. P. M. Crane (R)
14. J. N. Erlenborn (R)
15. Charlotte T. Reid (R)
16. J. B. Anderson (R)
17. L. C. Arends (R)
18. R. H. Michel (R)
19. T. F. Railsback (R)

20. P. Findley (R)
21. K. J. Gray (D)
22. W. L. Springer (R)
23. G. E. Shipley (D)
24. C. M. Price (D)

INDIANA
1. R. J. Madden (D)
2. E. F. Landgrebe (R)
3. J. Brademas (D)
4. J. E. Roush (D)*
5. E. Hillis (R)*
6. W. G. Bray (R)
7. J. T. Myers (R)
8. R. H. Zion (R)
9. L. H. Hamilton (D)
10. D. W. Dennis (R)
11. A. Jacobs, Jr. (D)

IOWA
1. F. Schwengel (R)
2. J. C. Culver (D)
3. H. R. Gross (R)
4. J. H. Kyl (R)
5. N. Smith (D)
6. W. Mayne (R)
7. W. J. Scherle (R)

KANSAS
1. K. G. Sebelius (R)
2. W. R. Roy (D)*
3. L. Winn, Jr. (R)
4. G. E. Shriver (R)
5. J. Skubitz (R)

KENTUCKY
1. F. A. Stubblefield (D)
2. W. H. Natcher (D)
3. R. Mazzoli (D)*
4. M. G. Snyder (R)
5. T. L. Carter (R)
6. J. C. Watts (D)
7. C. D. Perkins (D)

LOUISIANA
1. F. E. Hebert (D)
2. H. Boggs (D)
3. P. T. Caffery (D)
4. J. D. Waggonner, Jr. (D)
5. O. E. Passman (D)
6. J. R. Rarick (D)
7. E. W. Edwards (D)
8. S. O. Long (D)

MAINE
1. P. N. Kyros (D)
2. W. D. Hathaway (D)

MARYLAND
1. vacant
2. C. D. Long (D)
3. E. A. Garmatz (D)
4. P. S. Sarbanes (D)*
5. L. J. Hogan (R)
6. G. E. Byron (D)*
7. P. J. Mitchell (D)*
8. G. Gude (R)

MASSACHUSETTS
1. S. O. Conte (R)
2. E. P. Boland (D)
3. R. F. Drinan (D)*
4. H. D. Donohue (D)
5. F. B. Morse (R)
6. M. J. Harrington (D)
7. T. H. Macdonald (D)
8. T. P. O'Neill, Jr. (D)
9. Louise Day Hicks (D)*
10. Margaret M. Heckler (R)
11. J. A. Burke (D)
12. H. Keith (R)

MICHIGAN
1. J. Conyers, Jr. (D)
2. M. L. Esch (R)
3. G. Brown (R)
4. E. Hutchinson (R)
5. G. R. Ford (R)
6. C. E. Chamberlain (R)
7. D. W. Riegle, Jr. (R)
8. J. Harvey (R)
9. G. A. Vander Jagt (R)
10. E. A. Cederberg (R)
11. P. E. Ruppe (R)
12. J. G. O'Hara (D)
13. C. C. Diggs, Jr. (D)
14. L. N. Nedzi (D)
15. W. D. Ford (D)
16. J. D. Dingell (D)
17. Martha W. Griffiths (D)
18. W. S. Broomfield (R)
19. J. H. McDonald (R)

MINNESOTA
1. A. H. Quie (R)
2. A. Nelsen (R)
3. W. Frenzel (R)*
4. J. E. Karth (D)
5. D. M. Fraser (D)
6. J. M. Zwach (R)
7. B. Bergland (D)*
8. J. A. Blatnik (D)

MISSISSIPPI
1. T. G. Abernethy (D)
2. J. L. Whitten (D)
3. C. H. Griffin (D)
4. G. V. Montgomery (D)
5. W. M. Colmer (D)

MISSOURI
1. W. L. Clay (D)
2. J. W. Symington (D)
3. Leonor K. Sullivan (D)
4. W. J. Randall (D)
5. R. Bolling (D)
6. W. R. Hull, Jr. (D)
7. D. G. Hall (D)
8. R. H. Ichord (D)
9. W. L. Hungate (D)
10. B. D. Burlison (D)

MONTANA
1. R. G. Shoup (R)*
2. J. Melcher (D)

NEBRASKA
1. C. Thone (R)*
2. J. Y. McCollister (R)*
3. D. T. Martin (R)

NEVADA
   W. S. Baring (D)

NEW HAMPSHIRE
1. L. C. Wyman (R)
2. J. C. Cleveland (R)

NEW JERSEY
1. J. E. Hunt (R)
2. C. W. Sandman; Jr. (R)
3. J. J. Howard (D)
4. F. Thompson, Jr. (D)
5. P. Frelinghuysen (R)
6. E. B. Forsythe (R)*
7. W. B. Widnall (R)
8. R. A. Roe (D)
9. H. Helstoski (D)
10. P. W. Rodino, Jr. (D)
11. J. G. Minish (D)
12. Florence P. Dwyer (R)
13. C. E. Gallagher (D)
14. D. V. Daniels (D)
15. E. J. Patten (D)

NEW MEXICO
1. M. Lujan, Jr. (R)
2. H. L. Runnels (D)*

NEW YORK
1. O. G. Pike (D)
2. J. R. Grover, Jr. (R)
3. L. L. Wolff (D)
4. J. W. Wydler (R)
5. N. F. Lent (R)*
6. S. Halpern (R)
7. J. P. Addabbo (D)
8. B. S. Rosenthal (D)
9. J. J. Delaney (D)
10. E. Celler (D)
11. F. J. Brasco (D)
12. Shirley A. Chisholm (D)
13. B. L. Podell (D)
14. J. J. Rooney (D)
15. H. L. Carey (D)
16. J. M. Murphy (D)
17. E. I. Koch (D)
18. C. B. Rangel (D)*
19. Bella S. Abzug (D)*
20. W. F. Ryan (D)
21. H. Badillo (D)*
22. J. H. Scheuer (D)
23. J. B. Bingham (D)
24. M. Biaggi (D)
25. P. A. Peyser (R)*
26. O. R. Reid (R)
27. J. G. Dow (D)*
28. H. Fish, Jr. (R)
29. S. S. Stratton (D)
30. C. J. King (R)
31. R. C. McEwen (R)
32. A. Pirnie (R)
33. H. W. Robison (R)
34. J. H. Terry (R)*
35. J. M. Hanley (D)
36. F. Horton (R)
37. B. B. Conable, Jr. (R)
38. J. F. Hastings (R)
39. J. Kemp (R)*
40. H. P. Smith III (R)
41. T. J. Dulski (D)

NORTH CAROLINA
1. W. B. Jones (D)
2. L. H. Fountain (D)
3. D. N. Henderson (D)
4. N. Galifianakis (D)
5. W. D. Mizell (R)
6. L. R. Preyer (D)
7. A. A. Lennon (D)
8. E. B. Ruth (R)
9. C. R. Jonas (R)
10. J. T. Broyhill (R)
11. R. A. Taylor (D)

NORTH DAKOTA
1. M. Andrews (R)
2. A. A. Link (D)*

OHIO
1. W. J. Keating (R)*
2. D. D. Clancy (R)
3. C. W. Whalen, Jr. (R)
4. W. M. McCulloch (R)
5. D. L. Latta (R)
6. W. H. Harsha (R)
7. C. J. Brown (R)
8. J. E. Betts (R)
9. T. L. Ashley (D)
10. C. E. Miller (R)
11. J. W. Stanton (R)
12. S. L. Devine (R)
13. C. A. Mosher (R)
14. J. F. Seiberling, Jr. (D)*
15. C. P. Wylie (R)
16. F. T. Bow (R)
17. J. M. Ashbrook (R)
18. W. L. Hays (D)
19. C. J. Carney (D)*
20. J. W. Stanton (D)*
21. L. Stokes (D)
22. C. A. Vanik (D)
23. W. E. Minshall (R)
24. W. E. Powell (R)*

OKLAHOMA
1. P. Belcher (R)
2. E. Edmondson (D)
3. C. B. Albert (D)
4. T. Steed (D)
5. J. Jarman (D)
6. J. N. H. Camp (R)

OREGON
1. W. Wyatt (R)
2. A. Ullman (D)
3. Edith Green (D)
4. J. Dellenback (R)

PENNSYLVANIA
1. W. A. Barrett (D)
2. R. N. C. Nix (D)
3. J. A. Byrne (D)
4. J. Eilberg (D)
5. W. J. Green (D)
6. G. Yatron (D)
7. L. G. Williams (R)
8. E. G. Biester, Jr. (R)
9. J. H. Ware 3d (R)*
10. J. M. McDade (R)
11. D. J. Flood (D)
12. J. I. Whalley (R)
13. L. Coughlin (R)
14. W. S. Moorhead (D)
15. F. B. Rooney (D)
16. E. D. Eshleman (R)
17. H. T. Schneebeli (R)
18. R. J. Corbett (R)
19. G. A. Goodling (R)
20. J. M. Gaydos (D)
21. J. H. Dent (D)
22. J. P. Saylor (R)
23. A. W. Johnson (R)
24. J. P. Vigorito (D)
25. F. M. Clark (D)
26. T. E. Morgan (D)
27. J. G. Fulton (R)

RHODE ISLAND
1. F. J. St. Germain (D)
2. R. O. Tiernan (D)

SOUTH CAROLINA
1. vacant
2. F. Spence (R)*
3. W. J. B. Dorn (D)
4. J. R. Mann (D)
5. T. S. Gettys (D)
6. J. L. McMillan (D)

SOUTH DAKOTA
1. F. E. Denholm (D)*
2. J. Abourezk (D)*

TENNESSEE
1. J. H. Quillen (R)
2. J. J. Duncan (R)
3. LaMar Baker (R)*
4. J. L. Evins (D)
5. R. H. Fulton (D)
6. W. R. Anderson (D)
7. L. R. Blanton (D)
8. E. Jones (D)
9. D. H. Kuykendall (R)

TEXAS
1. W. Patman (D)
2. J. Dowdy (D)
3. J. M. Collins (R)
4. R. Roberts (D)
5. E. Cabell (D)
6. O. E. Teague (D)
7. W. R. Archer (R)*
8. B. Eckhardt (D)
9. J. Brooks (D)
10. J. J. Pickle (D)
11. W. R. Poage (D)
12. J. C. Wright, Jr. (D)
13. G. Purcell (D)
14. J. Young (D)
15. E. de la Garza (D)
16. R. C. White (D)
17. O. Burleson (D)
18. R. D. Price (R)
19. G. H. Mahon (D)
20. H. B. Gonzalez (D)
21. O. C. Fisher (D)
22. R. R. Casey (D)
23. A. Kazen, Jr. (D)

UTAH
1. K. G. McKay (D)*
2. S. P. Lloyd (R)

VERMONT
   R. T. Stafford (R)

VIRGINIA
1. T. N. Downing (D)
2. G. W. Whitehurst (R)
3. D. E. Satterfield III (D)
4. W. M. Abbitt (D)
5. W. C. Daniel (D)
6. R. H. Poff (R)
7. J. K. Robinson (R)*
8. W. L. Scott (R)
9. W. C. Wampler (R)
10. J. T. Broyhill (R)

WASHINGTON
1. T. M. Pelly (R)
2. L. Meeds (D)
3. Julia B. Hansen (D)
4. M. McCormack (D)*
5. T. S. Foley (D)
6. F. V. Hicks (D)
7. B. Adams (D)

WEST VIRGINIA
1. R. H. Mollohan (D)
2. H. O. Staggers (D)
3. J. Slack (D)
4. K. Hechler (D)
5. J. Kee (D)

WISCONSIN
1. L. Aspin (D)*
2. R. W. Kastenmeier (D)
3. V. W. Thomson (R)
4. C. J. Zablocki (D)
5. H. S. Reuss (D)
6. W. A. Steiger (R)
7. D. R. Obey (D)
8. J. W. Byrnes (R)
9. G. R. Davis (R)
10. A. E. O'Konski (R)

WYOMING
   T. Roncalio (D)*

* elected to office in 1970
all others: incumbents
returned to office in 1970

UNITED STATES CABINET

Secretary of State: WILLIAM P. ROGERS
Secretary of the Treasury: JOHN B. CONNALLY, JR.
Secretary of Defense: MELVIN R. LAIRD
Attorney General: JOHN N. MITCHELL
Postmaster General: WINTON M. BLOUNT
Secretary of the Interior: ROGERS C. B. MORTON
Secretary of Agriculture: CLIFFORD M. HARDIN
Secretary of Commerce: MAURICE H. STANS
Secretary of Labor: JAMES D. HODGSON
Secretary of Health, Education, and Welfare: ELLIOT L. RICHARDSON
Secretary of Housing and Urban Development: GEORGE W. ROMNEY
Secretary of Transportation: JOHN A. VOLPE

UNITED STATES SUPREME COURT

Chief Justice: WARREN E. BURGER (1969)
Associate Justices:
   HUGO L. BLACK (1937)
   WILLIAM O. DOUGLAS (1939)
   JOHN M. HARLAN (1955)
   WILLIAM J. BRENNAN, JR. (1956)
   POTTER STEWART (1958)
   BYRON WHITE (1962)
   THURGOOD MARSHALL (1967)
   HARRY A. BLACKMUN (1970)

EXECUTIVE OFFICE OF THE PRESIDENT

Director of Communications: HERBERT G. KLEIN
Counsellors: ROBERT H. FINCH, DONALD RUMSFELD
Assistants: PETER M. FLANIGAN, H. R. HALDEMAN
Assistant for Domestic Affairs: JOHN D. EHRLICHMAN
Assistant for National Security Affairs: HENRY A. KISSINGER
Counsel for Congressional Relations: CLARK MacGREGOR
Science Adviser: EDWARD E. DAVID, JR.
Special Assistant for Consumer Affairs: VIRGINIA H. KNAUER
Press Secretary: RONALD L. ZIEGLER
Personal Secretary: ROSE MARY WOODS
Social Secretary: LUCY ALEXANDER WINCHESTER
Office of Management and Budget: GEORGE P. SHULTZ, director
Council of Economic Advisers: PAUL W. MCCRACKEN, chairman
Central Intelligence Agency: RICHARD HELMS, director
Office of Economic Opportunity: FRANK C. CARLUCCI III, director
National Aeronautics and Space Administration: GEORGE M. LOW, acting administrator
Council on Environmental Quality: RUSSELL E. TRAIN, chairman

GOVERNORS OF THE UNITED STATES

ALABAMA	George C. Wallace (D)**	MONTANA	Forrest H. Anderson (D)
ALASKA	William A. Egan (D)**	NEBRASKA	J. J. Exon (D)**
ARIZONA	Jack Williams (R)*	NEVADA	D. N. O'Callaghan (D)**
ARKANSAS	Dale Bumpers (D)**	NEW HAMPSHIRE	Walter R. Peterson, Jr. (R)*
CALIFORNIA	Ronald Reagan (R)*	NEW JERSEY	William T. Cahill (R)
COLORADO	John A. Love (R)*	NEW MEXICO	Bruce King (D)**
CONNECTICUT	Thomas J. Meskill (R)**	NEW YORK	Nelson A. Rockefeller (R)*
DELAWARE	Russell W. Peterson (R)	NORTH CAROLINA	Robert W. Scott (D)
FLORIDA	Reubin Askew (D)**	NORTH DAKOTA	William L. Guy (D)
GEORGIA	Jimmy Carter (D)**	OHIO	John J. Gilligan (D)**
HAWAII	John A. Burns (D)*	OKLAHOMA	David Hall (D)**
IDAHO	Cecil D. Andrus (D)**	OREGON	Tom McCall (R)*
ILLINOIS	Richard B. Ogilvie (R)	PENNSYLVANIA	Milton J. Shapp (D)**
INDIANA	Edgar D. Whitcomb (R)	RHODE ISLAND	Frank Licht (D)
IOWA	Robert D. Ray (R)*	SOUTH CAROLINA	John C. West (D)**
KANSAS	Robert B. Docking (D)*	SOUTH DAKOTA	Richard S. Kneip (D)**
KENTUCKY	Louie B. Nunn (R)	TENNESSEE	Winfield K. Dunn (R)**
LOUISIANA	John J. McKeithen (D)	TEXAS	Preston Smith (D)*
MAINE	Kenneth M. Curtis (D)*	UTAH	Calvin L. Rampton (D)
MARYLAND	Marvin Mandel (D)*	VERMONT	Deane C. Davis (R)*
MASSACHUSETTS	Francis W. Sargent (R)*	VIRGINIA	Linwood Holton (R)
MICHIGAN	William G. Milliken (R)*	WASHINGTON	Daniel J. Evans (R)
MINNESOTA	Wendell R. Anderson (D)**	WEST VIRGINIA	Arch A. Moore, Jr. (R)
MISSISSIPPI	John Bell Williams (D)	WISCONSIN	Patrick J. Lucey (D)**
MISSOURI	Warren E. Hearnes (D)	WYOMING	Stanley K. Hathaway (R)*

* incumbent returned to office in 1970
** elected to office in 1970

NOBEL PRIZES

Chemistry: LUIS F. LELOIR, Argentina, Institute of Biochemical Research in Buenos Aires, for his work involving the chemical processes in which body sugar is broken down into simple carbohydrates.

Literature: ALEKSANDR I. SOLZHENITSYN, Soviet Union, for his novels based on his experiences in Russian prisons, depicting the struggle to survive under dehumanizing conditions; his books include *One Day in the Life of Ivan Denisovich*, *The Cancer Ward*, and *The First Circle*. He has been severely attacked by the present Soviet Government because of his anti-Stalinist writings. He had been expelled by the Soviet Writers' Union in 1969 but continues to live in his homeland. Solzhenitsyn did not appear at the award-presentation ceremonies in Sweden. He feared that if he left the Soviet Union, he would not be allowed to return.

Peace: NORMAN E. BORLAUG, U.S., director of the International Maize and Wheat Improvement Center of Mexico, for his research yielding improved strains of wheat and rice that will help solve the world hunger problem. "Dr. Borlaug, as the prime mover in the 'green revolution,' has made it possible for the developing countries to break away from hunger and poverty."

Physics: LOUIS E. F. NEEL, France, University of Grenoble, for his research in magnetism having important applications in the field of solid-state physics; and HANNES O. G. ALFVEN, Sweden, Institute of Technology in Stockholm and University of California in San Diego, for his work involving magnetohydrodynamics—the study of electricity-conducting gases in a magnetic field.

Physiology or Medicine: JULIUS AXELROD, U.S. National Institute of Mental Health; SIR BERNARD KATZ, Great Britain, University College in London; and ULF VON EULER, Sweden, Royal Caroline Institute in Stockholm, for their independent research in the chemistry of nerve transmission, leading to the possibility of influencing the nervous system to correct nervous and mental disorders.

Memorial Prize in Economics: PAUL A. SAMUELSON, U.S., Massachusetts Institute of Technology, for developing static and dynamic economic theory, raising the "level of scientific analysis in economic theory." His book *Economics*, published in 1948, has become a standard textbook in colleges and universities around the world.

PULITZER PRIZES

JOURNALISM

Cartoons: THOMAS F. DARCY, editorial cartoonist, *Newsday*.

Commentary: MARQUIS CHILDS, contributing editor, *St. Louis Post-Dispatch*, for his Washington, D.C., commentary.

Criticism: ADA LOUISE HUXTABLE, architecture critic, *The New York Times*, for distinguished architectural criticism.

Editorial Writing: PHILIP L. GEYELIN, editorial page editor, *The Washington Post*, for editorials on varied topics.

Feature Photography: DALLAS KINNEY, staff photographer, *Palm Beach Post*, for pictures illustrating a series on migrant workers in Palm Beach County.

Spot News Photography: STEVE STARR, staff photographer, Albany bureau, The Associated Press, for his picture of armed students at Cornell University in 1969.

International Reporting: SEYMOUR M. HERSH, freelance reporter, for report on alleged 1968 Songmy massacre in South Vietnam.

Local Reporting, general: THOMAS FITZPATRICK, reporter, *Chicago Sun-Times*, for account of his evening with the Weatherman faction of SDS during the October 1969 Chicago riot.

Local Reporting, special: HAROLD EUGENE MARTIN, publisher, *Montgomery-Alabama Journal*, for exposé about using Alabama prisoners for drug experiments.

National Reporting: WILLIAM J. EATON, Washington correspondent, *Chicago Daily News*, for reports about Judge Clement F. Haynsworth's alleged conflicts of interest.

Public Service Gold Medal: NEWSDAY, for its investigation and exposé of "secret land deals and zoning manipulations by public and political party office holders."

LETTERS AND MUSIC

Biography: T. HARRY WILLIAMS, for his biography *Huey Long*.

Drama: CHARLES GORDONE, for off-Broadway play *No Place to Be Somebody*.

Fiction: JEAN STAFFORD, for her book *Collected Stories*.

History: DEAN GOODERHAM ACHESON, for his book *Present at the Creation: My Years in the State Department*.

Music: CHARLES W. WUORINEN, for his electronic-music composition *Time's Encomium*.

Nonfiction: ERIK H. ERIKSON, for *Gandhi's Truth*, a study of militant nonviolence.

Poetry: RICHARD HOWARD, for his third volume of poems, *Untitled Subjects*.

DICTIONARY INDEX

A

Aaron, Hank, U.S. athlete, picture 325
Academy award winners 164
Accessories, things added to give style
    fashion 266–67
    for young people's rooms 273
ACTION 70, Girl Scout program 390
Advertising
    cigarette advertising banned on TV 176
Africa 64–73
    game parks 74–75
    summit conference 54
    See also names of countries
Afro-Asian Islamic Organization, picture 114–15
Agnew, Spiro T., U.S. vice-president 370, 373, pictures 278, 362
Agriculture 76–85
    See also names of countries

Airdex. An index, or measure, of air pollution. It is usually given in the form of a figure or series of figures and announced with weather reports in the newspaper or on radio or TV. The airdex reading tells the amounts of harmful substances (impurities) in the air. Often it records impurities such as carbon monoxide, sulfur dioxide, and soot separately. It reports whether each amount is large enough to be unhealthy.

Air fares, increased 348
Airplanes
    Israeli Air Force 260–61
    noise of jet planes, a health hazard 17
    pollution from 187, 188
    Soviet in Middle East 258–59
Air pollution 18–20, 27–29, 32, 187–88, picture 182
Air travel
    environmental problems 19
Akufo-Addo, Edward, president of Ghana 69
Akwei, Richard, Ghana diplomat, picture 360
Al-, for Arabic names see second part of name
Alberta, Canada, pollution, picture 142–43
Allen, James E., U.S. public official 158–59, picture 157
Allende Gossens, Salvador, Chilean president 54, 56, 214, 218–19
Allesandri Rodriguez, Jorge, former Chilean president 218
Alligator, animal, picture 184
American Institute of Architects headquarters, Washington, D.C. 106–07, picture 105
American League, baseball 322–24
American Motors Gremlin, small car, picture 351
American painting
    collection of early American painting 97
American Zionist Federation 293
America's Cup race, picture 319
Amiama Tio, Fernando, Dominican Republic official, picture 378
Amino acids, in biochemistry 298
    meteorite containing 294
Andrews, Tige, U.S. actor, picture 175
Animals
    African game parks 74–75
    endangered species 184
    harmed by pollution 186
Antihelium nuclei, antiparticle 299
Antimatter, particles 299
Anti-Semitism 293
Apartheid, in South Africa 71, 73
Aphrodite of Cnidus, claimed to be head of, picture 303
Apollo 13, moon flight 44, 312, pictures 45, 308
Arab-Israeli dispute 50, 53, 54, 60, 260
    cease fire 250, 253–54, 377–78
    United Nations efforts toward peace 358–59
Arafat, Yasir, Palestinian commando, picture 251
Arana Osorio, Carlos, Guatemalan president 219
Arava, Israeli plane, picture 261
Archeology, pictures 302–03
Architecture 102–07
    EXPO'70, pictures 122–25
Argentina 219, 221
Arkansas River Navigation Project 348
Arms race, in Middle East 359
Armstrong, Louis, U.S. musician, picture 175
Arthritis, advances in research 238
Arts 86–107
    United Nation's art objects 356
Arts and handicrafts hobbies 208, pictures 209
Ashe, Arthur, U.S. athlete 38
Ashton, George, and family, winner of New York super lottery, picture 274
Asia 108–19
    Pope Paul VI's visit to 291
    See also names of countries
Astro-chemistry 298
Astronomy, pictures 304–05
Atlantic Ocean, drilling missions in 300
Australia 126–31
Austria 201
Autobiography 226, pictures 225
Automobiles
    factor in air pollution 18, 20, 27–28, 32, 187–88
    General Motors strike 350
    General Motors XEP, picture 345
    model cars, picture 207
    racing 321
    small cars 350, pictures 351
Avant-garde dance 169
Aviation industry 348–49
Awards see Prizes and awards

B

Bacharach, Burt, U.S. composer 173
Bahrain Islands 254, 256–57
Balaguer, Joaquin, Dominican Republic president 387, picture 386
Ballet 169, picture 168
Baltimore Orioles, baseball team 322, 323, 324
Bandaranaike, Mrs. Sirimavo, Ceylon prime minister 46, 119
Bank of America tower, San Francisco, Calif. 104
Bantustans, homeland for South African blacks 71, 73
Barbados 384
Barre, Mohammed Siad, Somalia leader 69
Barzani, Mustafa, al-, Iraq Kurd leader, picture 254
Baseball 322–25
Basketball 326–27
Basques, people in northern Spain 60, 199
Beadwork, a hobby 208, pictures 209
Beatles, The, British musical group 171
Beethoven, Ludwig van, German composer 170
Begley, Ed, U.S. actor, picture 284

Berlin, Germany 202
Berrigan brothers, Catholic priests 292
Biafra 38, picture 39
    aftermath of civil war 68
Bible, new 290, picture 291
Biehl, Eugen, West German official, kidnaped 60
Biography 226
Biological sciences 298
Bird fossil, picture 295
Black, Hugo L., U.S. jurist, picture 373
Blackmun, Harry A., U.S. jurist 44, 46, 375, picture 373
Black Panthers
    Chicago 7 trial ends 41
    demonstration for equal rights, picture 367
Blacks
    document against white America 290
    game about blacks and whites 268
Black sound, in popular music 173
Blood analyzer, development of 241

Body language. The movements of a person's body that
    tell what is on his mind and, often, how he is likely
    to behave. Unlike sign language, body language is
    not a conscious attempt to communicate with an-
    other person. Instead it consists of very slight, un-
    conscious movements or gestures that indicate his
    feelings. It also includes particular ways of standing
    or sitting. To a person who is trained to understand
    body language, the movements and positions convey
    a meaning.

Boeing 747 348, picture 343
Bolivia 56, 221
Bombings, University of Wisconsin 52
Bones and muscles, exhibit of, picture 242
Books
    photography, 88, 90, pictures 90–91
    See also Literature
Boots, fashion 267
Boston Museum of Art
    centennial celebration exhibitions 97
Bourassa, Robert, Canadian official 137–38
Boxing 334
BOYPOWER '76 392
Boys' Clubs of America 394
Boy Scouts of America 392, picture 389
Brancusi, Constantin, Rumanian sculptor 100, picture
    87, 101
Brandt, Willy, West German chancellor 53, 192, 196, 202,
    picture 193
Brazil, picture 216
    kidnaping 223, picture 217
    World Soccer Cup 320
Breakthrough, Operation, housing operation 107
Brennan, William J. Jr., U.S. jurist, picture 373
Breughel, Pieter, Flemish artist 97
Brezhnev, Leonid I, Soviet leader 202
    U.S.–Soviet relations 379
British Guiana
    famous stamp sold 210–11
British Museum
    head, claimed to be Aphrodite, picture 303
Brooks, Angie, Liberian delegate to UN, picture 354
Bruce, David K., U.S. diplomat 50, 376
Buckley, James L., U.S. senator 371
Buckley, Sonja, U.S. doctor, picture 239
Budnick, Dan, U.S. photographer, picture 89
Burdick, Quentin, U.S. senator 371
Burger, Warren E., U.S. jurist, picture 373
Burma 118–19
    EXPO'70, Burmese Pavilion, picture 125
Burns, Arthur, U.S: public official, picture 368
Bush, George, U.S. public official 60

Business slowdown, United States 148
Bussing, of school children 370

C

Cabinet, of the United States 373, 404
Caetano, Marcelo, Portuguese premier, picture 195
Caldwell, Dean, U.S. mountain climber, picture 277
California
    Bank of America tower, San Francisco 104
    census, 1970 380
    Oakland Museum 102
Cambodia 43, 56
    United States troops in 44, 48, 112–13, 375–76, pic-
        tures 110, 112
Cambridge, Mass.
    Design Research Building 102, picture 103
Cameras 91
Camp Fire Girls 393
Campus unrest see Student unrest
Canada 134–43
    EXPO'70, Canadian Pavilion, picture 124
    Quebec separatists kidnap officials 56, 60, 134–37
    recognizes Red China 56
    scholastic photography awards 92
    stamps issued in 1970 211
    United States draft-age immigrants 290
Cancer
    advances in research 238–39, 298
Capitals of the world 398–403
Caribbean Free Trade Area (CARIFTA) 384
Carnegie Commission on Higher Education 158
Caro, Anthony, English sculptor 100, picture 101
Carswell, G. Harrold, U.S. jurist 38, 375
Cartoons
    economy of the United States 146
    education 154
    "hard-hats" demonstration 364
    Middle East crisis 248, 358
    pollution 189
    SALT 197
Casals, Jordi, U.S. doctor, picture 239
Cash, Johnny, U.S. singer 173
Casper, Billy, U.S. athlete 337
Castro, Fidel, Cuban prime minister 384, picture 385
Catalogues, Photography-book 88, 90
Catlin, George, U.S. artist
    "Kee-O-Kuk, Chief of the Sauk and Foxes," picture 96
Cease-fire, Middle East 50, 53, 54, 260
Ceausescu, Nicolae, Rumanian leader 205
Celibacy, for priests 291
Census, U.S., official count of people 380–81
Central America see Latin America
Central Conference of American Rabbis 293
Cereals, dry, nutrition of 81
Ceylon 119
    Bandaranaike, Mrs. Sirimavo 46
Chad, rebellion of Muslim tribesmen 69, picture 70
Charrière, Henri, French author 226, picture 225
Chavez, Cesar, U.S. labor leader 83
Cheetah, animal, picture 184
Chemistry 299
    Nobel prize winner 409
Chevrolet Vega, small car, picture 351
Chicago, Ill.
    John Hancock Center 102, 104
Chicago 7 trial 41
Chi Cheng, Taiwan athlete 332
Children see Young people
Chile 214, 218–19
    Allende Gossens, Salvador 54, 56
    U.S. attitude of neutrality 378

China, Communist 116
  Canada established diplomatic relations 56, 138
  entertainers in Tanzania, picture 72
  financing Tanzam railroad 71, picture 72
  Italy, relations with 58
  space satellite 44
  talks with United States 38
Choate, Robert B., Jr., American engineer 81, picture 80
Cholera, spread of 240
Choquette, Jerome, Canadian official 137
Church-Cooper Amendment 376
Cigarette smoking and cancer 239
Cincinnati Reds, baseball team 323, 324
Circulatory system, picture 243
Cities
  air pollution from automobiles 20
  capitals of the world 398–403
  game about problems in cities 268
  noise, a health hazard 17
Civil disorders
  Augusta, Georgia 46
  bomb blast at University of Wisconsin 52
  New York City 46
  Poland 60, 205
  Trinidad, picture 382
  See also Student unrest
Civil rights 370
  student rights 159
Clark, Kenneth, British historian 228, picture 227
Classical music 170–71
  rock music 171–72
Clay, Cassius, U.S. athlete, picture 318
Clean car race, by students 188; picture 187
Clothing
  American clothing worn in Southeast Asia, pictures 121
  fashion, 1970 264–67
Clubs see Youth organizations
Coffin, William Sloane, Jr., American clergyman 290
Coins and coin collecting 213
Cole, Michael, American actor, picture 175
Collecting and collections
  coins 213
  stamps, 211, pictures 207, 210
Colleges see Universities and colleges
Colombia 219
Colombo, Emilio, Italian premier 52, 201
Colonialism
  United Nations resolution 357–58
Color photography awards 92–95
Comets, Tago-Sato-Kisaka and 1970-F, pictures 305
Commemorative stamps 211, pictures 210
Commercials, television
  elimination from childrens shows proposed 176
Common Market see European Economic Community
Commonwealth, Caribbean 384
Communication
  Intelsat, commercial satellites 315
Communism
  China 116
  Southeast Asia 112–13, pictures 110
  Soviet Union and East Europe 202
  See also Marxism
Communist China see China, Communist
Community problems
  Boys' Clubs of America 394
Congress, United States see United States Congress
Connally, John B., Jr., U.S. public official 60, 373
Connecticut
  Knights of Columbus building 102, picture 104
Conservation, fur fashions 267
Consultation on Church Union (COCU) 290
Contemporary sculpture 100–01
Continental drift theory 300, 301

Cook, Captain James, British explorer 126
Corn
  blight in United States 77, 83, picture 81
  research developments 83
Costa Rica 40, 219, picture 220
Council on Environmental Quality 185
Country music 173
Courage, Piers, British athlete 321
Court, Margaret, Australian athlete, picture 318
Creative Photography, magazine 88
Crime and criminals
  anticrime legislation 371
  Chicago 7 trial ends 41
Cross, James, British official, kidnaped 56, 60, 137
Cuba, economy failing 384, 387, picture 385
Cub Scouts 392
Cuellar, Mike, American athlete 322, 324, picture 325
Cushing, Richard Cardinal, U.S. archbishop 292, picture 283
Cyprus 254
Czechoslovakia 204

D

Dahomey 69
Dairy and dairy products 78, 80, pictures 79, 85
  New Zealand's market in Great Britain 131
Dance 168–69
  Moiseyev Dance Company, picture 162

Dashiki. A man's sport shirt made of material having several colors. It has full, bell-shaped sleeves and a large front pocket.

Data bank. An organized collection of information. It contains facts and statistics about persons, organizations, or activities. Also, a storage place where this information is kept. The term was used often in 1970 during investigations by the U.S. Senate subcommittee on constitutional rights. The committee chairman, Sam J. Ervin, Jr., of North Carolina, accused the Army of maintaining a data bank on U.S. civilians. Most were active in politics or involved in political protest. He called the practice of keeping data banks a violation of the privacy of citizens.

Davidson, Bruce, U.S. photographer
  East 100th Street 88, picture 86
Davis, Angela, U.S. civil-rights militant, picture 279
Dayan, Moshe, Israeli official, picture 249
DC-10, jet plane 349
DDT, danger of 21–22, 81
Deaths 280–87
  See also De Gaulle, Nasser, Sukarno
Decoupage, a hobby 208
Deep Sea Drilling Project 300
Defense
  Australian contract to buy U.S. planes 128–29
  cutback in government spending 148
  Israeli Air Force 260–61
De Gaulle, Charles, French president 192, 199, 280–81, picture 193
De Kooning, Willem, U.S. artist, picture 86–87
Demonstrations
  United States, pictures 363, 366, 367
  See also Civil disorders; Student unrest
Deoxyribonucleic acid (DNA), research to cure diseases 298
Desegregation, pictures 156, 157
Design Research Building, Cambridge, Mass. 102, picture 103
Detergents, source of pollution 23–24, 186

Developing nations
 Fiji and Tonga become independent 126, 131, 132–33
 Gambia becomes a republic 44
 Guyana becomes a republic 40
 United Nation's goal for 357–58
Diana camera 91
Dinosaur Trailside Park, New York City 306
Diphtheria, outbreak of 241
Disease see Medicine and health
Disney's "The Aristocats," movie, picture 166–67
Dixon, Dean, American conductor 171, picture 170
DNA, research to cure diseases 298
Dog shows 330–31
Dominican Republic 387, picture 386
Dominis, John, U.S. photographer, picture 90–91
Douglas, William O., American jurist, picture 373
Downs, Wilbur, U.S. doctor, picture 239
Draft, or conscription
 counseling for students 161
Drama Critics Circle awards 181
Drinan, Father Robert, Catholic priest 292, picture 293
"Drive for Decency" 394
Drug addiction
 Canada 143
 lecture at Phoenix House, New York City, picture 241
 schools, problem in 161
Dubcek, Alexander, former Czechoslovakian leader 204

Dune buggy. A light automobile built for traveling or racing over desert and mountain country rather than for use on paved roads.

Dungan, Ralph, American diplomat 378
Dupont, Clifford, Rhodesian president, picture 73

E

Eagle, bird, picture 184
Earth Day 44, 182, pictures 183
Earthquake, in Peru, picture 216
Earth-resource measurements, by spacecraft 314
East Asia 116–17
East Germany see Germany
Eban, Abba, Israeli foreign minister, picture 377
Echeverria Alvarez, Luis, Mexican president 219, picture 221
Eclipse of sun 42, picture 304
Ecology 10–35, 182–91
Economic conditions
 farms and farm products 76–77, 81
 Soviet Union and East Germany 202
 United States 144–53, 368
 See also articles on individual countries
Economics
 Nobel memorial prize winner 409

Ecotactics. The science of improving the quality of man's environment by fighting pollution of the earth, including its air and its bodies of water. (Ecotactics, the title of a 1970 handbook of the Sierra Club, is defined by the editors as "the science of arranging and maneuvering all available forces in action against enemies of the earth.")

Ecuador 221
Education 154–61
 Boys' Clubs of America, scholarships and grants 394
 Museum of Medical Science, Houston, Texas 242–45
 Sesame Street, TV program 161, 176, 177–79
 West Indies 384, picture 383
 See also Libraries; Universities and colleges
EEC see European Economic Community

Effiong, Philip, Biafran leader, picture 64
Egypt see United Arab Republic
Eisenhower, Mamie, wife of Dwight D. Eisenhower, picture 275
Elections
 Conservatives win British elections 48
 environment was voters' concern 185
 pre-election recess periods, for students 159
 United States, off-year elections 370–71
 See also articles on various countries
Elementary schools
 open-classroom approach 161
Element 105, chemical element 299
Elephants, in Kruger National Park, picture 74
Elizabeth II, queen of Great Britain 126, picture 132
Emmy awards 176
Employment and unemployment
 business slowdown in United States 144, 151, picture 147, 149

Encounter group. In psychiatry, a rather small group of persons brought together for regular meetings, or encounters. The meetings encourage close social contact between members with open and frank confrontations. The experience in group behavior is thought to help many people recognize and solve their personality problems. This form of treatment is called "sensitivity training."

Energy, sun's energy necessary to living things 13
Environment 10–35, 182–91
 Dirty Water, game 268
 Great Barrier Reef, Australia, threatened 130
 pesticides 80–81
Environmental art 99
Environmental Protection Agency 81
Enzymes 298
Ethiopia, Muslims separatists are threat to 69–70
Ethnic problems
 movies about 164, 166
 non-whites in Great Britain 48
Europe 192–205
 East Europe 202–05
 See also articles on various countries
European Economic Community
 possible new members 197, 199
 Yugoslavia trade agreement signed 40
Evanston, Ill.
 Northwestern University Library 102
Explorer scouts 392
EXPO'70 122–25
 architecture 107

F

Fabrics, for young people's rooms 273
Falcon, bird, picture 184

Familygram. A radio message sent to a member of the U.S. Navy by a member or members of his family while he is at sea on a lengthy mission.

Family planning 16, 32
 Jamaica, picture 383
Farm clubs 393, 395, pictures 84–85, 389
Farming see Agriculture
Fashion 264–67, pictures 262–63
Feinbloom, William, American doctor, picture 237
Fertilizers, environmental problem 23
Festivals
 film festivals 167
 rock music 171, picture 172

Fiction 226
Figueres Ferrer, Jose, Costa Rican president 40, 219, picture 220
Fiji 56, 126, 131, 132–33
Films see Motion pictures
Finch, Robert H., U.S. official 48–49, 159, 373
Finland 201
First National Explorer Olympics 392
Flags, Fiji and Tonga 133
Floor coverings, for young people 272
Florida
 Boys' Clubs of America, picture 394
Flying Turtle, sculpture by Brancusi, picture 101
Focus, photography magazine 88
Food 76–85
 problem to feed world 15
Food-stamp program 81
Football 328–29
 Super Bowl champions 38, 329
Ford Pinto, small car, picture 351
Foreign policy, of nations
 U.S. aid to Latin America cut 214, 223
 See also articles on various countries
Fossils
 bird fossil, picture 295
 dinosaur tracks 306–07
Four-H (4-H) clubs 393, pictures 85
France
 Charles de Gaulle 192, 199, 280–81, picture 193
 fire in Saint Laurent du Pont 58
 French Polynesia 131
Franco, Francisco, Spanish head of state 60, picture 195
French Polynesia 131
Front de Liberation du Quebec (FLQ) 136–37
Furniture, for young people 270
Furs and conservation 267
Future Farmers of America 395, pictures 84–85, 389

G

Gambia
 becomes republic 44
Game parks, Africa 74–75
Games 268, pictures 263
Gandhi, Indira, India's prime minister 118
Gardner, Erle Stanley, U.S. author, picture 285
General Motors strike 350
Generation gap, game about the 268
Genetics
 artificial gene created 298
Geology
 ancient Saharan South Pole found 301
Germany 196
 East Germany 205
 leaders of East and West meet 42
 Soviet-West German treaty 53, 196, 202, 204, 205
 West Germany and Poland sign treaty 58
Ghana
 refugees from 73
 returned to civilian government 69
Ghetto
 game about people in the ghetto 268, picture 263
Ghiorso, Albert, U.S. scientist 299
Gibson, Kenneth A., Newark mayor 48–49
Gierek, Edward, Poland's Communist leader 60, 205
Giraffe, in Kruger National Park, picture 75
Girl Scouts of the U.S.A. 390–91, pictures 35, 389–91
Glencoe "Soil Saver," tractor 78
Glomar Challenger, research vessel 300
Glover, F. Scott, U.S. doctor, picture 245
Goldberg, Rube, American cartoonist, pictures 282
Golf 335, 337, picture 341

Gomulka, Wladyslaw, Poland's Communist leader
 resigned 60, 205
Goodell, Charles, U.S. public official 370–71
Gore, Albert, U.S. public official 370
Gorton, Sir John, Australian prime minister 131
Government, heads of
 nations of the world 398–403
Governors, United States 371, 408
Grading (marking) systems, for student work 161
Graham, Robin Lee, sailed alone around the world, picture 396
Grain
 research developments 83
 surplus in Canada 140, picture 141
Grammy awards 171
Grants, gifts and subsidies
 Boys' Clubs of America 394
Great Barrier Reef, Australia, threatened by starfish 130
Great Britain see United Kingdom of Great Britain and Northern Ireland
Greece, United States relations with 197
Greek Cypriots 254
Gross national product
 United States 151
Guatemala 44, 214, 219, 223
Guinea, invaded by Portuguese Guinea 60, 64, 69
Guyana, becomes republic 40

H

Hahnium, element 105, 299
Haile Selassie, Ethiopian emperor, picture 66
Hairstyles, 1970 264
Haise, Fred W., Jr., U.S. astronaut 44, 312, picture 45
Haiti 387
Hall, Gary, U.S. athlete 336
Hambro, Edvard, Norwegian president of UN General Assembly 356, pictures 353, 354
Handicrafts
 fashion styles 266
 hobbies 208, pictures 209
Harding, Warren, U.S. mountain climber, picture 277
Harlan, John M., U.S. jurist, picture 373
Haynes, Lloyd, U.S. actor, picture 175
Hays, Anna Mae, U.S. general, picture 275
Health see Medicine and health
Heartbeat, checking, picture 244
Heart transplants 238
Heath, Edward, British prime minister 48, 199, picture 194
Heath, James, American "Boy of the Year," picture 388
Hendrix, Jimi, U.S. rock singer, picture 173
Heyerdahl, Thor, Norwegian explorer, picture 276
Hickel, Walter J., U.S. public official 58, 373
High schools
 John Adams High School, Portland, Oregon 160–61
Hijacking of planes 349, pictures 343
 Palestinian commandos 54, 253, picture 248–49
 Soviet airliner 56
Hindus and Muslims, tension between 118
History, new books about 228
Hobbies 206–13
 arts and handicrafts 208, pictures 209
 coin collecting 213
 photography 92–95
 stamp collecting 210–12, pictures 207
Hockey 335, picture 341
Hodgson, James D., U.S. official 48–49, 373
Hoffman, Julius J., U.S. judge, picture 40
Hoisington, Elizabeth P., U.S. general, picture 275
Holyoake, Keith, New Zealand prime minister 131
Holzman, Red, U.S. basketball coach 326

Honor America Day 50
Horizon Club Conference 393
Horse racing 334, picture 334—35
House of Representatives, United States see United
    States Congress
Housing
    architectural design 102, 107, picture 106
Human behavior, study of, pictures 297
Hungary 205
Husak, Gustav, Czech Communist party head 205
Hussein, Jordanian king, picture 50
Hyaline-membrane disease 240

I

Ibos, a people of Biafra and Nigeria 38, 68, picture 39
Ice hockey 335, picture 341
Iceland 50, 201
Ice skating 334
Illinois
    John Hancock Center, Chicago 102, 104
    Northwestern University Library, Evanston 102
Immigration and emigration
    New Zealand 131, picture 129
Imperial Hotel, Tokyo, Japan 107
Income
    farm income 76—77
    See also articles on various countries
Independence, for Pacific islands 131, 132—33
India 118
Indiana
    St. Thomas Aquinas Church, Indianapolis 104, 106,
        picture 87
Indians, American
    demonstration for equal rights, picture 367
Indochina war see Vietnam war
Indonesia 113—14
Industries
    auto industry 350
    factories are source of air pollution 27—28, pictures
        25, 28—29
    See also articles on various countries
Inflation, United States 144, 150, 368
Insecticides, pollution by 21—22, 80—81
Integration see Desegregation
Intelsat, communications satellites 315
Interest rates 150
Interior design, for young people's rooms 270—73
International co-operation
    space co-operation 308, 313—14
International Farm Youth Exchangees 393
International relations see United Nations and articles
        on various countries
Iran 254, 256
Iraq 254
Ireland
    Paisley, Ian, Protestant leader, picture 200
Israel
    Israeli Air Force 260—61
    See also Arab-Israeli dispute
Italy 50, 201
    ancient tomb, Paestum, picture 303
    Colombo, Emilio 52
    Communist China, relations with 58

J

Jacklin, Tony, British golfer 337
Jackson, George, U.S. black militant and author 228,
    picture 225
Jackson State College, Mississippi 46—47, 154, 158, 369

Jamaica 384, picture 383
Japan 117
    architecture 107
    EXPO'70 122—25
Jarring, Gunnar, United Nations mediator 50, 53, 54,
    358, pictures 359
Jaw and teeth, picture 244—45
Jewish Defense League (JDL) 293
Jews and Judaism 60, 293, picture 289

Job action. An organized slowdown in work, arranged
    by a labor union. The action is a way of putting
    pressure on an employer to agree to a union's de-
    mands. Often it takes the form of holding union
    meetings during what are usually working hours.

Joffrey Ballet 169, picture 168
John Hancock Center, Chicago, Ill. 102, 104
Jonathan, Leabua, leader of Lesotho 71, picture 67
Jones Act upheld (prohibiting movement of cargo in
    foreign ships) 348
Joplin, Janis, U.S. rock singer, picture 173
Jordan 50, 53
    civil war 54
    Palestinian commandos 253—54; pictures 247, 251
Journalism, Pulitzer prizes 409

K

"Kee-O-Kuk, Chief of the Sauk and Foxes" by George
    Catlin, picture 96
Kelsay, Merrill, Star Farmer of America award winner,
    picture 395
Kent State University, Ohio 46—47, 154, 158, 368—69,
    picture 155
Kenya
    Asians expelled from country 70, 73
Kenyatta, Jomo, president of Kenya 70, picture 69
Keratomalacia, disease 241
Kerr, Clark, American educator 158
Khorana, H. Gobind, American chemist 298, picture 294
Khrushchev Remembers, new book 224
Kidd, Billy, U.S. athlete, picture 339
Kidnapings
    Eugen Biehl, kidnaped by Basques 60
    Latin America 44, 221, 223, pictures 217, 222
    Pierre Laporte and James Cross, in Canada 56, 60,
        136, picture 135
Kidney transplants 238
Kienast quintuplets, picture 274
Knicks (New York Knickerbockers) 326
Knights of Columbus building, New Haven, Conn. 102,
    picture 104
Kosygin, Aleksei, Soviet premier 53, 202, picture 193
Kruger National Park 74—75
Kunstler, William, U.S. lawyer 41
Kurdish nationalism 254
Kuwait 254, 256

L

Labor
    farm workers organized 83
    unemployment, U.S. 148, 151, pictures 147, 149
    See also Strikes
Laird, Melvin, U.S. official, pictures 112, 375, 379
Land use policy, to save environment 32, 190—91
Laos
    Vietnamese Communist attack 113, picture 110
Laporte, Pierre, Canadian official murdered 56, 136,
    picture 135

Lassa fever, new virus 239, pictures 236, 239
Latin America 214–23
  U.S. attitude of neutrality 378
  See also articles on various countries
Lebanon 53
Lee, Will, U.S. actor, picture 177
Legislation
  environmental bills 185
  laws passed by Congress 371
Leinsdorf, Erich, American conductor, picture 397
Lenin's birth celebration, picture 203
Lesotho, coup d'etat and political unrest 71
Levingston, Roberto Marcelo, Argentinian president 221
Lewis, Henry, U.S. conductor 171
Libya 38, 254
Life
  search for life's beginning in space 298
Life cycle 13, picture 12
Life Library of Photography 90, pictures 90–91
LIFT (Low Inventories for Tomorrow) program, Canada 140
Light and sound sculpture 101
Lindsay, John, New York City mayor, picture 353
Lin Piao, Chinese leader 116
Lions, in African national park, picture 75
Lipton, Peggy, U.S. actress, picture 175
Literature 224–29
  children's 230–35
  Nobel prize winner 409
  Pulitzer prizes 409
Little, Cleavon, U.S. actor, picture 181
Little League World Series, pictures 340
Lodge, Henry Cabot, U.S. diplomat 376
Lombardi, Vince, U.S. football coach, picture 284
London, England
  garbage strike 199, picture 198
Long, Loretta, U.S. actress, pictures 177, 179

Longuette. A woman's skirt, dress, or coat reaching below the knee. The term was first used by fashion designers and stores in 1970. They did not specify an exact length for the longuette. Therefore the term includes the more precise term midi.
  See also Midi

Lon Nol, Cambodian premier 112
Los Angeles, California
  automotive pollutants have decreased 20
Lottery, winners of super lottery, picture 274
Lovell, James A., Jr., U.S. astronaut 44, 312, picture 45

Low profile. A position or role that does not attract great attention. In international politics, a nation is said to maintain a low profile when it does not take sudden, dramatic, or far-reaching actions toward other nations.

Lunar rocks, analysis of 315
Lunar rover, U.S. moon vehicle, picture 311
Luna spacecraft, Soviet unmanned craft 54, 308, 312–13, picture 309–10
Lung capacity machine, picture 243
Lunokhod 1, Soviet vehicle on moon 58, 313, pictures 310–11

M

Machines and machinery
  environmental problems 18–20
  farm machinery 78, picture 79
Magazines, photography 88, picture 89
Makarova, Natalya, Soviet ballerina 54, 169

Malaysia 114–15
Manapouri, Lake, New Zealand 131
Manhattan, SS, tanker 348
Manson, Charles, U.S. hippie cult leader, picture 279
Mao Tse-tung, Chinese leader 116
Maps
  Africa 65
  Cambodia 45
  Europe 193
  Fiji and Tonga 133
  Latin America 215
  Middle East 246
  Southeast Asia 108
Maravich, "Pistol" Pete, U.S. athlete, picture 327
Marshall, Thurgood, U.S. jurist, picture 373
Marxism, in Chile 214, 218–19
Massachusetts
  Design Research Building, Cambridge 102, picture 103
Mass transit program 346–47
Matisse, Henri, French artist 97, 99
Matter and antimatter 299

Maxi or **Maxicoat.** A long outer coat that flares, or widens, very gradually toward the bottom. In women's models the hem of the skirt is no more than an inch or two above the ankle, and sometimes it reaches the ankle. In men's the hemline is about a foot above the ankle. Picture 265

McCartney, Paul, British composer and singer 171
McGovern-Hatfield Amendment 376
McGrady, Marty, U.S. athlete 332, picture 333
McGrath, Bob, U.S. actor, picture 177
McLaren, Bruce, New Zealand athlete 321
Medicine and health 236–41
  Australia's new health plan 130
  Museum of Medical Science, Houston, Texas 242–45
  Nobel prize winner 409
  noise, hazard to health 17
Medina, Ernest, U.S. Army officer, picture 376
Mediterranean Sea, drilling missions in 300

Megacity. A city having a population of a million or more persons.

Meier, Richard, U.S. architect 107
Meir, Golda, Israeli prime minister, picture 51
Mendoza y Amor, Benjamin, Bolivian attacker of Pope Paul VI 291, picture 289
Merchant ships, building of 348, picture 344–45
Mercury, animals' food contaminated by 186
Mercury fungicides, danger of 236
Meteor, Soviet weather satellites 315
Meteorology, weather satellites 314–15
Metropolitan Museum of Art, New York City
  centennial celebration exhibitions 86–87, 97
Metropolitan Opera, New York City 170
Mexico 219, picture 221
  border disputes with United States 52
Mexico, Gulf of, oil spills, picture 186
Michals, Duane, U.S. photographer 88

Middle American. A member of a new and increasing group within the U.S. middle-class, holding clearly defined attitudes and ideals. Politically and socially, middle Americans are thought to be conservative, extremely patriotic, and opposed to challenging the authority or actions of the government. They favor conventional dress and behavior at all times.
  Middle Americans include some 40,000,000 persons who in the last 15 years have risen from low or modest income levels to average annual in-

Middle American (cont.)
comes of about $12,500 for a family of four. The rise in their standard of living is measured by an increase in ownership of their own homes and automobiles.

Middle East 246–57
United Nations efforts toward peace 358–59
U.S. proposals for cease-fire 377–78
See also Arab-Israeli dispute

Midi. Also midiskirt. A dress or coat whose skirt extends about three to five inches below the knee of the wearer, or approximately to midpoint of the calf of the leg. Picture 265

Mildred and William Dean Howells, sculpture by Saint-Gaudens 100
Millett, Kate, U.S. feminist and author 229, picture 228
Mines and mining
Australia 130, picture 129
Mini-midiskirt controversy 264, picture 265
Mints, United States
tourist facilities at 213
Mishima, Yukio, Japanese author, picture 116
Missiles
Russian-made in Middle East, picture 259
Mitchell, Martha, wife of U.S. attorney general, picture 278
Models, railroad and cars, picture 206–07
Modules, housing units 107, picture 106
Moe, Karen, U.S. athlete, picture 336
Moiseyev Dance Company, picture 162
Molniya, Soviet communications satellites 315
Monkey, in Kruger National Park, picture 75
Moon
eclipse of sun, pictures 304
flight to the moon 312
Moore, Melba, U.S. actress, picture 181
Morris, Robert, U.S. sculptor 100–01
Morton, Rogers C. B., U.S. public official 373
Moscow, capital of U.S.S.R.
school children, picture 195
Moscow Treaty, between West Germany and Russia 53, 196, 202, 204, 205
Moss, Frank, U.S. senator 371
Motion pictures 164–67
Academy awards 164
Moynihan, Daniel, U.S. official 370, picture 157
Muhammed Ali, U.S. athlete, picture 318
Muscat and Oman 50
Museums
Boston Museum of Art 97
Metropolitan Museum of Art, New York City 86–87, 97
Museum of Medical Science, Houston, Texas 242–45
Music 170–73
awards 171, 409
World Youth Orchestra, picture 397
Muskie, Edmund, U.S. senator 371
Muslims and Hindus, tension between 118

N

Nairobi, Kenya, street scene, picture 70–71
Nasser, Gamal Abdel, United Arab Republic president 50, 54, 246, 253, pictures 55, 247, 280
death cancels U.S. show of force 377
National Communicable Disease Center, Atlanta, Ga., picture 240
National Council of Churches 290
National Environmental Policy Act of 1969 185
National Guard, United States 368–69

National League, baseball 322–24
Nations of the world, with statistics 398–403
NATO see North Atlantic Treaty Organization
Natural resources, conservation of 32, 189
Naxalites, terrorist group in India 118
Negroes see Blacks
Neighborhood Youth Corps 152, pictures 153
Nerve gas, dumped off Florida coast 52
Netsch, Walter, U.S. architect 102
New Brunswick, Canada 138
New Guinea 131
New Haven, Conn.
Knights of Columbus building 102, picture 104
New Jersey
census, 1970 380
dinosaur tracks 306–07
News
TV coverage under attack 174, 176
New York
census, 1970 380
New York City
air pollution, picture 182
Dinosaur Trailside Park 306–07
Jewish demonstration against Soviet Union, picture 289
open-admissions policy for City University 158
United Nations anniversary celebrations 356–58
Westyard Building 104, picture 105
New Zealand 126, 131, picture 130
Nicklaus, Jack, U.S. golfer 337
Nigeria 54
end and aftermath of civil war 38, 68
Nikolayev, Andrian, Soviet cosmonaut, picture 309, 313
Nimbus, weather satellites 315
1970-F, comet, picture 305
Nixon, Richard M., U.S. president, pictures 49, 61, 117, 144, 312, 355, 362, 365, 369, 380, 388
aid to Latin America curtailed 214, 223
cabinet 373
cites U.S. commandos, picture 111
civil rights 370
commission on student unrest 159
countries visited 377
election 1970, 370–71
inflation 368
student unrest 368–69
U.S.–Soviet relations 379
Vietnam war and Cambodia 376, picture 45
Yugoslavia, visit to 202, picture 203
Nixon Doctrine, in foreign affairs 376
Nobel prizes 409
Noise, a pollutant 187
health hazard 17

No-knock. Referring to the provision of a law that permits policemen with search warrants to enter the residence of suspected lawbreaker without knocking or otherwise announcing themselves. The best-known such provision is in the 1970 U.S. Drug Abuse Control Act. The warrant is issued to the police by a judge or magistrate when he has reason to believe that drugs such as heroin are possessed by the person whose residence is to be raided, and that to knock first would give the person time to get rid of the drugs.

North Atlantic Treaty Organization 197
Northwestern University Library, Evanston, Ill. 102
Northwest Passage, tankers proved too costly to operate in 348
Nova Scotia, Canada 138
Nuclear power plants
pollution from 29

Nuclear weapons
  bombs exploded in French Polynesia 131
Nutrition, dry cereals 81

O

Oakland Museum, California 102
Obituaries see Deaths
Obote, Milton, Uganda president, picture 67
Ocean
  pollution in the ocean 25, 186–87
Oceania 126, 131, 132–33
Oceanography 300
Off-Broadway theater 180, 181
Oil pollution 186
  ocean polluted by oil 26
Oman 257
Open-admissions policy, for colleges 158
Opera 170
Orangerie, sculpture by Caro 100, picture 101
Orchestral music 170–71
Organization of African Unity
  summit meeting, picture 66
Organ transplantation 238
Ovando Candia, Alfredo, Bolivian president 221

P

Pacific Islands 126, 131, 132–33
Paestum, Italy, ancient tomb, picture 303
Painting 96–99
Paisley, Ian, Protestant leader in Northern Ireland, picture 200
Pakistan
  cyclone and flood 58, 118, pictures 59, 109, 118–19
Palestinian commandos 253–54, pictures 247, 251
  clash with Israeli forces 53
  hijacked planes 54, 349
  Lebanon 46
  Switzerland 40
Pants and knickers, fashion 264
Papua 131
Paris peace talks, on Vietnam war 376, picture 111
Parks
  African game parks 74–75
Pastrana Borrero, Misael, Colombian president 219
Paul VI, pope 291, 292
  attempted assassination 58
Peace
  Nobel prize winner 409
Peace talks
  Middle East 54, 60
  Vietnam war 376, picture 111
Pele (Edson Arantes do Nascimiento), Brazilian soccer champion 320
Penn Central Transportation Company, bankruptcy 150–51, 346
Persian Gulf area 254, 256–57
Personalities, pictures 274–79
Peru, earthquake 46, picture 216
Pesticides see Insecticides
Petroleum, highlights in industry 348
  See also Oil pollution
Petrouchka, ballet 169, picture 168
Phantom fighter-bomber, picture 260

Philadelphia Plan. A program of the Nixon administration, first used in Philadelphia, designed to increase the hiring of blacks and other members of minority groups. Under the plan, contractors engaged in construction-trades projects that cost $500,000 or

Philadelphia Plan (cont.)
  more, and that are paid for wholly or in part by the Federal government, must agree to hire a certain number of minority-group workers, as set by the government. By 1972 the number is scheduled to increase to 26 percent of the total work force of the project.

Philately 210–12, picture 207
Philippines
  attempted assassination of Pope Paul VI 291, picture 289
Philympia, British stamp exhibition 211
Phoenix House, New York City, picture 241
Photography 88–91
  awards 92–95
Physical sciences see Chemistry; Physics
Physicians, need of more 241
Physics 299
  Nobel prize winner 409
Physiology see Medicine and health
Piene, Otto, U.S. artist
  "sky ballets" in Washington, D.C., picture 99
Planet Uranus, picture 305
Plankton
  insecticides danger to 22
Plastic flower making, a hobby 208, picture 209
Plate tectonics theory 300
Platz, Elizabeth, U.S. minister, picture 288
Plaza, Galo, official of Organization of American States, picture 378
Poetry 229
Poland
  civil disorder and purge of Gomulka 60, 205
  treaty with West Germany 58, 196, 205
Politics
  books about 228
  TV free time devoted to politics 174
Pollution
  Canada 140, 143
  Dirty Water, game 268
  United States 18–35, 182–91
  See also Air pollution; Oil pollution; Water pollution
Polywater, or water II 299
Pompidou, Georges, French president 199, picture 357
Popular music 171–73
Population
  census, 1970 380–81
  nations of the world 398–403
Population explosion 15–16, 32, pictures 14–16, 383
Portuguese Guinea 60, 64, 69
Post Office, U.S. see United States Postal Service
Pouliot, Francois, Canadian diplomat, picture 360
Powell, Boog, U.S. athlete 322, picture 323
Powell, Enoch, British politician 48
Power plants, source of air pollution 27
Preakness Stakes, horse race, picture 334–35
Presidential miniatures, on coins, picture 213
Presidential Task Force, recommendations of 81
Prince Edward Island, Canada 138
Prisoners of war, proposals for release 376
Prizes and awards
  architecture 107
  entertainment awards 171
  Future Farmers of America awards 395
  literature for children 232–33
  Nobel prizes 409
  photography 90, 92–95
  Pulitzer prizes 409
Prokoshkin, Yuri, Soviet scientist 299
Protein synthesis, picture 296
Protestantism 290, picture 288
Public Broadcasting Service (PBS) 176

Publishing see Books; Literature
Puerto Rico, U.S. Navy target practice 387
Pulitzer prizes 409
Pulsa, group of U.S. sculptors 101
Purlie, play 181, picture 180

Q

"Quality of life," concern for 185, 188–89
Quebec, Canada 136–38
    separatists kidnap officials 56, 60, 136, picture 135
Quintuplets, born to New Jersey couple 40, picture 274

R

Races of man, civil rights 370
Racing
    auto racing 321
    horse racing 334, picture 334–35
Rail Passenger Service Act 346
Railroads 346–47
    model railroad set, picture 206
Razak, Tun Abdul, Malaysian leader, picture 115
Realistic style, of painting 99

Re-entry corridor. The path taken by a spacecraft on its return to earth. The path must permit the craft to re-enter the earth's atmosphere without burning up in the atmosphere and without skipping back into outer space.

Refugees
    African refugees 73, picture 68
    Palestinian refugee camp, picture 252
Reich, Charles A., U.S. author 229, picture 227
Rejection phenomenon, in heart transplants 238
Religion 288–93
Rembrandt, Harmensy van Rijn, Dutch artist 97
Repertory theater 181
Reproduction process, picture 245
Reuther, Walter P. U.S. labor leader, picture 285
Rhodesia, Republic of
    conflict over racial issue 73
    declared itself a republic 42
Ribonucleic acid (RNA), research for cancer cure 298
Richardson, Elliot L., U.S. official 48–49, 373

Right on. An exclamatory phrase used to show enthusiastic agreement or strong approval. It is often the equivalent of "That's great" or "I'm with you 100 per cent."

Rindt, Jochen, Austrian athlete 321
RNA, research for cancer cure 298
Robinson, Frank, U.S. athlete 322, 323, 324
Robinson, Kenneth, Outstanding Teenager of America, picture 397
Robinson, Matt, U.S. actor, picture 177
Roche, Kevin, U.S. architect 102, 104
Rock music and music groups 171–73
Rogers, William P., U.S. official, picture 378
    Middle East cease-fire 50
Roman Catholic Church 291–92, picture 289
Rosati, James, U.S. sculptor 101
Rose, Ben, U.S. photographer, picture 91
Rosewall, Ken, Australian athlete 338
Ruckelshaus, William D., U.S. public official, picture 185
Rumania 205
Rumor, Mariano, Italian premier 201
Russell, Louis B., Jr., heart transplant recipient, picture 238

S

Sadat, Anwar al-, president, United Arab Republic 56, 253
Sahara, ancient South Pole found in 301
Said, Qabus ibn, sultan of Oman, picture 257
Saint-Gaudens, Augustus, U.S. sculptor 100
Saint Thomas Aquinas Church, Indianapolis, Ind. 104, 106, picture 87

SALT. Strategic Arms Limitation Talks. The long-range disarmament talks between representatives of the United States and Soviet Union, begun late in 1969, are designed to explore ways to reduce offensive and defensive weapons of both nations. A particular aim is the limitation of nuclear missiles and strategic bombing planes. See also 197, 379
    cartoon 197

SAM. Surface-to-air missile, a missile fired from the ground and designed to knock down enemy aircraft while they are approaching a target up to many miles distant. One type is for use against low-flying craft, and another for use against airplanes approaching at high altitudes.

San Francisco, California
    Bank of America tower 104
    United Nations anniversary celebrations 356
San Francisco Opera 170
Satellites, man-made
    China, Communist 116
    See also Space exploration
Sato, Eisaku, Japanese premier 117
Saudi Arabia 254, 256
Scholastic photography awards 92–95
School-lunch program 81
Schumann, Maurice, French diplomat, picture 357
Schweickart, Russell, U.S. astronaut, picture 313
Science
    ancient Saharan South Pole found 301
    dinosaurs 306–07
    See also Biological sciences; Chemistry, etc.
Scott, George C., U.S. actor 164, picture 165
Scranton, William, U.S. public official 158, 369
Sculpture 100–01
    head, claimed to be Aphrodite, picture 303
    model-metal sculpture, picture 207
Sea-floor spreading theory 300
Seattle Opera Company 170
Seeger, Pete, U.S. folk singer, picture 178
Senate, United States see United States Congress
Separatism, in Canada 136–37
Sesame Street, educational TV program 161, 176, 177–79
Sevastyanov, Vitaly, Soviet cosmonaut, picture 309
Sewage, water pollutant 24–25
Sharaf, Abdul Hamid, Jordanian diplomat, picture 358
Ships and shipping 348, picture 344–45
    Soviet warships in Mediterranean 258
    wreck of 18th-century ship, picture 302
Shostakovich, Dimitri, Soviet composer 170–71
Shultz, George P., U.S. official 48–49, 373

Sick-out. A situation that results when a large number of employees of a company or industry stay away from work, after reporting that they are ill. The result of this planned absenteeism is a work slow-down or stoppage. It is a way of protesting against conditions that the workers want to change.

Sihanouk, Norodom, Cambodian leader 43, 112

Silent majority. The great majority of Americans who do not take part in demonstrations or public protests against existing conditions, especially the war in Southeast Asia. They are considered by their silence to be in agreement with the government. The term first gained popularity when it was used by President Richard Nixon in a speech on Vietnam protests, on Nov. 3, 1969. He contrasted "the great silent majority" with a "vocal minority" of protesters.

Singapore 115
Skating, Ice 334
Skeleton, picture 242
Skiing 339
Skylab, space station 316–17
Slataper, Eugene L., U.S. doctor, picture 243
Smithville Youth Program 393
Smog, polluted air 27, 187–88
Soccer 320
   Brazil's victory celebration, picture 216
Social problems, books about 228–29
Solid waste pollution 24–25, 30, 189, pictures 13, 30–31, 34, 188
Somalia, nationalizes some industries 69
South Africa
   apartheid policy 38, 46, 71, 73
South America see Latin America
South Asia 118–19
Southeast Asia 112–13, pictures 110–13
   American influence in, pictures 120–21
   Australian troops in Singapore and Malaysia 128

Southern strategy. A plan of political action in the U.S. said to be designated to make the Republican party strong in the southern United States. The South for years elected Democrats almost without exception. The long-range purpose of the Southern strategy is to switch this regular support to the Republicans. The short-range goal, especially in the 1972 presidential election, is to head off the entry of a third-party candidate by eliminating the need of Southerners for a more conservative third choice. The Nixon administration denied that it has followed such a Southern strategy. But its opponents charge the administration has granted special favors to the South.

South Pole
   ancient pole found in Sahara 301
Soviet Union see Union of Soviet Socialist Republics
Soviet-West German treaty 53, 196, 202, 204, 205
Soyuz 9, Soviet spacecraft 312, picture 309
Space, outer, search for life in space 298
Space exploration 308–17
   Apollo 13 mission 44, picture 45
   cutback in space program 148
   Luna 16 landed on moon 54
   Soyuz 9, 48
Space stations 314, 316–17
Spain
   Basque crisis 199
   United States military bases in 52, 197
Sports
   books about 229
   See also names of sports
SST (supersonic transport) controversy 187, 349
Stacy, Hollis, U.S. athlete, picture 341
Stamps and stamp collecting 210–12, picture 207
Star Farmer of America Award 395
Stewart, Potter, U.S. jurist, picture 373
Stock market
   unease over activity 149–50
Stoph, Willi, East German premier 196
Strategic Arms Limitation Talks see SALT
Strelkov, Aleksandr, Soviet dancer, picture 162
Strikes
   garbage strike, London 199 picture 198
   postal service 42
   United Automobile Workers 151, 350
   See also Labor
Student unrest
   Kent State and Jackson State College 46–47
   United States 158–59, 368, 376, picture 155
   See also Civil disorders
Submarines, Australian, picture 128
Subsidy, for farmers 83
Suburbs, of cities
   census, 1970 380
Sudan 69, 254
Suharto, Indonesian president, 113 picture 114–15, 357
Sukarno, former president of Indonesia 114
Sun
   eclipse of sun, pictures 304
   living things need sun's energy 13
   solar corona, picture 296
Supersonic transport plane see SST controversy
Supreme Court, United States 373, 375, 408
   major decisions 372, 374
Surplus farm products 83
Swahili, national language of Kenya 70
Sweden 201
Swigert, John L., Jr., U.S. astronaut 44, 312, picture 45
Swimming 336
Switzerland
   Arab guerilla groups 40
   EXPO'70, Swiss Pavilion, picture 122
Syria 254

T

Tago-Sato-Kisaka comet, picture 305
Taimur, Said ibn, sultan of Oman, picture 256
Tange, Kenzo, Japanese architect 107
Tanzam railroad, Africa 71, picture 72
Tanzania, railroad through Zambia started 71
Tarr, Curtis W., U.S. official 42, picture 275
Tauf'ahau Tupou IV, king of Tonga, picture 132
Taut, Stanley, U.S. doctor 237
Taxation and taxes
   church property 290
   Tax Reform Act, U.S. 78
   tax reform in Canada 140
   United States 151
Tax Reform Act, U.S. 78
Tekoah, Josef, Israeli delegate to UN, picture 359
Television 174–76
   Emmy awards 176
   Sesame Street 161, 176, 177–79
Temin, Howard, U.S. biologist 298
Tennis 338
Terpsichore's Progress, dance exhibition 169
Texas
   Museum of Medical Science, Houston 242–45
Thant, U, UN secretary-general, pictures 352, 353, 356
Theater 180–81
   awards 181
Thermal (heat) pollution 29
   harmful to fish and plants 186
Thomas, Michael Tilson, U.S. conductor 171
Thomas, Taryn, Little Miss America, picture 397
Thompson, Benjamin, U.S. architect 102
Tie-dyeing, a hobby 208, picture 209
Tight-money policy 150

Time-Life Books 90, pictures 90–91
Tito, president of Yugoslavia 202, 204, picture 203
Tonga 126, 131, 132–33
   independence 48
Tony award winners 181
Topical stamp collecting, pictures 212
Toronto, Canada, land control proposed 143
Torres, Juan Jose, Bolivian president 56, 221
Touré, Sékou, president of Guinea 64, 69
Tourism, African national parks 74–75
   See also names of various countries
Tower of the Sun, EXPO'70, picture 123
Tower of Youth, EXPO'70, picture 124
Track and field, sports 332
Trade and commerce
   Caribbean Free Trade Area (CARIFTA) 384
   Japan and United States 117
   Yugoslavia signed agreement with EEC 40
Transportation 342–49
   environment problems 18–20
Trinidad and Tobago, civil unrest in 384, picture 382
Triticale, cross between rye and barley 83
Trudeau, Pierre Elliott, Canadian prime minister 56, 134, 138, pictures 134, 139
Tucker, Richard, U.S. opera singer 170
Tupamaro guerrillas, Uruguayan terrorists 223, picture 222
Turkey, earthquake 42
Turkish Cypriots 254
Tydings, Joseph, U.S. senator 370

U

Uganda, Asians expelled from country 70, 73
Ulbricht, Walter, East German leader 205
Unemployment 368
Union of Soviet Socialist Republics 202–05
   China, relations with 116
   Jews in Soviet Union 60, 293
   Luna 16 landed on moon 54
   Middle East, involvement in 250, 258–59, 260
   Moiseyev Dance Company, picture 162
   photography exhibit 90
   plane hijacked 56, picture 343
   school children, picture 195
   space flights 308, 312–15, pictures 309–10
   treaty with West Germans 53
   United States, relations with 379

Unisex. Close similarity in appearance between young men and women, or boys and girls, with respect to fashion (clothing) or hair styling. Making no distinction as to sex; appropriate to both sexes (as in unisex dress; a unisex hairdo).

United Arab Republic 50, 53, 54, 250, 253–54, 260
   Sadat, Anwar al- made president 56, 253
   U.S. proposals for a cease-fire 377–78
United Kingdom of Great Britain and Northern Ireland 199
   Conservatives win British elections 48
United Nations 42, 352–59
   member nations and chief representatives 404
   World Youth Assembly 360–61
United States 362–81
   census 1970, 380–81
   Middle East, involvement in 250, 253, 260
   space programs 308–17
United States Congress 370–71
   membership list 405–07
United States Postal Service 52, 211, 371
   strike 42

University and colleges
   basketball 326
   open-admissions policy 158
   See also Student unrest
Uranium
   Canada 140
   discovered in Northern Territory, Australia 130
Uranus, planet, picture 305
Uruguay, kidnaping 223, picture 222

V

Van Gogh, Vincent, Dutch artist 99
Velasco Ibarra, Jose Maria, Ecuadorian president 221
Velazquez, Diego, Spanish painter
   "The Slave of Velazquez" picture 98
Venera, Soviet spacecraft 313
Verso, Edward, U.S. dancer, picture 168
Video-cassette system, TV playback unit, picture 174
Vietcong, Vietnamese communists 376
Vietnam
   Future Farmers of America program 395
Vietnamization, of the Vietnam war 376
Vietnam war 375–76, picture 364
   Australian troops 128
   Cambodia 43, 44, 48, pictures 110–13
   Laos 112–13, pictures 110–13
   students voice sentiments, pictures 159
   troop withdrawal pledged by Nixon 44
Virgin Islands 387
Viruses, advances in research 238, 239
   research to cure diseases 298
Vogel, Mitch, U.S. actor, picture 163
Volpe, John, U.S. public official, picture 342
Von Spreti, Karl, West German diplomat, kidnaped 44, 223
Voting, age reduction legislation 371

W

Wallenda, Karl, high-wire artist, picture 277
Wall treatment, for young people's rooms 272
Walsh, James E., U.S. clergyman 50
Walsh, Rewa C., Miss Teenage America, picture 397
Walsh-Healey Act 17
War Measures Act, Canada 56, 136
War movies 164, picture 165
Washington, D.C.
   American Institute of Architects headquarters 106–07, picture 105
   "sky ballet" by Otto Piene, picture 99
Wasserberg, Gerald J., U.S. scientist 315
Water pollution 23–26, 29, 32, 186–87

Weatherman. A member of a small group of far left-wing American students whose goal is revolutionary change in the United States. They hope to alter U.S. foreign policy, race relations, and social and economic structure by direct action, including force and terrorism. The group includes the most radical and action-minded members of Students for a Democratic Society (SDS), the left-wing student organization that in 1969 was split by a struggle for power between this group and a more moderate one. The radical group seized control of the SDS national headquarters and became known as Weatherman.

Weather satellites 314–15
Weaver, Earl, Star Farmer of America award winner, picture 395

Weinglass, Leonard, U.S. lawyer 41
West Germany see Germany
West Indies 382–87
West Indies, University of, Trinidad, picture 383
Westyard Building, New York City 104, picture 105
Wheat surplus, in Canada 140
White, Byron, U.S. jurist, picture 373
White, Robert I., U.S. educator 369
Wildenstein, Alec, U.S. art collector, picture 98
Wildlife
    African game parks 74–75
    wildlife and pets photography awards, pictures 92–95
Williams, Clarence III, U.S. actor, pictures 175
Williams, Harrison, U.S. senator 371
Wilson, Flip, U.S. comedian, picture 175
Wilson, Harold, British prime minister
    visit to United States 38
Window treatment, for young people's rooms 273
Witt, Peter N., U.S. scientist, picture 297
Women
    ordination of women 290, picture 288
    United States generals, pictures 275

Women's Liberation Movement. A movement that seeks
    a new and improved status, or position, for women.
    The new status would apply particularly to dealings
    between women and men. It would bring liberation
    from what followers of the movement regard as a
    second-class standing for. women in the present
    society, built and dominated by men. The move-
    ment's goal includes not only women's guaranteed
    legal equality with men but equality in employ-
    ment opportunity, in pay scales in government
    service, family management, and in all other mat-
    ters affecting both sexes. See also 370, picture 366
    women's studies 161

Wool, New Zealand 131, picture 130
World Series results, in baseball 322, 323, 324
World's Fair EXPO'70, Japan 122–25
World Soccer Cup 320
World Youth Assembly 360–61
World Youth Orchestra, picture 397
Wright, Rebecca, U.S. dancer, picture 168

X

XEP, battery-driven car, picture 345

Y

Yablonski, Joseph A., U.S. labor official 38
Yost, Charles, U.S. ambassador to UN, picture 61, 353
Young people
    books for boys and girls 230–35
    commission on student unrest 159
    decorating rooms for young people 270–73
    drug abuse 161, picture 241
    help to improve environment, pictures 33–35
    in the news, pictures 396–97
    movies about 164
    photography awards 92–95
    Sesame Street, TV program 161, 176, 177–79
    sports, pictures 340–41
    UN World Youth Assembly 360–61
    U.S. draft age immigrants in Canada 290
Youth see Young people
Youth organizations 388–95, pictures 84–85
    Boys' Clubs of America 394
    Boy Scouts of America 392, picture 389
    Camp Fire Girls 393
    4-H clubs 393, pictures 85
    Future Farmers of America 395, pictures 84–85, 389
    Girl Scouts of the U.S.A. 390–91, pictures 389–91
    Neighborhood Youth Corp 152, pictures 153
Yugoslavia 202, 204
    signed trade agreement with EEC 40

Z

Zambia
    railroad through Tanzania started 71
Zayyat, Mohammad al-, Egyptian official, picture 53
Zionism 293
Zond, Soviet spacecraft 313

ILLUSTRATION CREDITS

The following list credits, by page, the sources of illustrations used in THE NEW BOOK OF KNOWLEDGE ANNUAL. Credits are listed illustration by illustration—left to right, top to bottom. Wherever appropriate, the name of the photographer or artist has been listed with the source, the two being separated by a dash. When two or more illustrations appear on one page, their credits are separated by semicolons.

10– NASA; NASA; Loebel—Frederic
11 Lewis, Inc.; Dennis Brack—Black Star; Multi-Media Photography; *St. Louis Post Dispatch*—Black Star
12 Miller Pope
13 Owen Franken
14 National Wildlife
15 Raghubir Singh—Nancy Palmer; National Wildlife
16 Raghubir Singh—Nancy Palmer; National Wildlife
18 Keegar—Photo Trends
19 Ambassador College
21 Teresa Zabala—Nancy Palmer
22 National Wildlife
23 National Wildlife
24 Jewel Stores; Paul Stephanus—DPI
25 National Wildlife
26 Christopher R. Harris—Black Star; Shell Oil
27 National Wildlife
28 Dennis Brack—Black Star
29 National Wildlife
30 James Pickerell—Black Star
33 DPI
34 Ambassador College; Reynolds Aluminum Company
35 Girl Scouts of America; DPI
36 George Sottung
38 Wide World
39 Miriam Reik—Bethel Agency
40 Wide World
41 © 1970 Verna Sadock, NBC News
42 Werner Wolff—Black Star
43 Ray Cranbourne—Empire News—Black Star; UPI
44 Wide World
45 UPI
46 John A. Darnell, *Life* magazine © 1970
47 UPI
48 Central Press—Pictorial Parade
49 Steve Northup—Camera 5; Forte—Pictorial Parade; Paul Conklin—PIX; UPI
50 Rene Burri—Magnum; G. Sipahioglu—PIX
51 Diana Davies—Bethel
52 *London Daily Express*—Pictorial Parade
53 Wide World
54 *The Sun*, London—Pictorial Parade
55 Photoreporters
56 UPI
57 UPI
58 Paul Conklin—PIX
59 UPI
60 Eastfoto
61 UPI
62 Agenzia Dufoto—Photoreporters; Bruno Barbey—Magnum; Bob West; UPI
63 Chalais—Camera Press—PIX; Lief Engberg—Photoreporters; Renee Falche Rebuffat—Rapho-Guillumette; ABC-TV; Fairchild Aerial Survey
64 UPI

65 George Buctel
66 UPI
67 UPI
68 UPI
70 *Paris Match*—Pictorial Parade
71 Marc and Evelyn Bernheim—Rapho-Guillumette
72 Camerapix—Nancy Palmer
73 UPI
74 Satour
75 Satour
76 Standard Oil Co.
78 Bob Coffman
79 Norman Reeder; Dick Braun
80 UPI
81 Dick Seim
82 Bob Fitch—Black Star
84 Future Farmers of America
85 Future Farmers of America; 4-H Clubs
86 Bruce Davidson © 1970 Magnum Photos; Metropolitan Museum of Art
87 The Solomon R. Guggenheim Museum, N.Y.; Balthazar Korab from Woolen Assoc.
89 Dan Budnik, *1971 Photography Annual*, published by Ziff-Davis
90 John Dominis, *The Camera*, published by Time-Life Books
91 Ben Rose, *Light and Film*, published by Time-Life Books
92 Eden Steiger, 13, 1970 Scholastic Magazines-Kodak Photography Awards
93 Kenneth Valastro, 15, 1970 Scholastic Magazines-Kodak Photography Awards
94 Tom Schneider, 16, 1970 Scholastic Magazines-Kodak Photography Awards; Doug Crockett, 16, 1970 Scholastic Magazines-Kodak Photography Awards
95 Tom Schneider, 16, 1970 Scholastic Magazines-Kodak Photography Awards; Laurie Baker, 16, 1970 Scholastic Magazines-Kodak Photography Awards
96 National Collection of Fine Arts, Smithsonian Institution
98 Photoreporters
99 *The New York Times*
100 National Portrait Gallery, Smithsonian Institution
101 The Solomon R. Guggenheim Museum, New York; Private Collection, courtesy Andre Emmerich Gallery
103 Ezra Stoller
104 Chalmer Alexander
105 Norman McGrath; Robert D. Harvey Studio
106 National Homes, Lafayette, Indiana
108 George Buctel
109 Camera Press—PIX; Simonpietri—Gamma—Photoreporters
110 UPI
111 UPI; Wide World
112 UPI; Terence Khoo—Black Star
113 UPI
114 UPI

115 David Channer—Camera Press—PIX
116 Pana—Black Star; Eiji Miyazawa—Black Star
117 UPI
118 Liason
120 Chalais—Camera Press—PIX; Daniell—Photoreporters
121 P. J. Griffiths—Magnum; Van Bucher—Photo Researchers
122 Japan Air Lines
123 Fuji Film
124 Japan Trade Center; Japan Air Lines; Paolo Koch—Black Star
125 Expo'70
126 *Sydney Morning Herald*
127 Colin Davey—Camera Press—PIX
128 *Sydney Morning Herald*
129 *London Daily Express*—Pictorial Parade
130 B. Williams—Camera Press—PIX
132 Colin Davey—Camera Press—PIX
133 *London Daily Express*—Pictorial Parade; George Buctel
134 UPI
135 Riboud—Magnum; UPI; Photoreporters
136 Cartier-Bresson—Magnum; UPI
137 UPI
139 UPI
141 DeWys
142 DeWys
144 Wide World
145 © The New York Times Co.
146 Scott Long, *The Minneapolis Tribune* 1970
147 *The New York Times*; Werner Wolff—Black Star
148 Elliott Erwitt—Magnum
149 Constantine Manos—Magnum
150 Gene Daniels—Black Star
152 Manpower Administration, U.S. Department of Labor
153 Manpower Administration, U.S. Department of Labor
154 Robert Day
155 © 1970 Tarentum, Pa., *Valley Daily News;* photo by John P. Filo
156 UPI
157 UPI
159 UPI
160 UPI
162 David Bier, courtesy Hurok Concerts, Inc.
163 A Cinema Center Film Presentation, a National General Pictures Release; 20th Century-Fox Studios
165 20th Century-Fox
166 © Walt Disney Productions 1970
168 Herbert Migdoll
170 UPI
172 David Gahr
173 David Gahr; Nancy Palmer
174 Sony Corporation
175 ABC-TV; ABC-TV; ABC-TV; NBC-TV
177 Children's TV Workshop
178 Children's TV Workshop
179 Children's TV Workshop
180 Zodiac

182 DPI
183 LeRoy Henderson—Black Star
184 Arthur Ambler, Audubon Society; Mark Boulton, Audubon Society; Anthony Mercieca, Audubon Society; Rohmer Beard, Audubon Society
185 UPI
186 UPI; Photo Trends
187 National Air Pollution Control Administration
188 Bruce Davidson—Magnum
189 Henry Martin
190 Elliot Erwitt—Magnum
191 Georg Gerster—Rapho-Guillumette
192 George Buctel
193 UPI; Photoreporters
194 UPI
195 UPI; Camera Press—PIX
197 Osrin in the Cleveland Plain Dealer
198 UPI
200 UPI
201 Photoreporters
203 Bunte—Camera Press—PIX
204 UPI
206 Ewing Galloway
207 Harold M. Lambert—Frederick Lewis; Bob S. Smith—Rapho-Guillumette; Sybil Shelton—DPI
209 Joanne Woodring; Joanne Woodring; Allen Reuben; Julian Wasser for Time
214 Joachim Jentschke—Black Star
215 George Buctel
216 UPI
217 Manchete from Pictorial Parade; UPI
218 Frederic Ohringer—Nancy Palmer
219 UPI
220 Wide World; UPI
221 UPI
222 Manchete from Pictorial Parade
223 UPI
224 Publifoto—PIX
225 William Morris; William Morrow and Co.; © by World Entertainers Ltd. Published by Coward-McCann and Bantam Books; Vaughn Covington
227 Janet Stone; Harper & Row Publishers; Random House; Random House
228 C. Shigioshi Hobori; Doubleday
229 Little Brown
230 From Alexander and the Wind-Up Mouse. © 1969 by Leo Lionni. Published by Pantheon
232 From The Judge. Text © 1969 by Harve Zemach. Pictures © 1969 by Margot Zemach. Published by Farrar, Straus and Giroux.
233 From Sounder. Text © 1969 by William H. Armstrong. Illus. © 1969 by James Barkley. Published by Harper & Row
234 From Journey Outside. © 1969 by Mary Q. Steele. Published by the Viking Press
236 UPI
237 UPI
238 The New York Times
239 UPI
240 UPI
241 UPI
242 Dick Kenyon, Medical Tribune
243 Dick Kenyon, Medical Tribune
244 Dick Kenyon, Medical Tribune
245 Dick Kenyon, Medical Tribune
246 George Buctel
247 Photoreporters
248 Yardley in the Baltimore Sun; Pictorial Parade
249 Diana Davies—Bethel
250 UPI
251 Photoreporters
252 Photoreporters; Rapho-Guillumette
253 Photoreporters
255 Camera Press—PIX
256 Camera Press—PIX
257 The New York Times
258 Tass from Sovfoto
259 U.S. Navy; UPI
260 Israeli Sun—PIX
261 London Daily Express—PIX; Israeli Sun—PIX
262 UPI
263 The New York Times; UPI; Western Publishing Co., Inc.
265 John Dominis, Life magazine © Time Inc.
266 Anne-Marie Barden
267 Anne-Marie Barden
268 Western Publishing Co. Inc.; Urban Systems, Inc.
269 Psychology Today; Psychology Today; Western Publishing Co., Inc.
270 Conso Publishing Co.
271 John T. Hill; Conso Publishing Co.
272 Conso Publishing Co.
273 Conso Publishing Co.
274 Wide World
275 UPI
276 Lief Engberg—Photoreporters
277 UPI
278 UPI
279 UPI
280 Ihrt—Black Star; AGIP—Pictorial Parade; Bureau—Gamma—PIX
281 © Karsh, Ottawa—Rapho-Guillumette
282 Wally McNamee, Newsweek; UPI
283 UPI
284 Pictorial Parade; Arnold Sachs—Pictorial Parade
285 UPI; Burton Berinsky—Pictorial Parade
288 UPI
289 UPI; Ted Rozumalski—Black Star
291 Religious News Service; UPI
292 UPI
293 Yigal Mann—PIX
294 UPI
295 American Museum of Natural History
296 UPI
297 UPI
301 Rhodes W. Fairbridge
302 UPI
303 American Museum of Natural History; UPI
304 UPI
305 UPI
306 The New York Times
307 Bill Ray, Life magazine © Time Inc.
308 UPI
309 Sovfoto; UPI
310 Sovfoto
311 Sovfoto; NASA
312 NASA
313 NASA
314 Radiation, Inc.
315 General Electric
316 NASA
317 Miller Pope; NASA; NASA
318 Ken Regan—Camera 5; Ben Rosenblatt
319 UPI
320 Manchete—Pictorial Parade
321 Peter Borsari—Camera 5
322 Wide World; UPI
323 Ken Regan—Camera 5
325 UPI
326 UPI
327 George Kalinsky
328 UPI
329 UPI
330 UPI; Evelyn Shafer
331 Tom McLaughlin
332 UPI
333 UPI
334 UPI
335 UPI
336 UPI
337 UPI
338 UPI
339 UPI
340 UPI
341 The New York Times
342 UPI
343 London Daily Express—Pictoral Parade; Werner Wolff—Black Star; Pan American
344 Bethlehem Steel
345 General Motors
346 Guy Gillette—Photo Researchers
349 McDonnell Douglas Corp.
350 Gene Daniels—Black Star
351 General Motors; American Motors; Ford Motor Co.
352 Max Machol, UN
353 UN; Russell Reif—Pictorial Parade
354 UPI
355 UPI
356 UPI
357 UPI
358 Peb in The Philadelphia Inquirer
359 UN
360 UN
361 UN
362 Ken Regan—Camera 5
363 DPI
364 Conrad © The Los Angeles Times 1970; John Robaton—Camera 5
365 UPI
366 UPI; Bob West
367 UPI
368 UPI
369 UPI
370 UPI
371 UPI
373 UPI
375 UPI
376 UPI
377 UPI
378 UPI
379 UPI
380 The New York Times
381 Blaise Zito
382 UPI
383 Franklynn Peterson—Black Star; Bijur—Monkmeyer Press
385 Pictorial Parade
386 Harry Benson—Black Star; UPI
388 UPI
389 Reynolds Aluminum; Girl Scouts of America; Future Farmers of America
390 Girl Scouts of America
392 Boy Scouts
393 4-H Clubs; Camp Fire Girls
394 Boys' Clubs of America
395 Archie L. Hardy, Future Farmers of America
396 Wide World
397 The New York Times; The New York Times; UPI; The New York Times

Cover photo: Roy Whitehouse from Shostal Associates

Endpaper photos: Lida Moser—DPI; Herbert Lanks—PIX; Charles Harbutt—Magnum; Elliott Erwitt—Magnum; Herbert Lanks—PIX; George W. Martin—DPI

If man cheats the earth, the earth will cheat man.
Chinese proverb